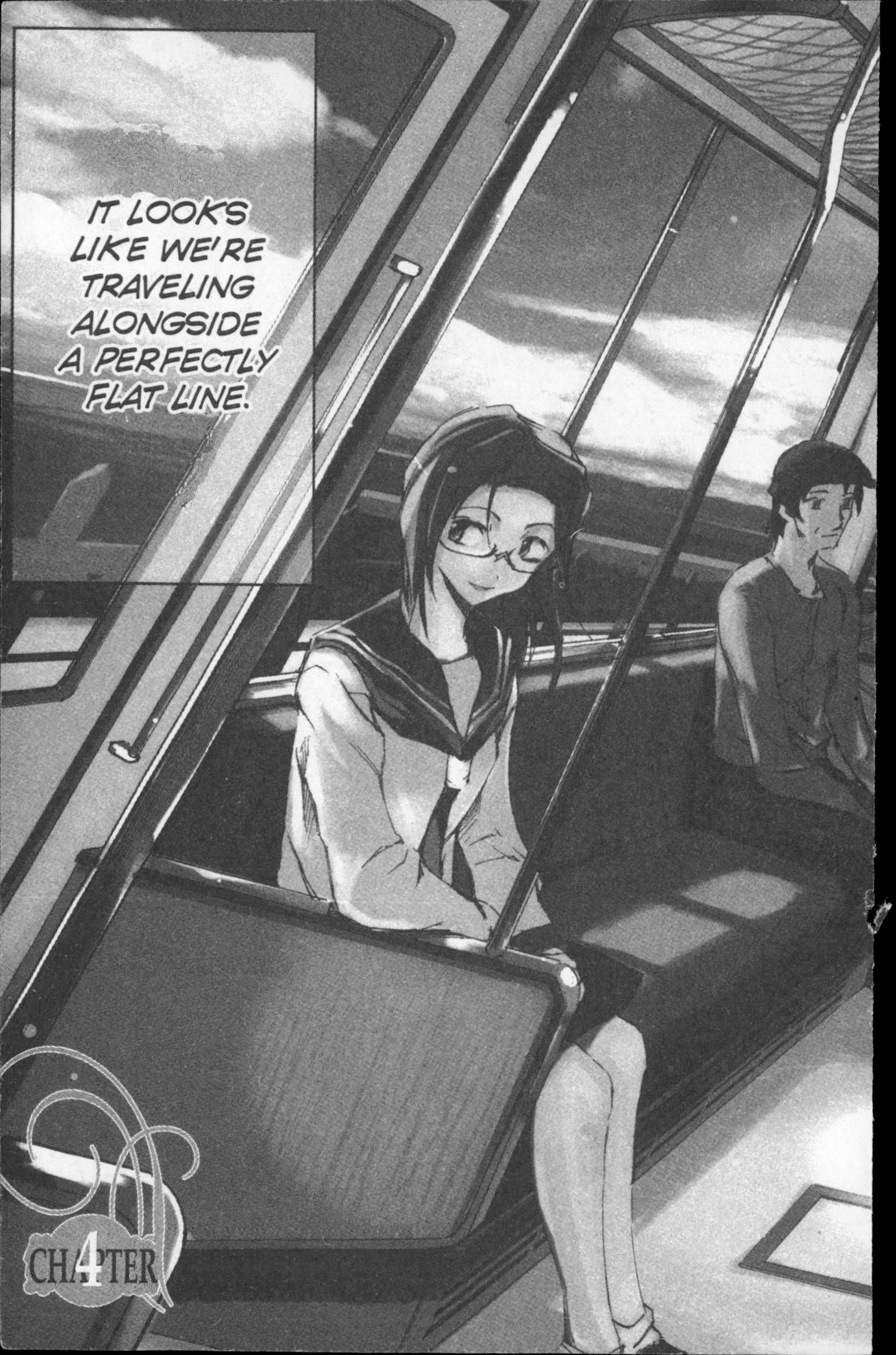
IT LOOKS LIKE WE'RE TRAVELING ALONGSIDE A PERFECTLY FLAT LINE.
CHAPTER 4

THE GIRL WHO RUNS THROUGH TIME

Yasutaka Tsutsui

time is
time was
time is not......

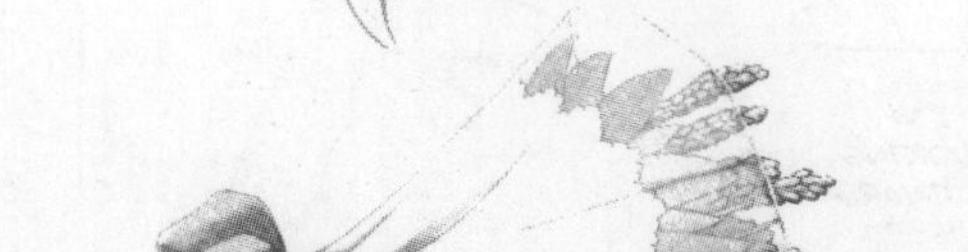

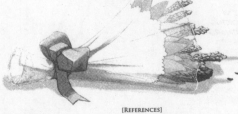

[REFERENCES]

"A TRAVELER IN TIME"
BY ALISON UTTLEY, 1939

TRANSLATED INTO JAPANESE
BY AKIRA ONO, 1980

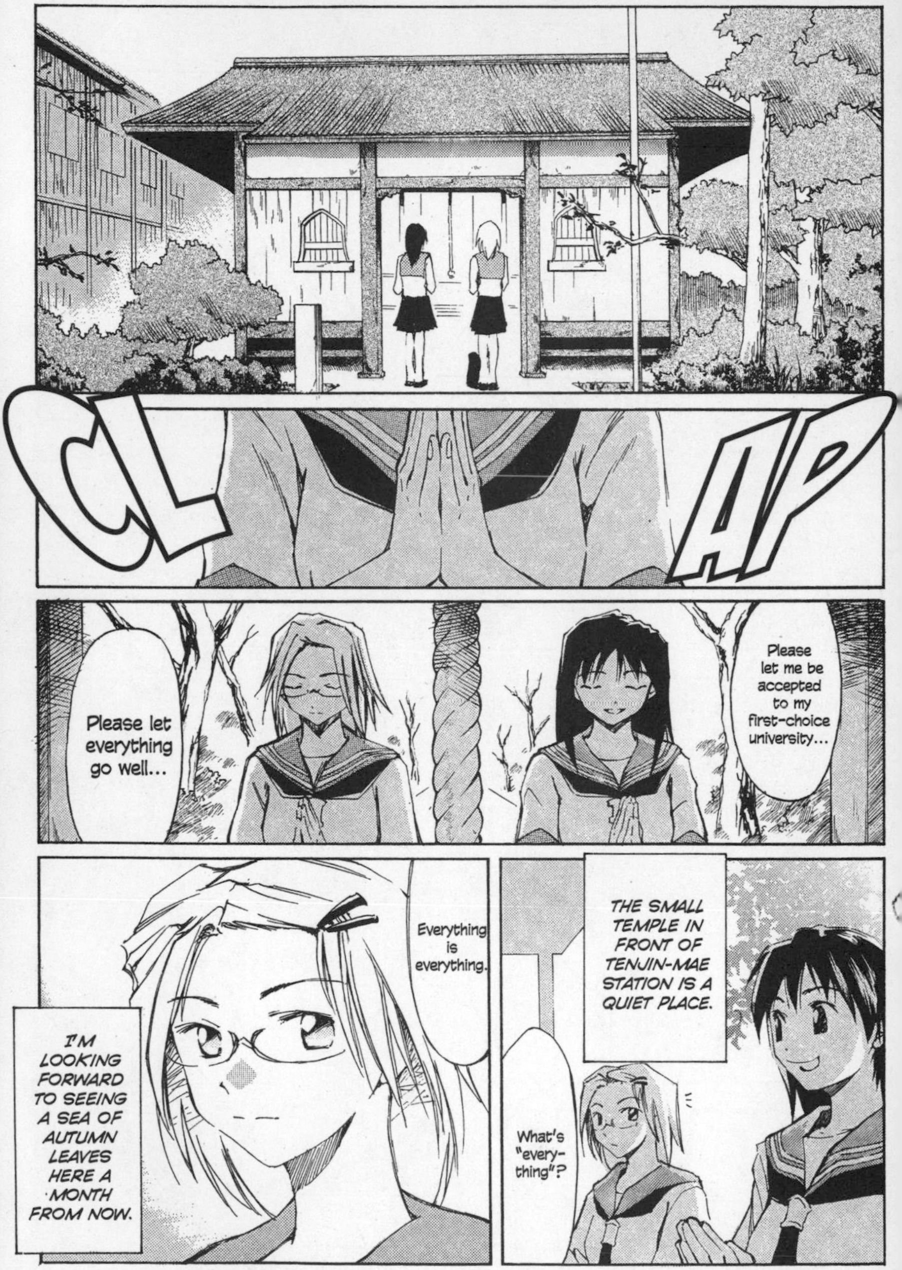
CLAP
Please let me be accepted to my first-choice university...
Please let everything go well...
THE SMALL TEMPLE IN FRONT OF TENJIN-MAE STATION IS A QUIET PLACE.
What's "every-thing"?
Everything is everything.
I'M LOOKING FORWARD TO SEEING A SEA OF AUTUMN LEAVES HERE A MONTH FROM NOW.

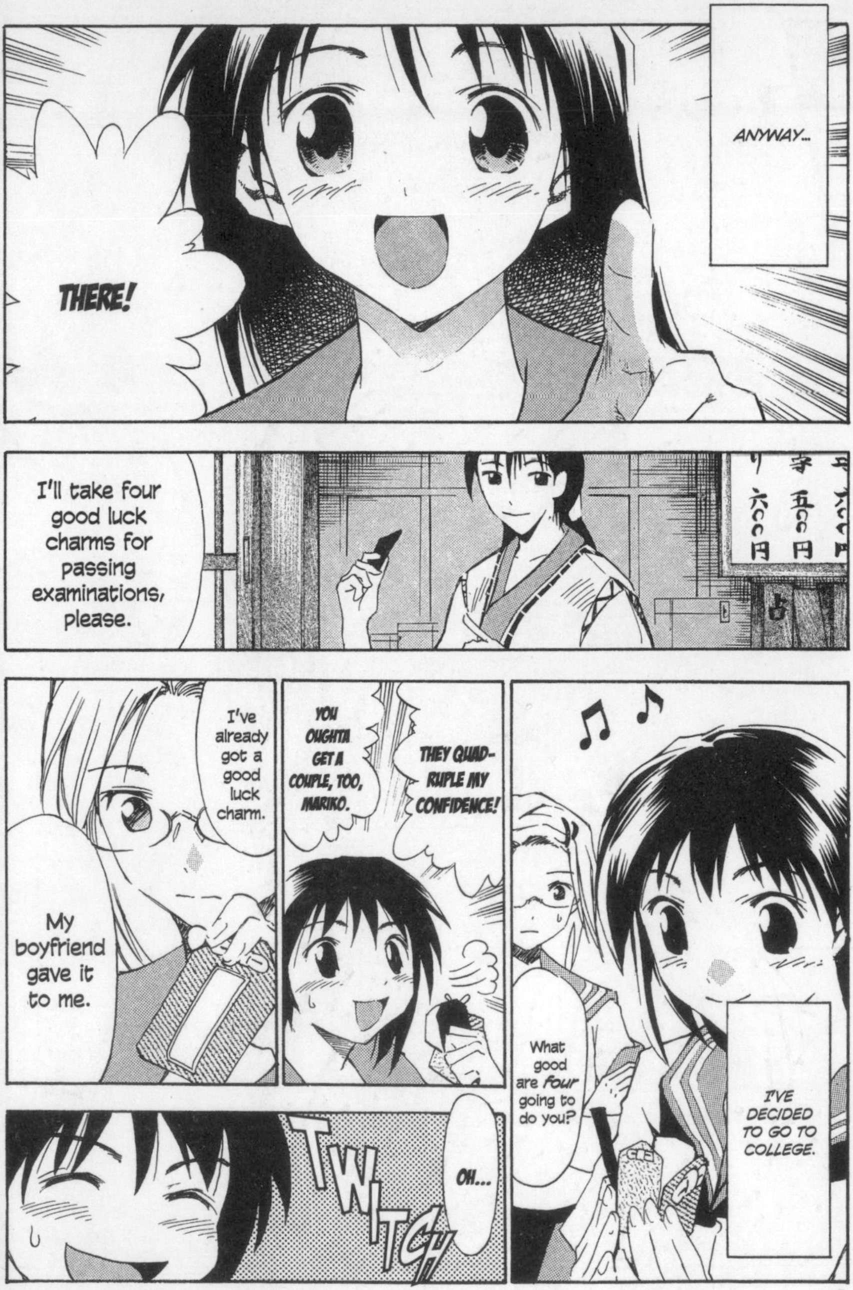
ANYWAY...
THERE!
I'll take four good luck charms for passing examinations, please.
I'VE DECIDED TO GO TO COLLEGE.
What good are *four* going to do you?
THEY QUADRUPLE MY CONFIDENCE!
YOU OUGHTA GET A COUPLE, TOO, MARIKO.
I've already got a good luck charm.
My boyfriend gave it to me.
OH...
TWITCH

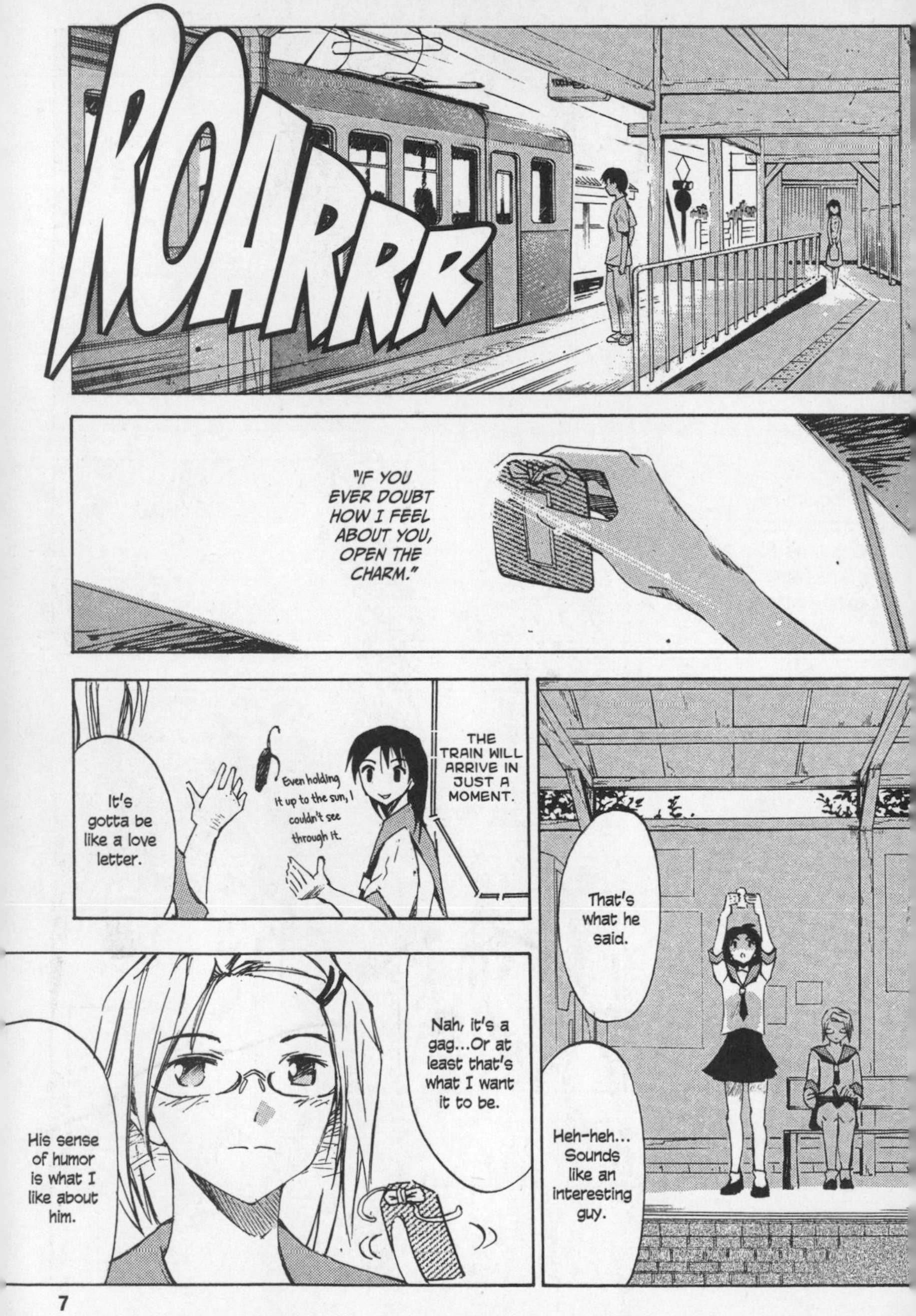
ROARRR
"IF YOU EVER DOUBT HOW I FEEL ABOUT YOU, OPEN THE CHARM."
That's what he said.
Heh-heh... Sounds like an interesting guy.
THE TRAIN WILL ARRIVE IN JUST A MOMENT.
Even holding it up to the sun, I couldn't see through it.
It's gotta be like a love letter.
Nah, it's a gag...Or at least that's what I want it to be.
His sense of humor is what I like about him.

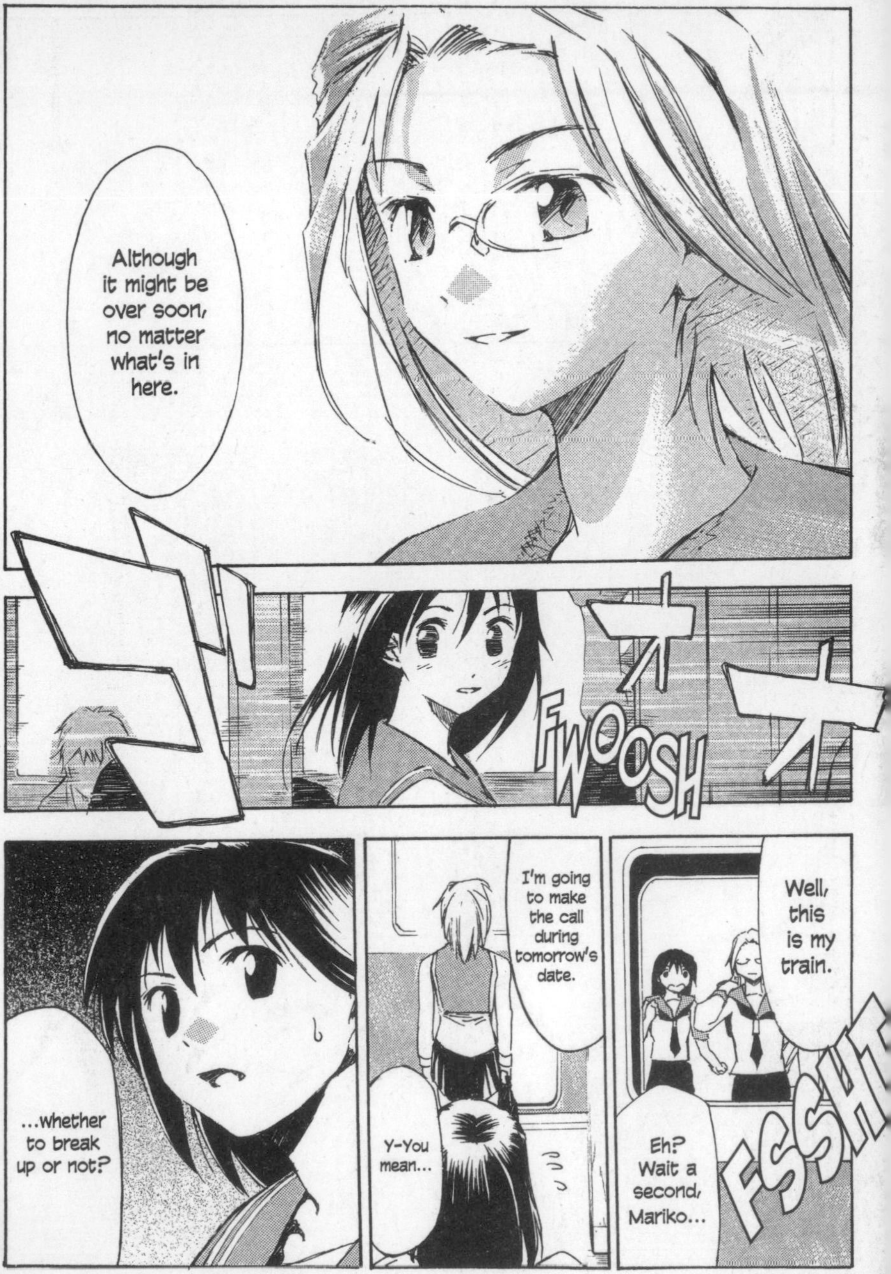
Although it might be over soon, no matter what's in here.
FWOOSH
Well, this is my train.
Eh? Wait a second, Mariko...
FSSHT
I'm going to make the call during tomorrow's date.
Y-You mean...
...whether to break up or not?

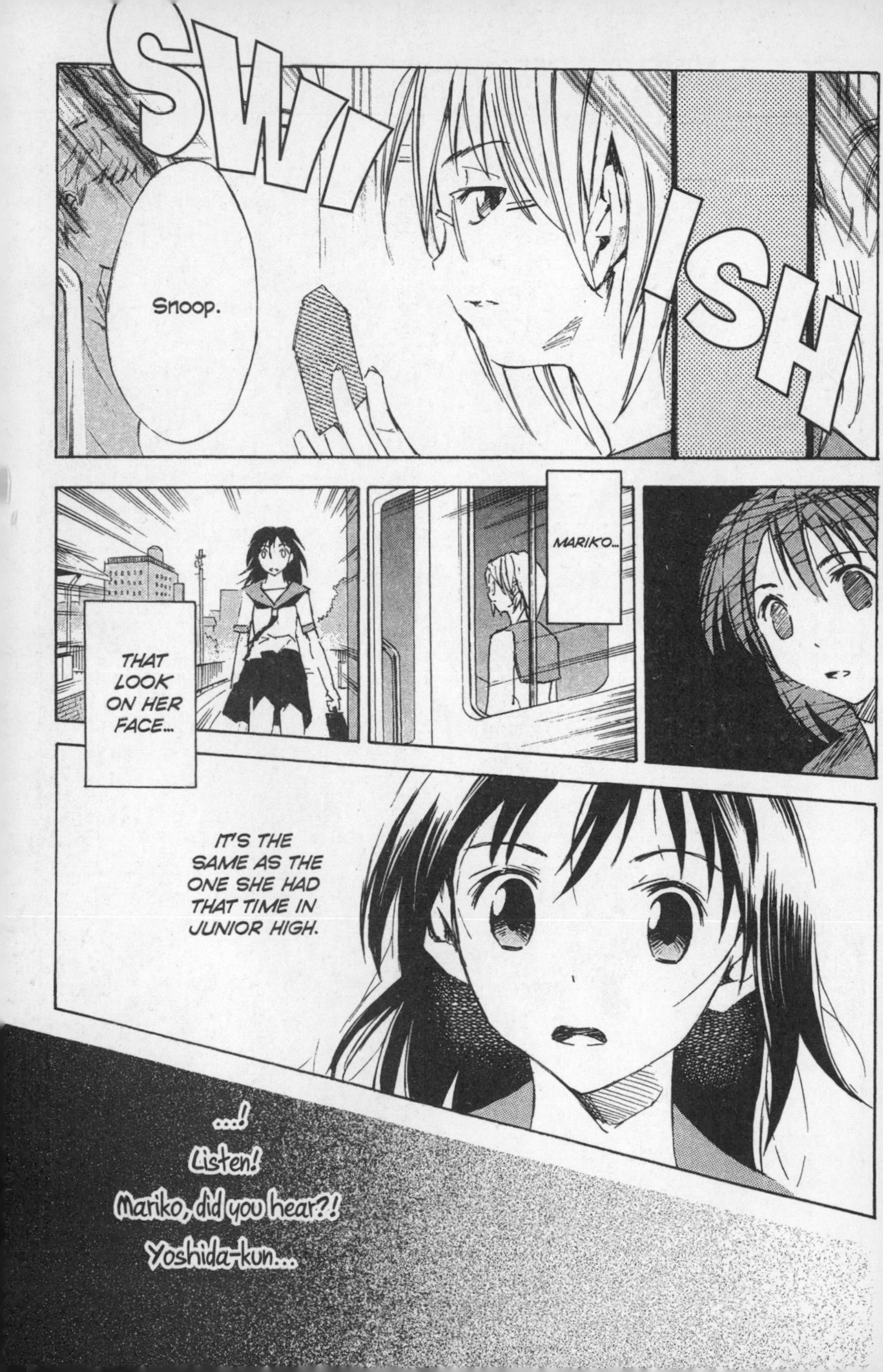
SWISH
Snoop.
MARIKO...
THAT LOOK ON HER FACE...
IT'S THE SAME AS THE ONE SHE HAD THAT TIME IN JUNIOR HIGH.
...!
Listen!
Mariko, did you hear?!
Yoshida-kun...

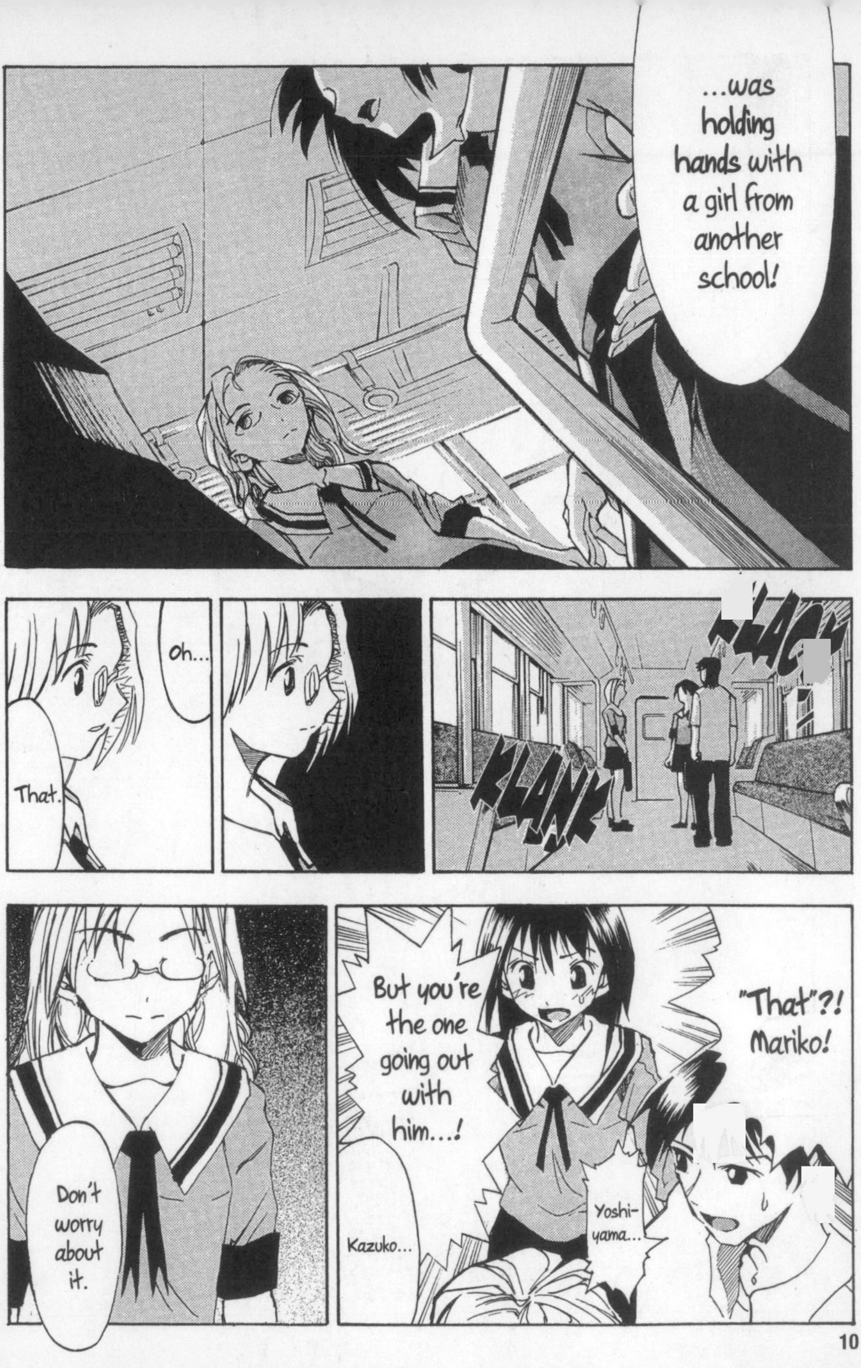
...was holding hands with a girl from another school!
KLANK
Oh...
That.
"That"?! Mariko!
But you're the one going out with him...!
Yoshi-yama...
Kazuko...
Don't worry about it.

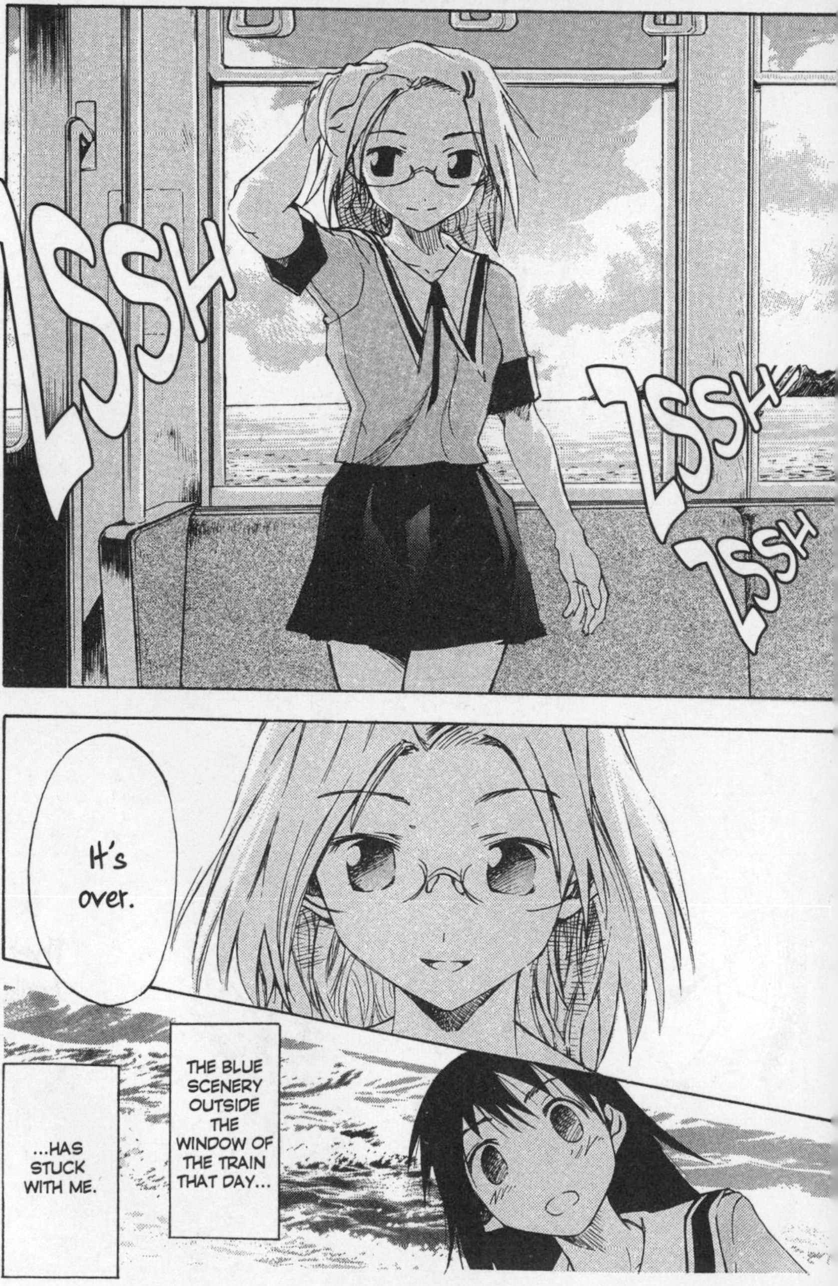
ZSSH
ZSSH
ZSSH
It's over.
THE BLUE SCENERY OUTSIDE THE WINDOW OF THE TRAIN THAT DAY...
...HAS STUCK WITH ME.

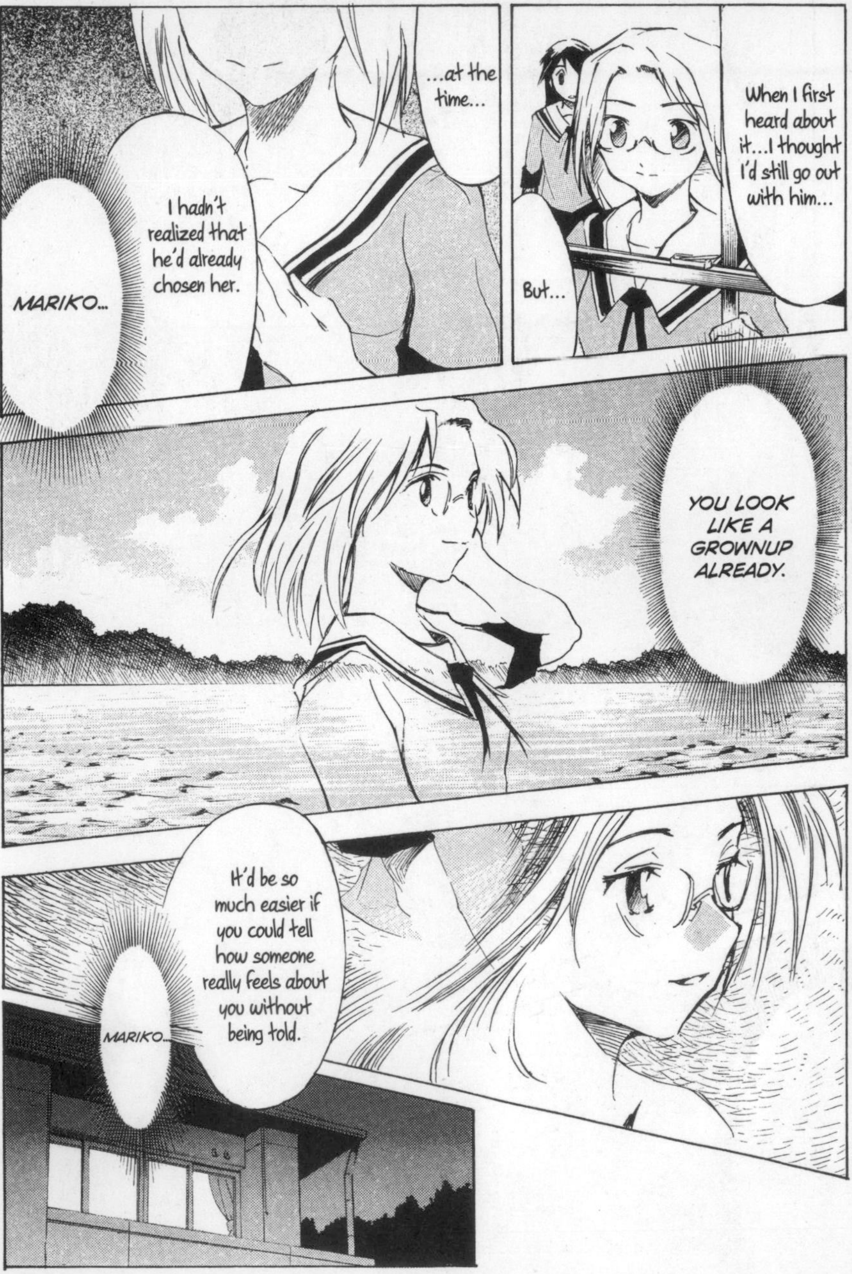
When I first heard about it...I thought I'd still go out with him...
But...
...at the time...
I hadn't realized that he'd already chosen her.
MARIKO...
YOU LOOK LIKE A GROWNUP ALREADY.
It'd be so much easier if you could tell how someone really feels about you without being told.
MARIKO...

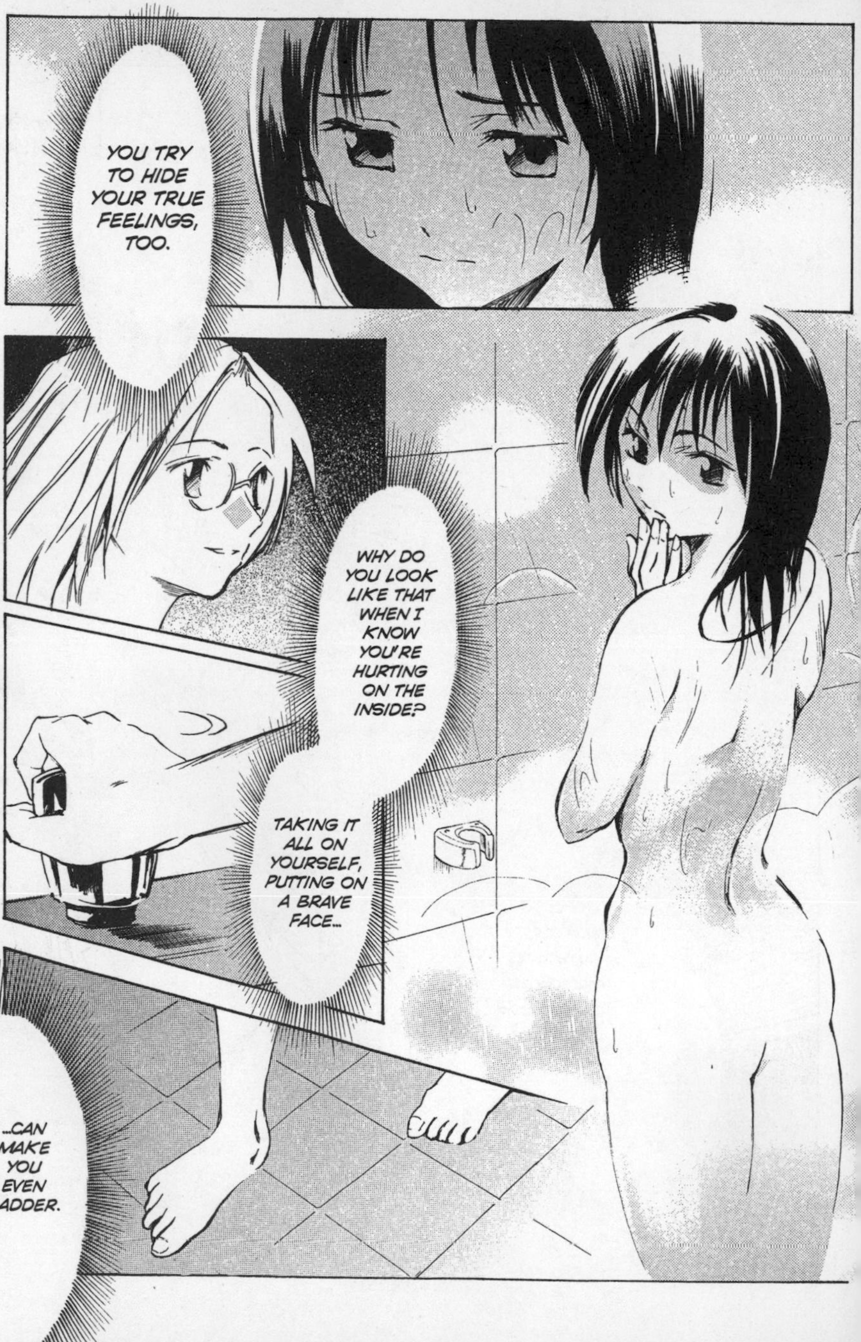
YOU TRY TO HIDE YOUR TRUE FEELINGS, TOO.
WHY DO YOU LOOK LIKE THAT WHEN I KNOW YOU'RE HURTING ON THE INSIDE?
TAKING IT ALL ON YOURSELF, PUTTING ON A BRAVE FACE...
...CAN MAKE YOU EVEN SADDER.

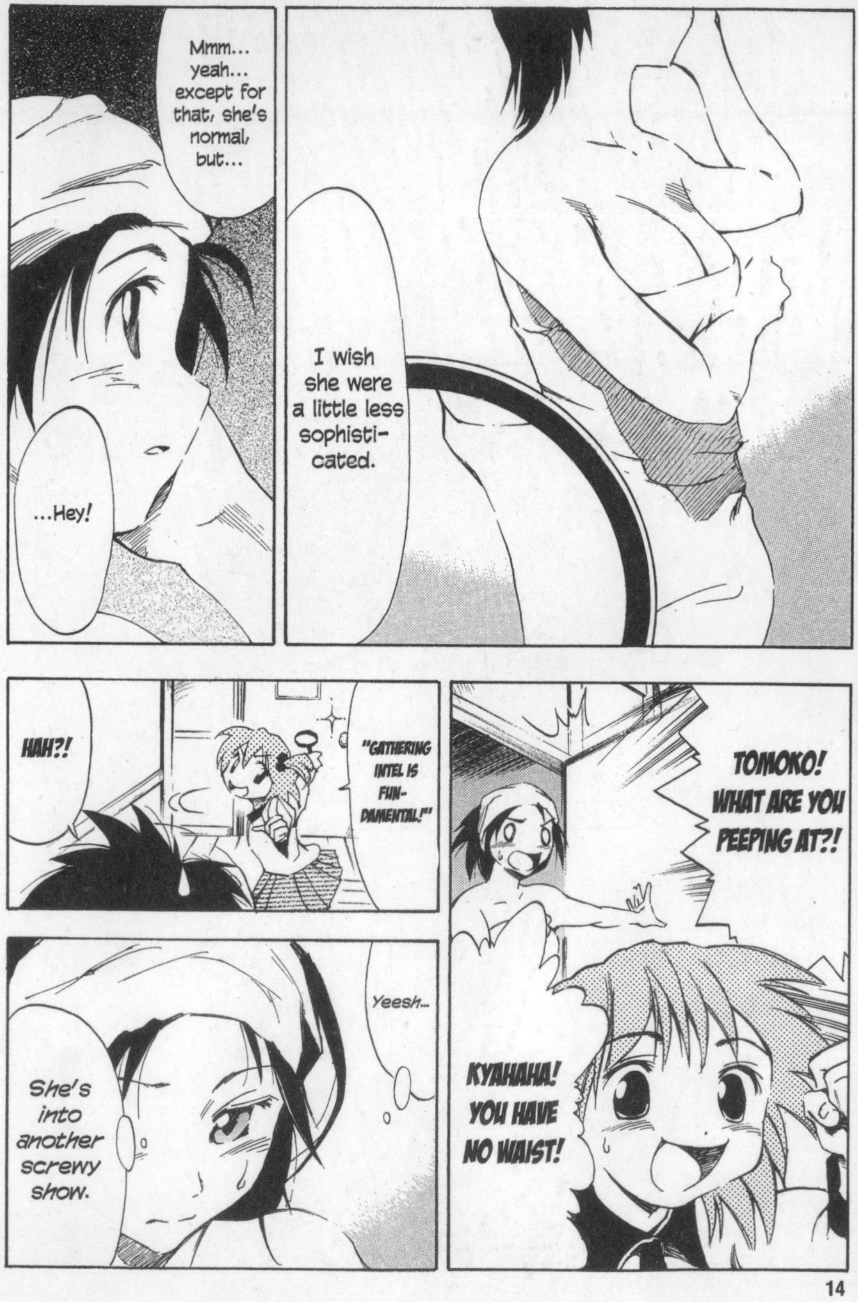

I wish she were a little less sophisticated.
Mmm... yeah... except for that, she's normal, but...
...Hey!
TOMOKO! WHAT ARE YOU PEEPING AT?!
KYAHAHA! YOU HAVE NO WAIST!
"GATHERING INTEL IS FUNDAMENTAL!"
HAH?!
Yeesh...
She's into another screwy show.

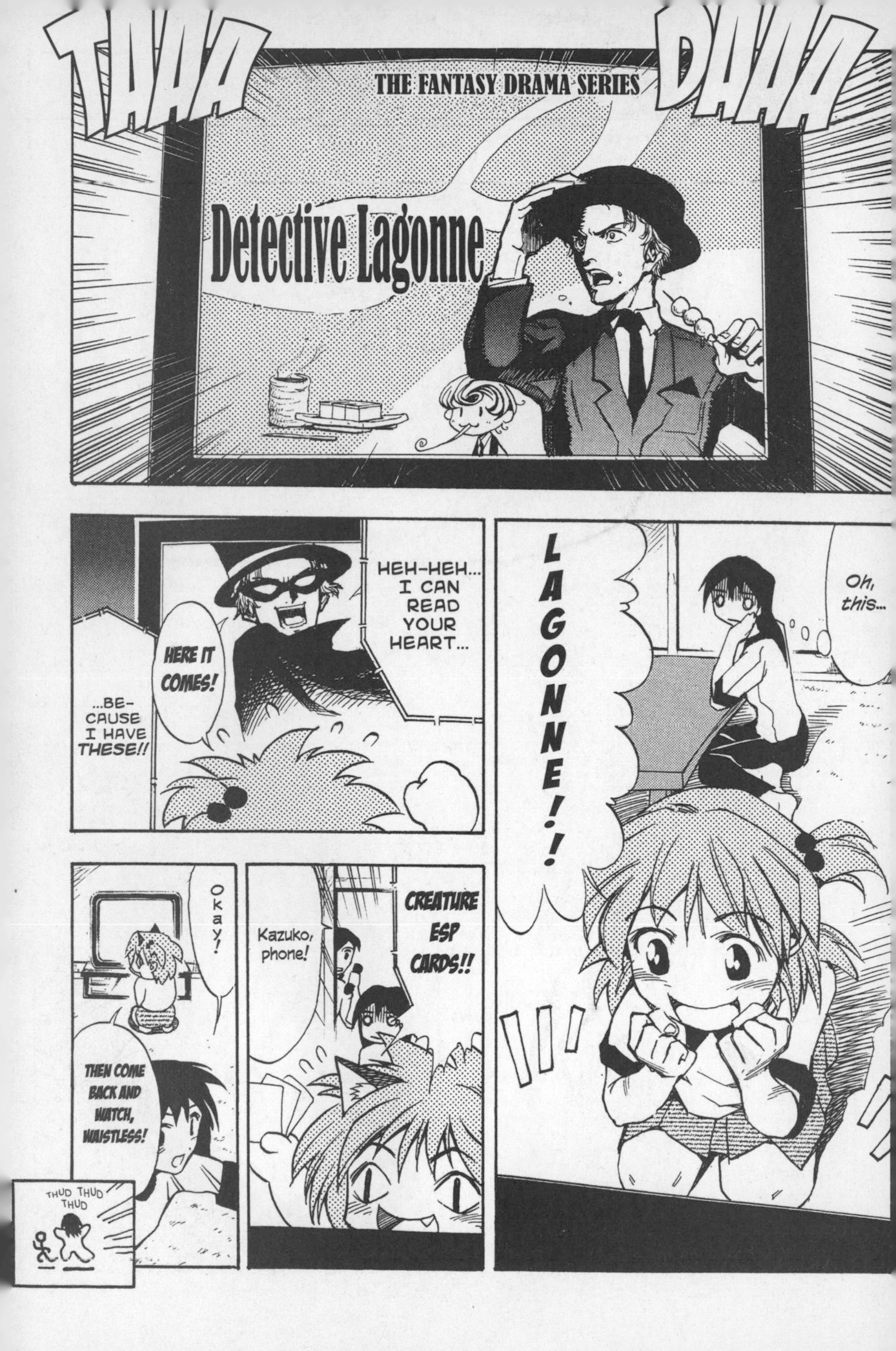
TAAA
DAAA
THE FANTASY DRAMA SERIES
Detective Lagonne
Oh, this...
LAGONNE!!
HEH-HEH... I CAN READ YOUR HEART...
HERE IT COMES!
...BE-CAUSE I HAVE THESE!!
CREATURE ESP CARDS!!
Kazuko, phone!
Okay!
THEN COME BACK AND WATCH, WAISTLESS!
THUD THUD THUD

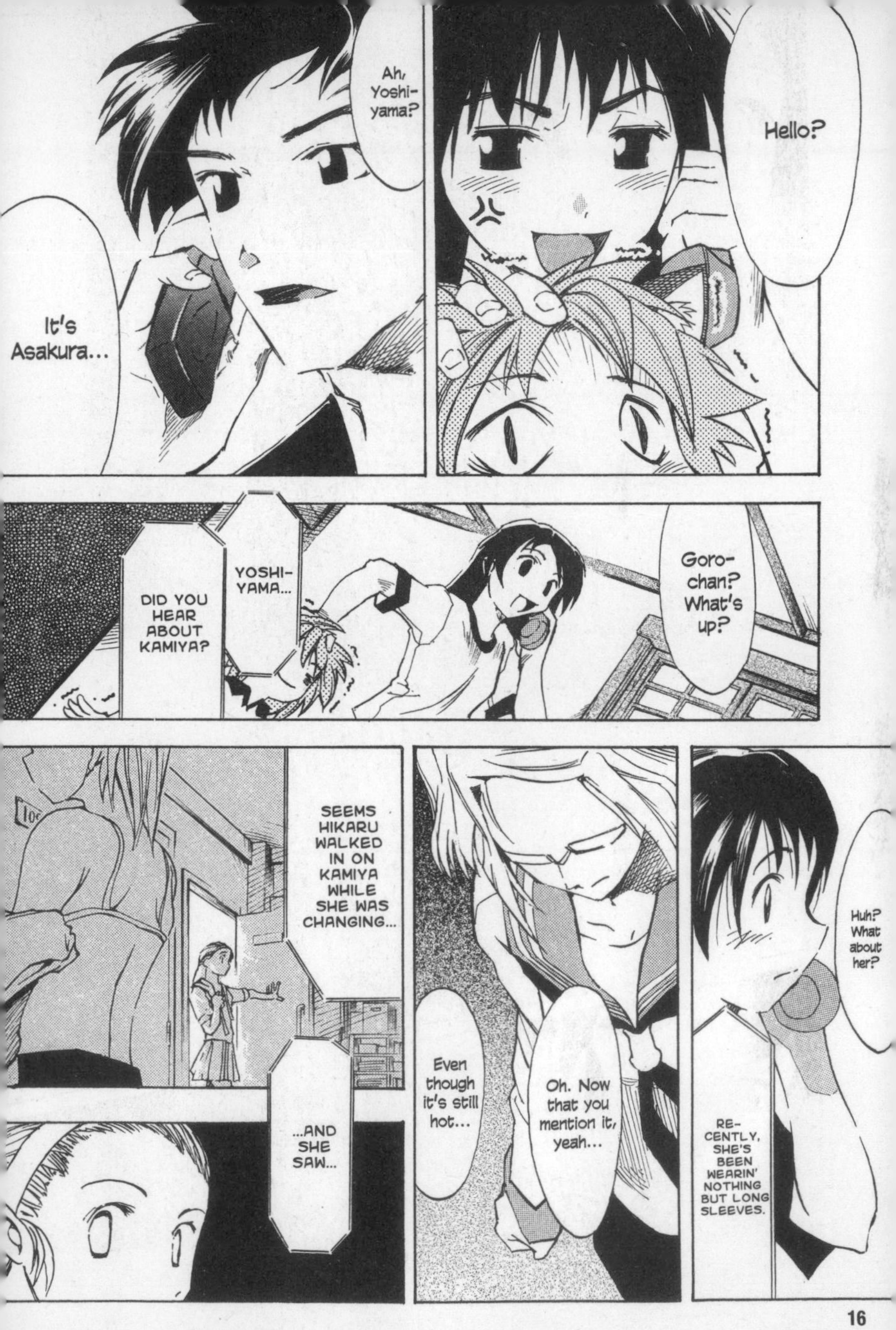
Hello?
Ah, Yoshi-yama?
It's Asakura...
Goro-chan? What's up?
YOSHI-YAMA...
DID YOU HEAR ABOUT KAMIYA?
Huh? What about her?
RE-CENTLY, SHE'S BEEN WEARIN' NOTHING BUT LONG SLEEVES.
Oh. Now that you mention it, yeah...
Even though it's still hot...
SEEMS HIKARU WALKED IN ON KAMIYA WHILE SHE WAS CHANGING...
...AND SHE SAW...

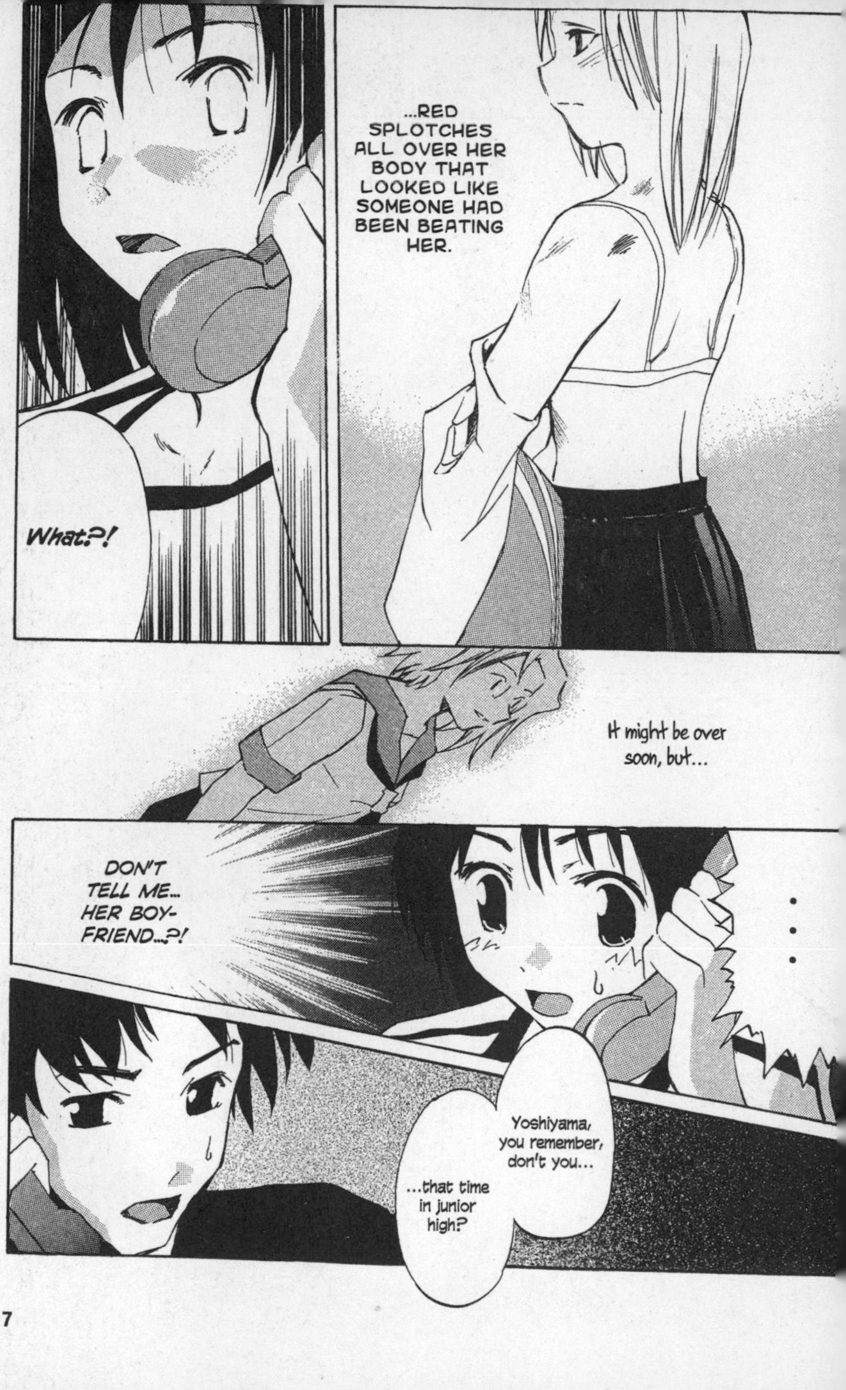
...RED SPLOTCHES ALL OVER HER BODY THAT LOOKED LIKE SOMEONE HAD BEEN BEATING HER.
What?!
It might be over soon, but...
DON'T TELL ME... HER BOY-FRIEND...?!
Yoshiyama, you remember, don't you...
...that time in junior high?

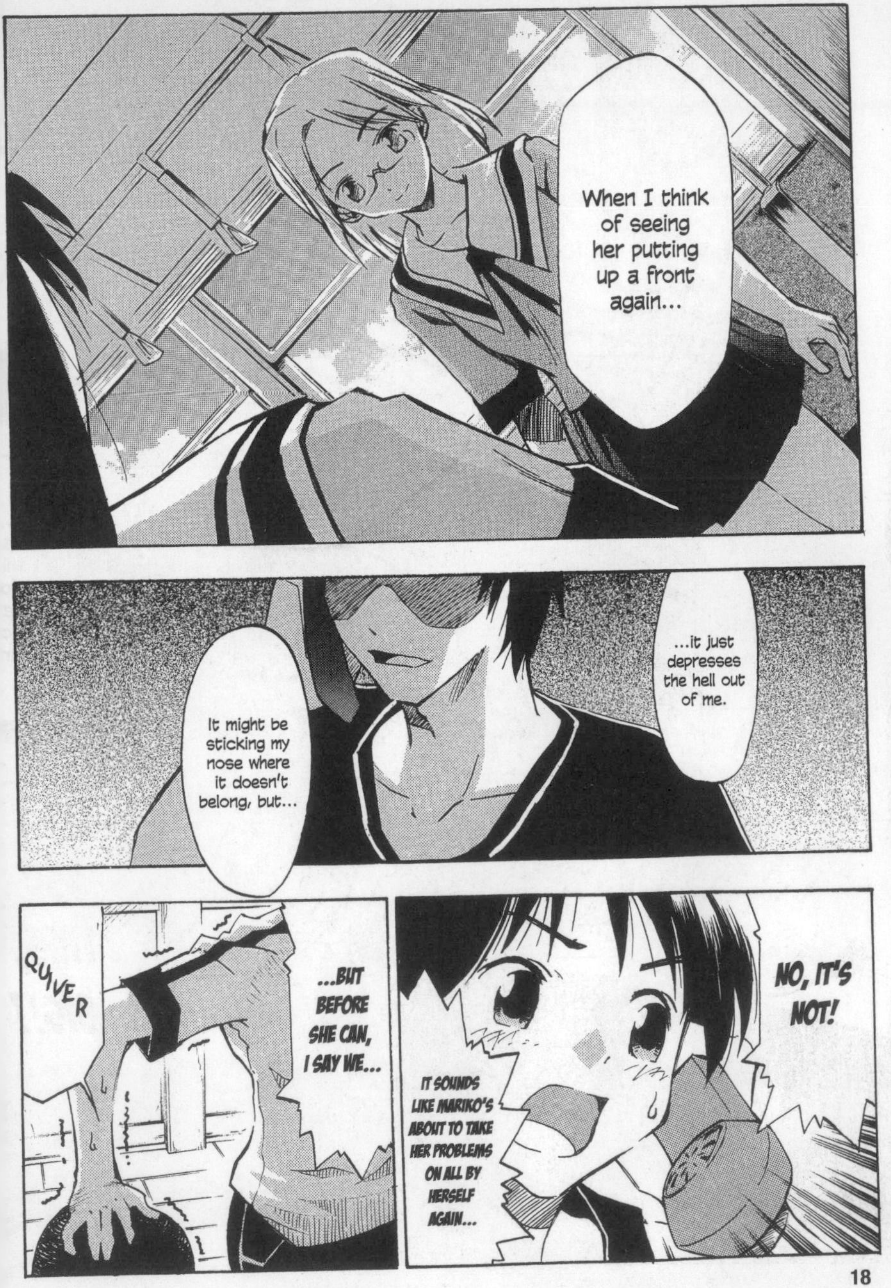
When I think of seeing her putting up a front again...
...it just depresses the hell out of me.
It might be sticking my nose where it doesn't belong, but...
NO, IT'S NOT!
IT SOUNDS LIKE MARIKO'S ABOUT TO TAKE HER PROBLEMS ON ALL BY HERSELF AGAIN...
...BUT BEFORE SHE CAN, I SAY WE...
QUIVER

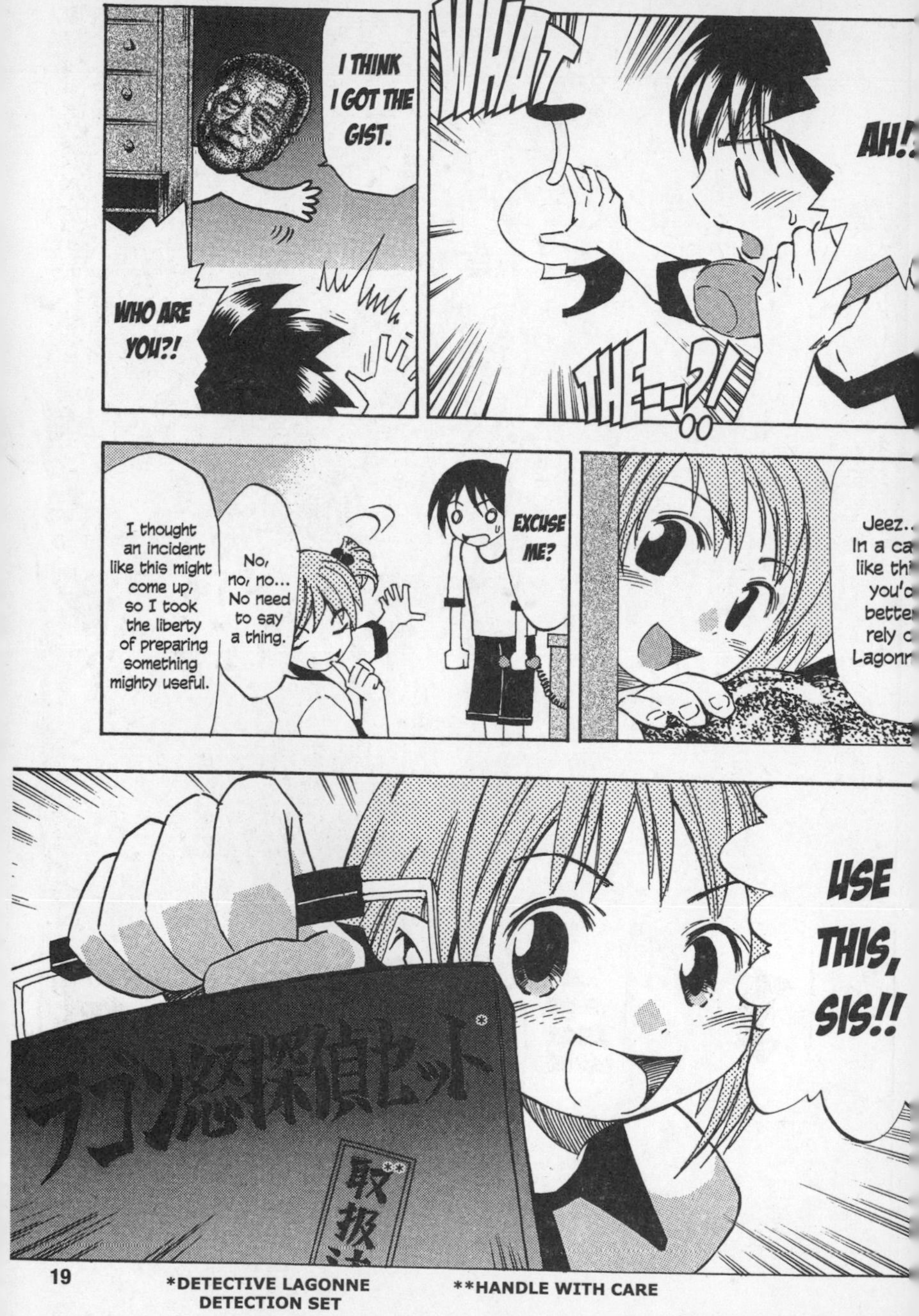

WHAT
AH!?
THE---?!
I THINK I GOT THE GIST.
WHO ARE YOU?!
Jeez.. In a ca like thi you'c bette rely c Lagonn
EXCUSE ME?
No, no, no... No need to say a thing.
I thought an incident like this might come up, so I took the liberty of preparing something mighty useful.
USE THIS, SIS!!

*DETECTIVE LAGONNE DETECTION SET

**HANDLE WITH CARE

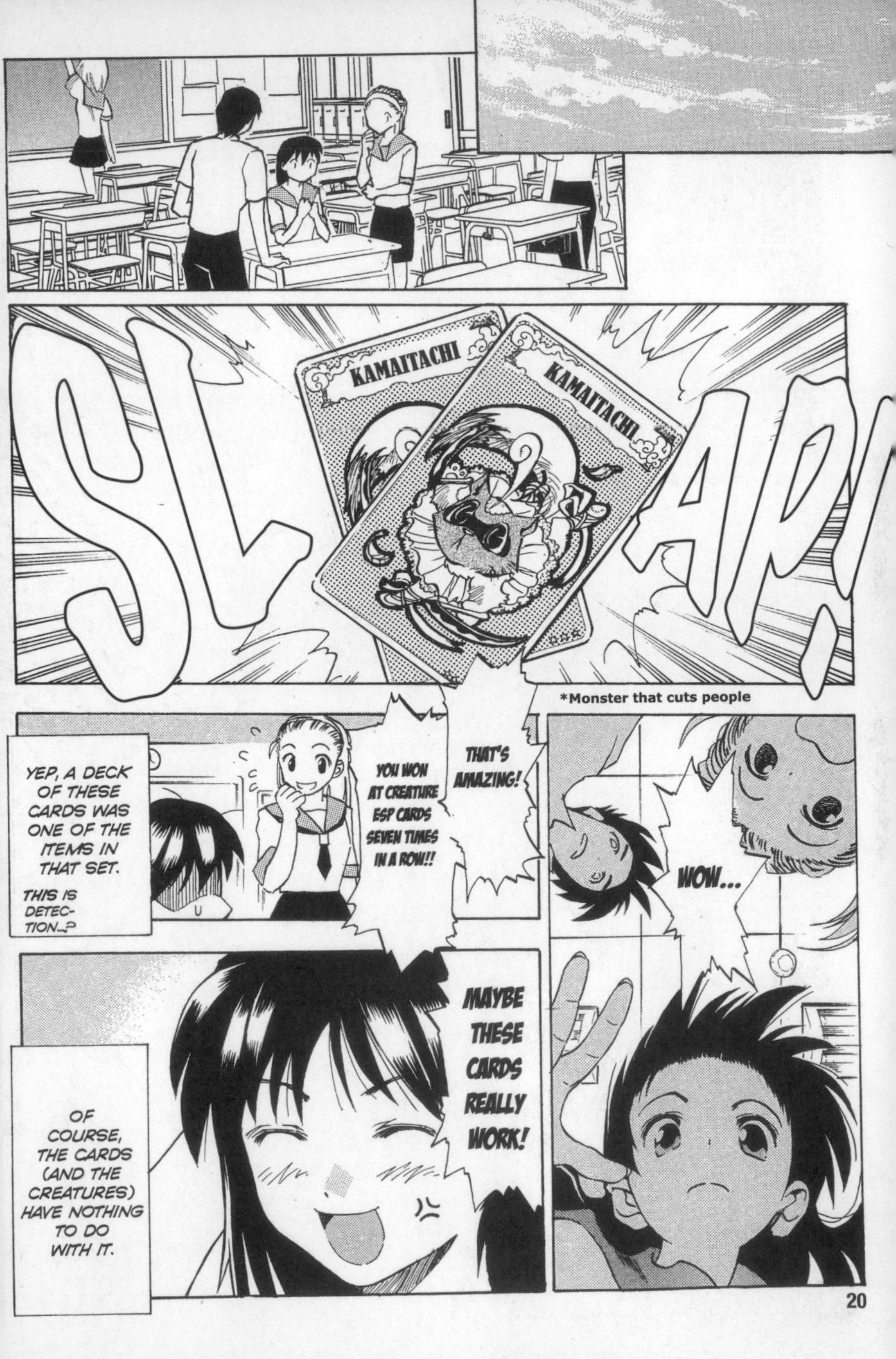

SLAP!
KAMAITACHI
KAMAITACHI
*Monster that cuts people
WOW...
THAT'S AMAZING!
YOU WON AT CREATURE ESP CARDS SEVEN TIMES IN A ROW!!
YEP, A DECK OF THESE CARDS WAS ONE OF THE ITEMS IN THAT SET.
THIS IS DETECTION...?
MAYBE THESE CARDS REALLY WORK!
OF COURSE, THE CARDS (AND THE CREATURES) HAVE NOTHING TO DO WITH IT.

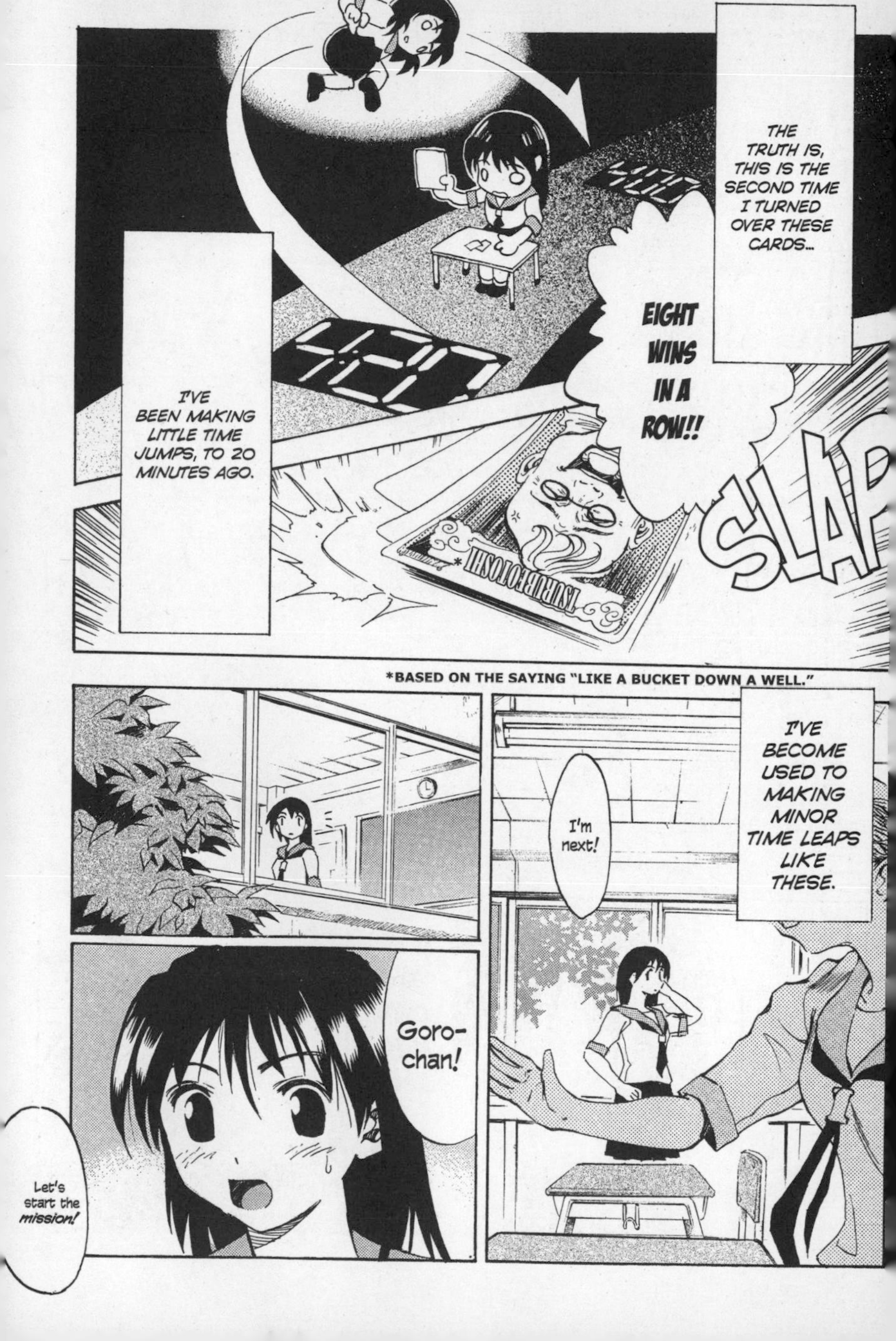
THE TRUTH IS, THIS IS THE SECOND TIME I TURNED OVER THESE CARDS...
EIGHT WINS IN A ROW!!
SLAP
TSURUBEOTOSHI*
I'VE BEEN MAKING LITTLE TIME JUMPS, TO 20 MINUTES AGO.
I'VE BECOME USED TO MAKING MINOR TIME LEAPS LIKE THESE.
I'm next!
Goro-chan!
Let's start the *mission!*

*BASED ON THE SAYING "LIKE A BUCKET DOWN A WELL."

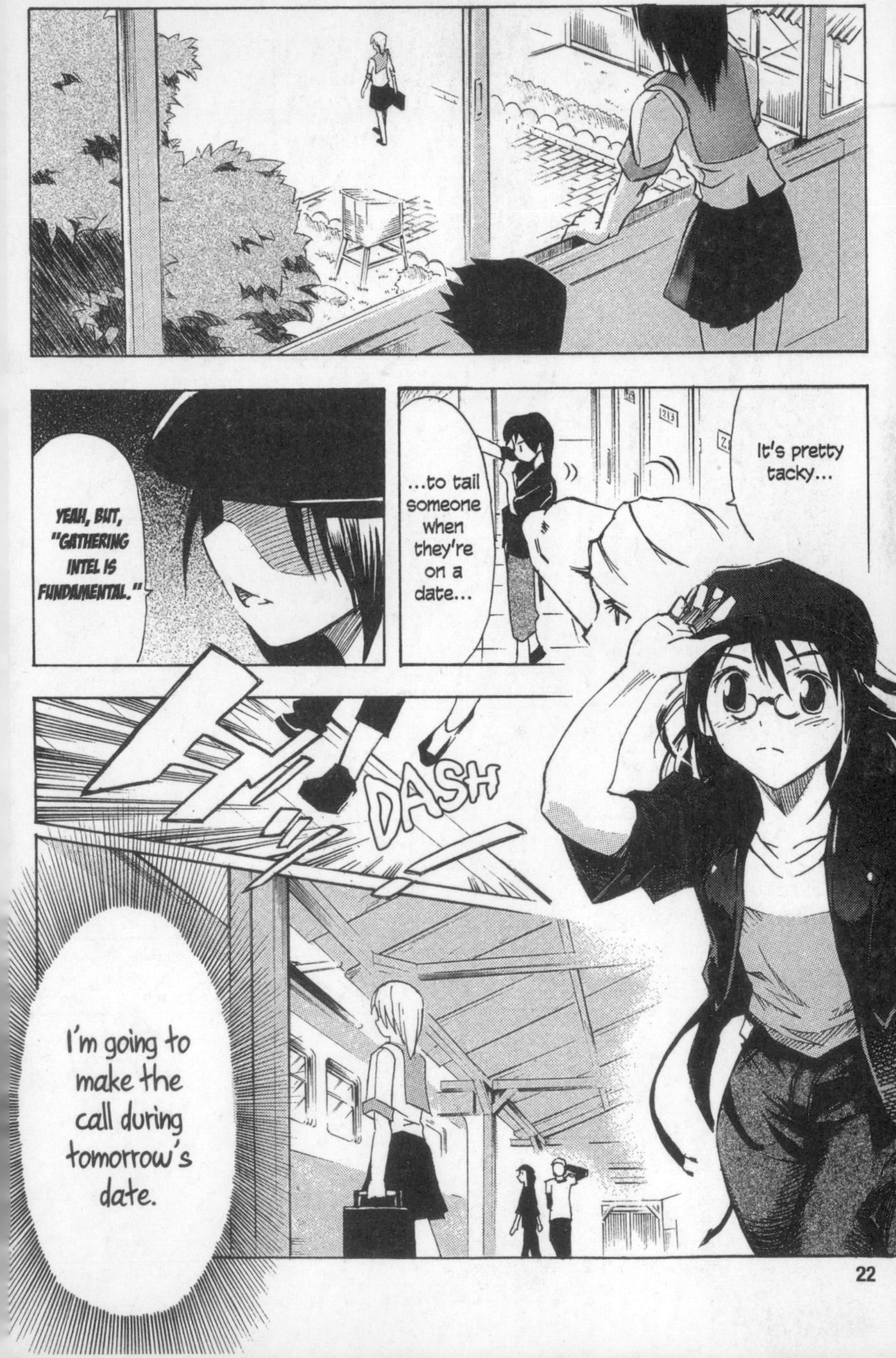
It's pretty tacky...
...to tail someone when they're on a date...
YEAH, BUT, "GATHERING INTEL IS FUNDAMENTAL."
DASH
I'm going to make the call during tomorrow's date.

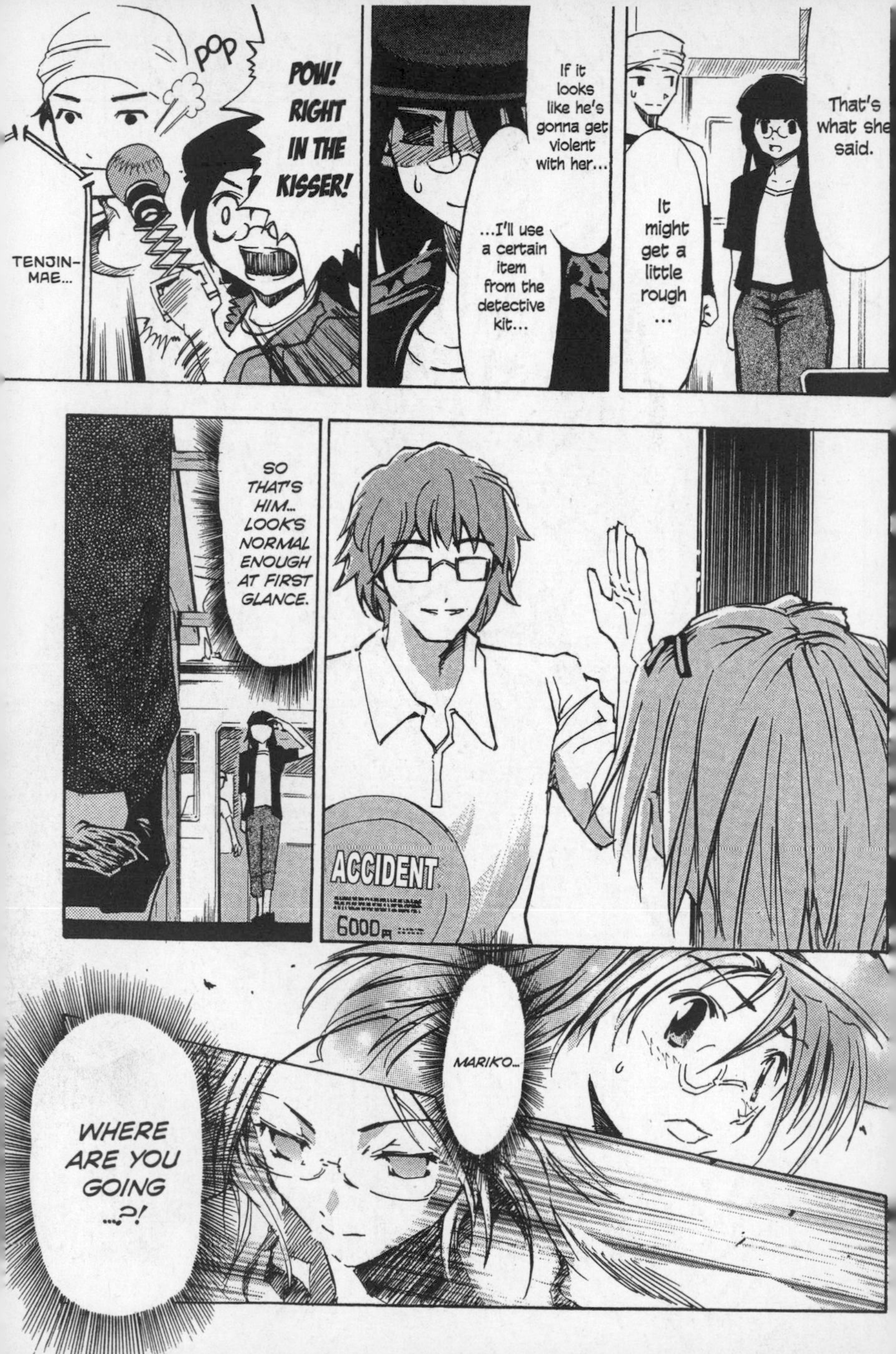

That's what she said.
It might get a little rough...
If it looks like he's gonna get violent with her...
...I'll use a certain item from the detective kit...
POP
POW! RIGHT IN THE KISSER!
TENJIN-MAE...
ACCIDENT
6000
SO THAT'S HIM... LOOKS NORMAL ENOUGH AT FIRST GLANCE.
MARIKO...
WHERE ARE YOU GOING ...?!

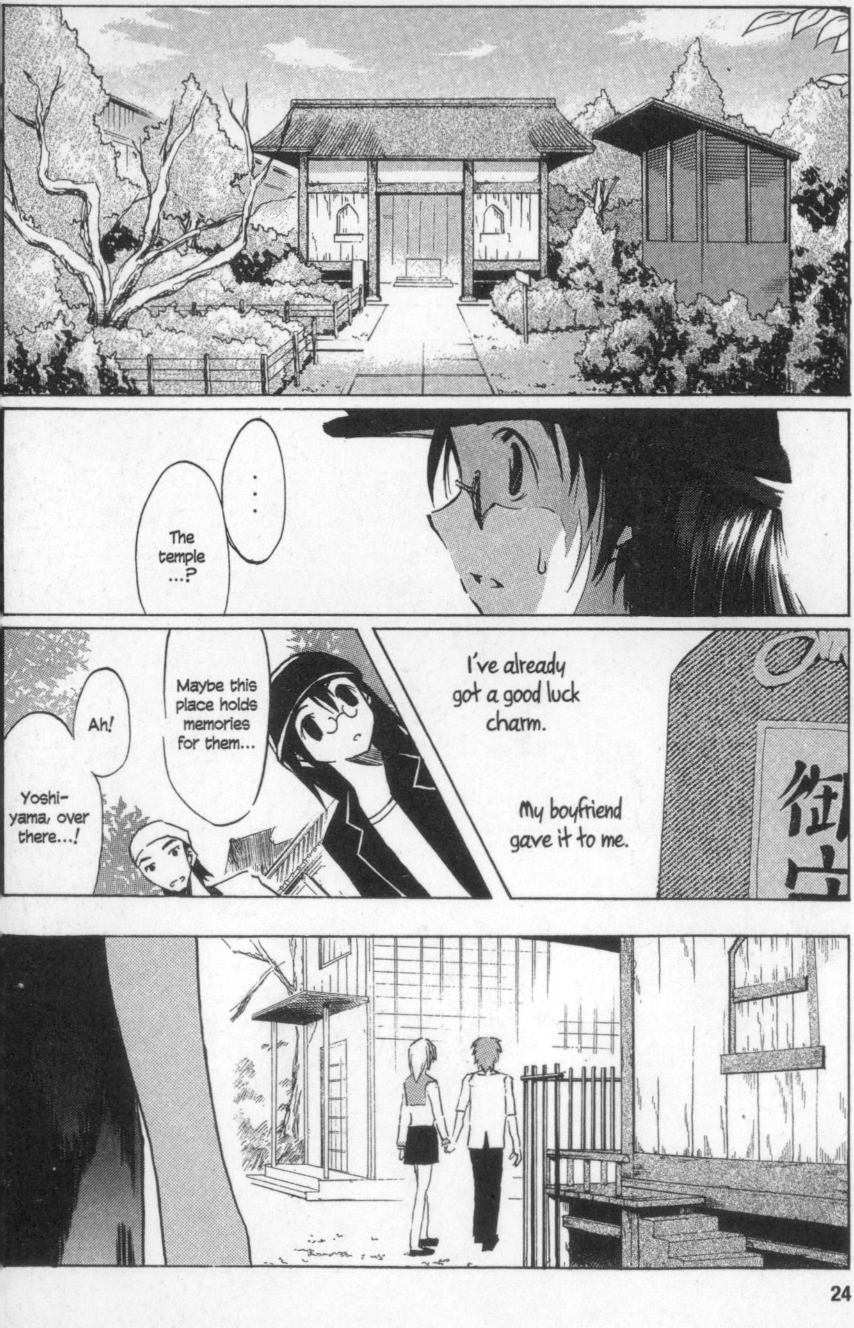
...
The temple ...?
I've already got a good luck charm.
My boyfriend gave it to me.
Maybe this place holds memories for them...
Ah!
Yoshi-yama, over there...!

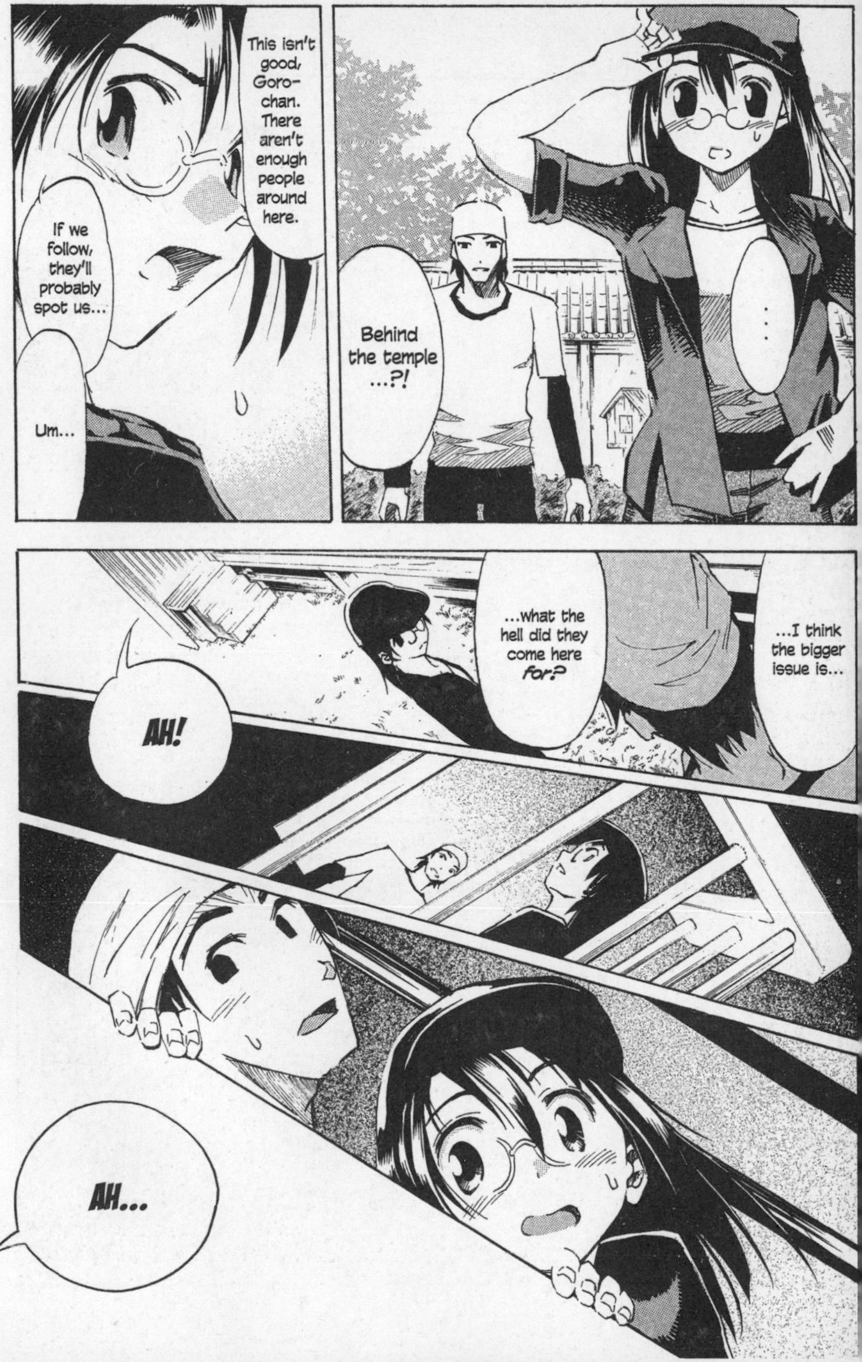
...
Behind the temple ...?!
This isn't good, Goro-chan. There aren't enough people around here.
If we follow, they'll probably spot us...
Um...
...I think the bigger issue is...
...what the hell did they come here for?
AH!
AH...

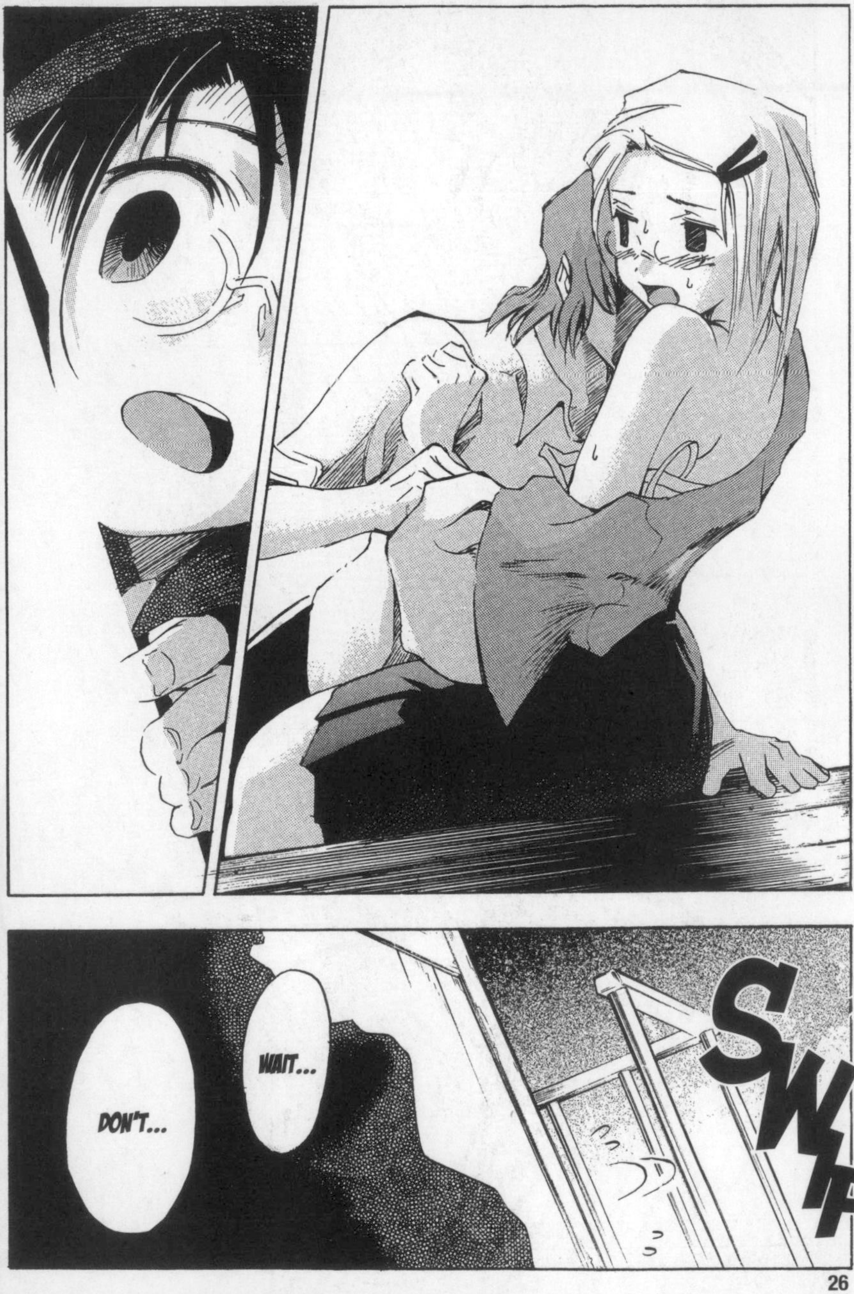
SWIP
WAIT...
DON'T...

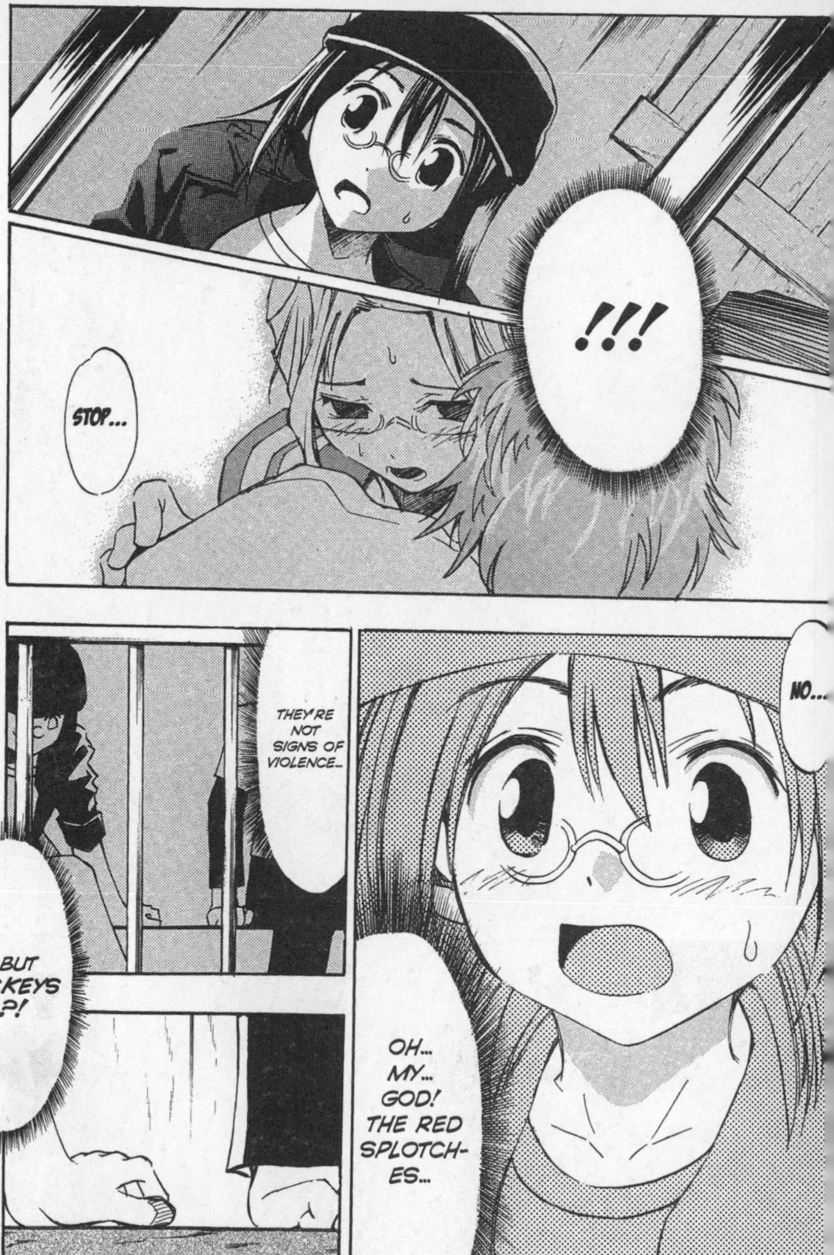
!!!
STOP...
NO...
OH... MY... GOD! THE RED SPLOTCH-ES...
THEY'RE NOT SIGNS OF VIOLENCE...
...BUT HICKEYS ?!

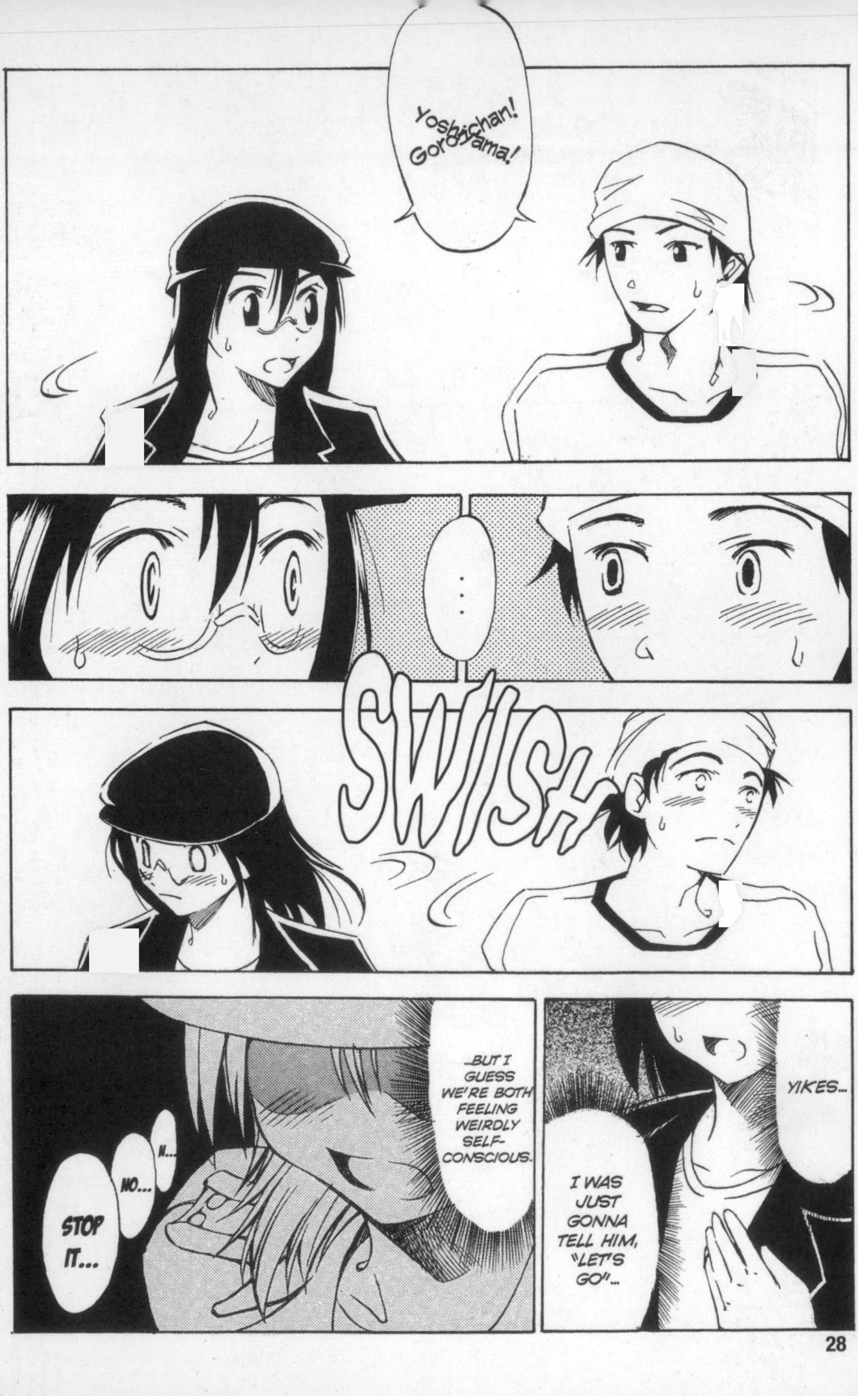
Yoshichan!
Goroyama!
....
SWISH
YIKES...
I WAS JUST GONNA TELL HIM, "LET'S GO"...
...BUT I GUESS WE'RE BOTH FEELING WEIRDLY SELF-CONSCIOUS.
N...
NO...
STOP IT...

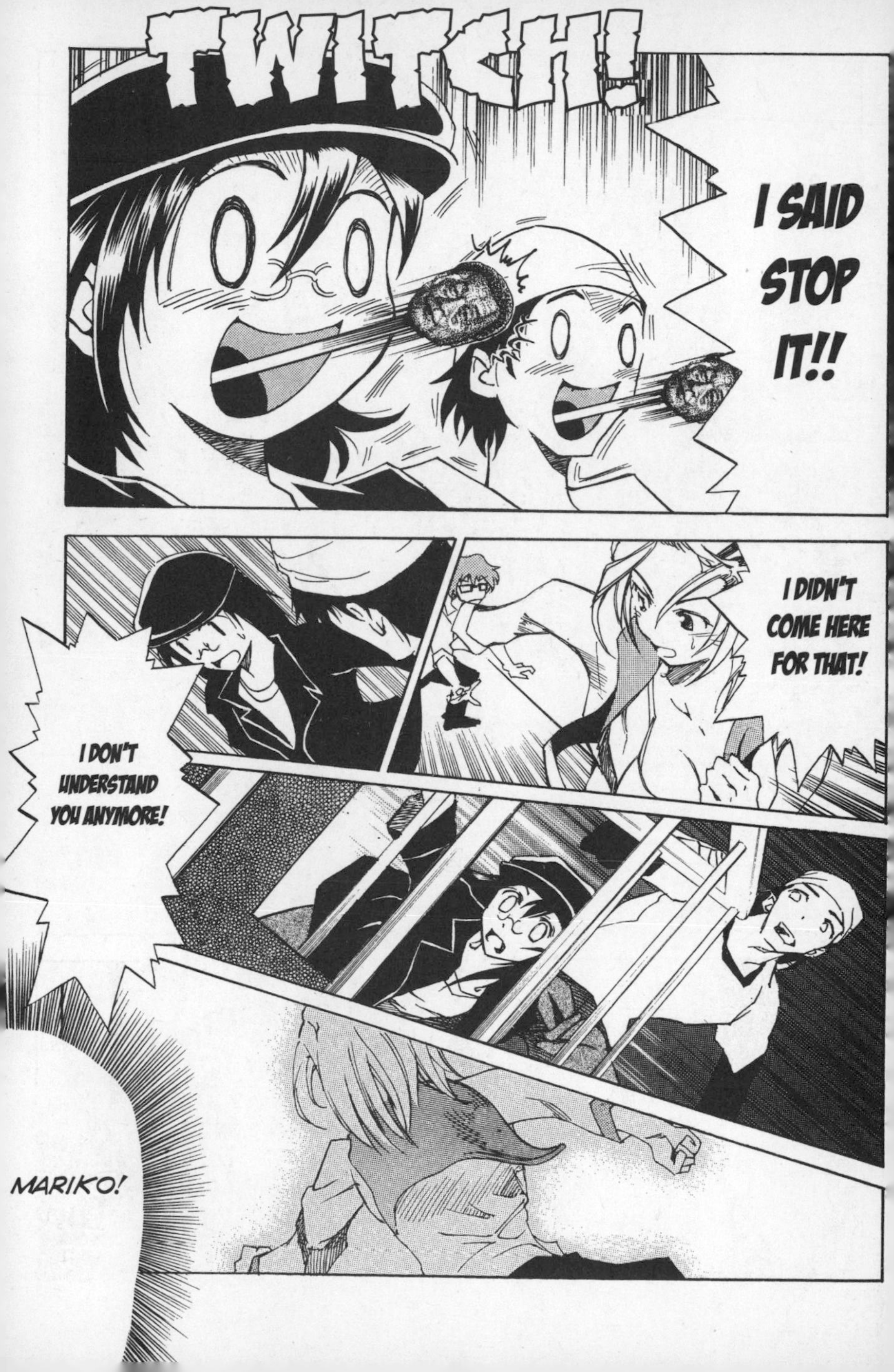
TWITCH!
I SAID STOP IT!!
I DIDN'T COME HERE FOR THAT!
I DON'T UNDERSTAND YOU ANYMORE!
MARIKO!

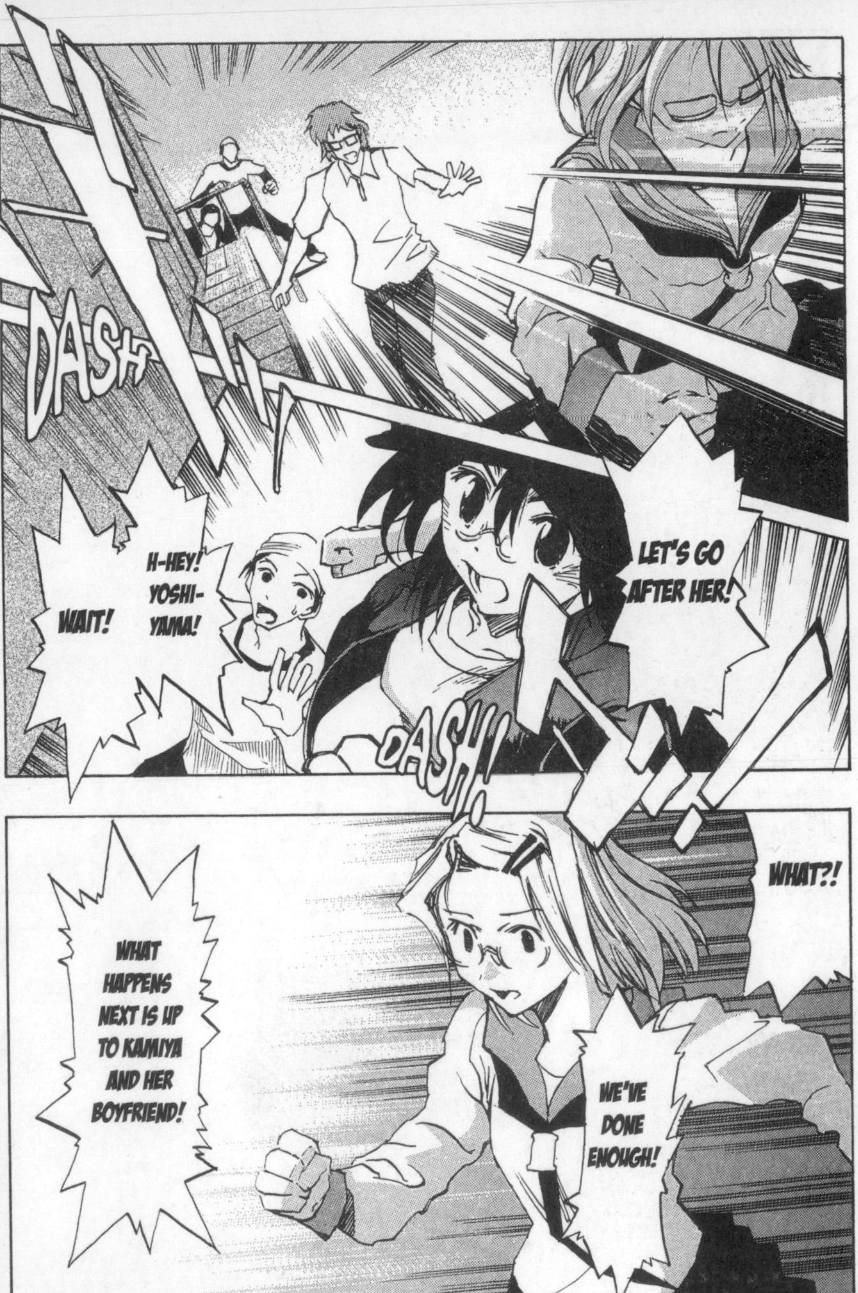
DASH
LET'S GO AFTER HER!
H-HEY! YOSHI-YAMA!
WAIT!
DASH!
WHAT?!
WE'VE DONE ENOUGH!
WHAT HAPPENS NEXT IS UP TO KAMIYA AND HER BOYFRIEND!

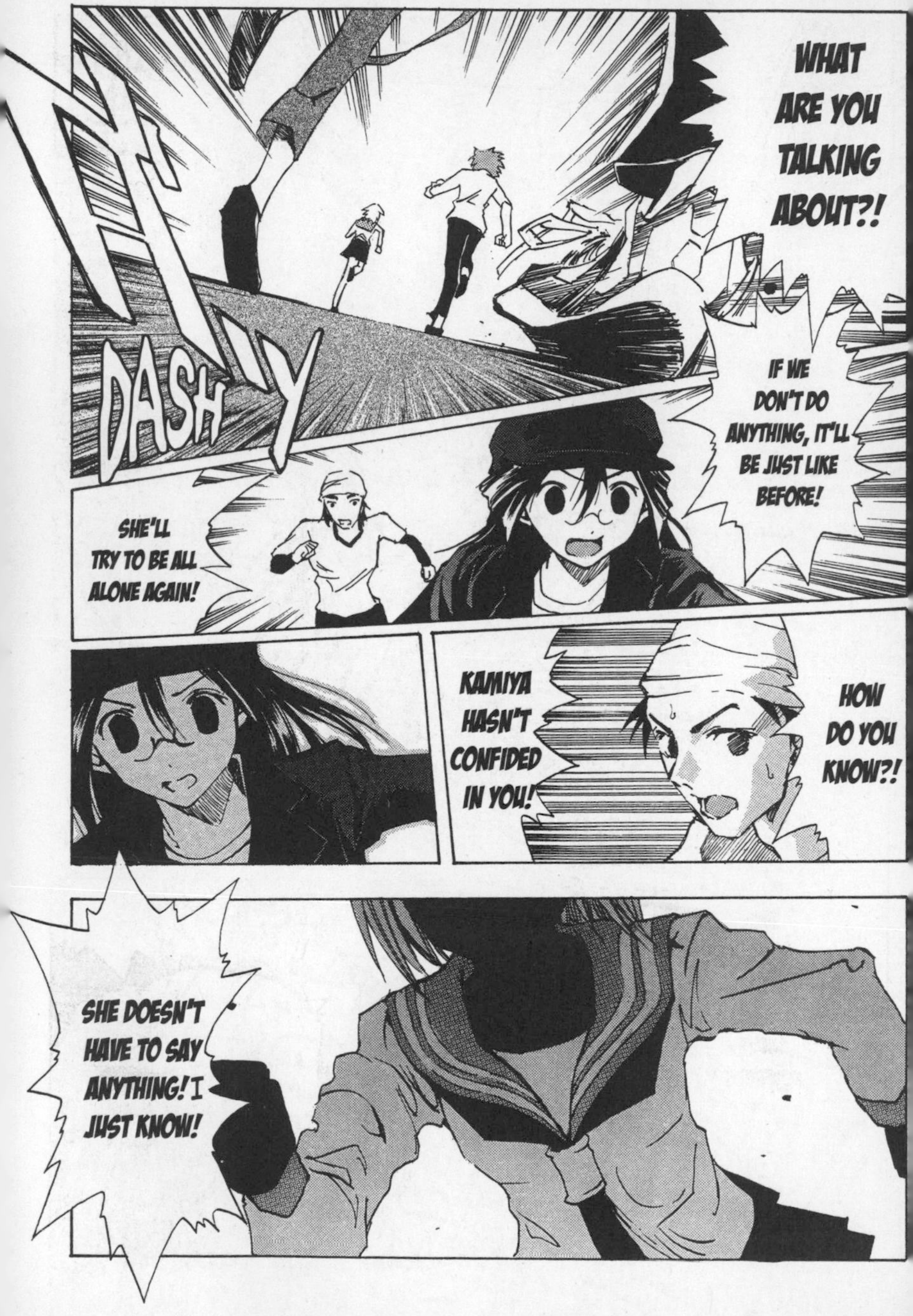
WHAT ARE YOU TALKING ABOUT?!
DASH
IF WE DON'T DO ANYTHING, IT'LL BE JUST LIKE BEFORE!
SHE'LL TRY TO BE ALL ALONE AGAIN!
KAMIYA HASN'T CONFIDED IN YOU!
HOW DO YOU KNOW?!
SHE DOESN'T HAVE TO SAY ANYTHING! I JUST KNOW!

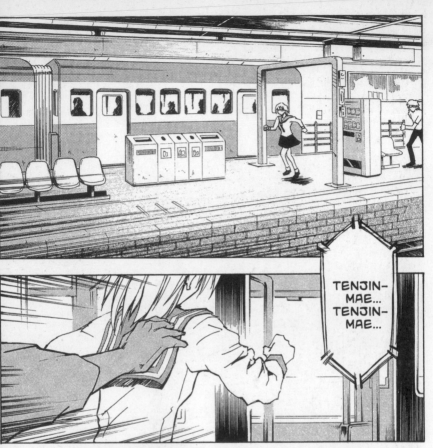

TENJIN-MAE...
TENJIN-MAE...

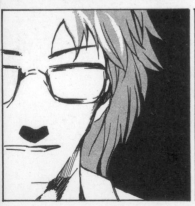

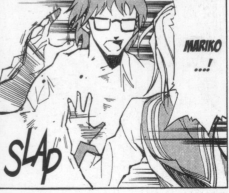

MARIKO...!

SLAP

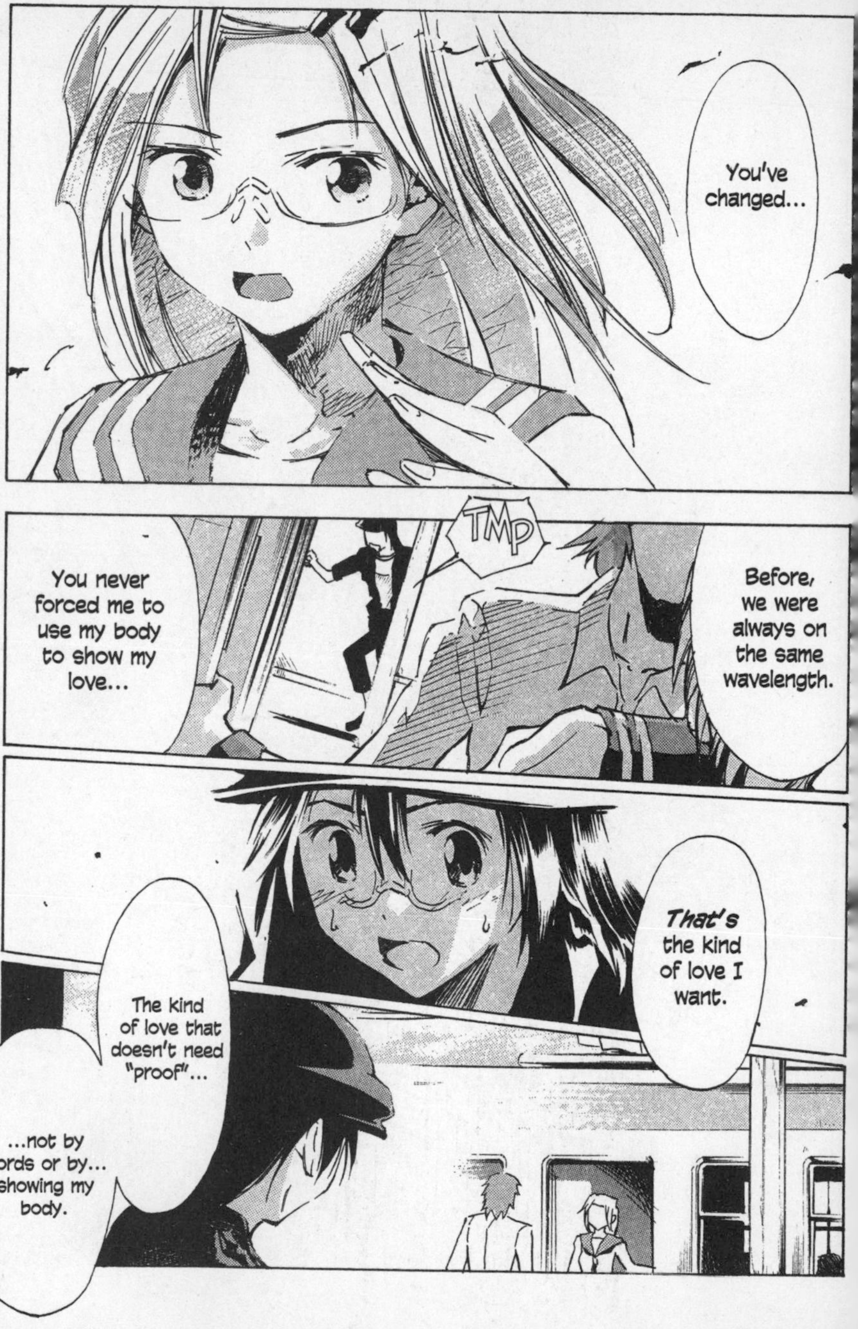
You've changed...
Before, we were always on the same wavelength.
TMP
You never forced me to use my body to show my love...
That's the kind of love I want.
The kind of love that doesn't need "proof"...
...not by words or by... showing my body.

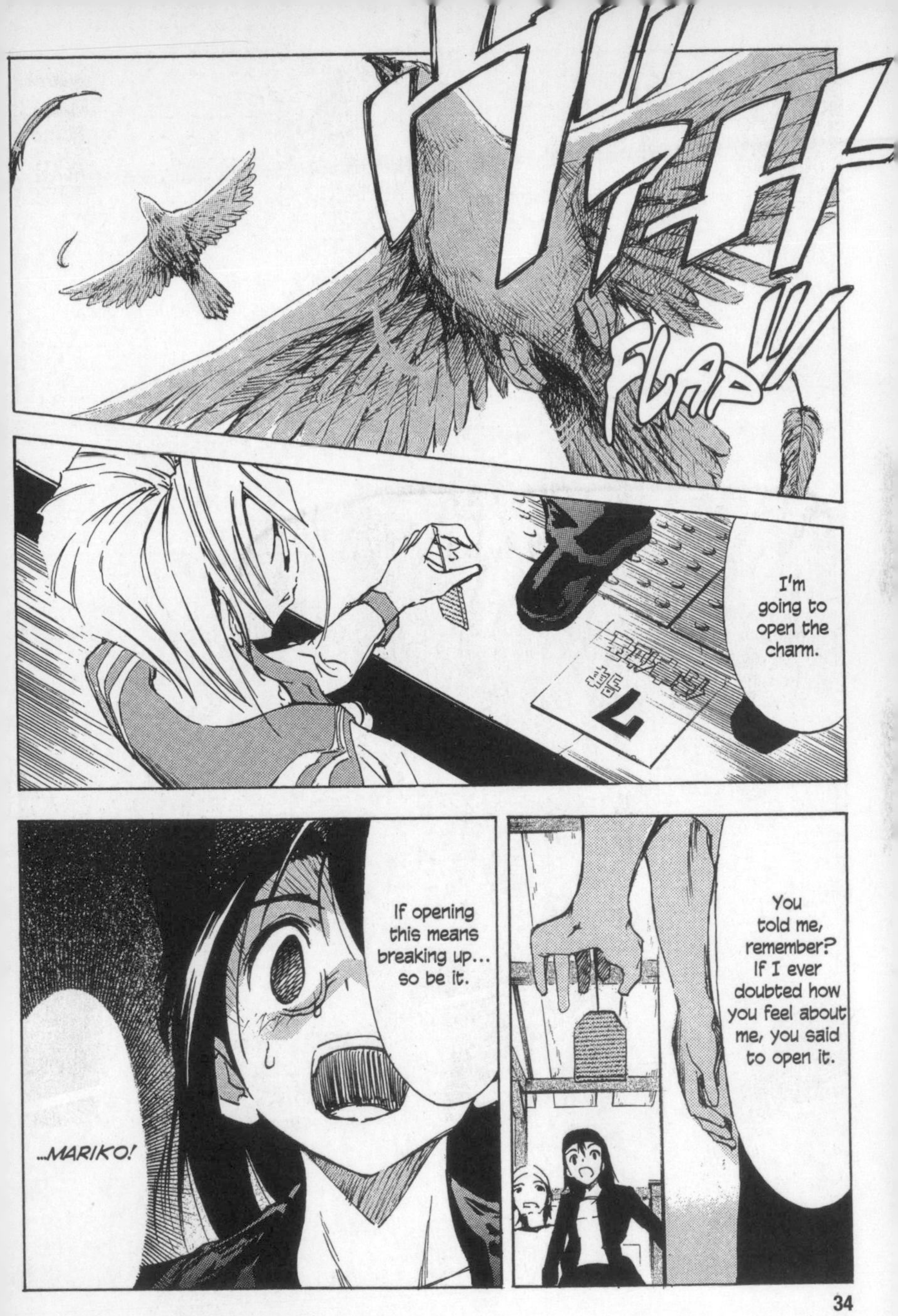
FLAP!!
I'm going to open the charm.
You told me, remember? If I ever doubted how you feel about me, you said to open it.
If opening this means breaking up... so be it.
...MARIKO!

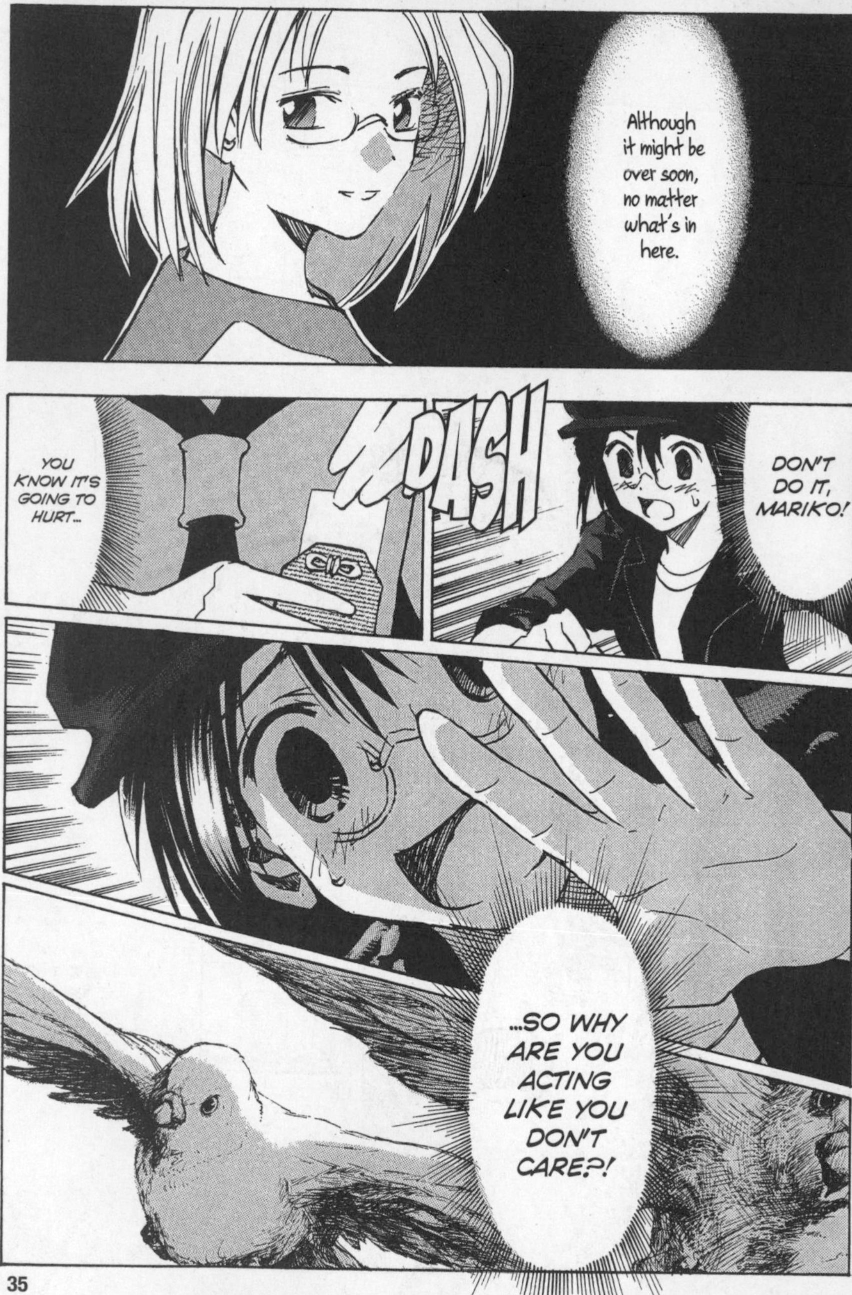
Although it might be over soon, no matter what's in here.
DON'T DO IT, MARIKO!
DASH
YOU KNOW IT'S GOING TO HURT...
...SO WHY ARE YOU ACTING LIKE YOU DON'T CARE?!

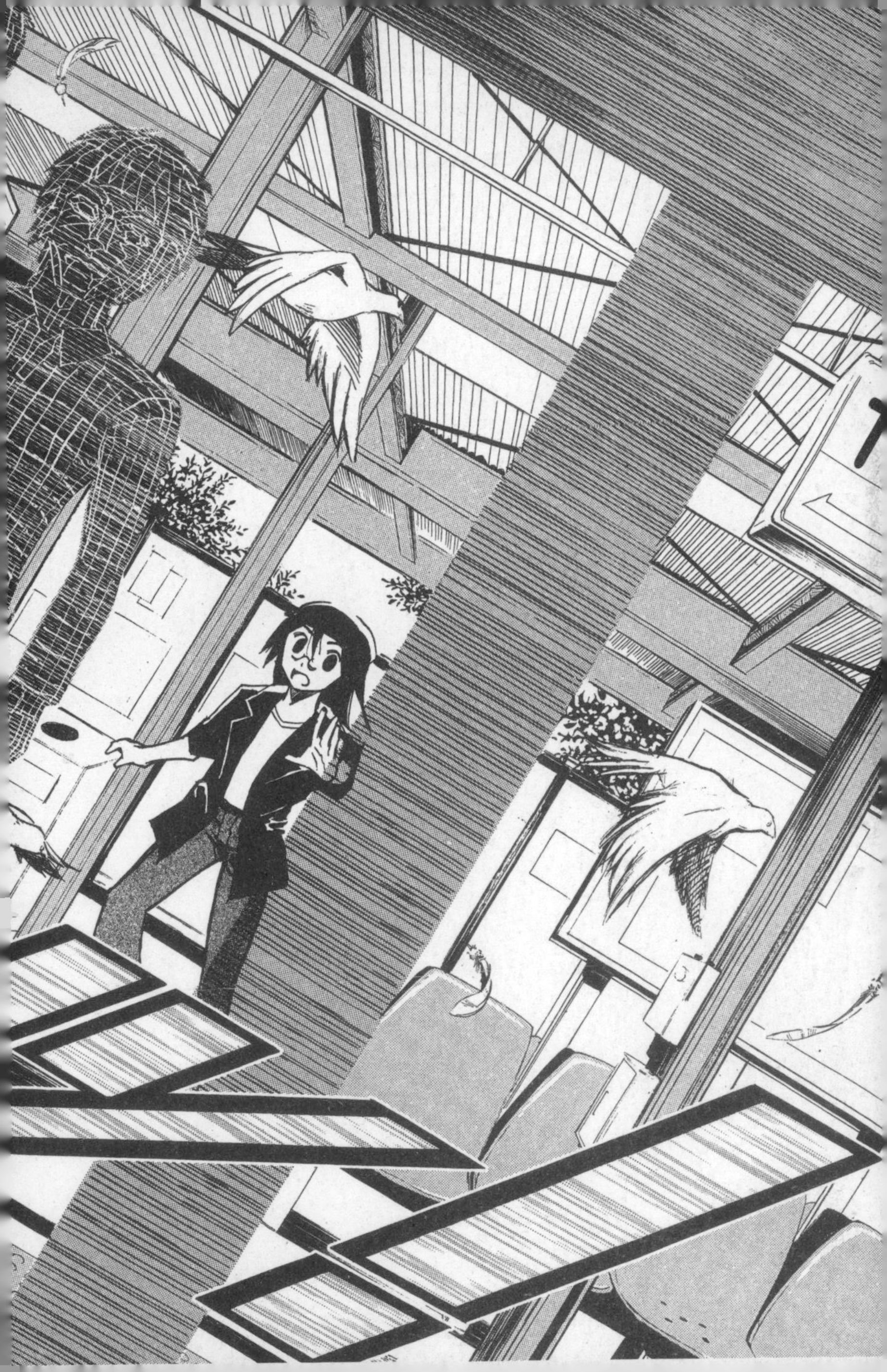

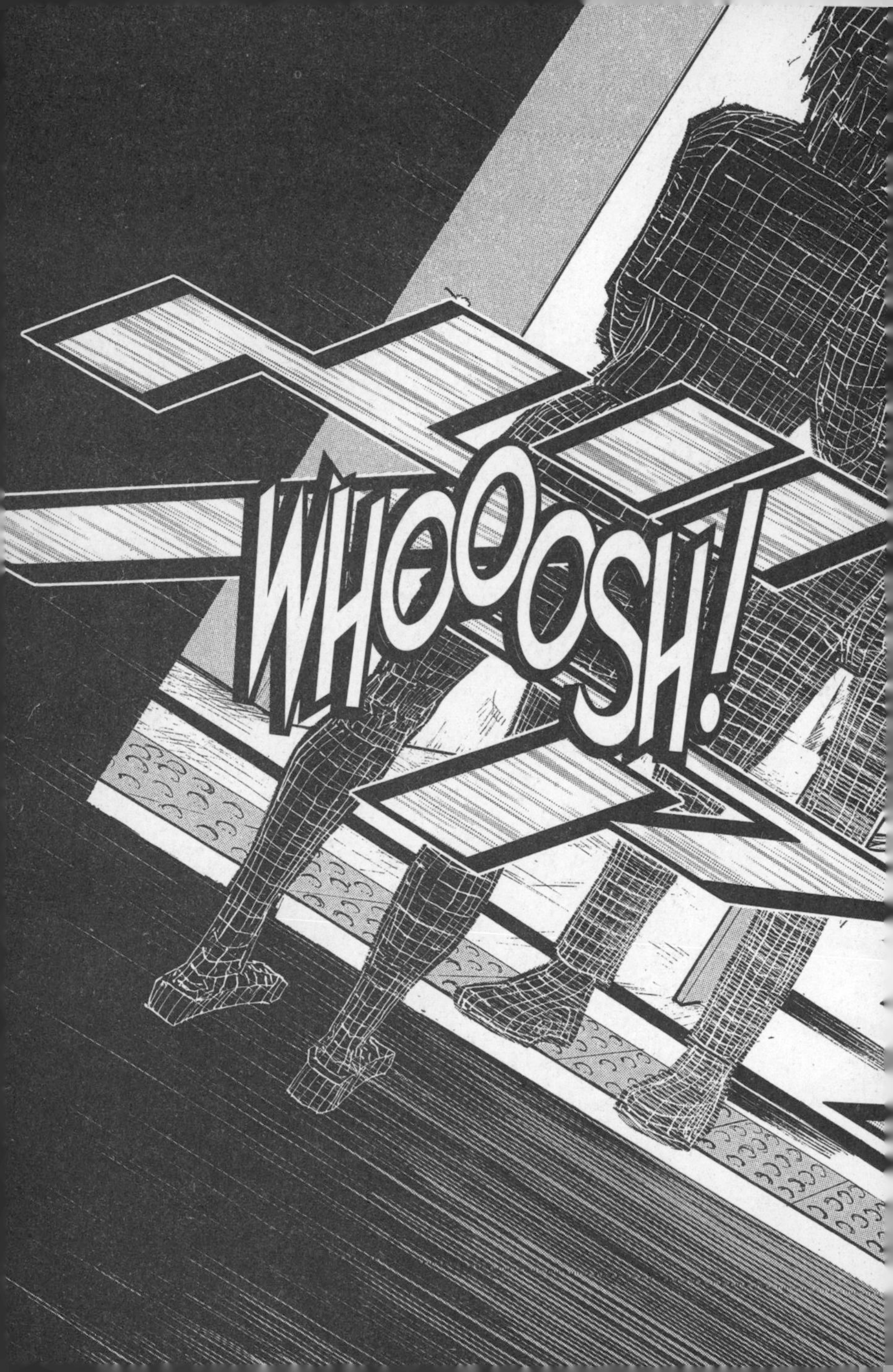
WHOOOOSH!

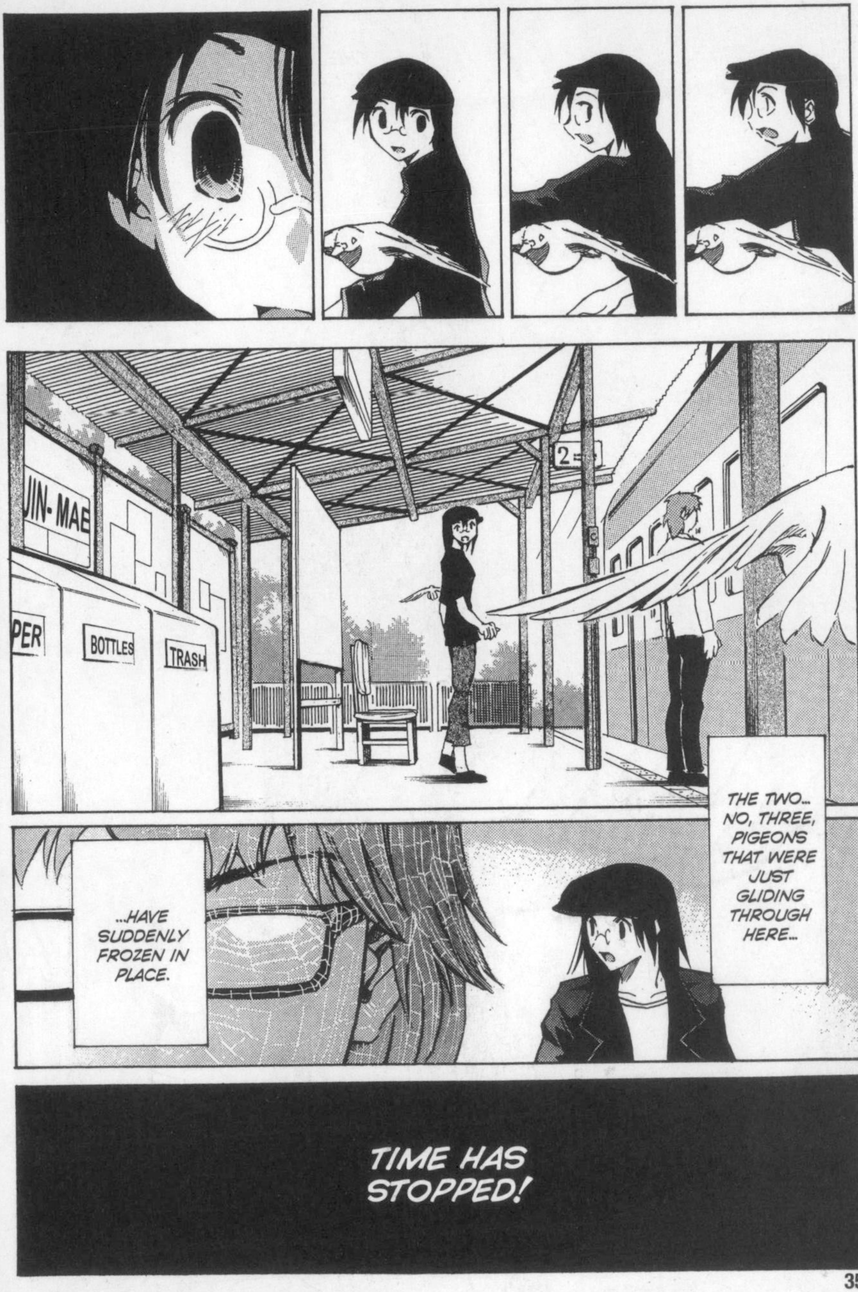
JIN- MAE
PER
BOTTLES
TRASH
THE TWO... NO, THREE, PIGEONS THAT WERE JUST GLIDING THROUGH HERE...
...HAVE SUDDENLY FROZEN IN PLACE.
TIME HAS STOPPED!

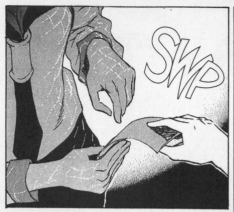

SWP

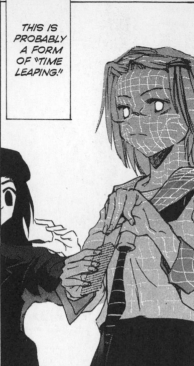

THIS IS PROBABLY A FORM OF "TIME LEAPING."

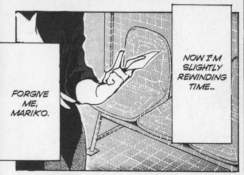

NOW I'M SLIGHTLY REWINDING TIME...

FORGIVE ME, MARIKO.

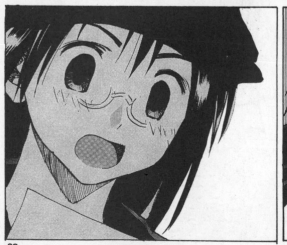

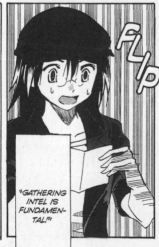

FLIP

"GATHERING INTEL IS FUNDAMENTAL!"

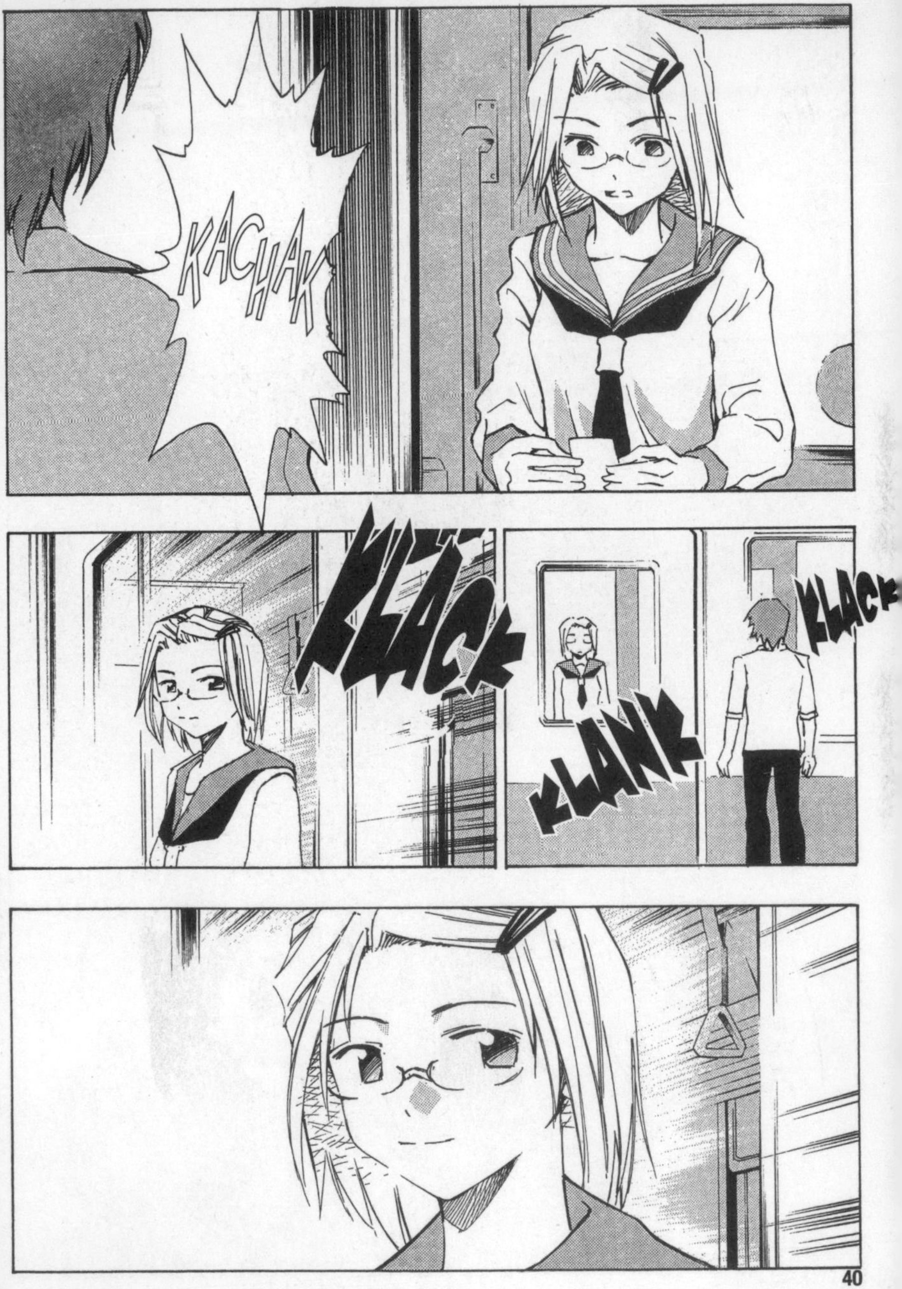
KACHAK
KLACK
KLANK
KLACK

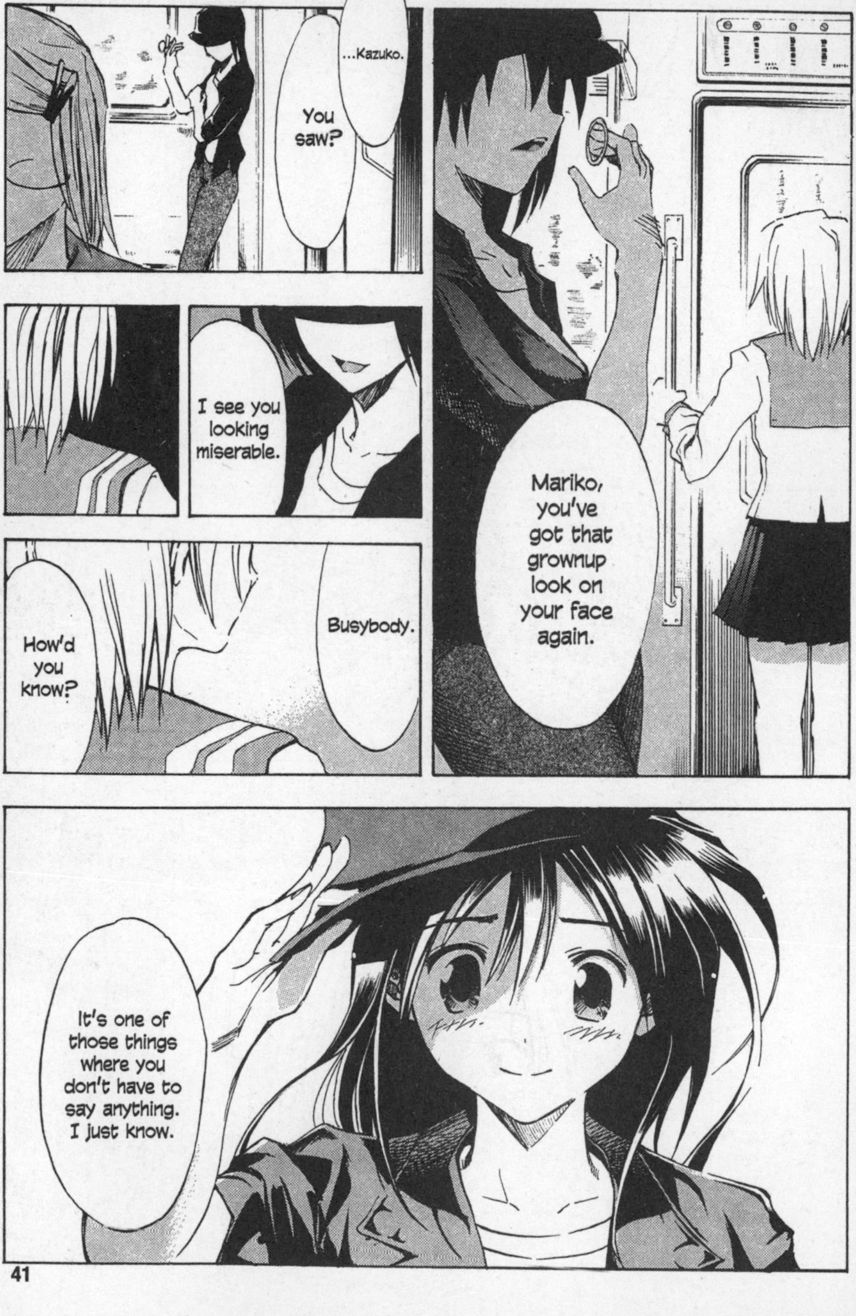
Mariko, you've got that grownup look on your face again.
...Kazuko.
You saw?
I see you looking miserable.
Busybody.
How'd you know?
It's one of those things where you don't have to say anything. I just know.

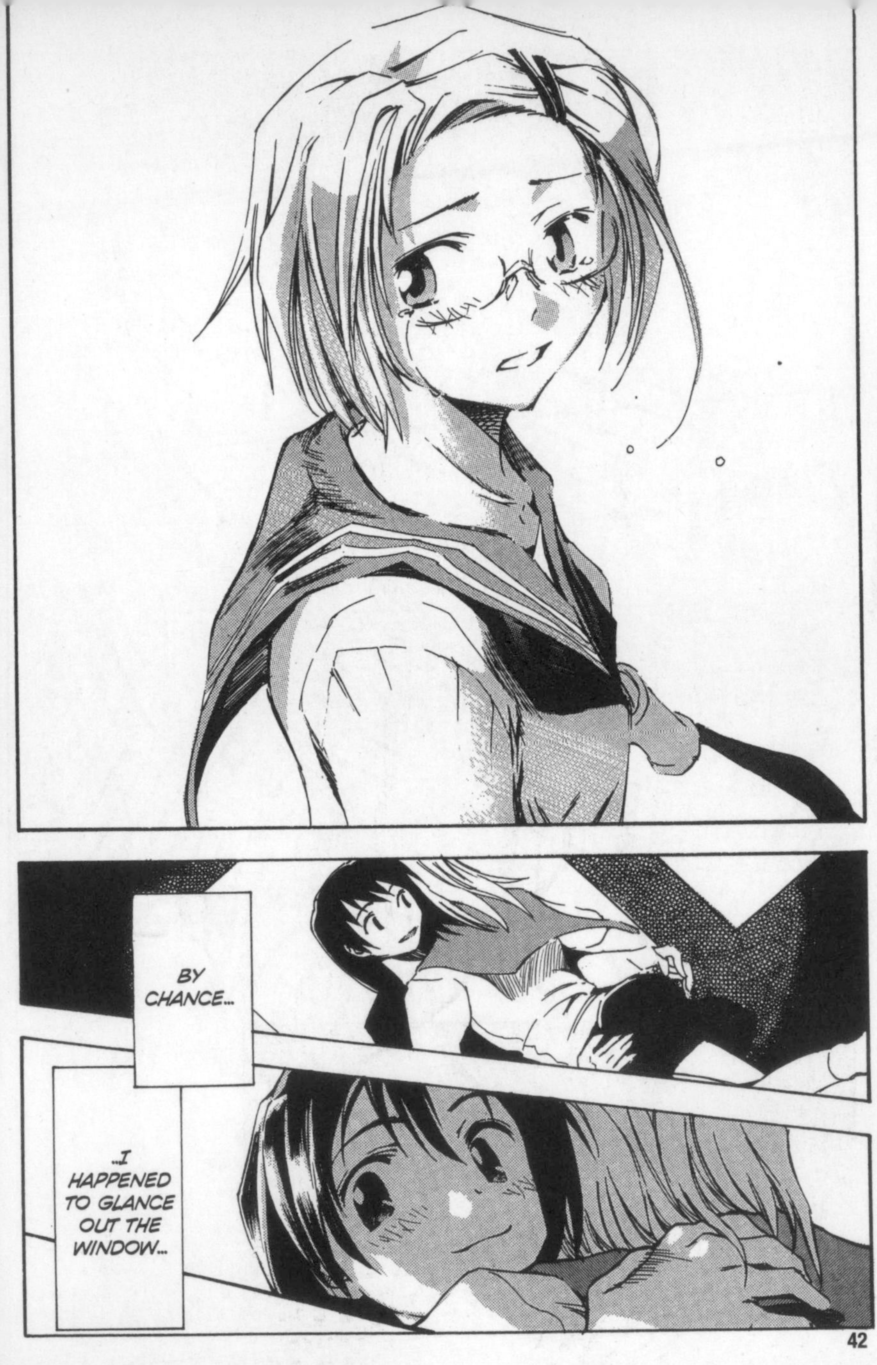
BY CHANCE...
...I HAPPENED TO GLANCE OUT THE WINDOW...

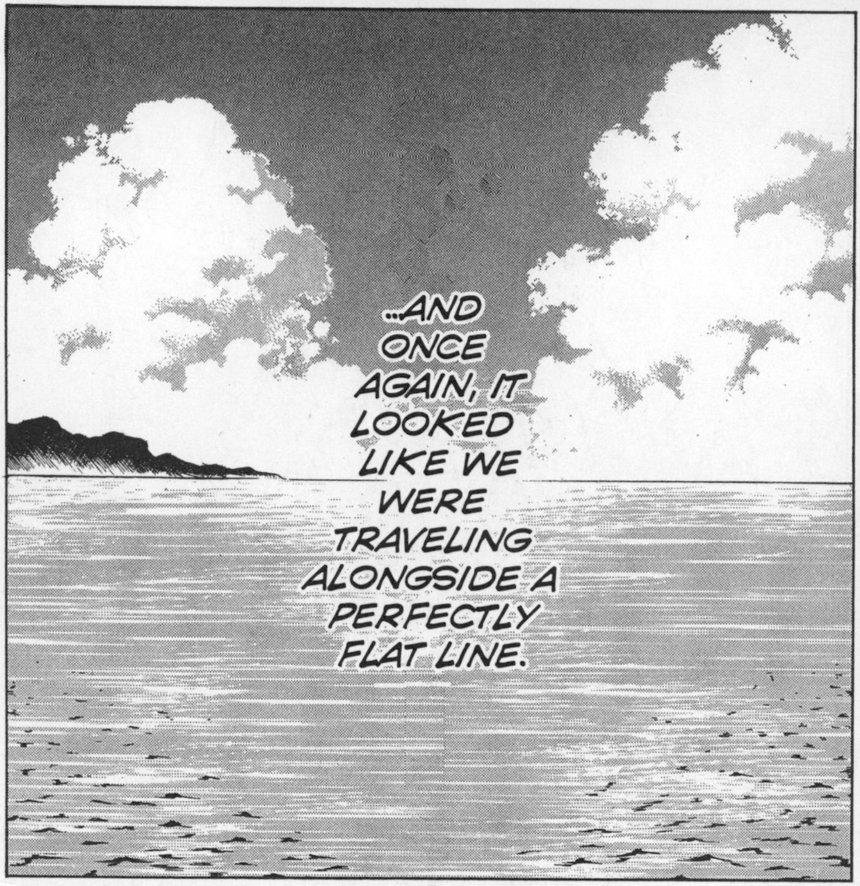
...AND ONCE AGAIN, IT LOOKED LIKE WE WERE TRAVELING ALONGSIDE A PERFECTLY FLAT LINE.

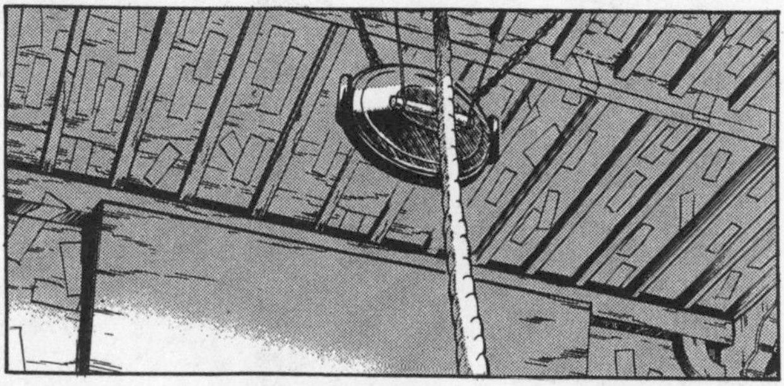

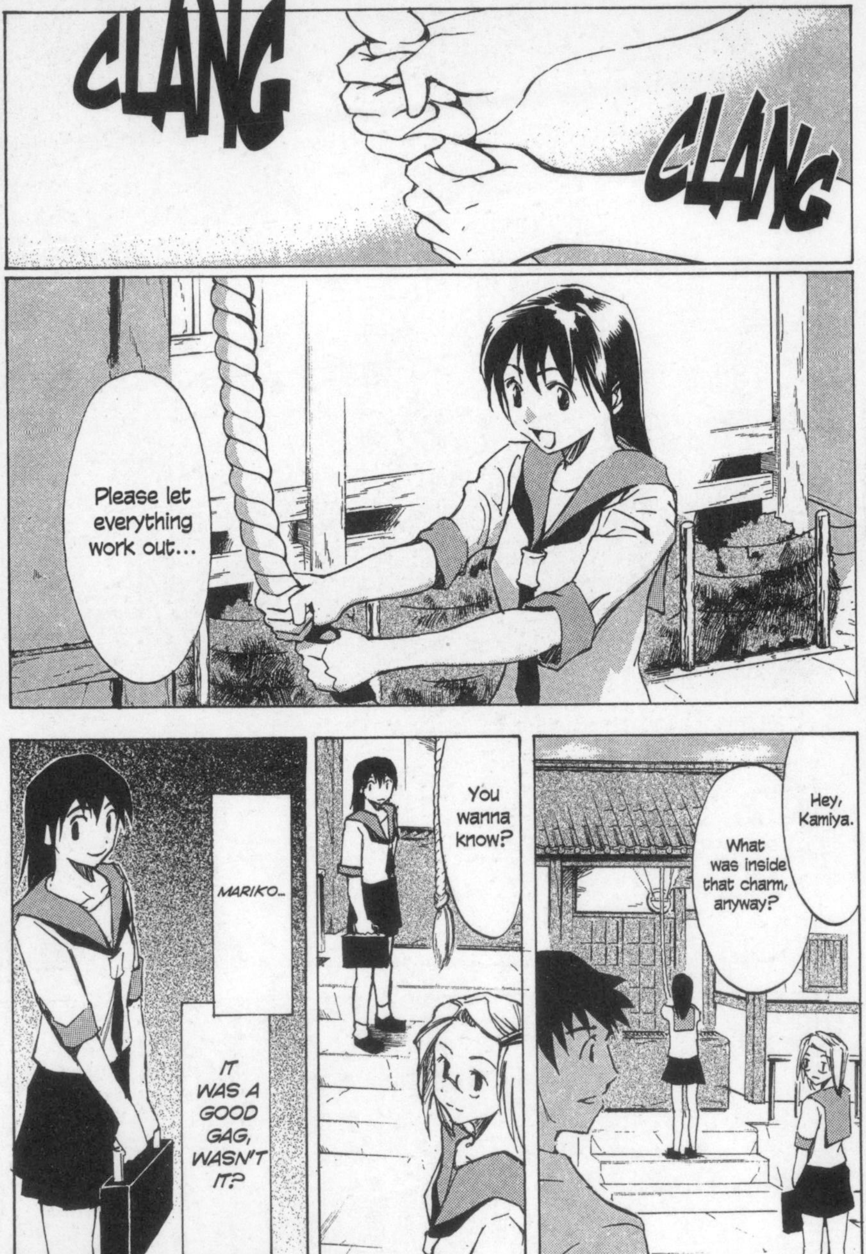
CLANG
CLANG
Please let everything work out...
Hey, Kamiya.
What was inside that charm, anyway?
You wanna know?
MARIKO...
IT WAS A GOOD GAG, WASN'T IT?

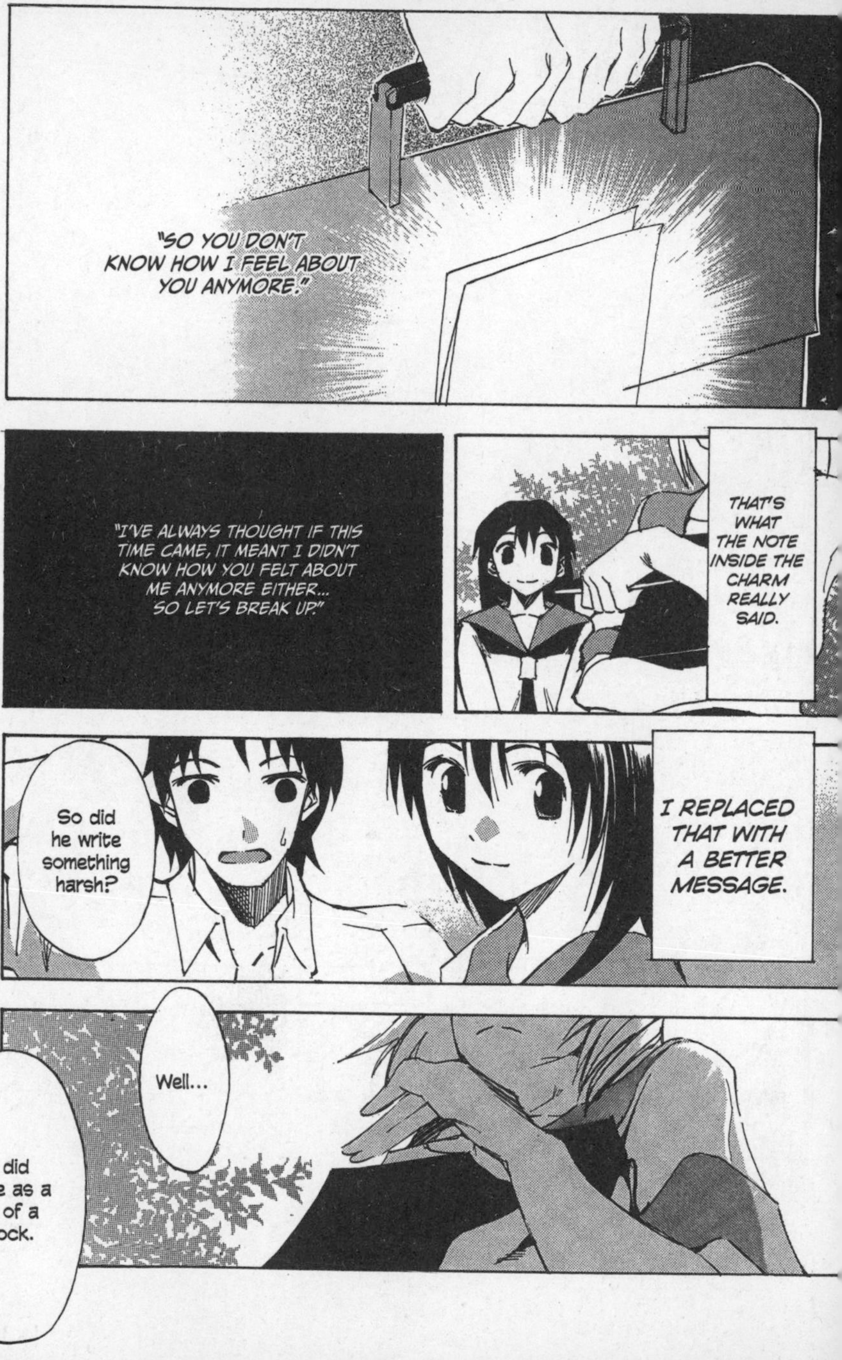
"SO YOU DON'T KNOW HOW I FEEL ABOUT YOU ANYMORE."
THAT'S WHAT THE NOTE INSIDE THE CHARM REALLY SAID.
"I'VE ALWAYS THOUGHT IF THIS TIME CAME, IT MEANT I DIDN'T KNOW HOW YOU FELT ABOUT ME ANYMORE EITHER... SO LET'S BREAK UP."
I REPLACED THAT WITH A BETTER MESSAGE.
So did he write something harsh?
Well...
It did come as a bit of a shock.

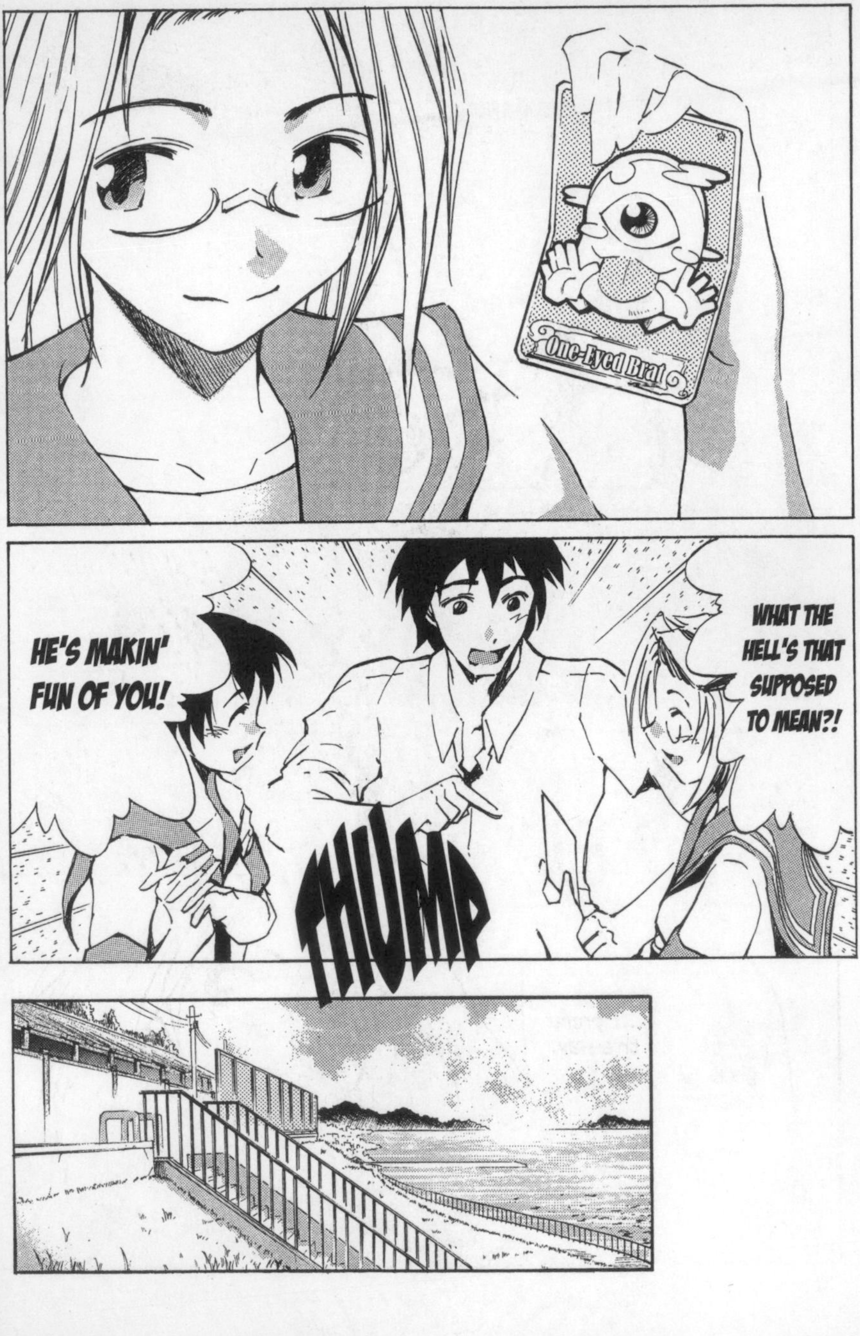
One-Eyed Brat
WHAT THE HELL'S THAT SUPPOSED TO MEAN?!
HE'S MAKIN' FUN OF YOU!
THUMP

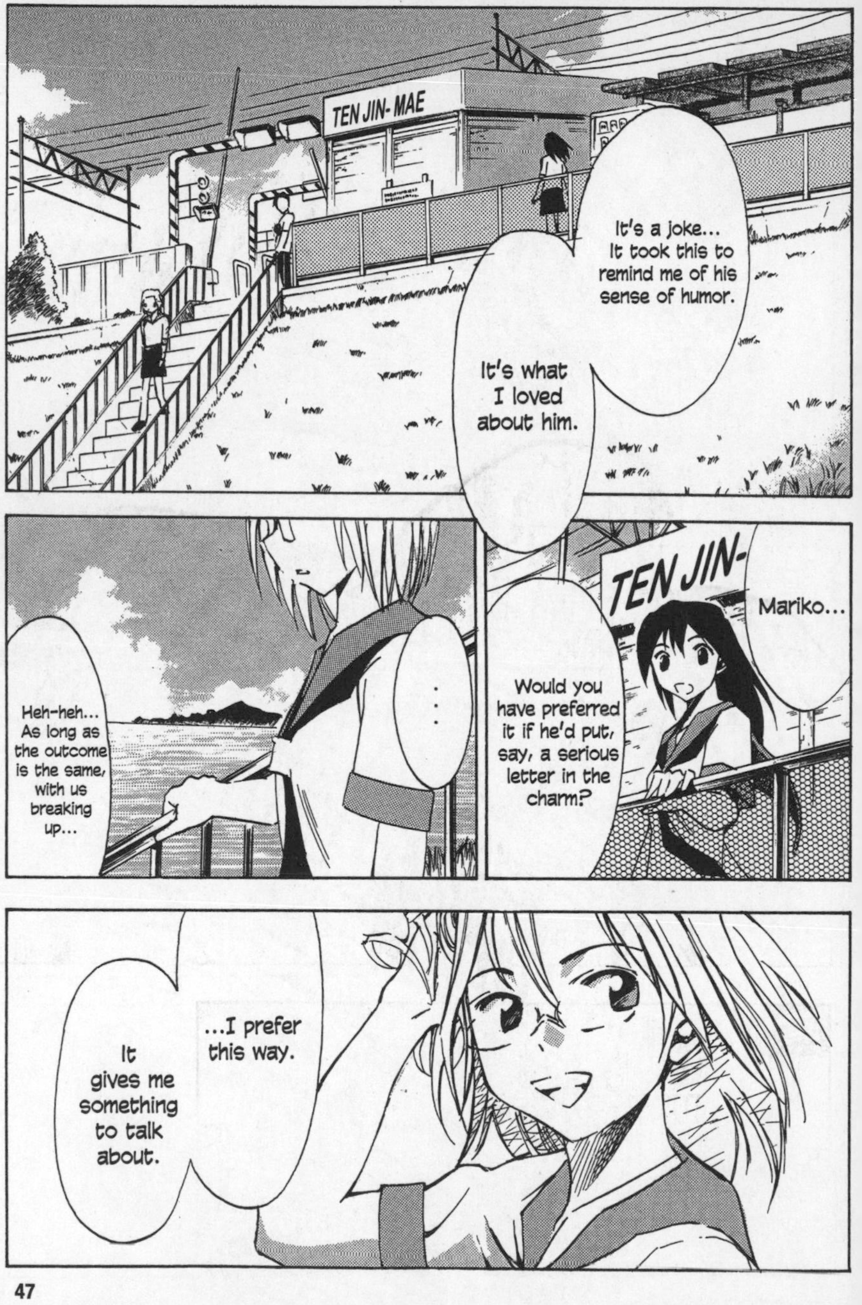
TEN JIN- MAE
It's a joke... It took this to remind me of his sense of humor.
It's what I loved about him.
TEN JIN-
Mariko...
Would you have preferred it if he'd put, say, a serious letter in the charm?
. . .
Heh-heh... As long as the outcome is the same, with us breaking up...
...I prefer this way.
It gives me something to talk about.

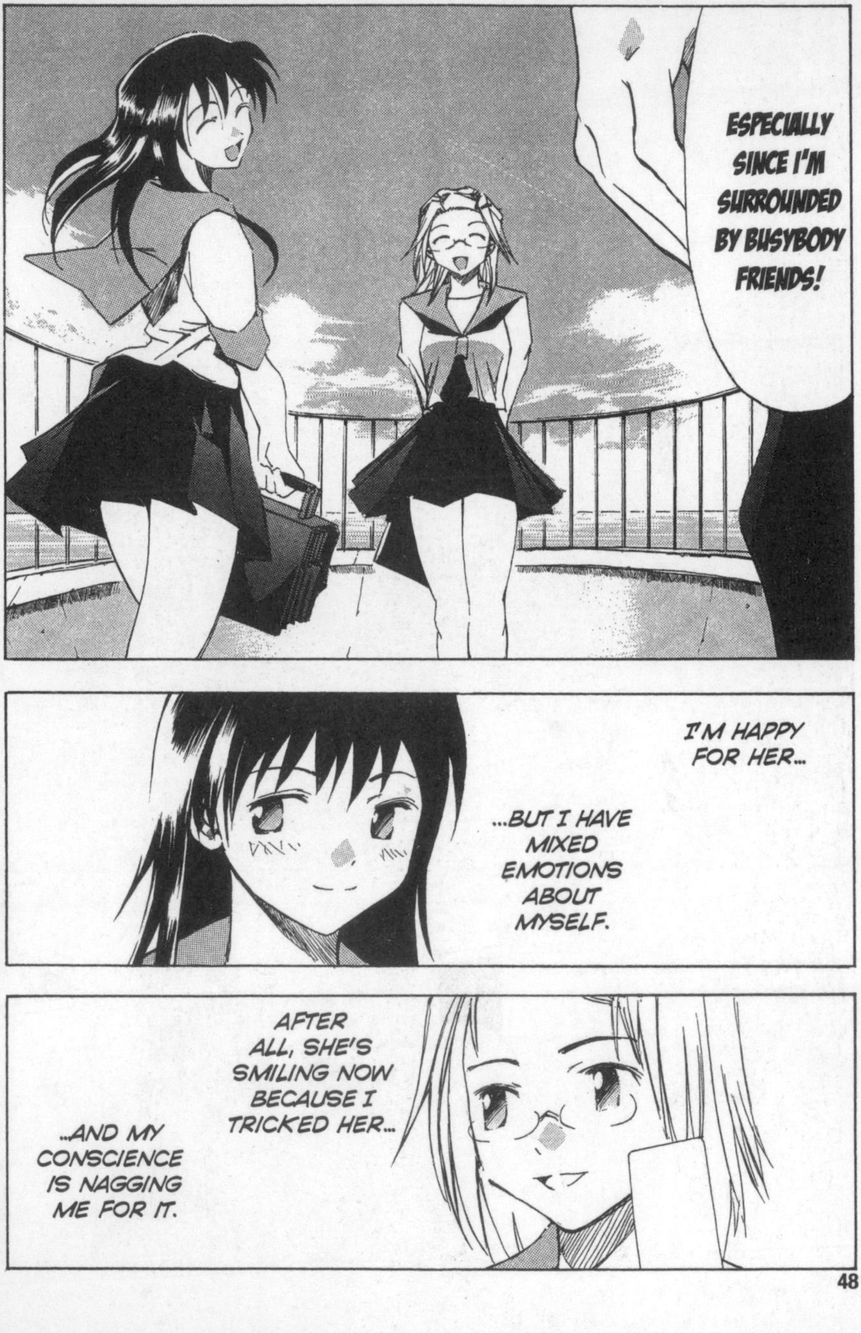
ESPECIALLY SINCE I'M SURROUNDED BY BUSYBODY FRIENDS!
I'M HAPPY FOR HER...
...BUT I HAVE MIXED EMOTIONS ABOUT MYSELF.
AFTER ALL, SHE'S SMILING NOW BECAUSE I TRICKED HER...
...AND MY CONSCIENCE IS NAGGING ME FOR IT.

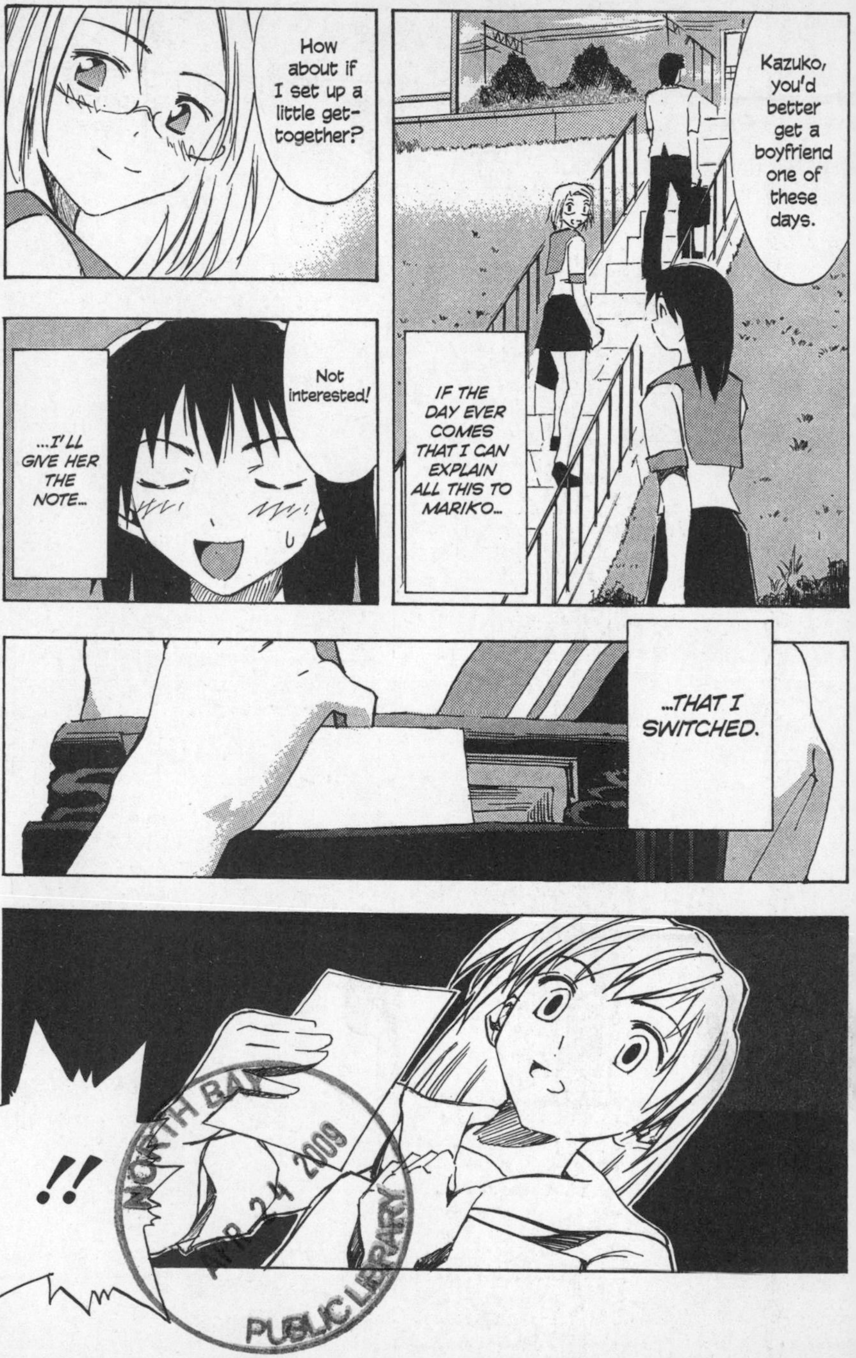
Kazuko, you'd better get a boyfriend one of these days.
IF THE DAY EVER COMES THAT I CAN EXPLAIN ALL THIS TO MARIKO...
How about if I set up a little get-together?
Not interested!
...I'LL GIVE HER THE NOTE...
...THAT I SWITCHED.
!!

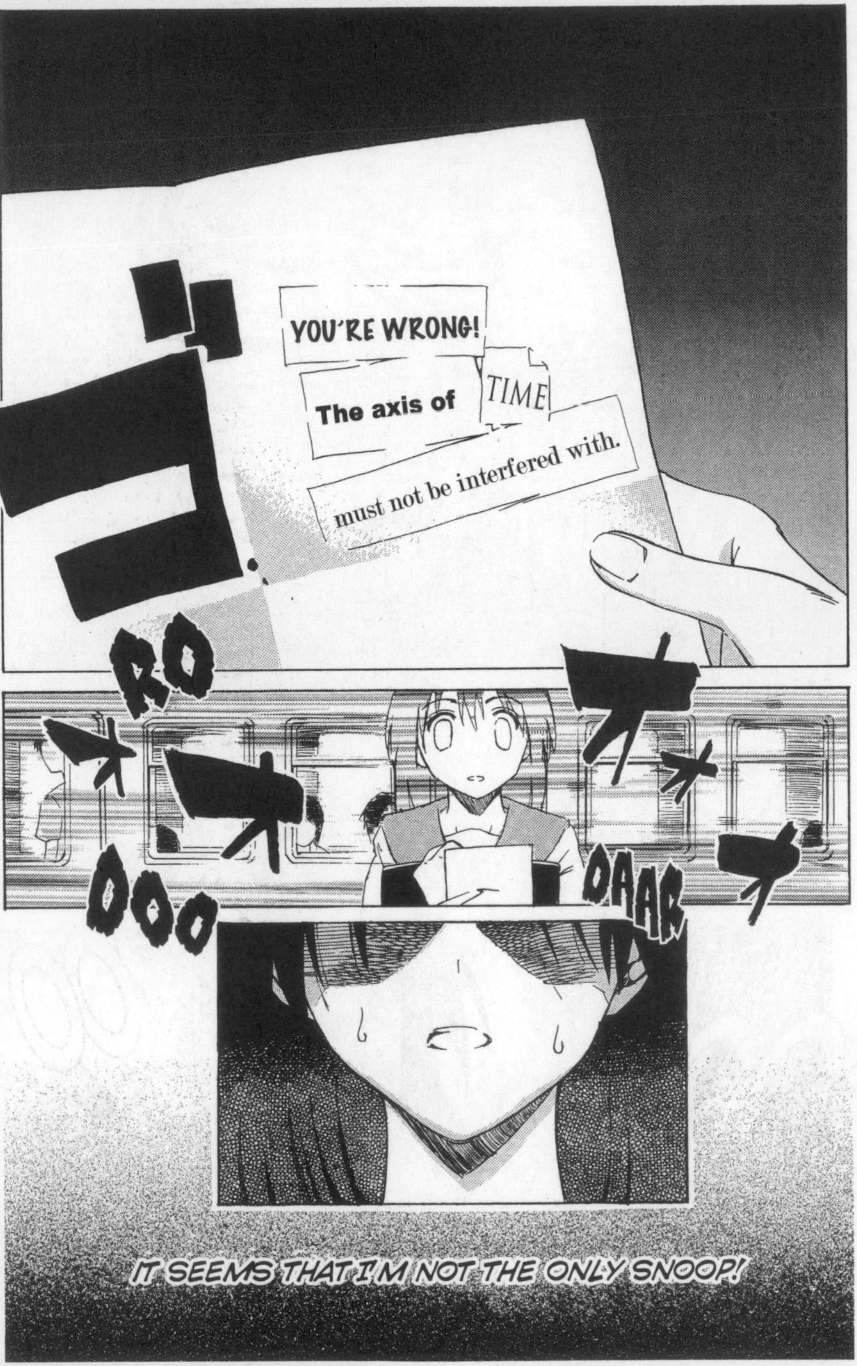
ゴ
YOU'RE WRONG!
The axis of TIME
must not be interfered with.
OAAR
ROOOO
IT SEEMS THAT I'M NOT THE ONLY SNOOP!

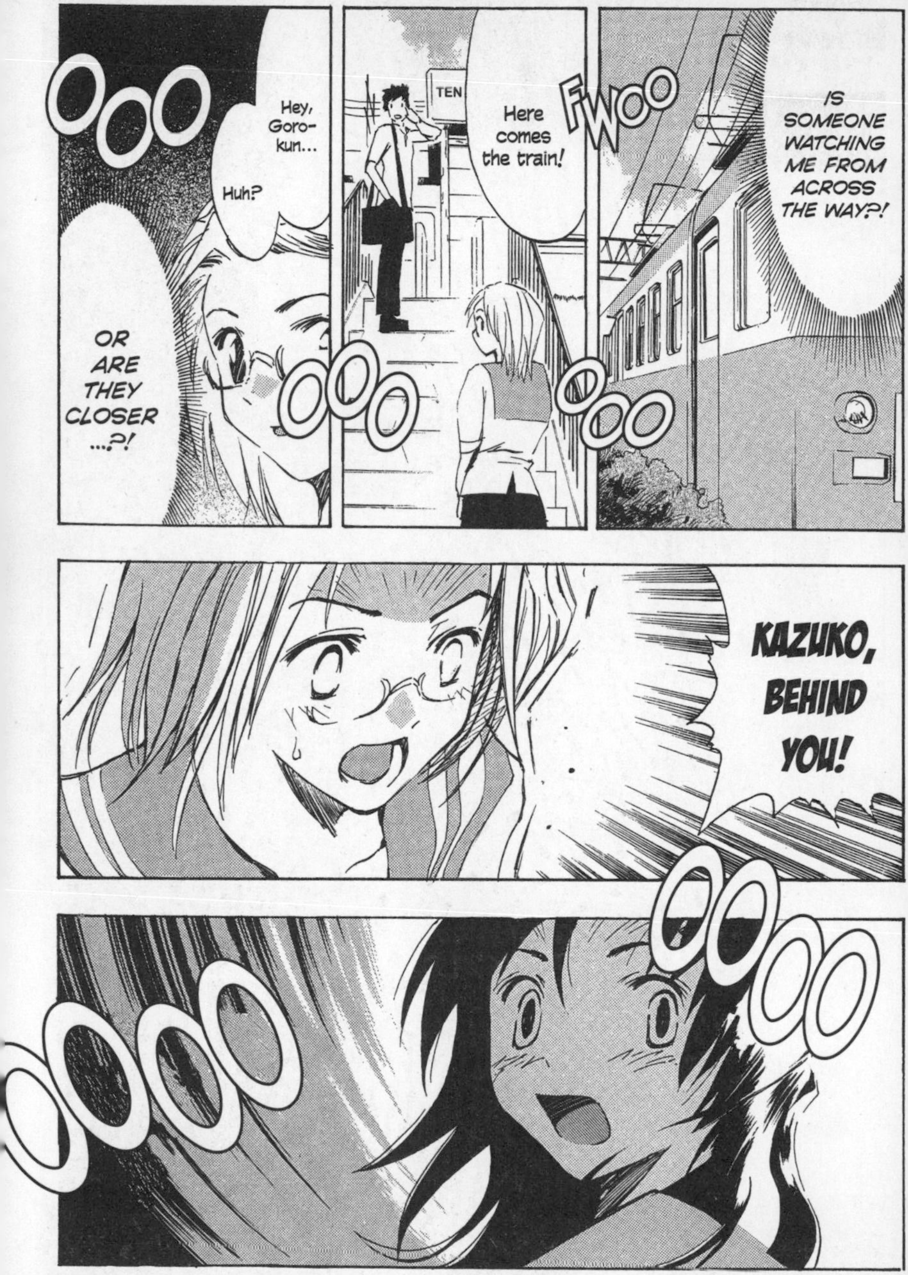
IS SOMEONE WATCHING ME FROM ACROSS THE WAY?!
FWOO
OOO
TEN
Here comes the train!
OOO
Hey, Goro-kun...
Huh?
OR ARE THEY CLOSER ...?!
OOO
KAZUKO, BEHIND YOU!
OOOO
OOOO

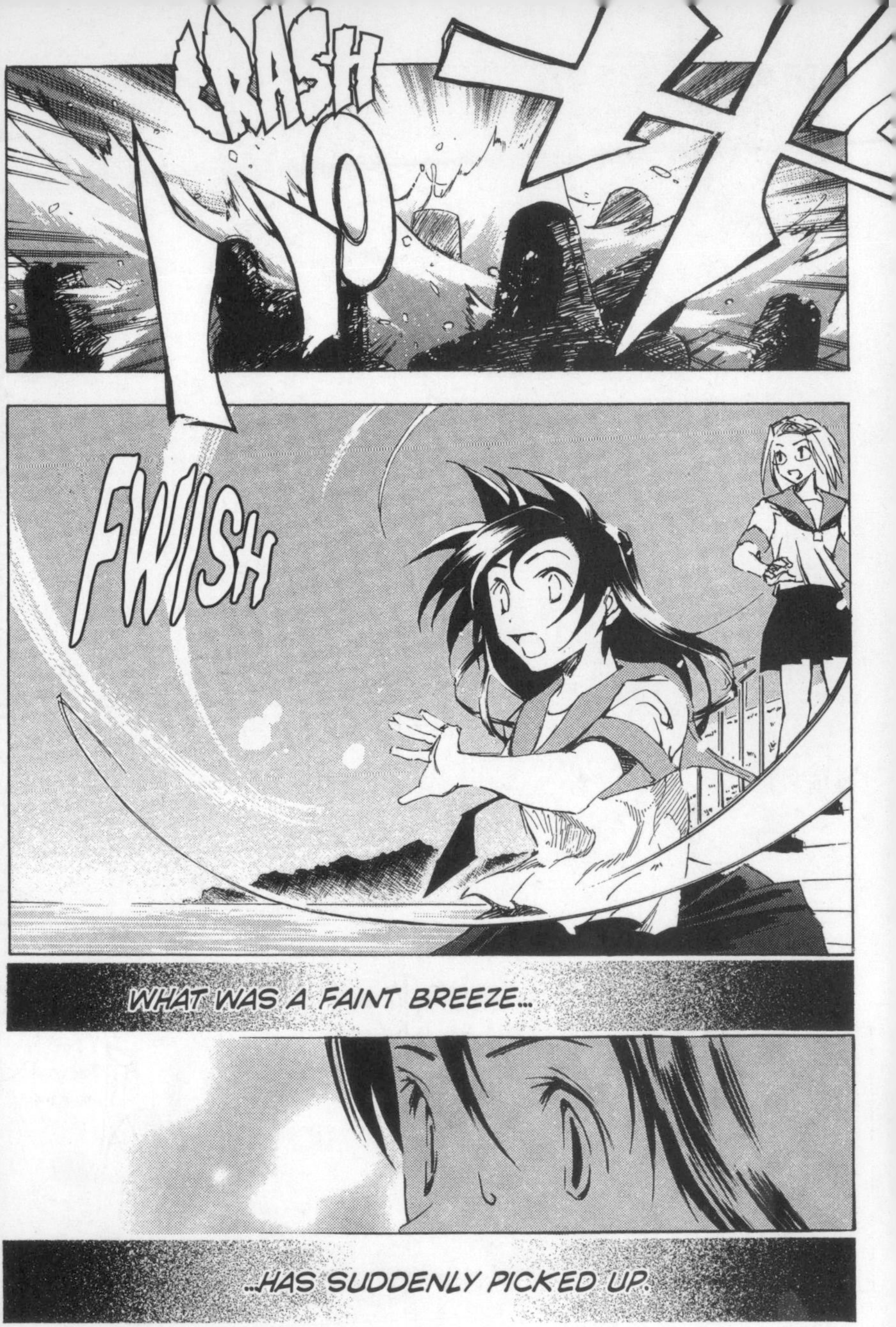
CRASH
FWISH
WHAT WAS A FAINT BREEZE...
...HAS SUDDENLY PICKED UP.

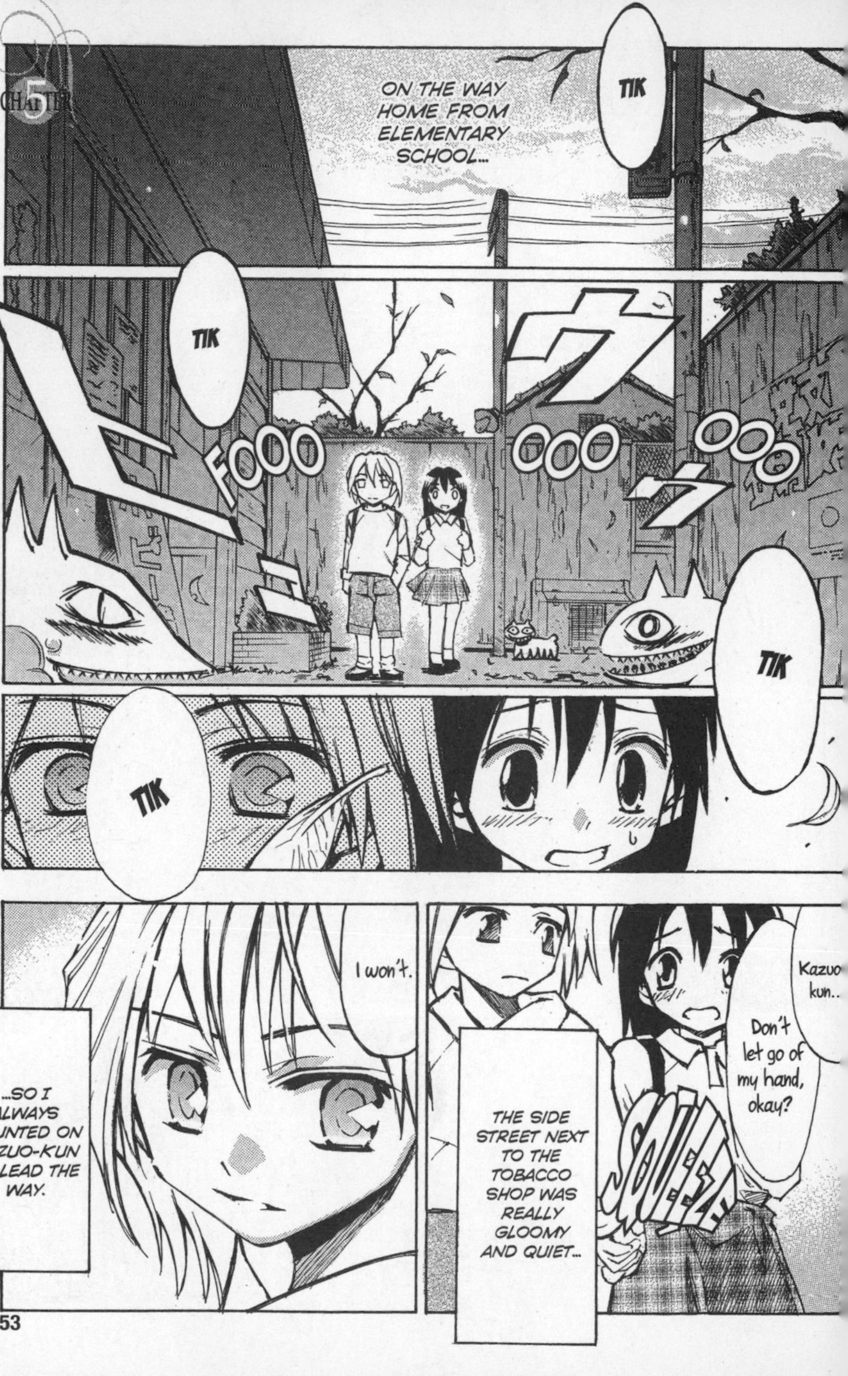
TIK
ON THE WAY HOME FROM ELEMENTARY SCHOOL...
TIK
FOOOOOOOOO
TIK
TIK
Kazuo kun..
Don't let go of my hand, okay?
SQUEEZE
THE SIDE STREET NEXT TO THE TOBACCO SHOP WAS REALLY GLOOMY AND QUIET...
I won't.
...SO I ALWAYS COUNTED ON KAZUO-KUN TO LEAD THE WAY.

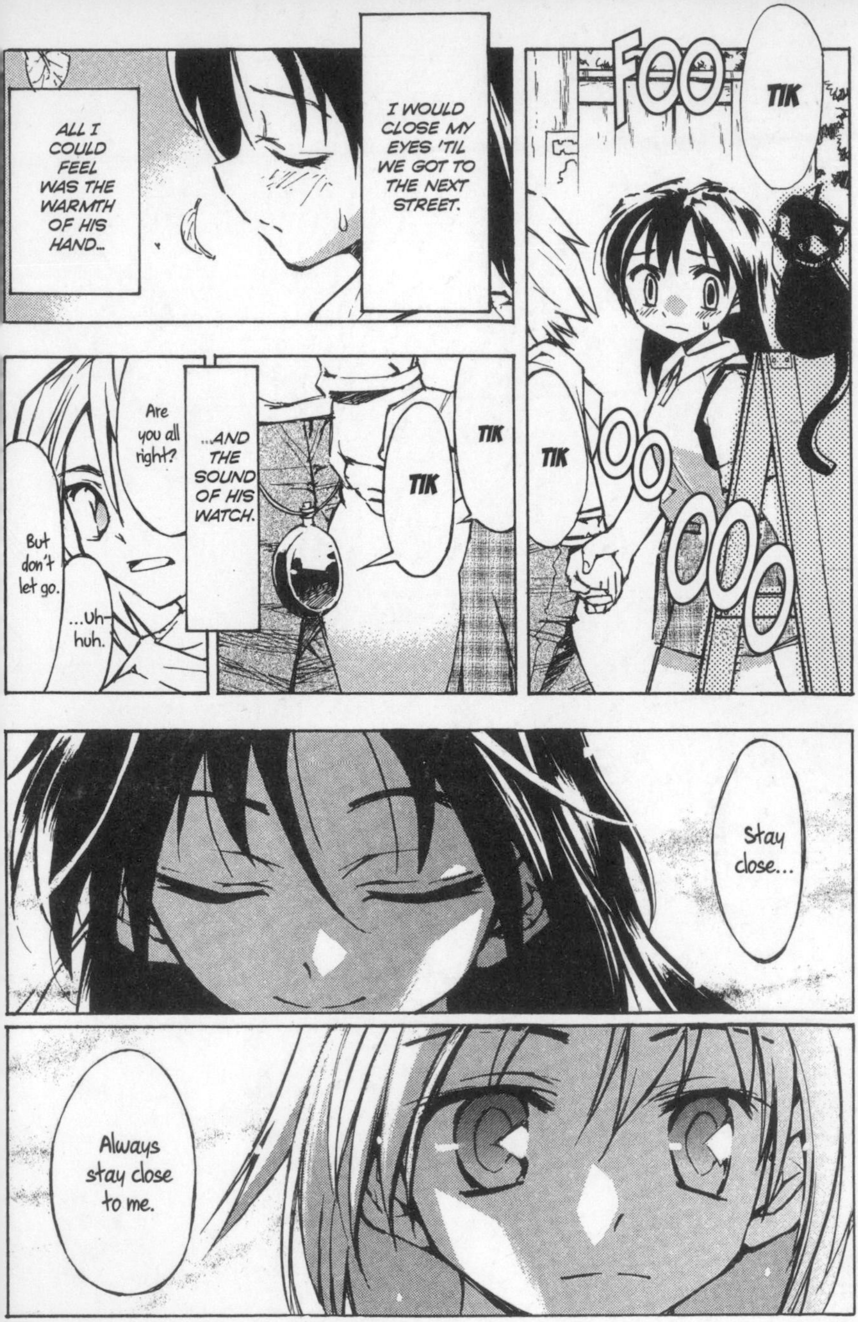
FOO
TIK
OOOOOO
TIK
I WOULD CLOSE MY EYES 'TIL WE GOT TO THE NEXT STREET.
ALL I COULD FEEL WAS THE WARMTH OF HIS HAND...
TIK
TIK
...AND THE SOUND OF HIS WATCH.
Are you all right?
But don't let go.
...Uh-huh.
Stay close...
Always stay close to me.

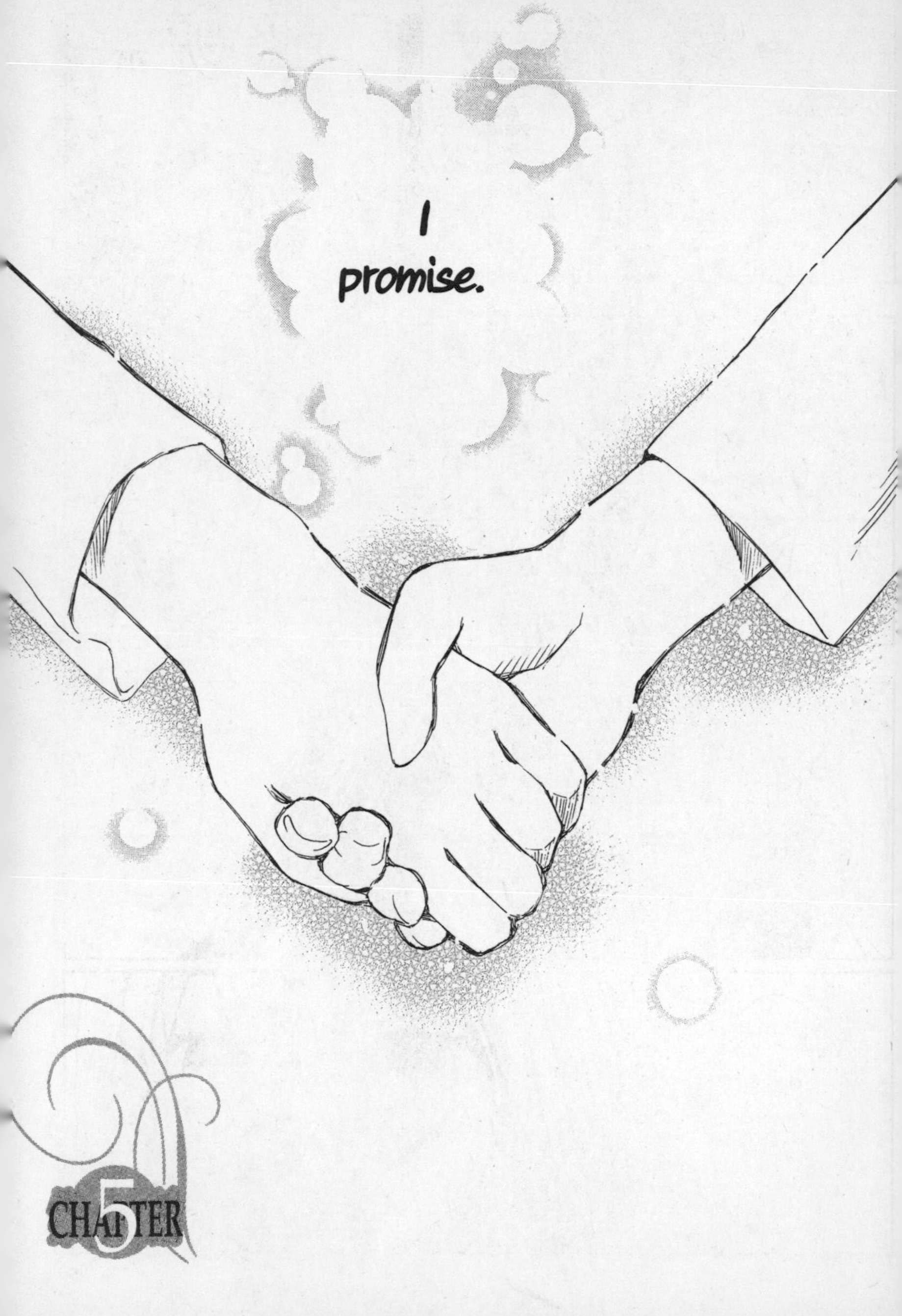
I promise.
CHAPTER 5

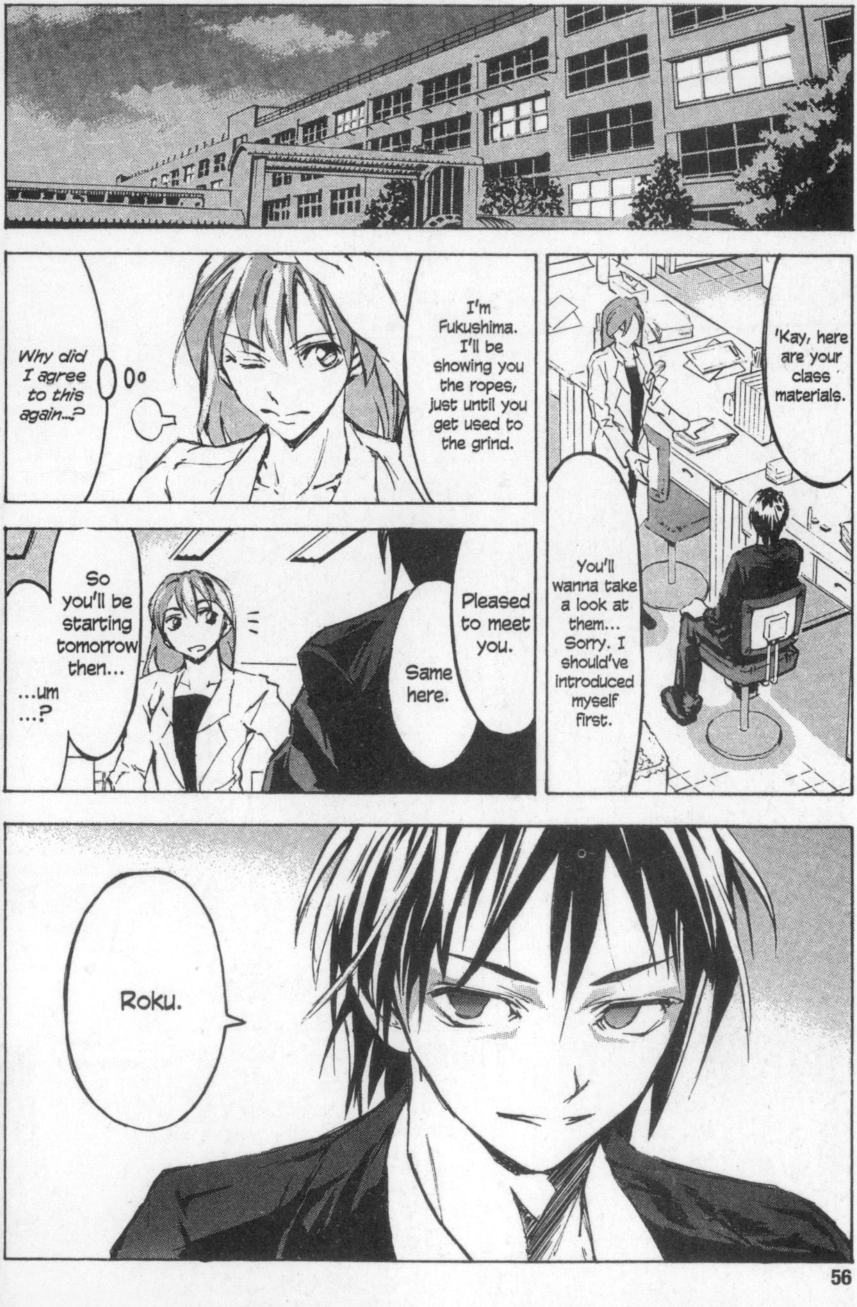

'Kay, here are your class materials.
You'll wanna take a look at them... Sorry. I should've introduced myself first.
I'm Fukushima. I'll be showing you the ropes, just until you get used to the grind.
Why did I agree to this again...?
Pleased to meet you.
Same here.
So you'll be starting tomorrow then...
...um ...?
Roku.

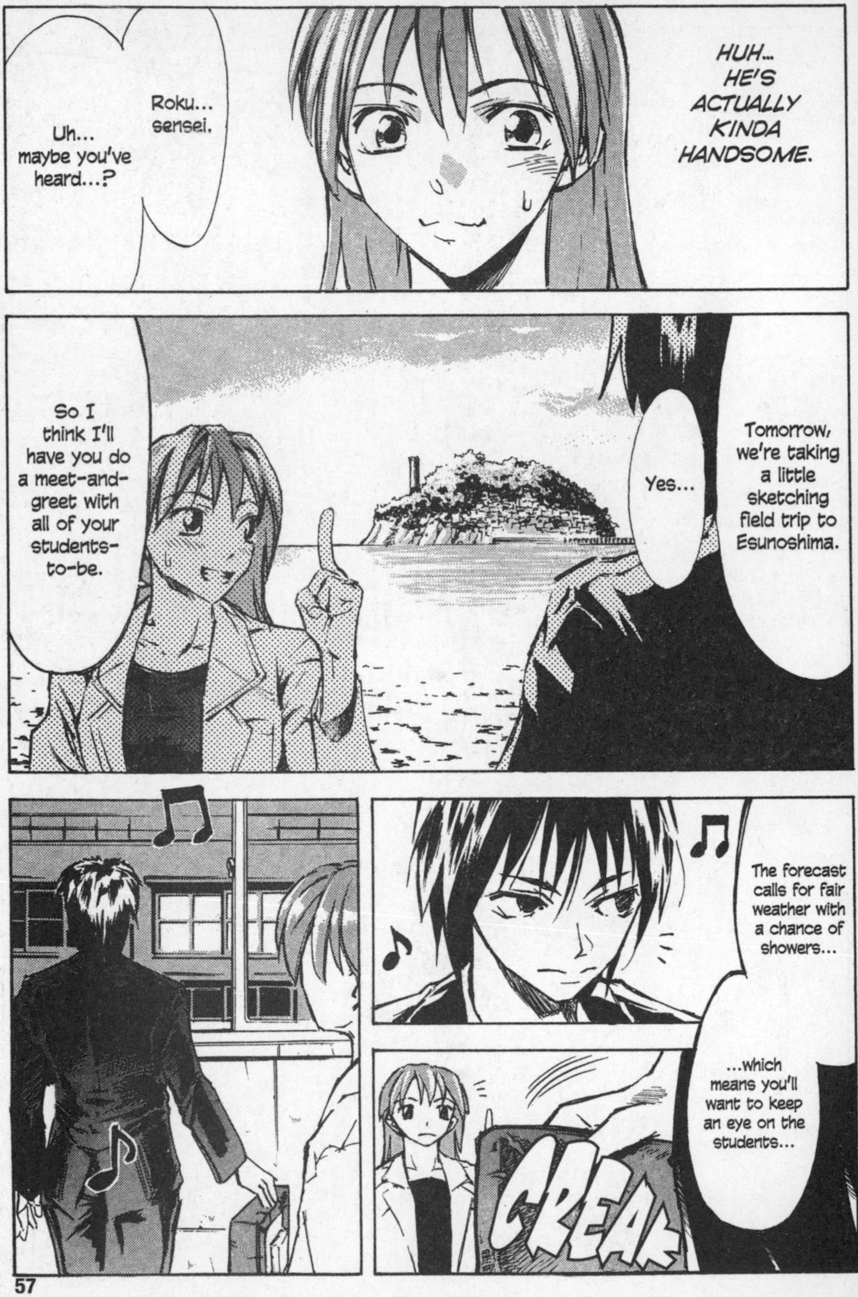
HUH... HE'S ACTUALLY KINDA HANDSOME.
Roku... sensei.
Uh... maybe you've heard...?
Tomorrow, we're taking a little sketching field trip to Esunoshima.
Yes...
So I think I'll have you do a meet-and-greet with all of your students-to-be.
The forecast calls for fair weather with a chance of showers...
...which means you'll want to keep an eye on the students...
CREAK

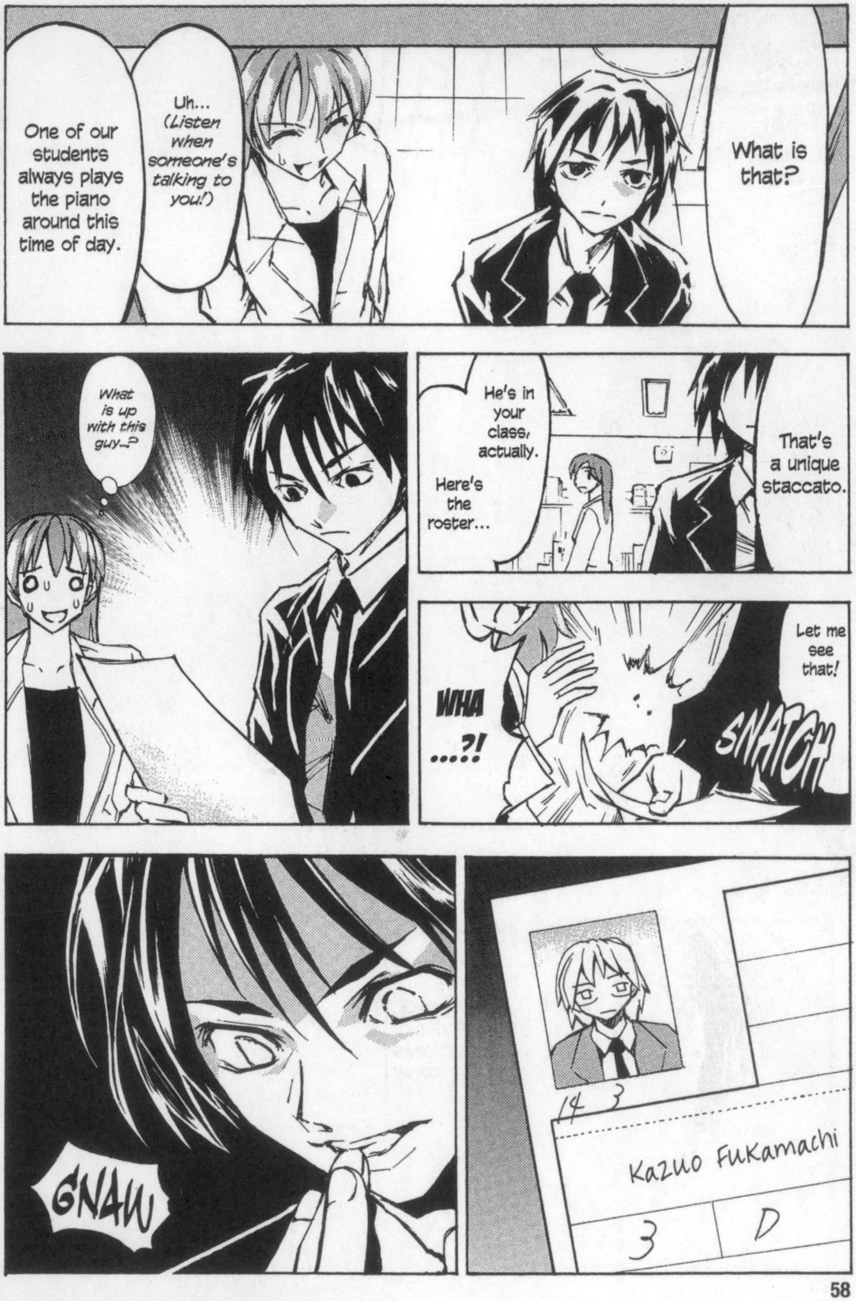
What is that?
Uh... (Listen when someone's talking to you!)
One of our students always plays the piano around this time of day.
That's a unique staccato.
He's in your class, actually.
Here's the roster...
Let me see that!
SNATCH
WHA...?!
What is up with this guy...?
14 3
Kazuo Fukamachi
3 D
GNAW

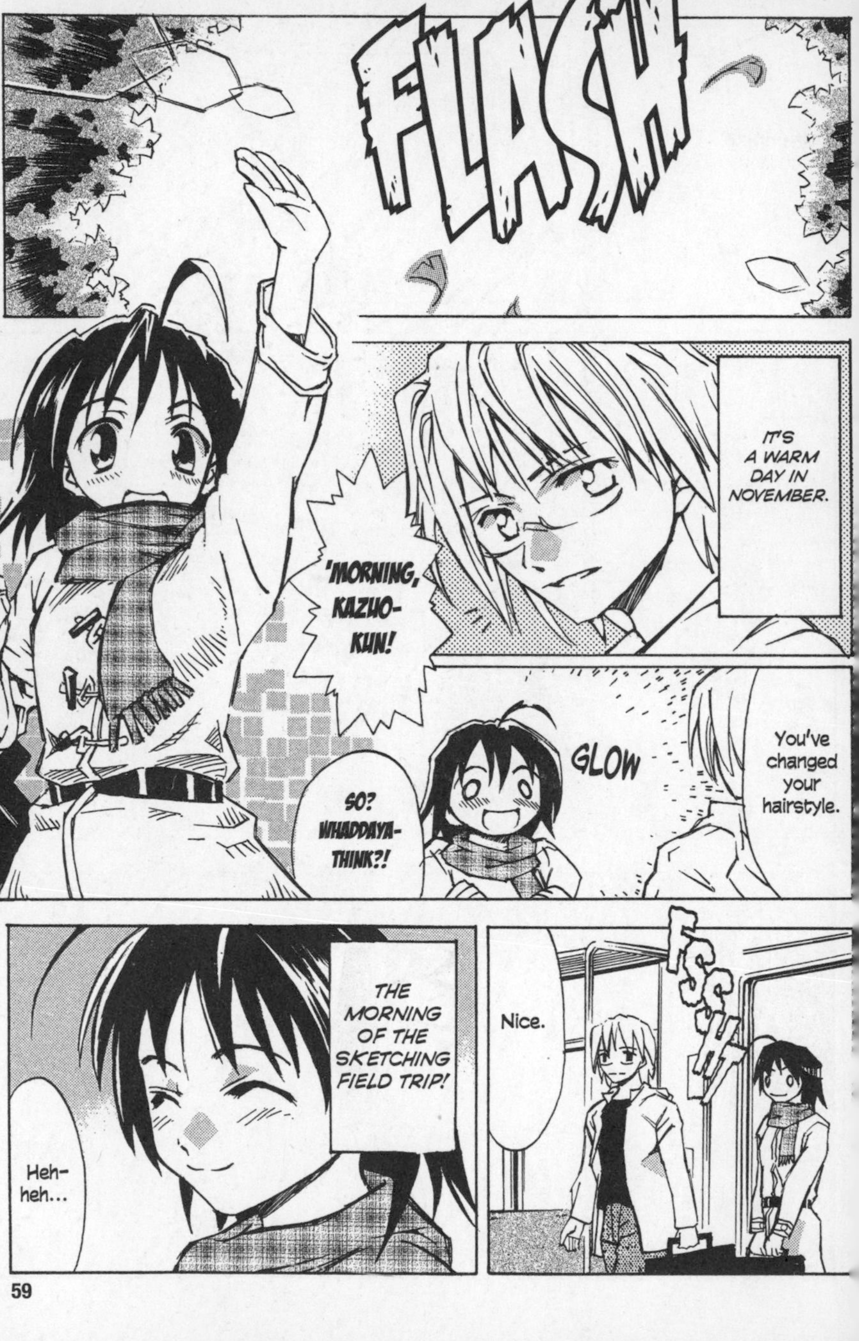
FLASH
IT'S A WARM DAY IN NOVEMBER.
'MORNING, KAZUO-KUN!
You've changed your hairstyle.
GLOW
SO? WHADDAYA-THINK?!
FSSH
Nice.
THE MORNING OF THE SKETCHING FIELD TRIP!
Heh-heh...

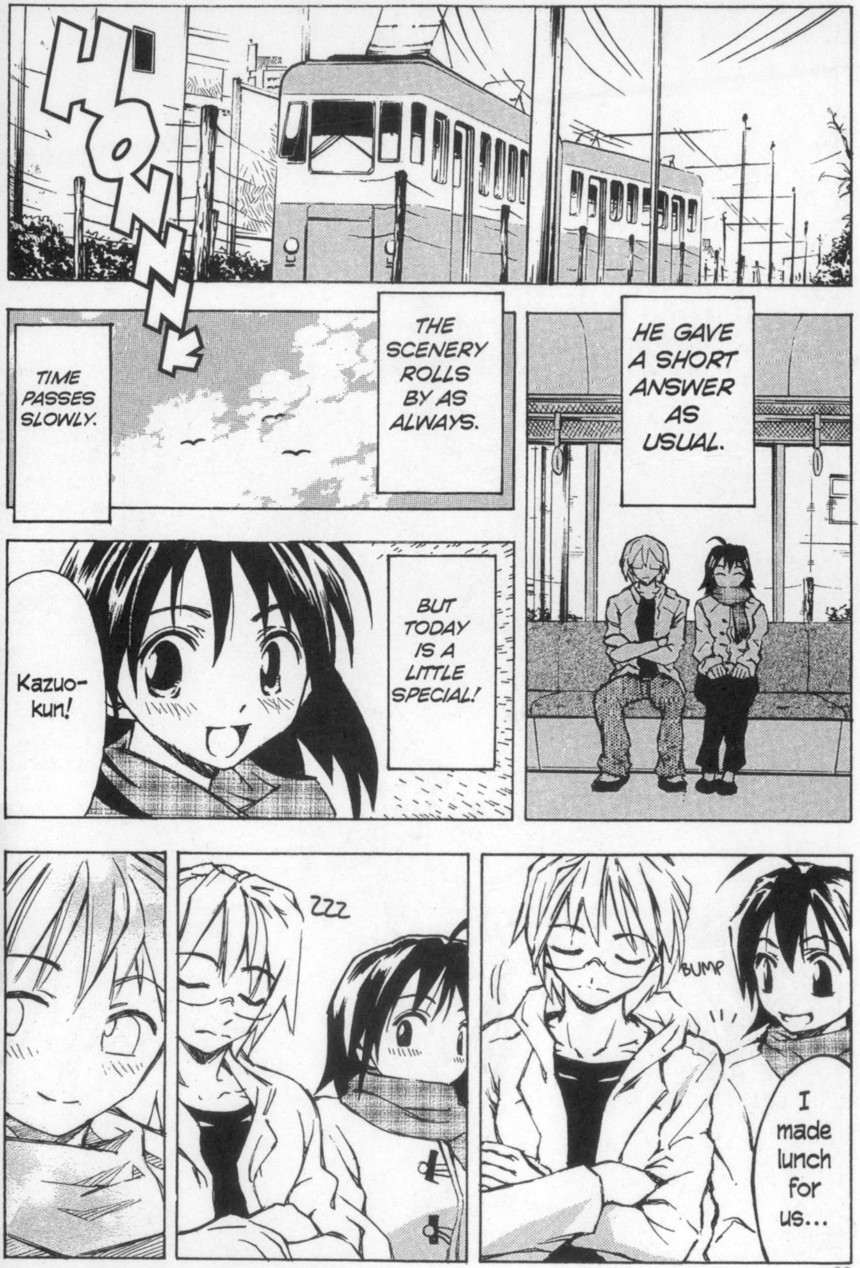
HONNK
HE GAVE A SHORT ANSWER AS USUAL.
THE SCENERY ROLLS BY AS ALWAYS.
TIME PASSES SLOWLY.
BUT TODAY IS A LITTLE SPECIAL!
Kazuo-kun!
BUMP
I made lunch for us...
ZZZ

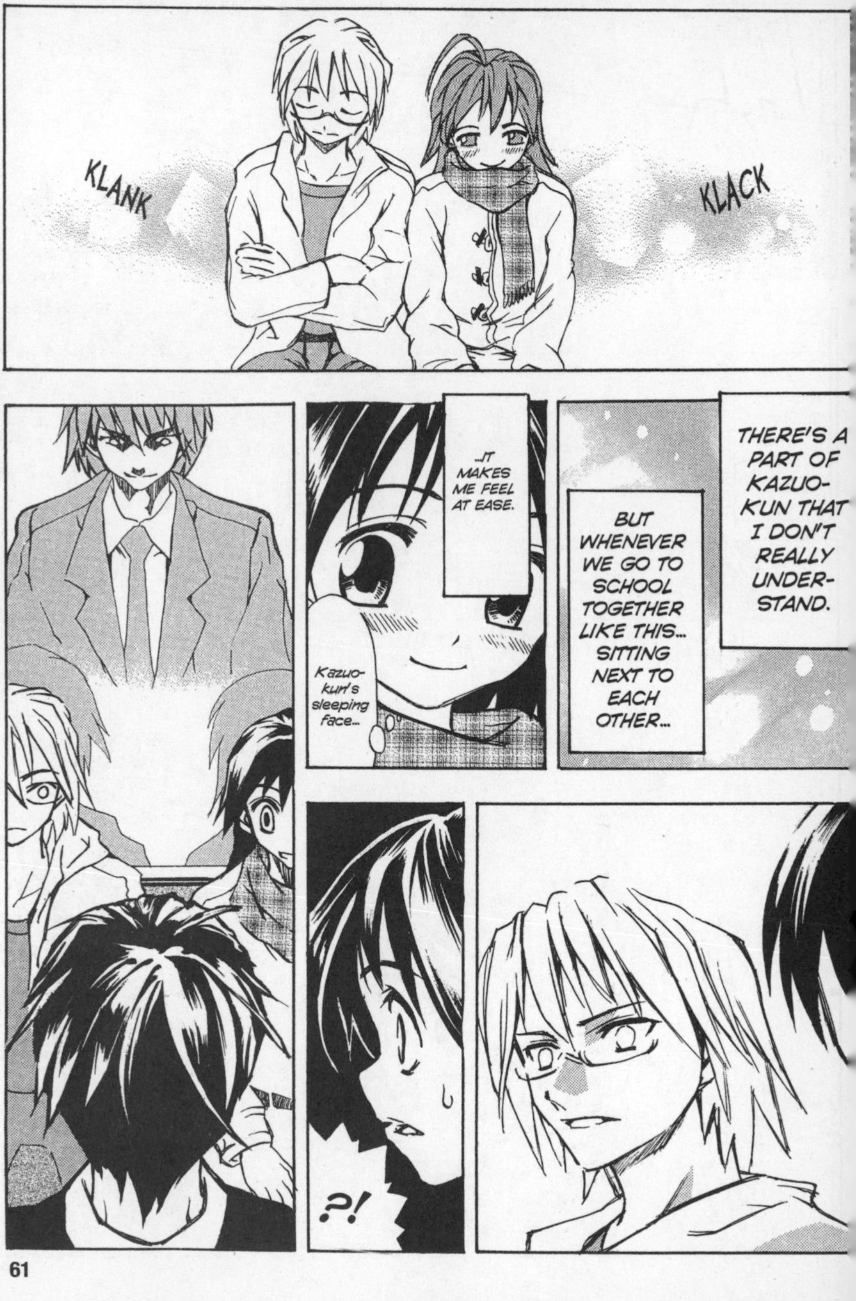
KLACK
KLANK
THERE'S A PART OF KAZUO-KUN THAT I DON'T REALLY UNDER-STAND.
BUT WHENEVER WE GO TO SCHOOL TOGETHER LIKE THIS... SITTING NEXT TO EACH OTHER...
...IT MAKES ME FEEL AT EASE.
Kazuo-kun's sleeping face...
?!

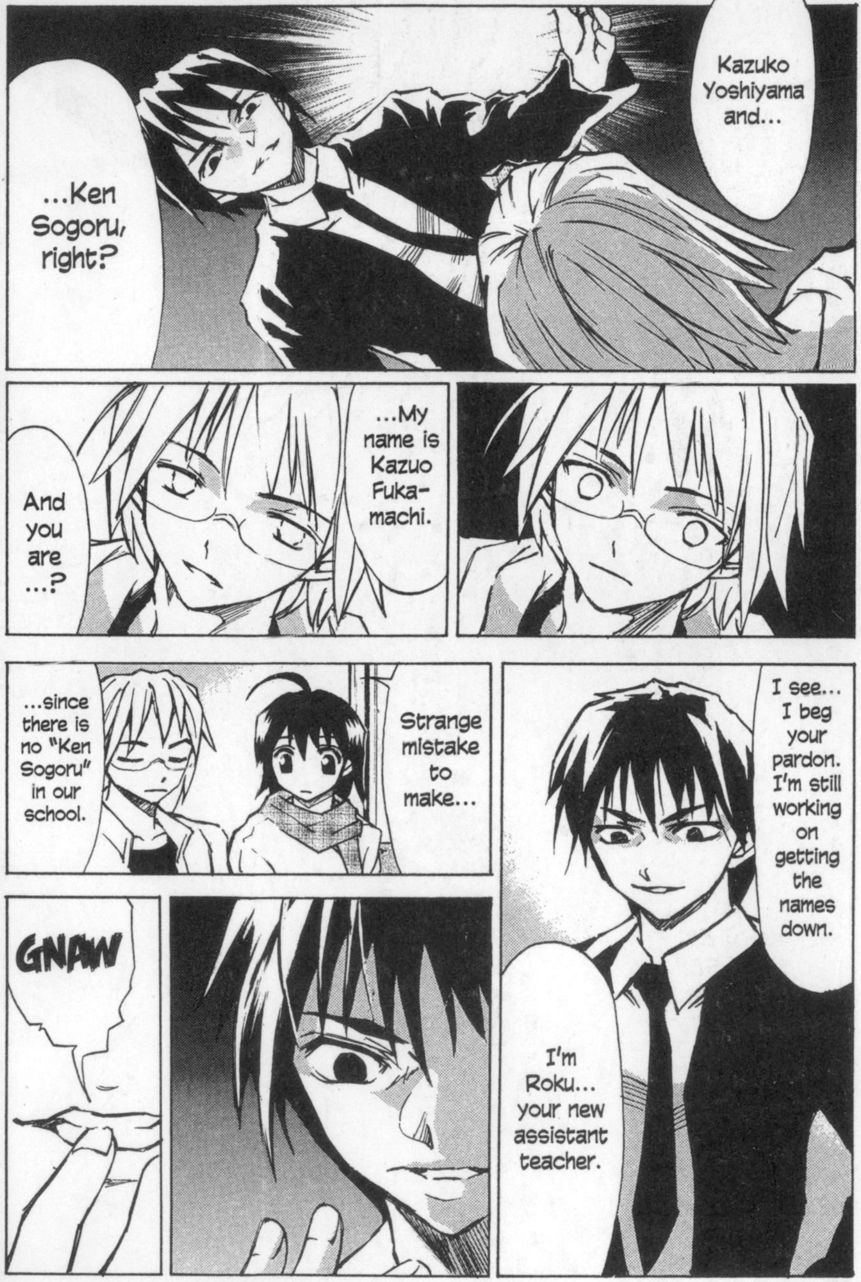
Kazuko Yoshiyama and...
...Ken Sogoru, right?
...My name is Kazuo Fuka-machi.
And you are ...?
I see... I beg your pardon. I'm still working on getting the names down.
I'm Roku... your new assistant teacher.
Strange mistake to make...
...since there is no "Ken Sogoru" in our school.
GNAW

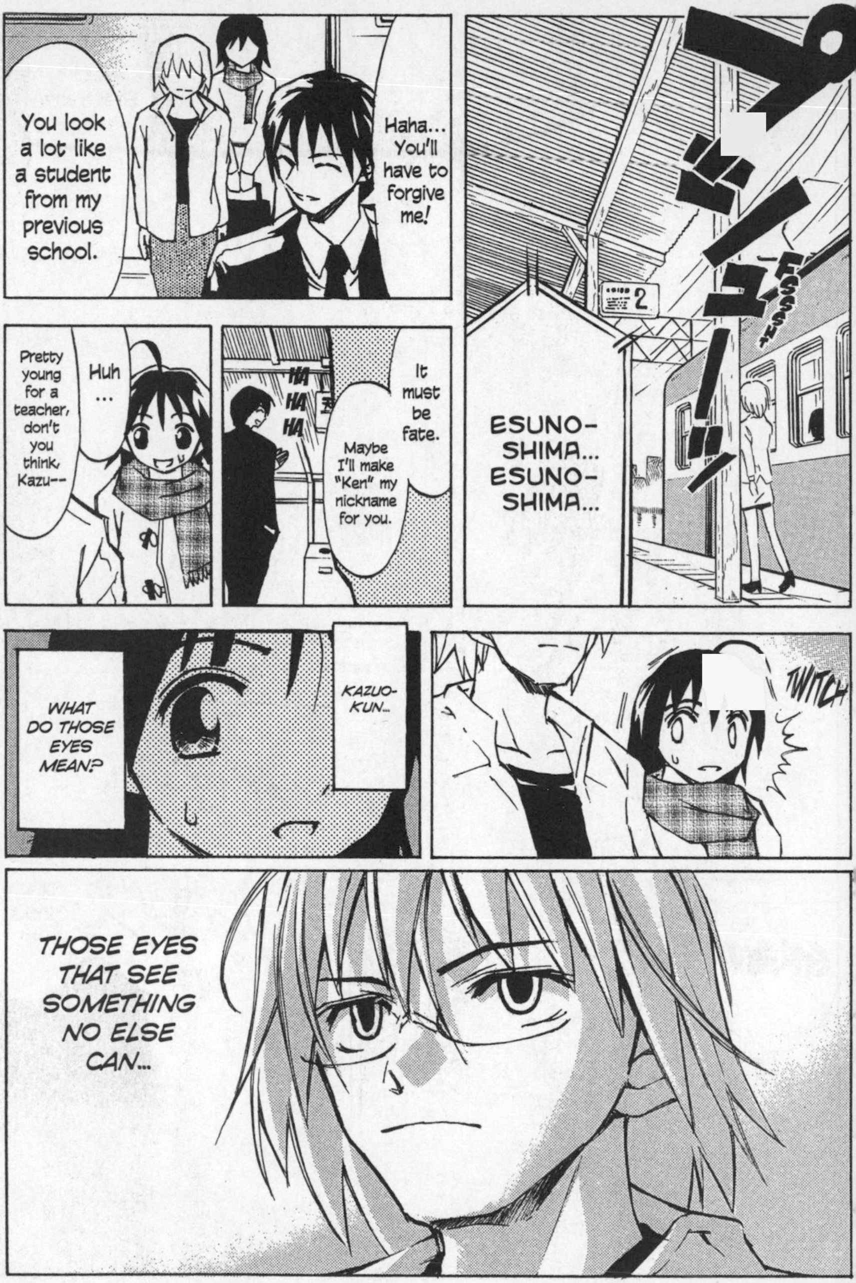
FSSSHT
ESUNO-SHIMA... ESUNO-SHIMA...
Haha... You'll have to forgive me!
You look a lot like a student from my previous school.
It must be fate.
Maybe I'll make "Ken" my nickname for you.
HA HA HA
Huh ...
Pretty young for a teacher, don't you think, Kazu--
TWITCH
KAZUO-KUN...
WHAT DO THOSE EYES MEAN?
THOSE EYES THAT SEE SOMETHING NO ELSE CAN...

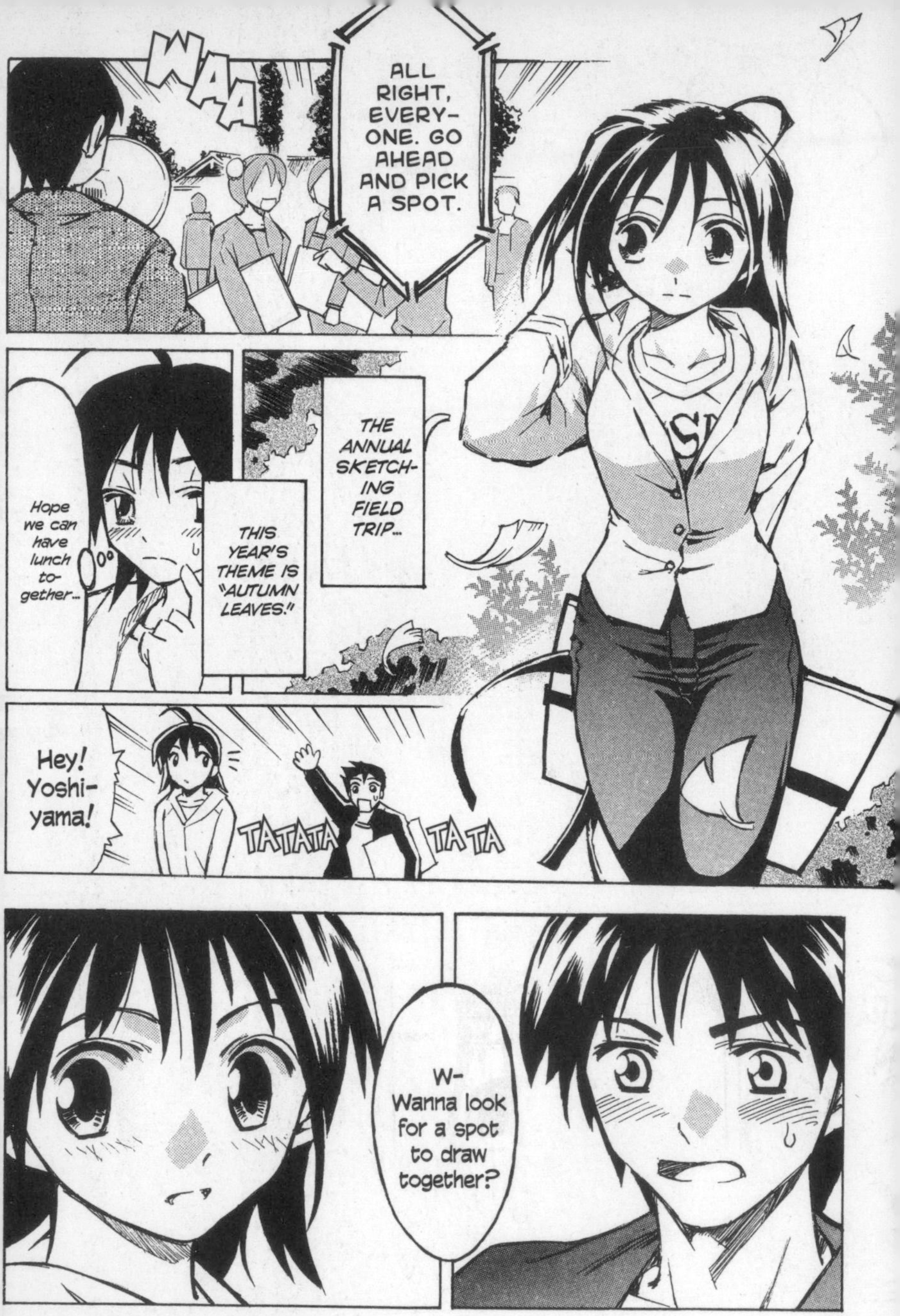
ALL RIGHT, EVERY-ONE. GO AHEAD AND PICK A SPOT.
WAA
THE ANNUAL SKETCH-ING FIELD TRIP...
THIS YEAR'S THEME IS "AUTUMN LEAVES."
Hope we can have lunch to-gether...
TATATA
TA TA
Hey! Yoshi-yama!
W-Wanna look for a spot to draw together?

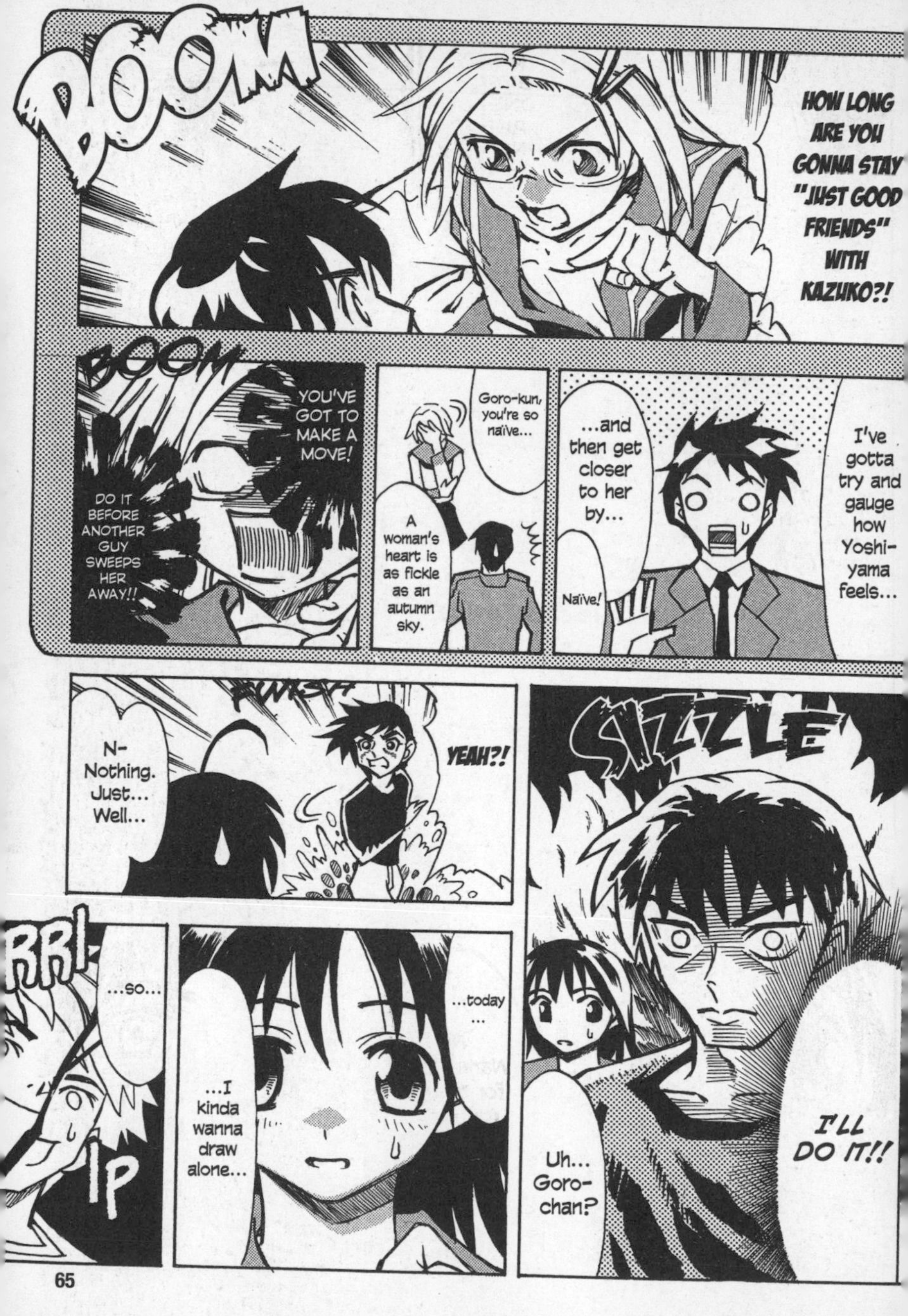
BOOM
HOW LONG ARE YOU GONNA STAY "JUST GOOD FRIENDS" WITH KAZUKO?!
I've gotta try and gauge how Yoshiyama feels...
...and then get closer to her by...
Naïve!
Goro-kun, you're so naïve...
A woman's heart is as fickle as an autumn sky.
BOOM
YOU'VE GOT TO MAKE A MOVE!
DO IT BEFORE ANOTHER GUY SWEEPS HER AWAY!!
SIZZLE
I'LL DO IT!!
Uh... Goro-chan?
YEAH?!
N-Nothing. Just... Well...
...today...
...I kinda wanna draw alone...
RRI
IP
...so...

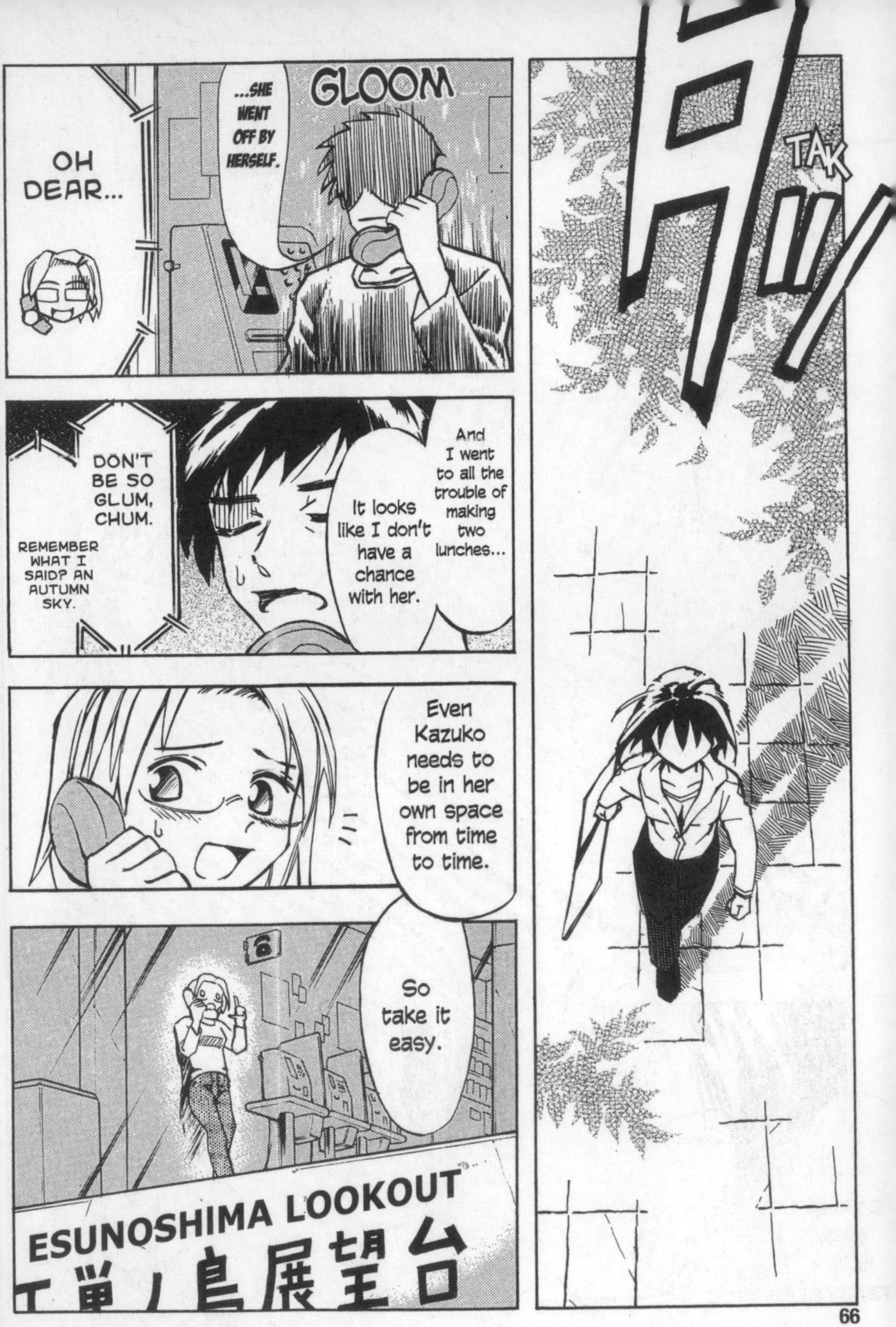
TAK
GLOOM
...SHE WENT OFF BY HERSELF.
OH DEAR...
And I went to all the trouble of making two lunches...
It looks like I don't have a chance with her.
DON'T BE SO GLUM, CHUM.
REMEMBER WHAT I SAID? AN AUTUMN SKY.
Even Kazuko needs to be in her own space from time to time.
So take it easy.
ESUNOSHIMA LOOKOUT

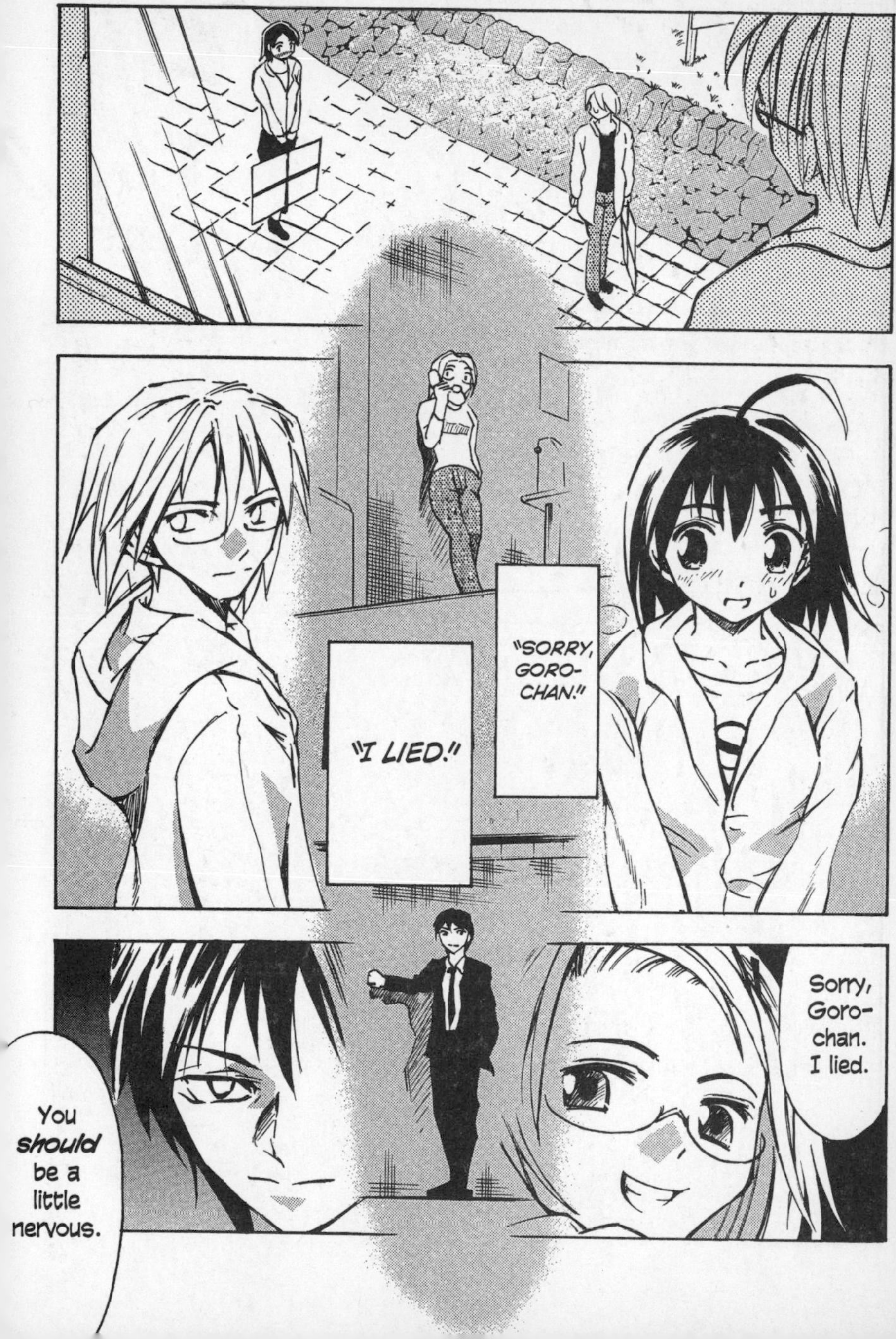
"SORRY, GORO-CHAN!"
"I LIED!"
Sorry, Goro-chan. I lied.
You *should* be a little nervous.

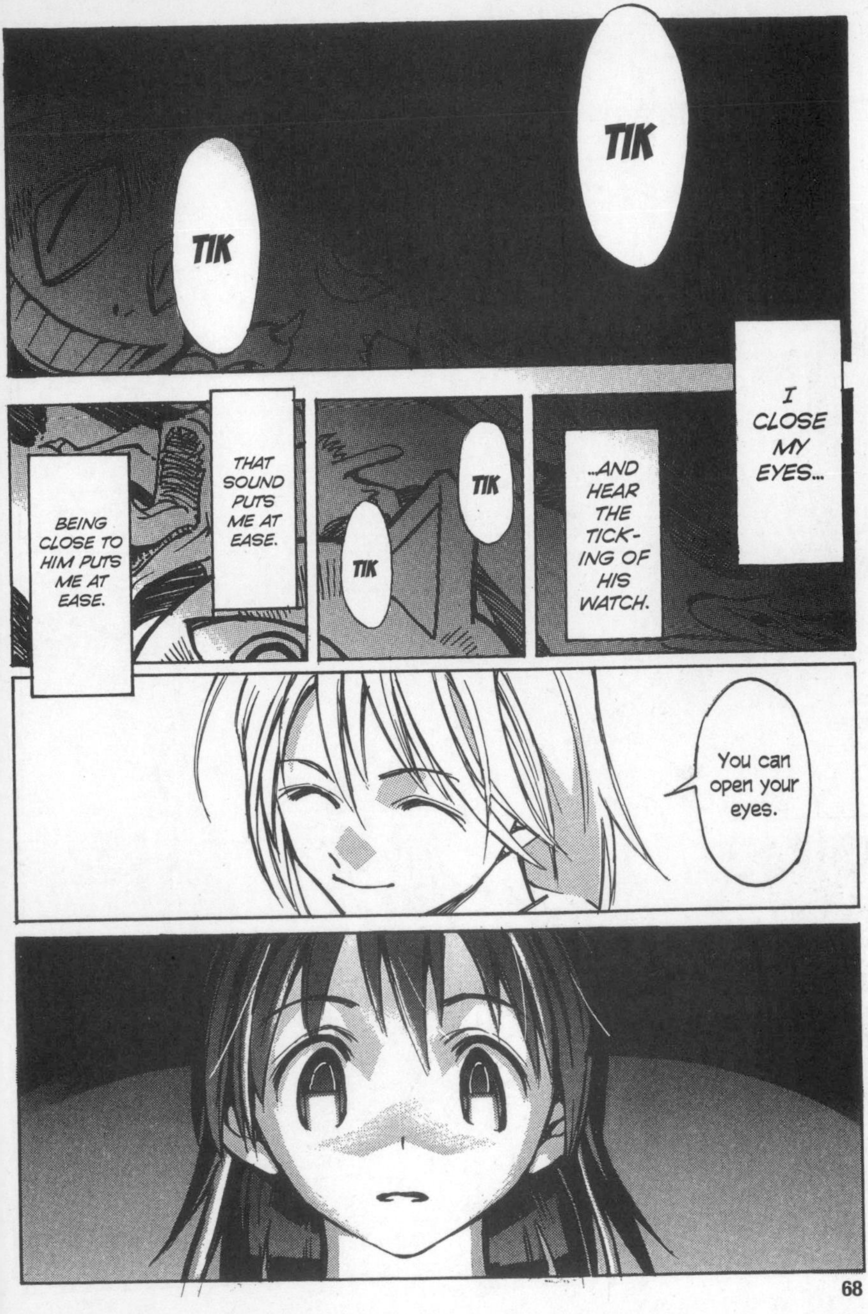
TIK
TIK
I CLOSE MY EYES...
...AND HEAR THE TICKING OF HIS WATCH.
TIK
TIK
THAT SOUND PUTS ME AT EASE.
BEING CLOSE TO HIM PUTS ME AT EASE.
You can open your eyes.

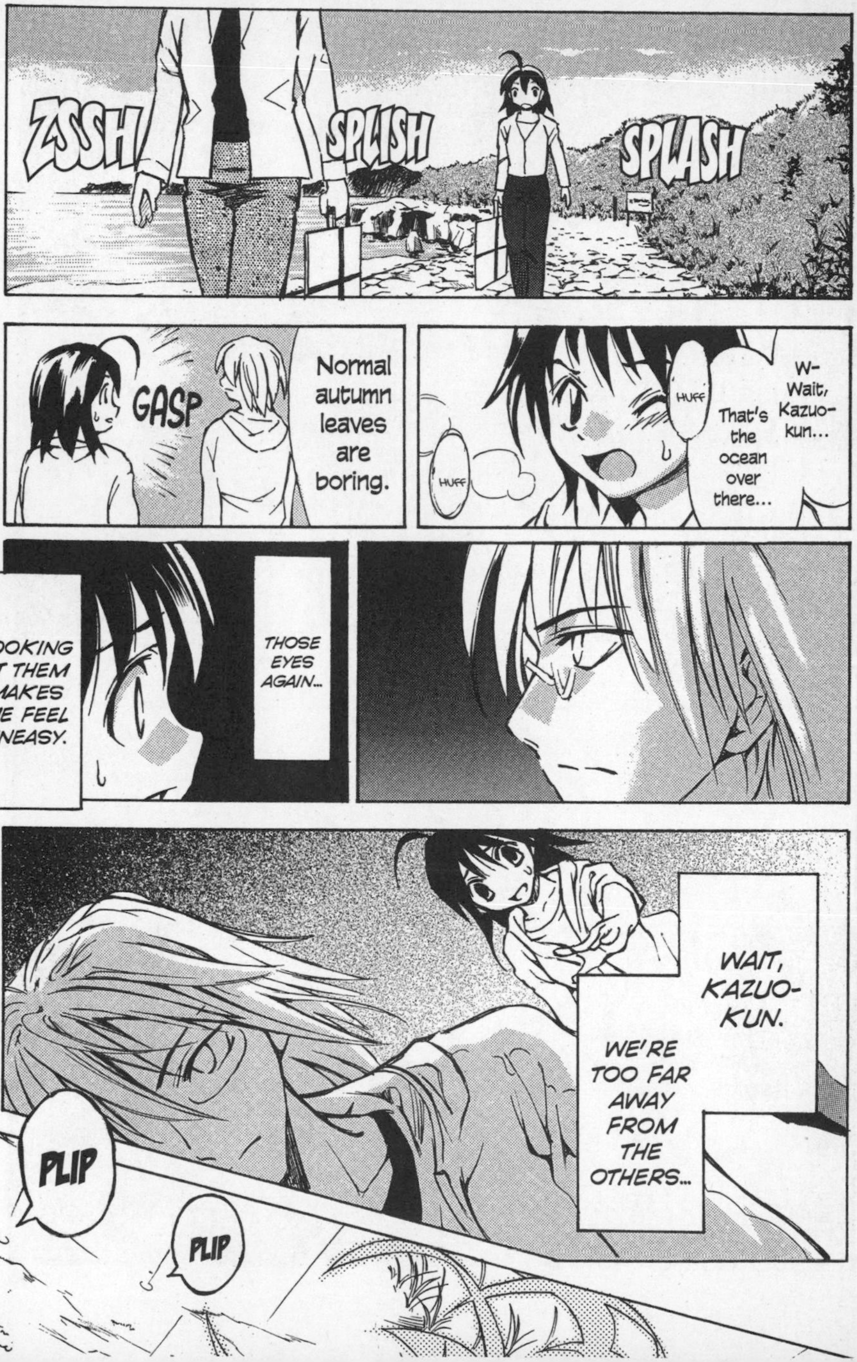
SPLASH
SPLISH
ZSSH
W-Wait, Kazuo-kun...
That's the ocean over there...
HUFF
HUFF
Normal autumn leaves are boring.
GASP
THOSE EYES AGAIN...
LOOKING AT THEM MAKES ME FEEL UNEASY.
WAIT, KAZUO-KUN.
WE'RE TOO FAR AWAY FROM THE OTHERS...
PLIP
PLIP

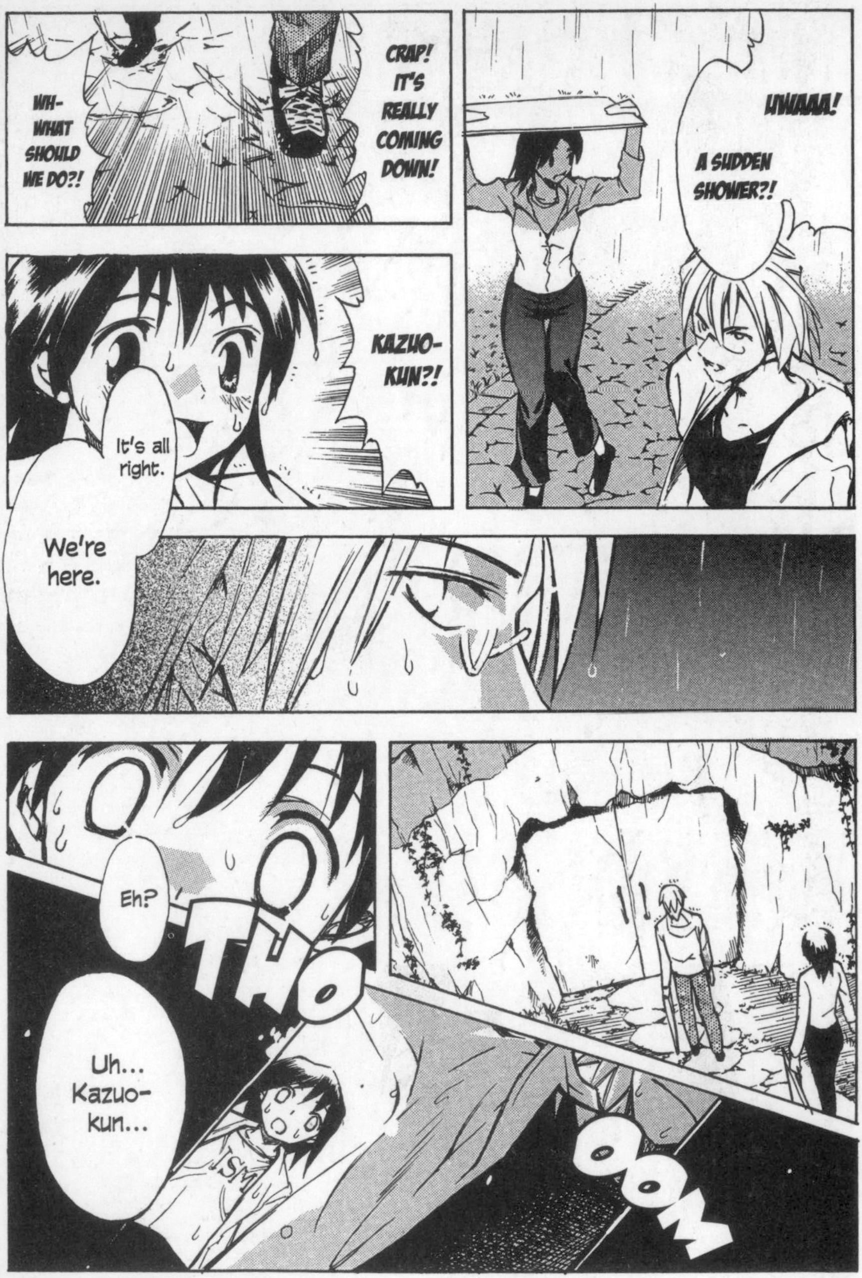
UWAAA!
A SUDDEN SHOWER?!
CRAP! IT'S REALLY COMING DOWN!
WH-WHAT SHOULD WE DO?!
KAZUO-KUN?!
It's all right.
We're here.
Eh?
THOOOM
Uh... Kazuo-kun...

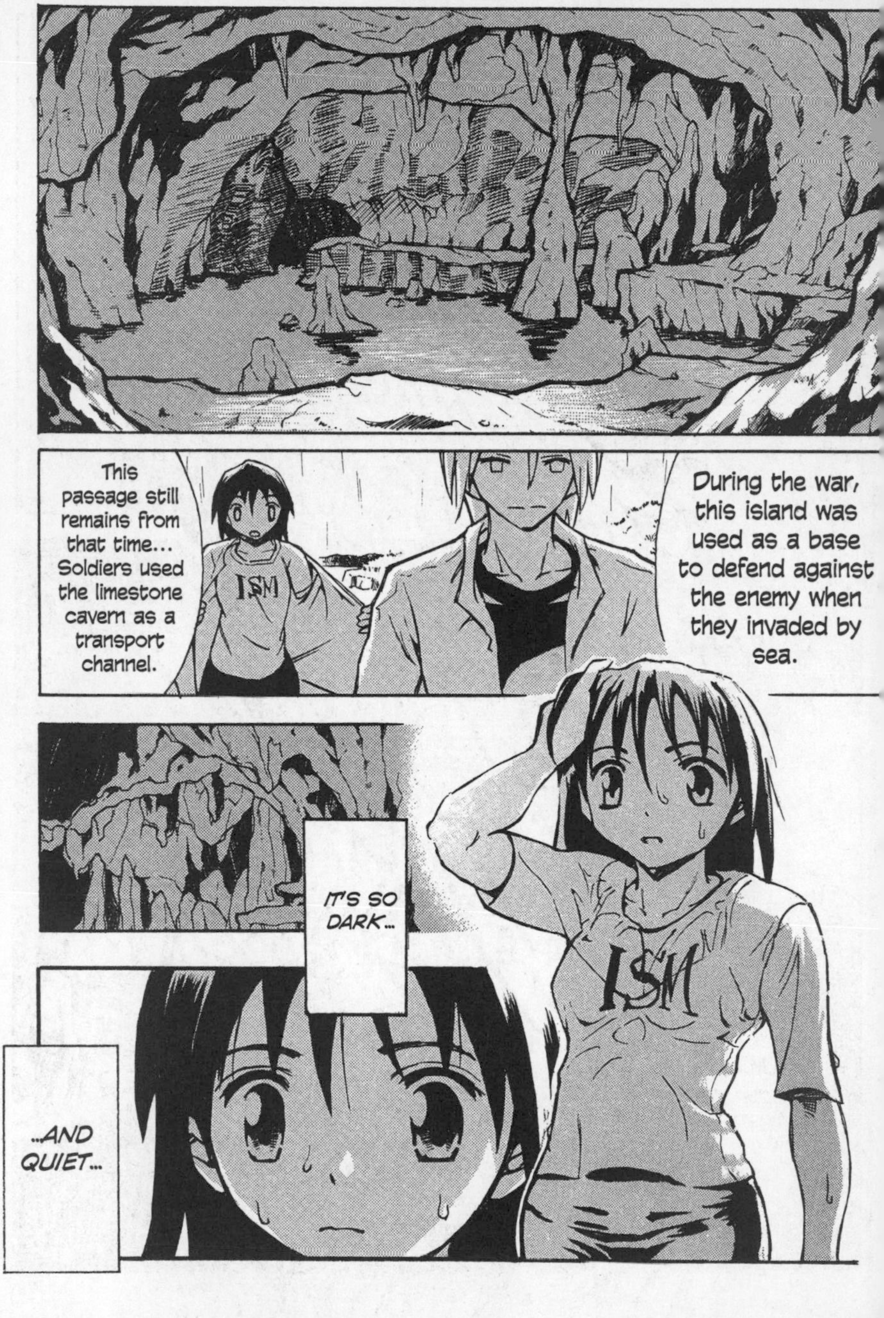
During the war, this island was used as a base to defend against the enemy when they invaded by sea.
This passage still remains from that time... Soldiers used the limestone cavern as a transport channel.
ISM
IT'S SO DARK...
...AND QUIET...
ISM

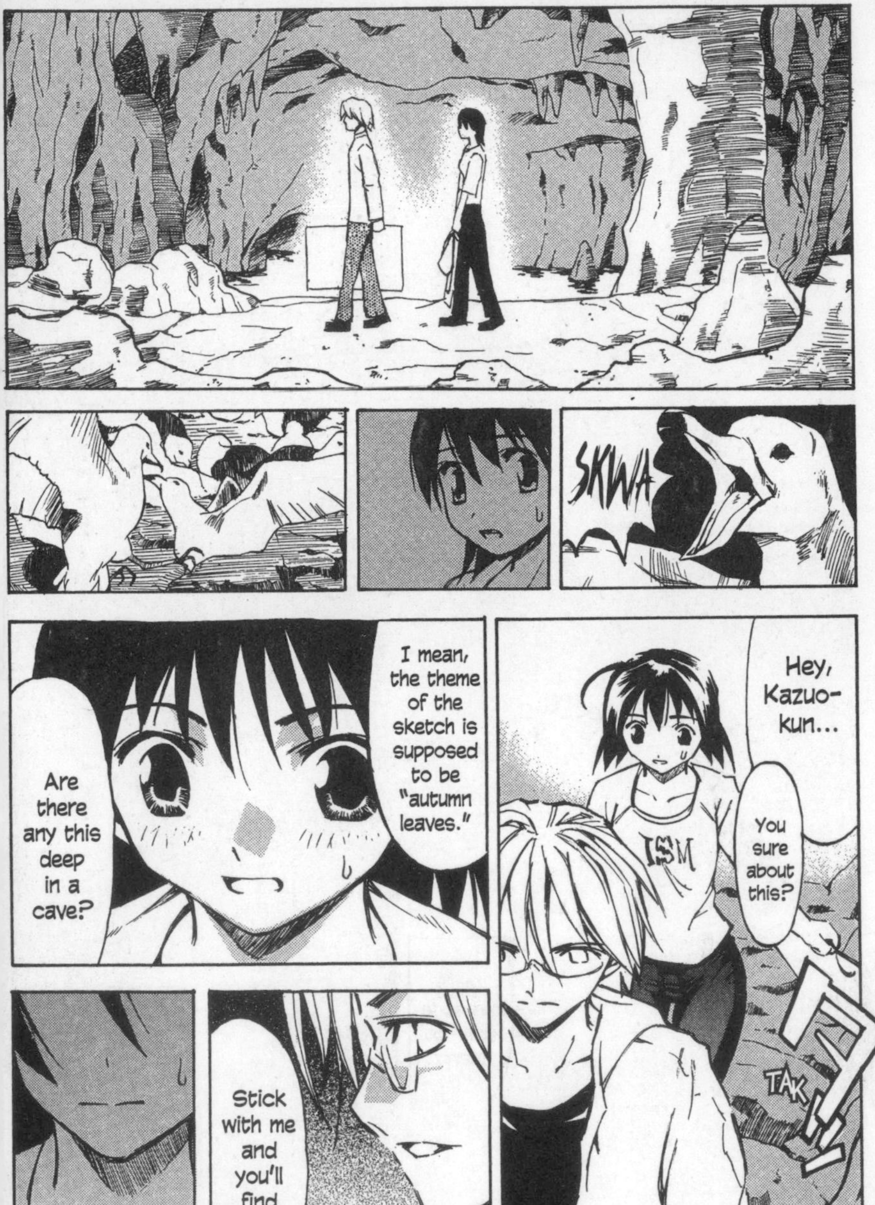
SKWA
Hey, Kazuo-kun...
You sure about this?
TAK
I mean, the theme of the sketch is supposed to be "autumn leaves."
Are there any this deep in a cave?
Stick with me and you'll find out.

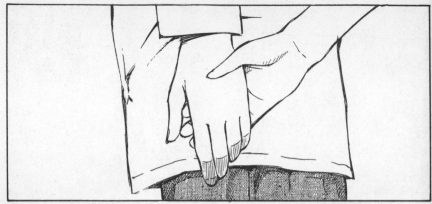

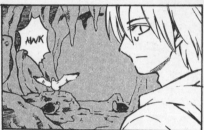

AWK

Just don't let go of my hand.

I will...

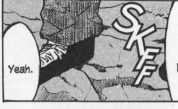

SKFF

Your watch sounds a lot louder in here...

Yeah.

That's because it's not quartz.

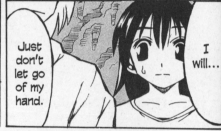

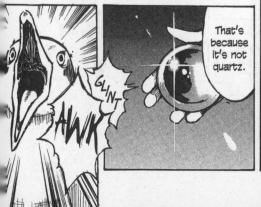

GLINT

AWK

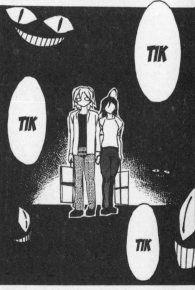

TIK

TIK

TIK

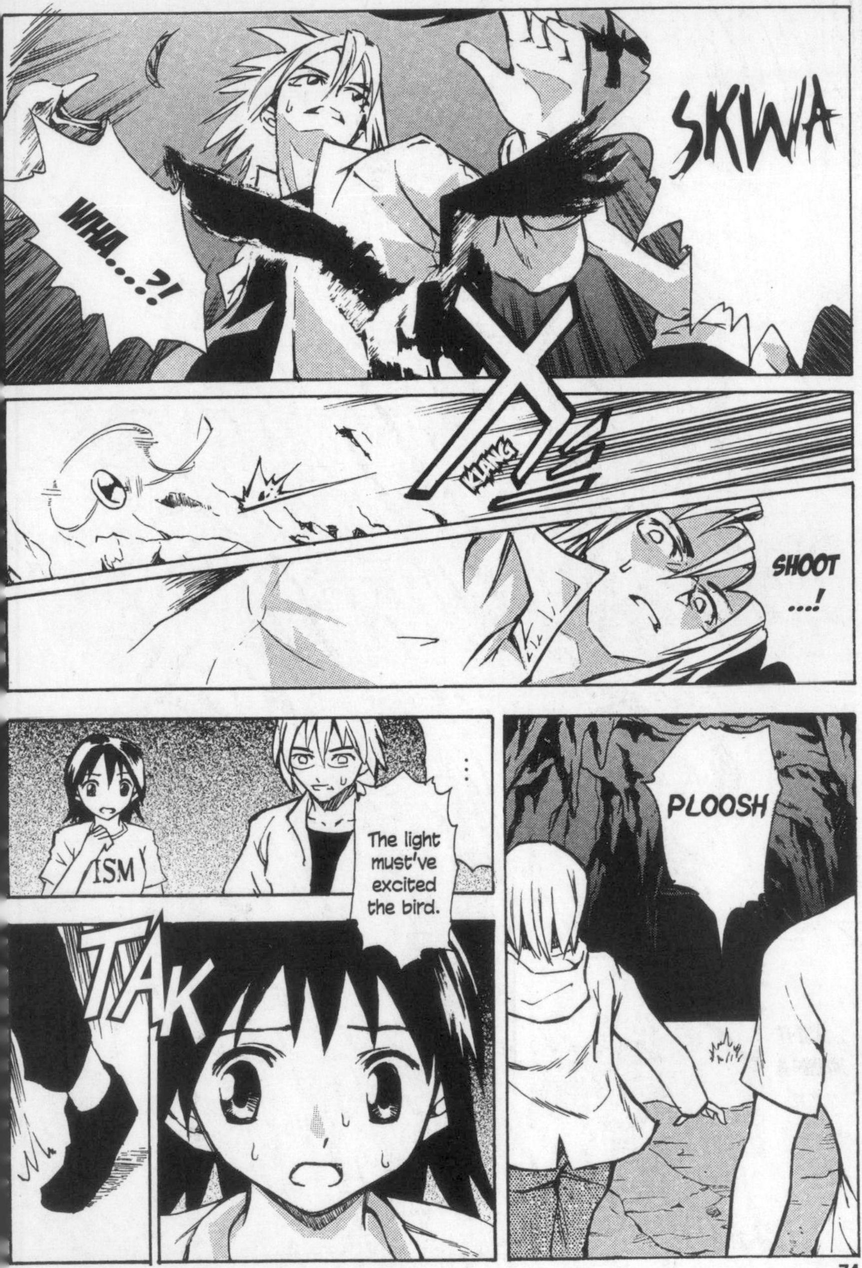
SKWA
WHA...?!
KLANG
SHOOT
...!
PLOOSH
...
The light must've excited the bird.
TAK

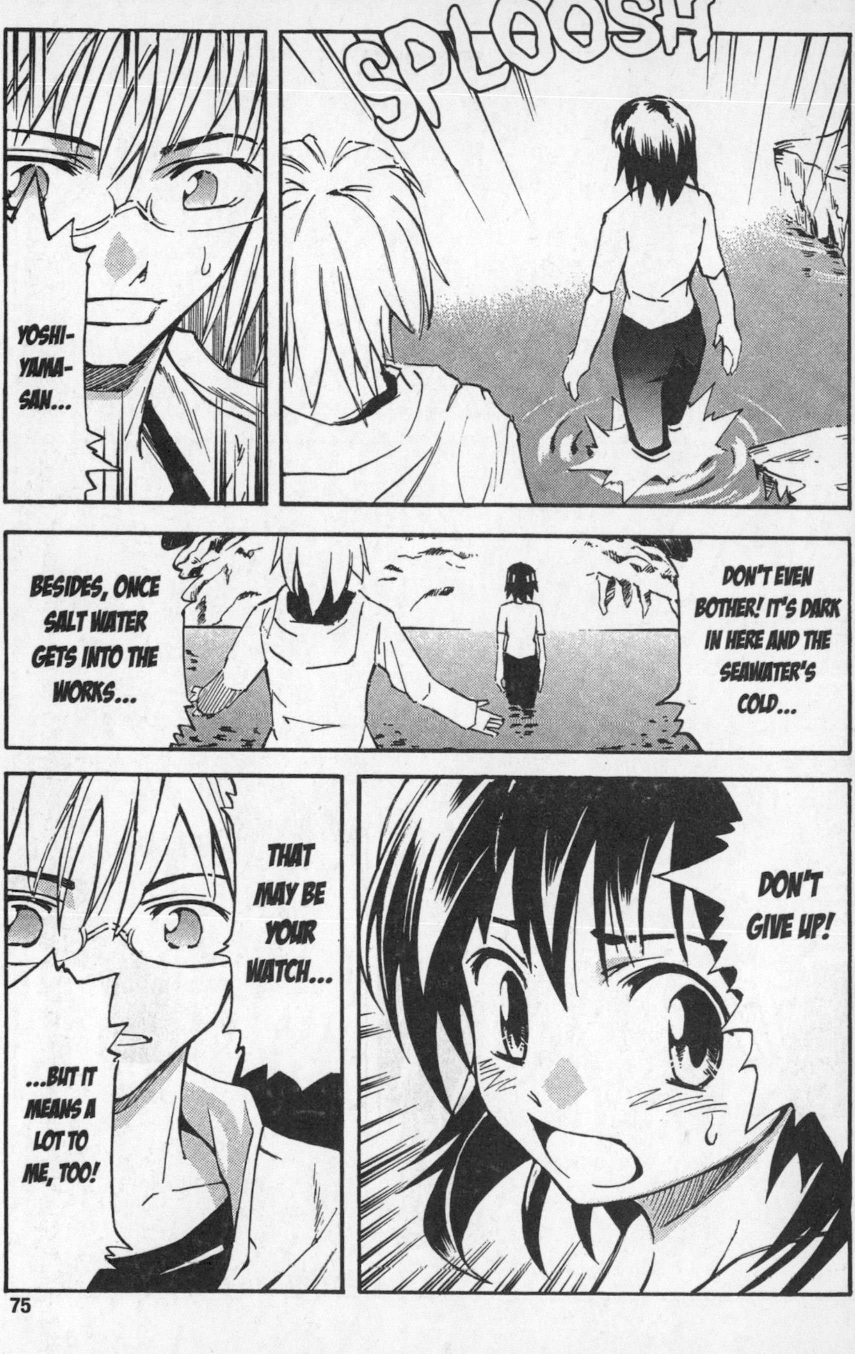
SPLOOSH
YOSHI-YAMA-SAN...
DON'T EVEN BOTHER! IT'S DARK IN HERE AND THE SEAWATER'S COLD...
BESIDES, ONCE SALT WATER GETS INTO THE WORKS...
DON'T GIVE UP!
THAT MAY BE YOUR WATCH...
...BUT IT MEANS A LOT TO ME, TOO!

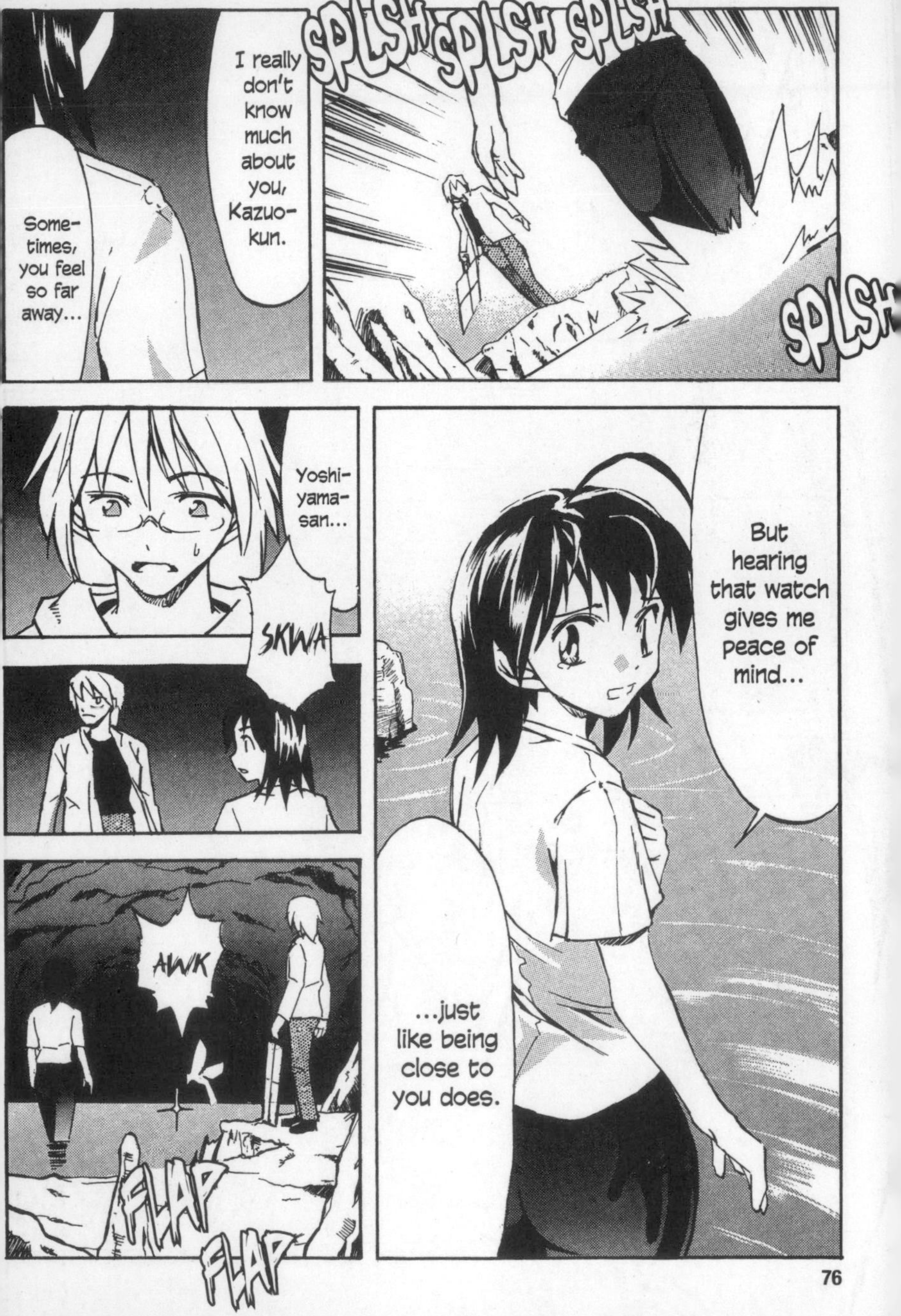
SPLSH SPLSH SPLSH
SPLSH
I really don't know much about you, Kazuo-kun.
Some-times, you feel so far away...
But hearing that watch gives me peace of mind...
...just like being close to you does.
Yoshi-yama-san...
SKWA
AWK
FLAP
FLAP

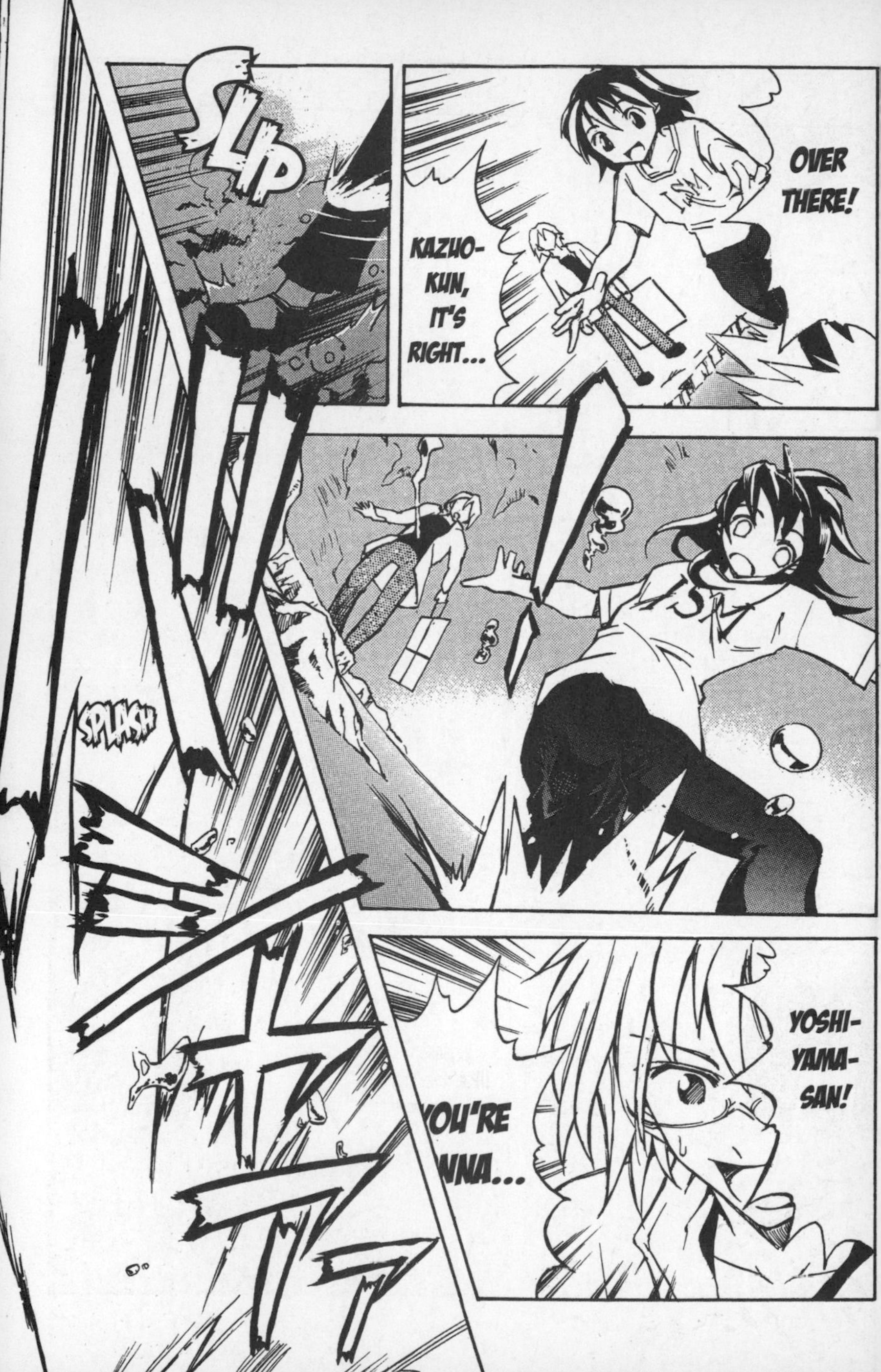
OVER THERE!
KAZUO-KUN, IT'S RIGHT...
SLIP
YOSHI-YAMA-SAN!
YOU'RE
NNA...
SPLASH

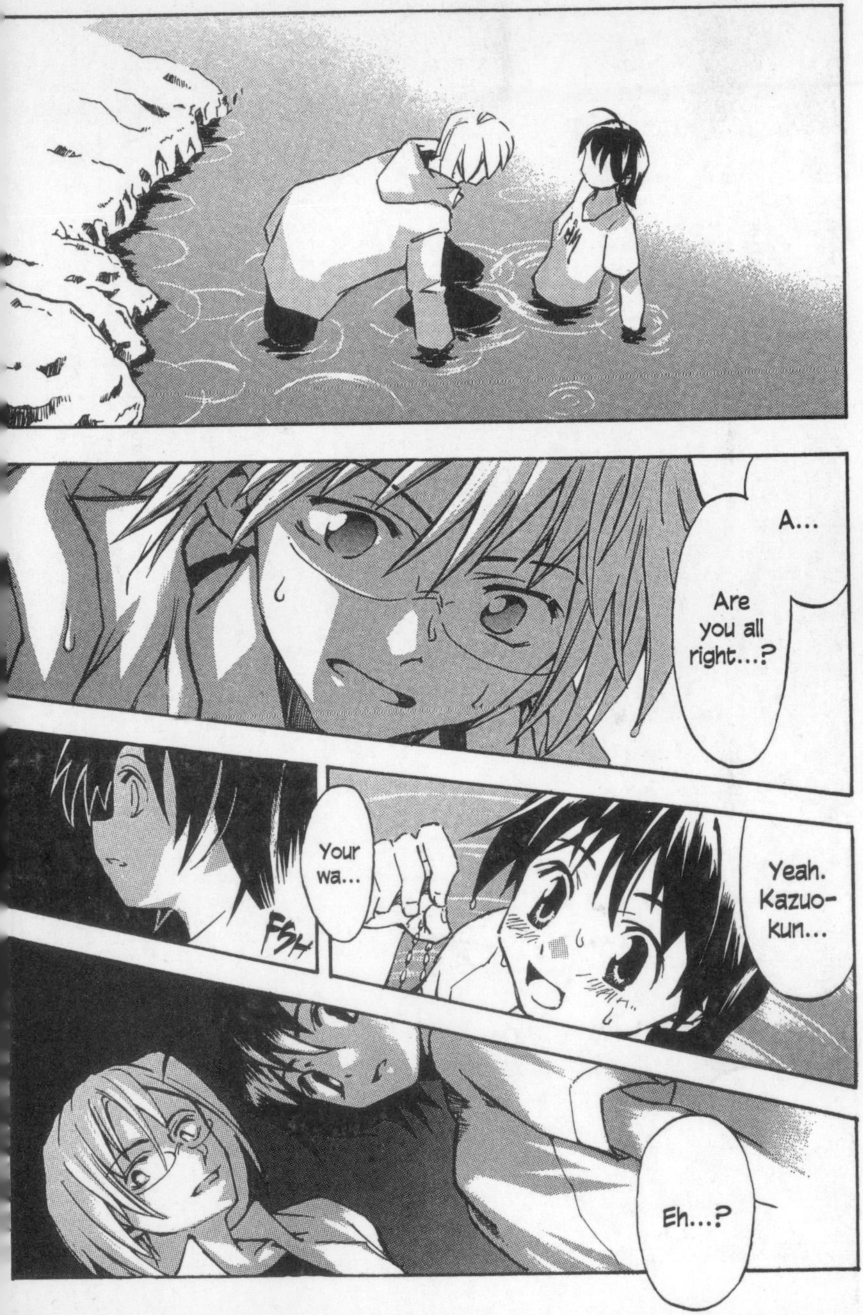
A...
Are you all right...?
Yeah. Kazuo-kun...
Your wa...
FSH
Eh...?

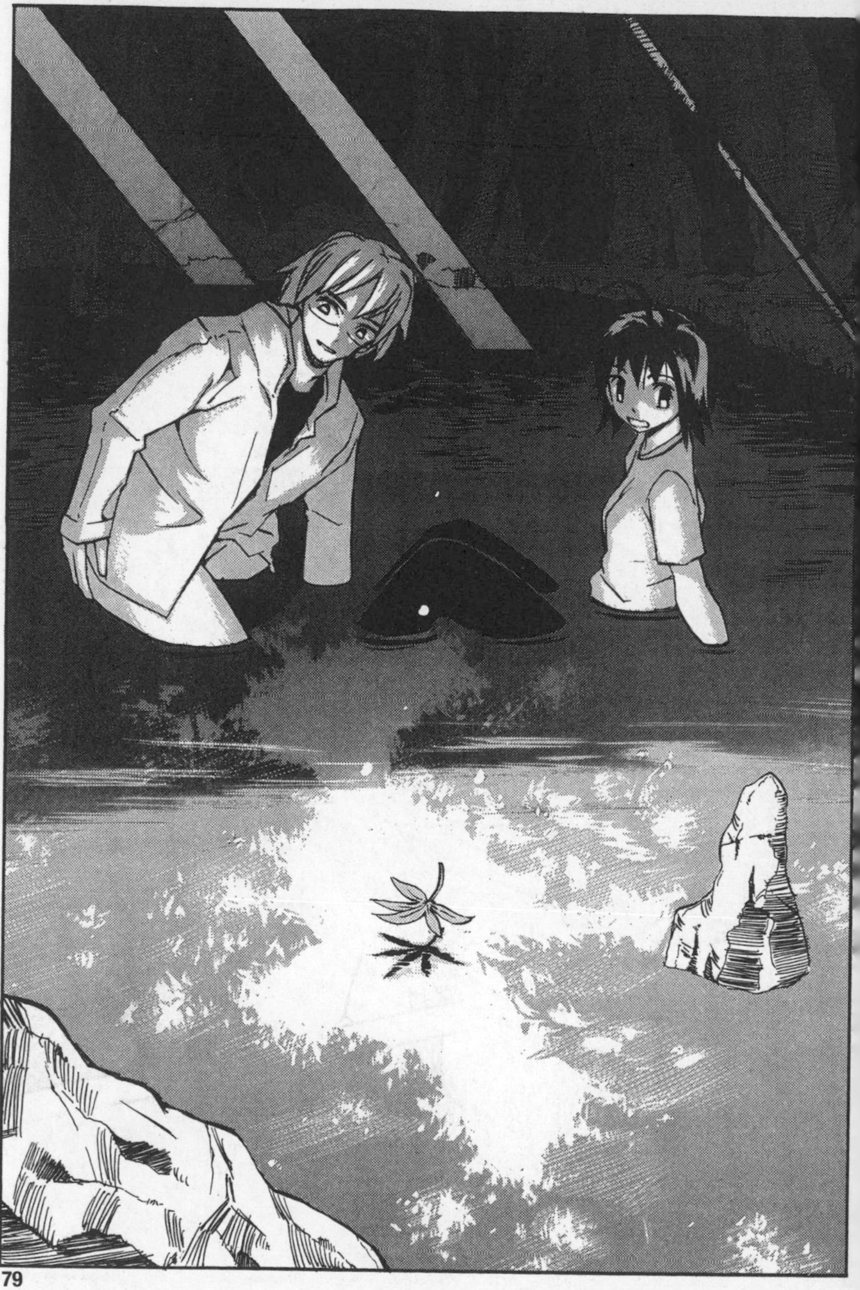

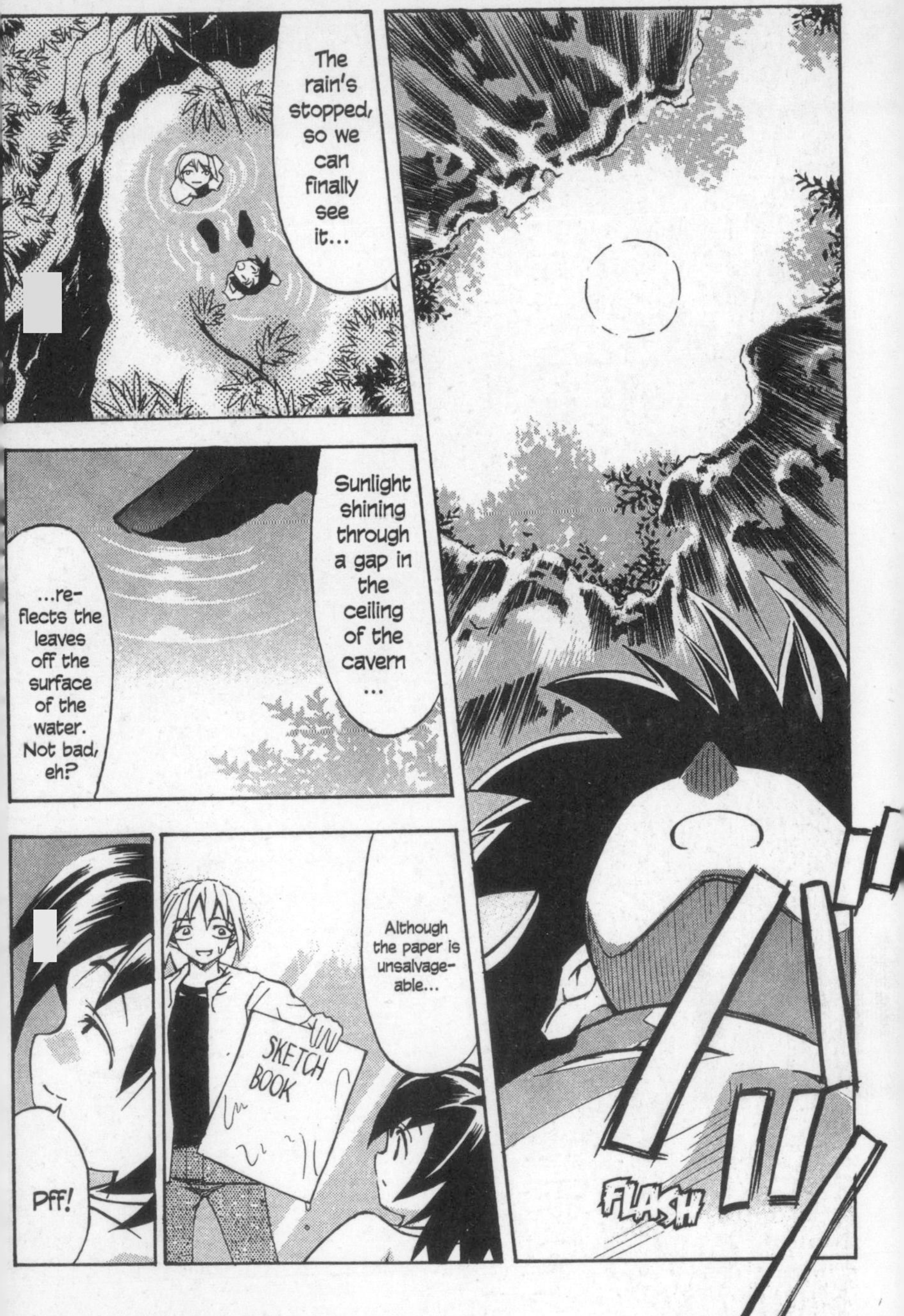
FLASH
The rain's stopped, so we can finally see it...
Sunlight shining through a gap in the ceiling of the cavern ...
...re-flects the leaves off the surface of the water. Not bad, eh?
Although the paper is unsalvage-able...
SKETCH BOOK
Pff!

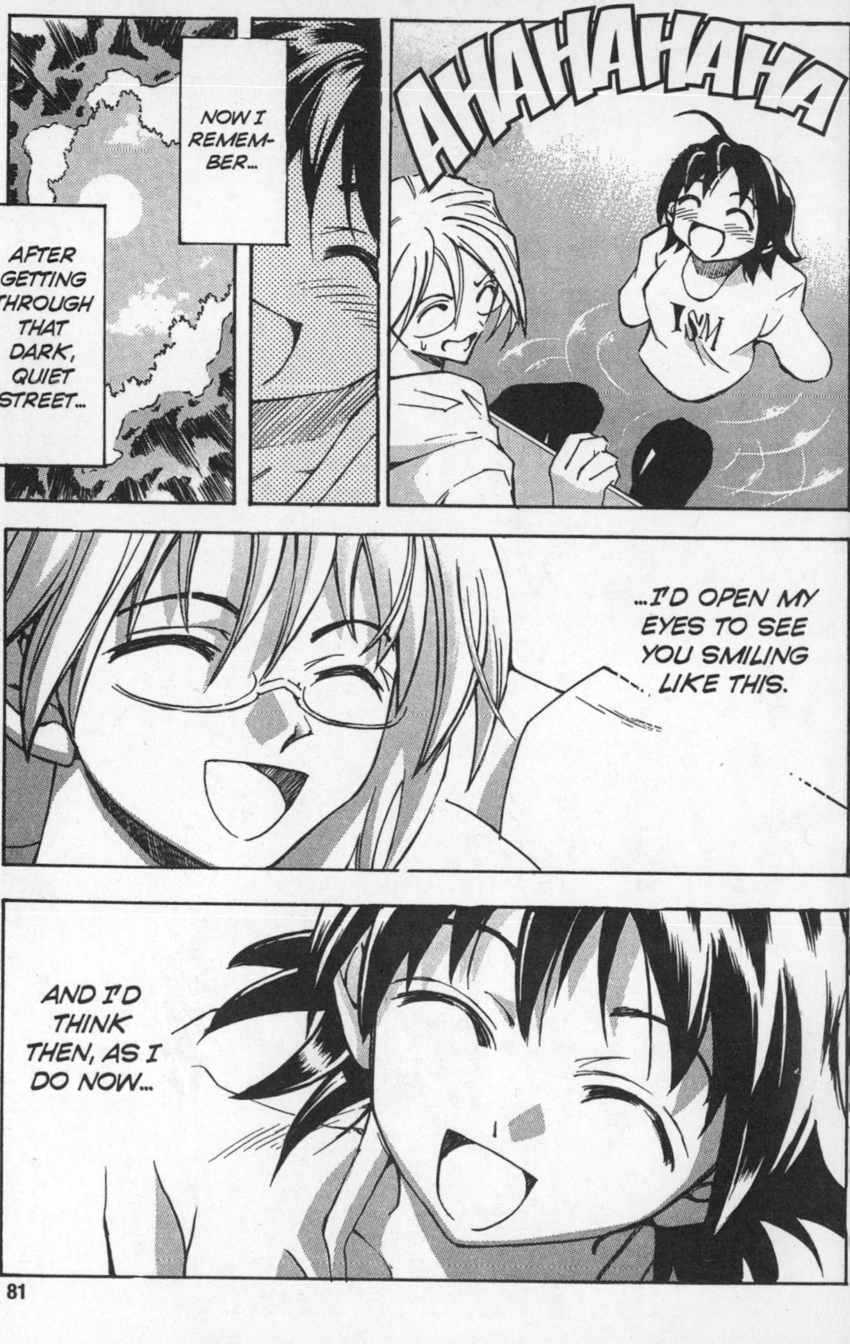
AHAHAHAHAHA
NOW I REMEMBER...
AFTER GETTING THROUGH THAT DARK, QUIET STREET...
ISM
...I'D OPEN MY EYES TO SEE YOU SMILING LIKE THIS.
AND I'D THINK THEN, AS I DO NOW...

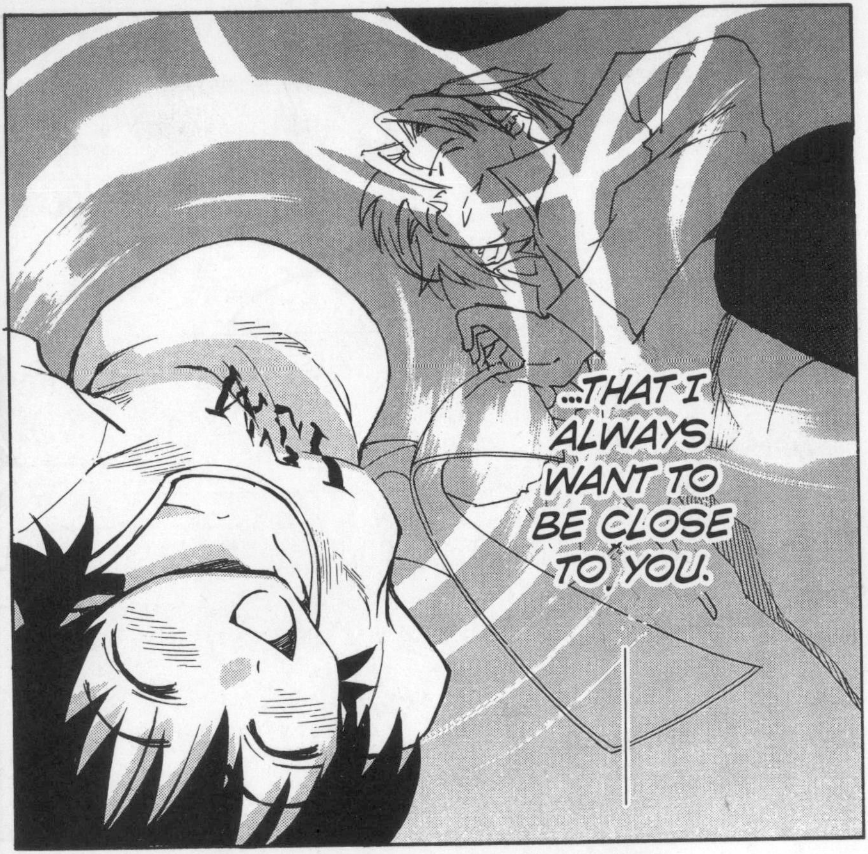
...THAT I ALWAYS WANT TO BE CLOSE TO YOU.

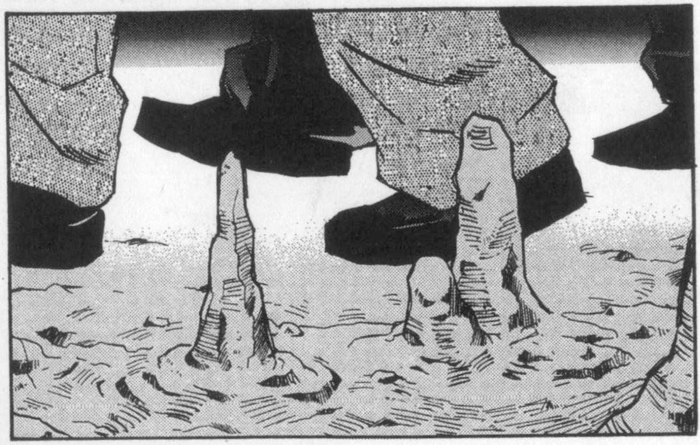

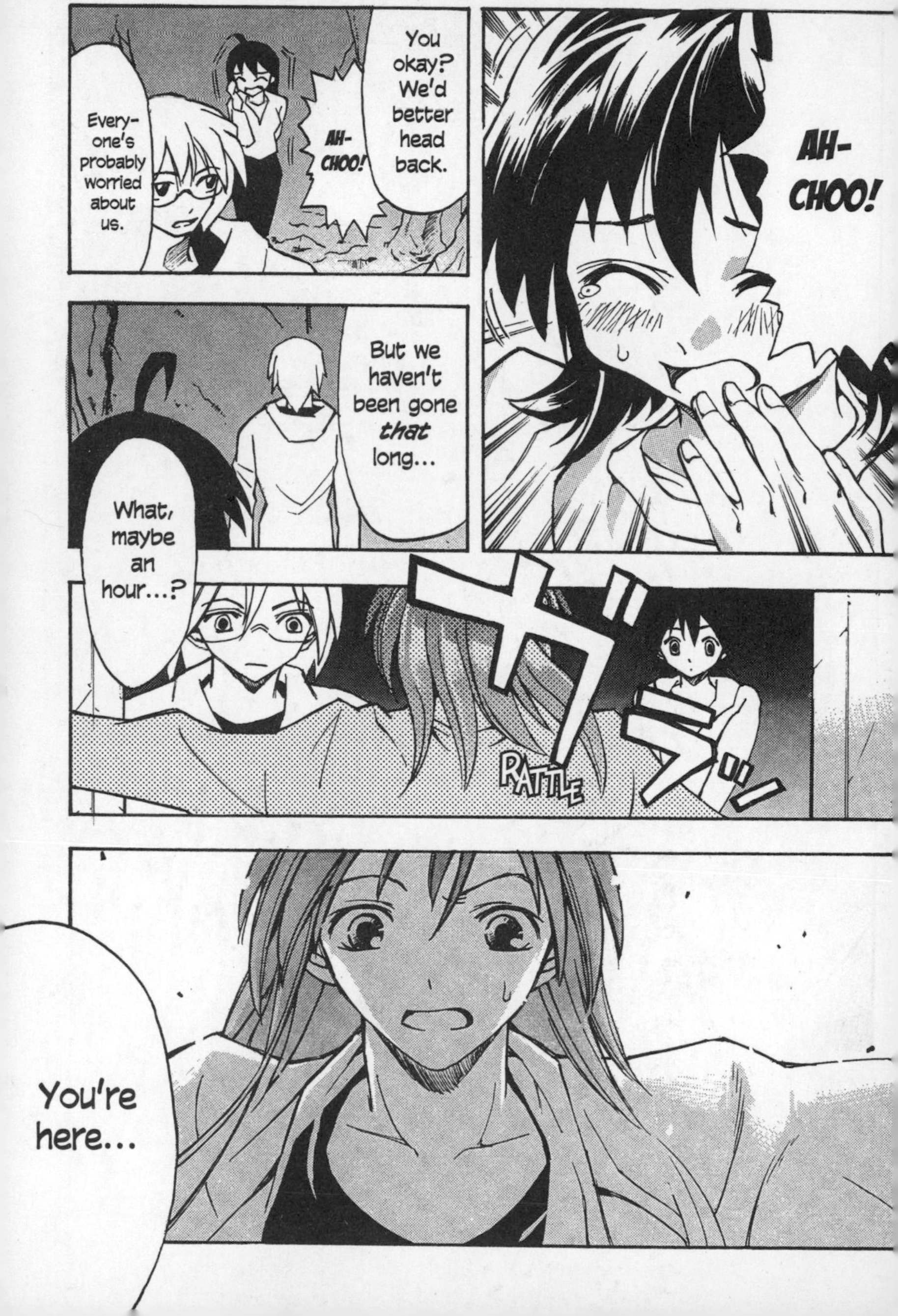
AH-CHOO!
You okay? We'd better head back.
AH-CHOO!
Every-one's probably worried about us.
But we haven't been gone *that* long...
What, maybe an hour...?
ガラッ
RATTLE
You're here...

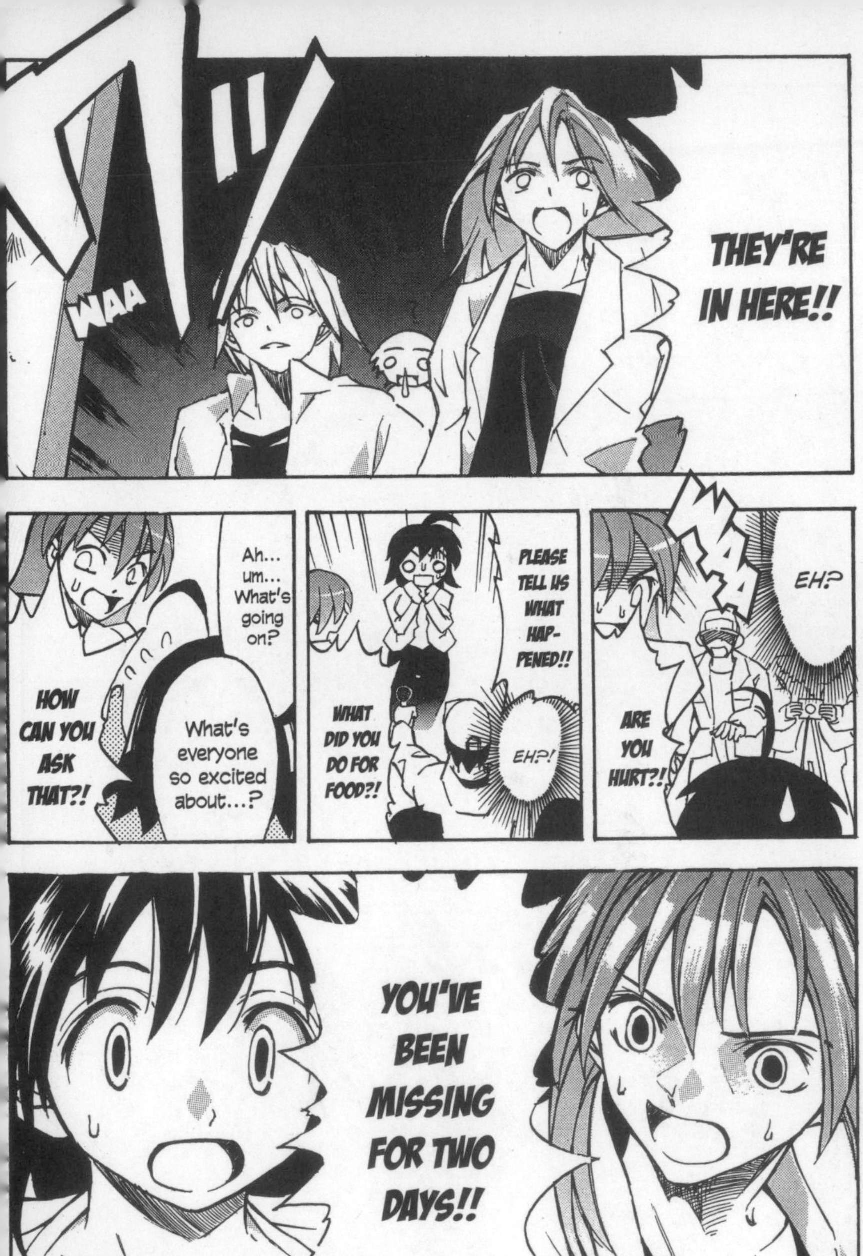
THEY'RE IN HERE!!
WAA
WAA
EH?
ARE YOU HURT?!
PLEASE TELL US WHAT HAP-PENED!!
EH?!
WHAT DID YOU DO FOR FOOD?!
Ah... um... What's going on?
HOW CAN YOU ASK THAT?!
What's everyone so excited about...?
YOU'VE BEEN MISSING FOR TWO DAYS!!

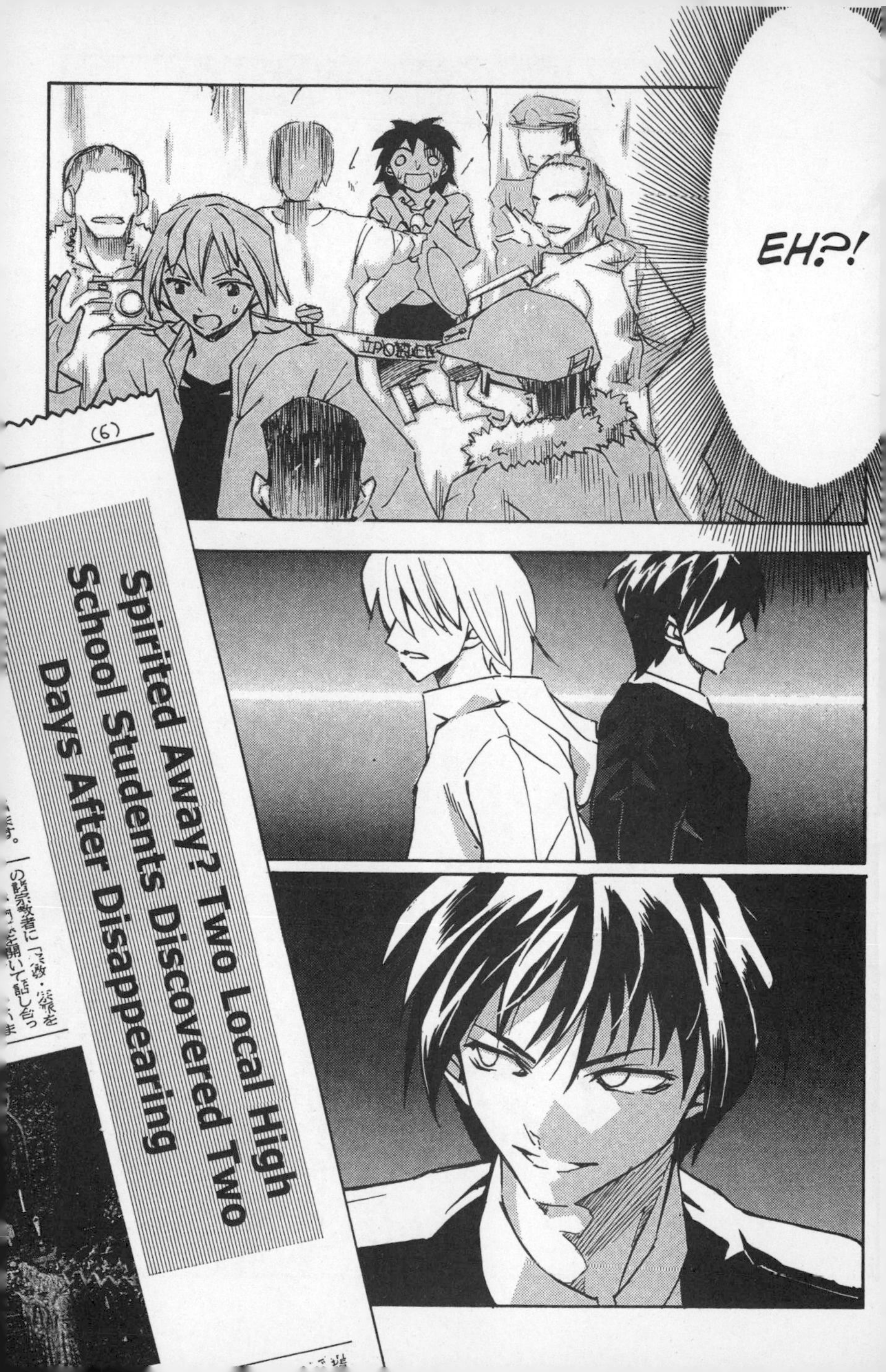
EH?!
(6)
Spirited Away? Two Local High School Students Discovered Two Days After Disappearing

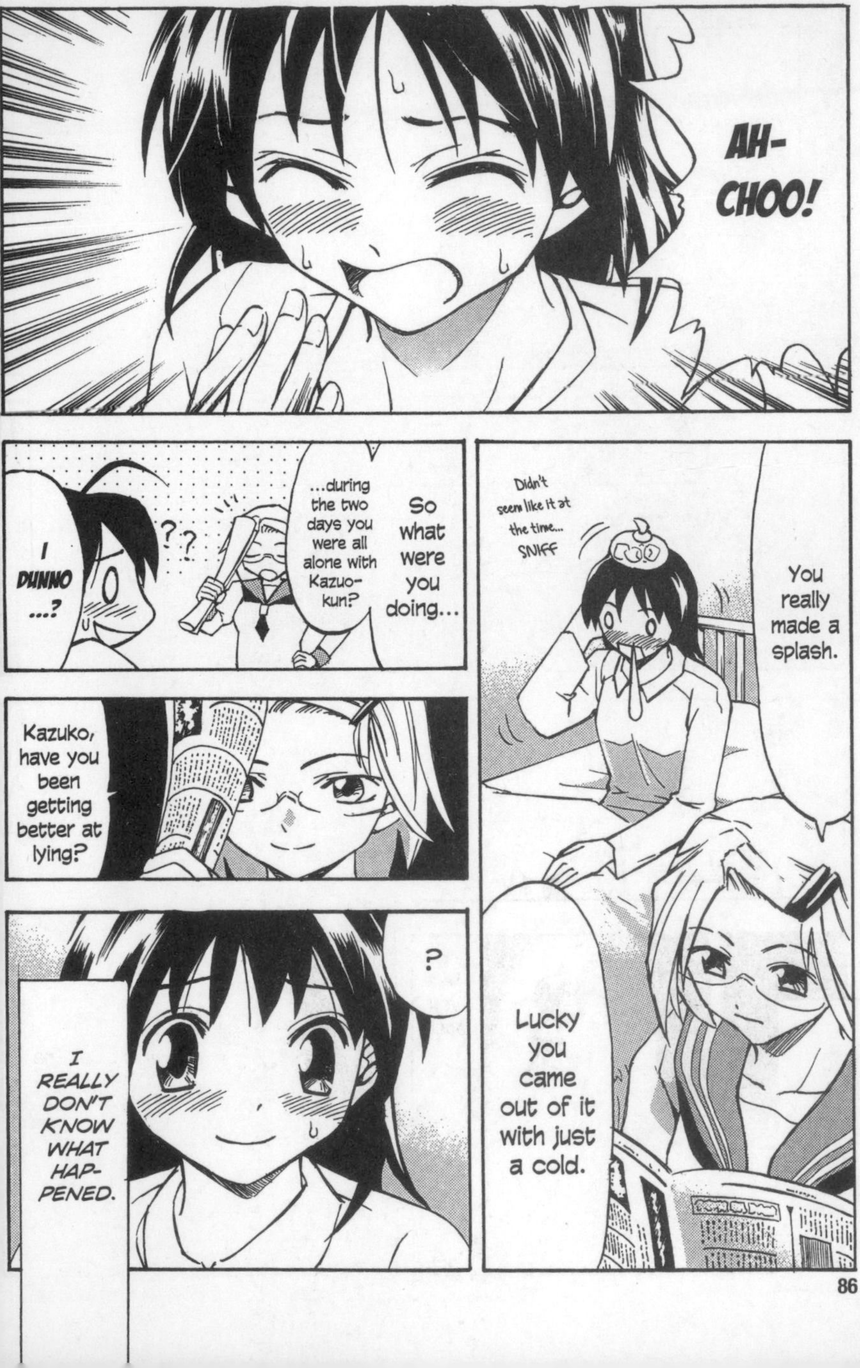
AH-CHOO!
You really made a splash.
Didn't seem like it at the time... SNIFF
Lucky you came out of it with just a cold.
So what were you doing...
...during the two days you were all alone with Kazuo-kun?
I DUNNO ...?
Kazuko, have you been getting better at lying?
?
I REALLY DON'T KNOW WHAT HAP-PENED.

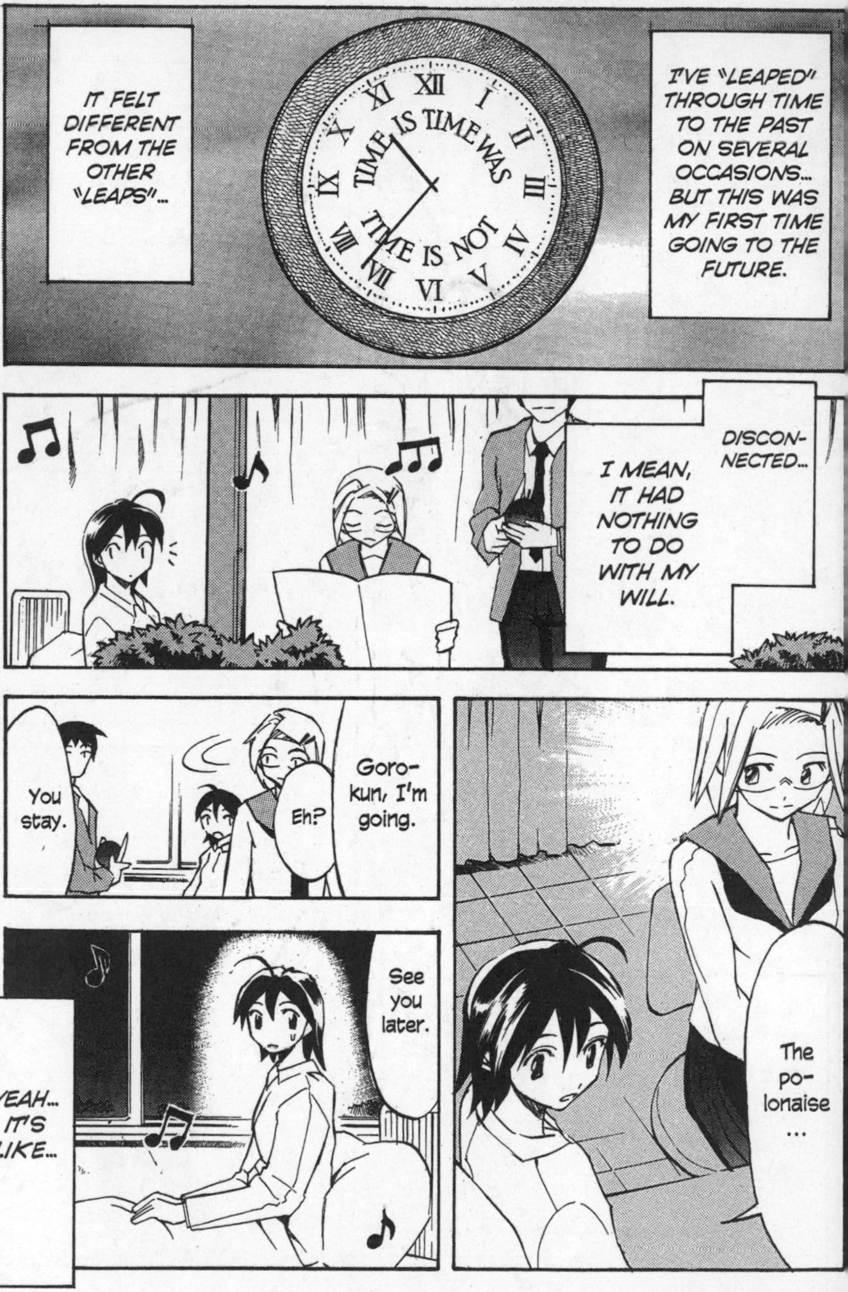
I'VE "LEAPED" THROUGH TIME TO THE PAST ON SEVERAL OCCASIONS... BUT THIS WAS MY FIRST TIME GOING TO THE FUTURE.
TIME IS TIME WAS TIME IS NOT
IT FELT DIFFERENT FROM THE OTHER "LEAPS"...
DISCONNECTED...
I MEAN, IT HAD NOTHING TO DO WITH MY WILL.
The polonaise...
Goro-kun, I'm going.
Eh?
You stay.
See you later.
YEAH... IT'S LIKE...

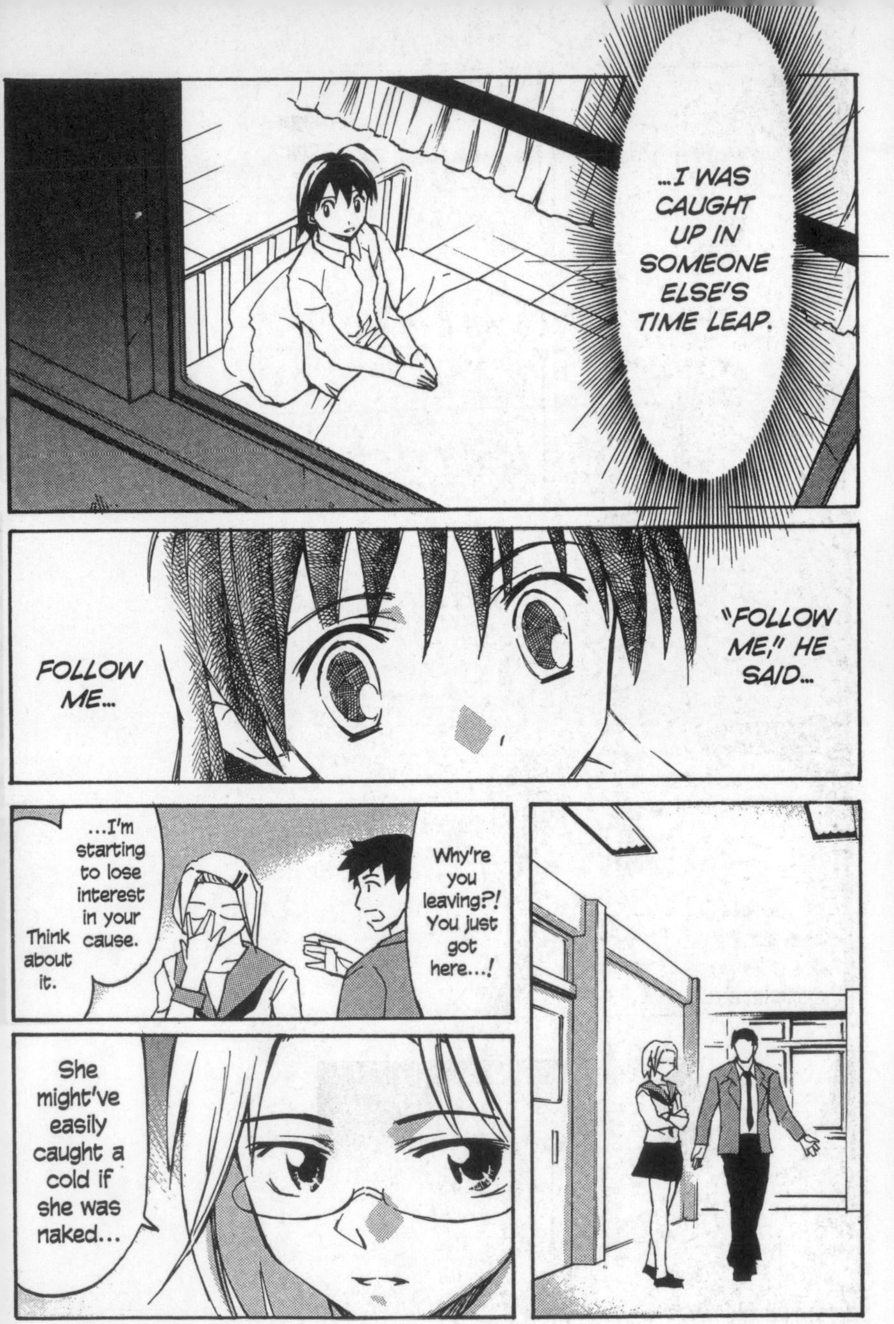
...I WAS CAUGHT UP IN SOMEONE ELSE'S TIME LEAP.
"FOLLOW ME," HE SAID...
FOLLOW ME...
Why're you leaving?! You just got here...!
...I'm starting to lose interest in your cause.
Think about it.
She might've easily caught a cold if she was naked...

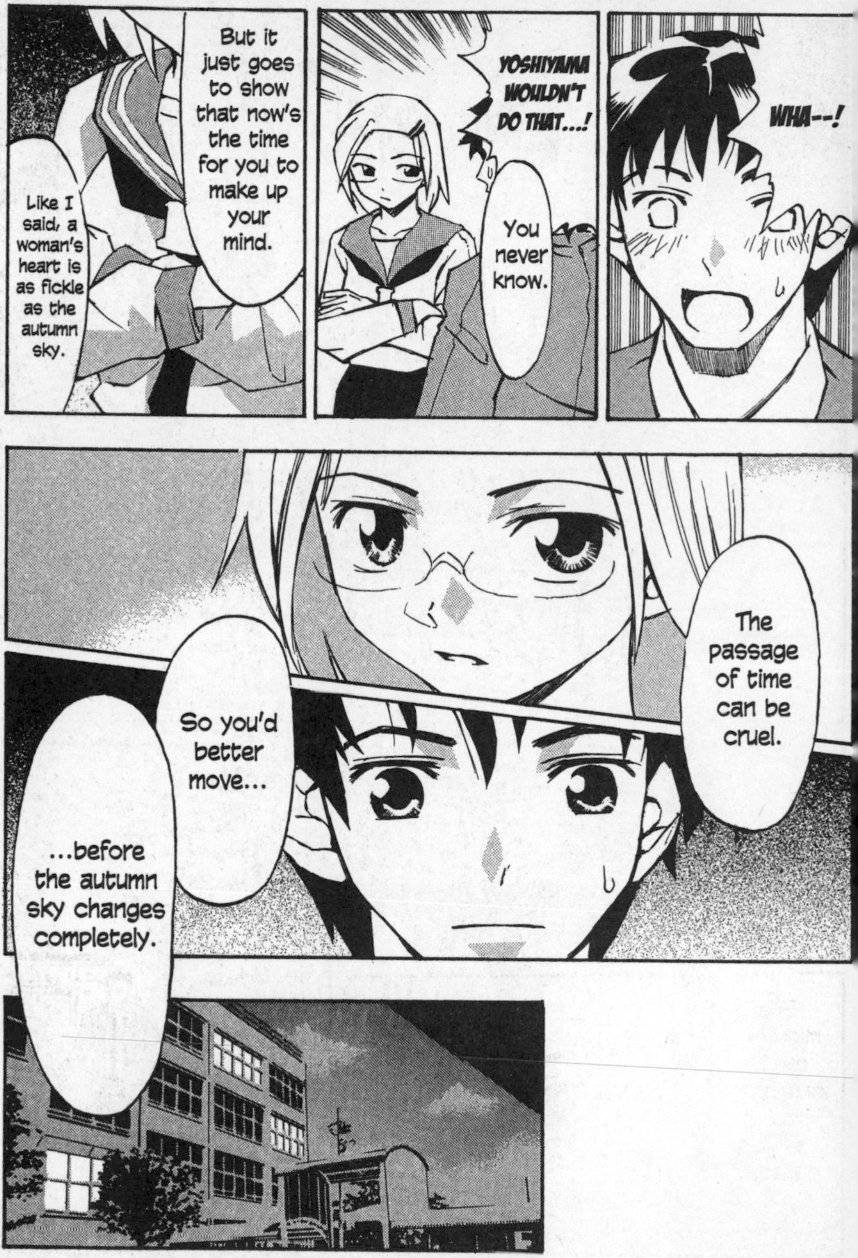
WHA--!
YOSHIYAMA WOULDN'T DO THAT...!
You never know.
But it just goes to show that now's the time for you to make up your mind.
Like I said, a woman's heart is as fickle as the autumn sky.
The passage of time can be cruel.
So you'd better move...
...before the autumn sky changes completely.

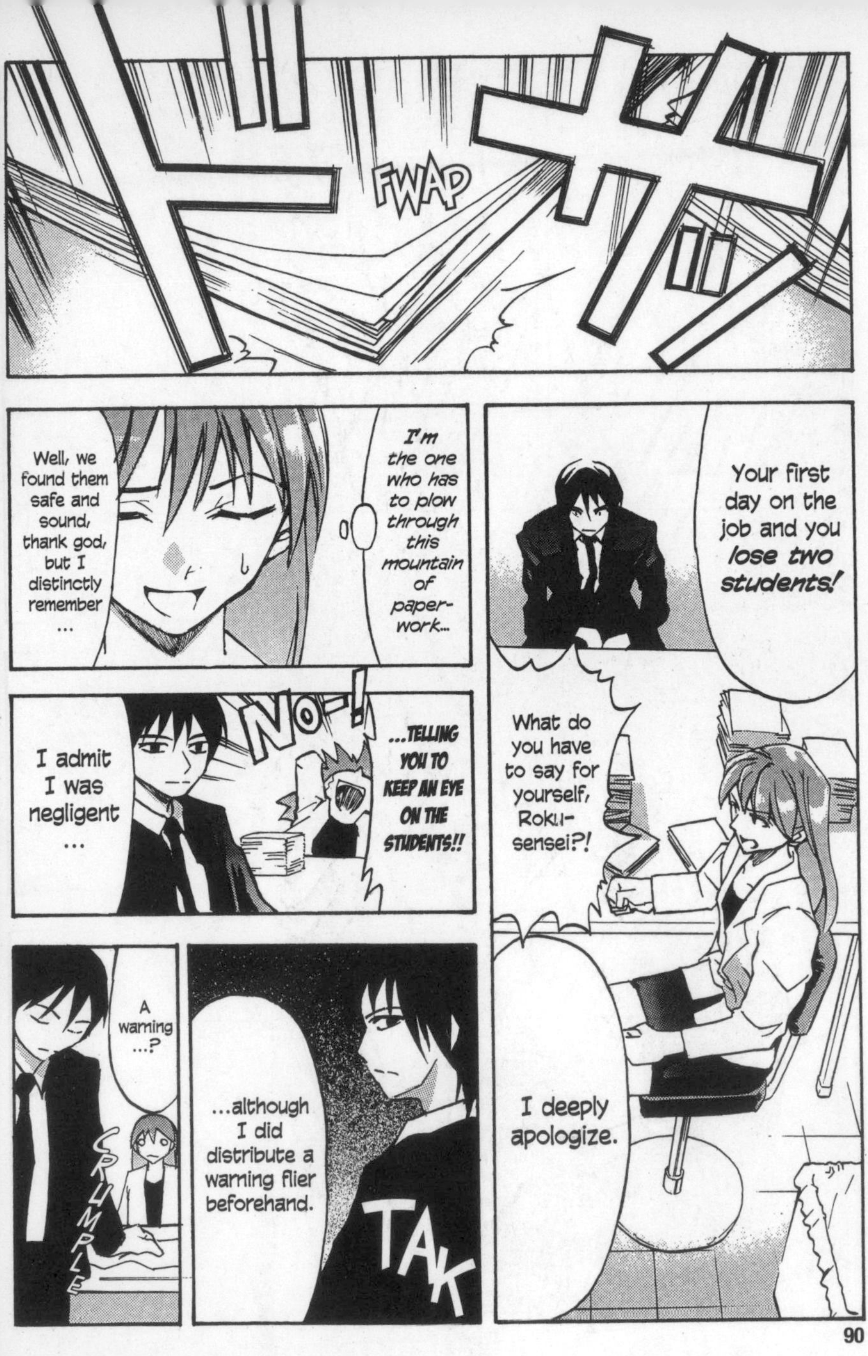
FWAP
Your first day on the job and you *lose two students!*
What do you have to say for yourself, Roku-sensei?!
I deeply apologize.
I'm the one who has to plow through this mountain of paper-work...
Well, we found them safe and sound, thank god, but I distinctly remember ...
...TELLING YOU TO KEEP AN EYE ON THE STUDENTS!!
NO-!
I admit I was negligent ...
...although I did distribute a warning flier beforehand.
TAK
A warning ...?
CRUMPLE

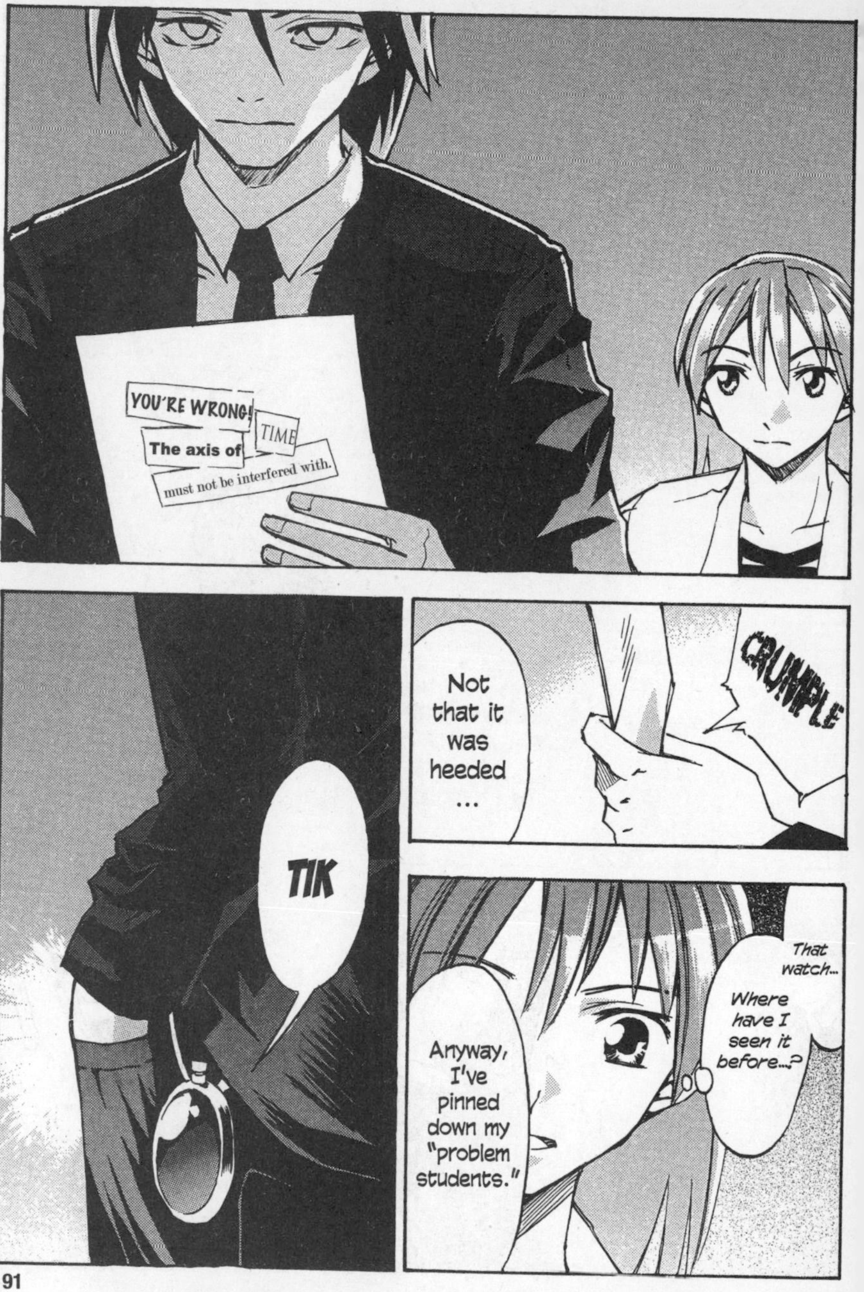
YOU'RE WRONG!
TIME
The axis of
must not be interfered with.
CRUMPLE
Not that it was heeded ...
That watch... Where have I seen it before...?
Anyway, I've pinned down my "problem students."
TIK

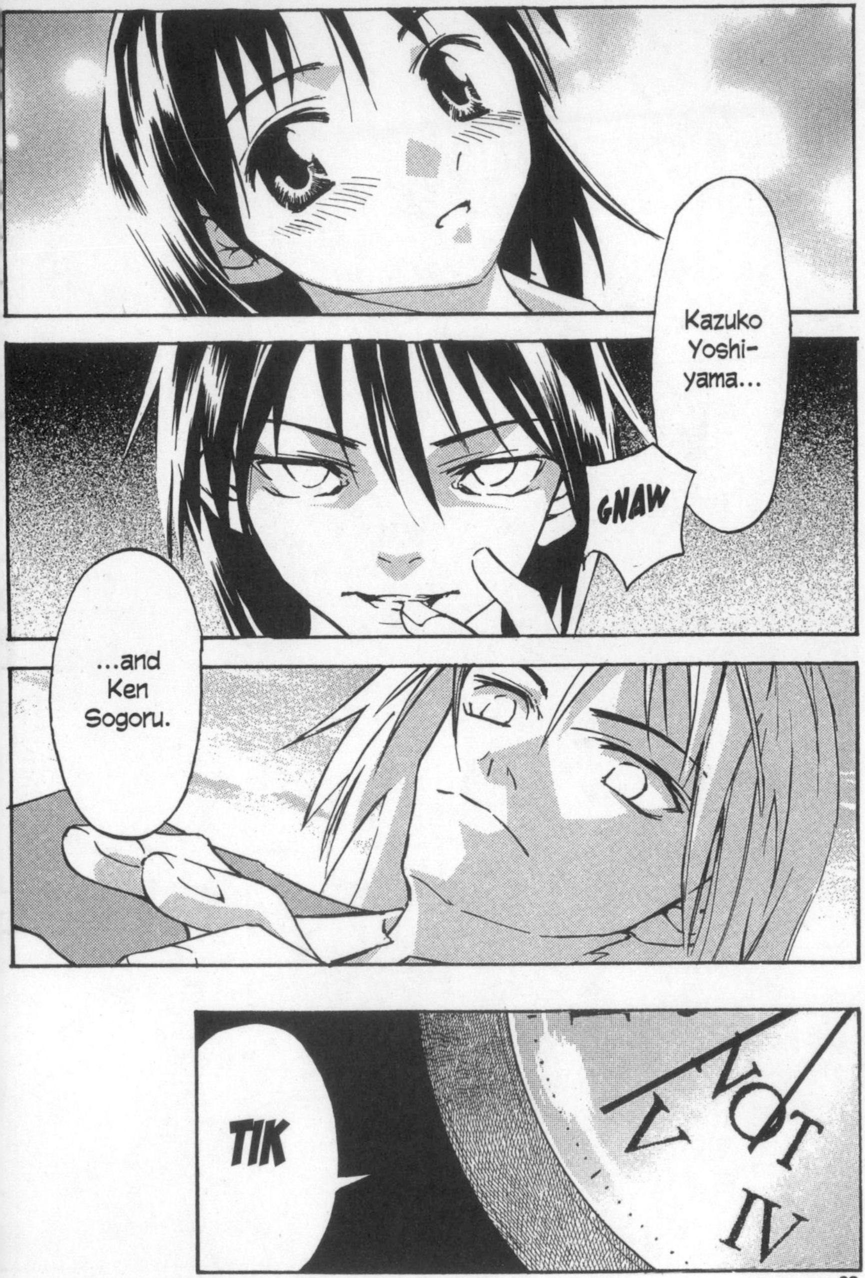
Kazuko Yoshi-yama...
GNAW
...and Ken Sogoru.
TIK

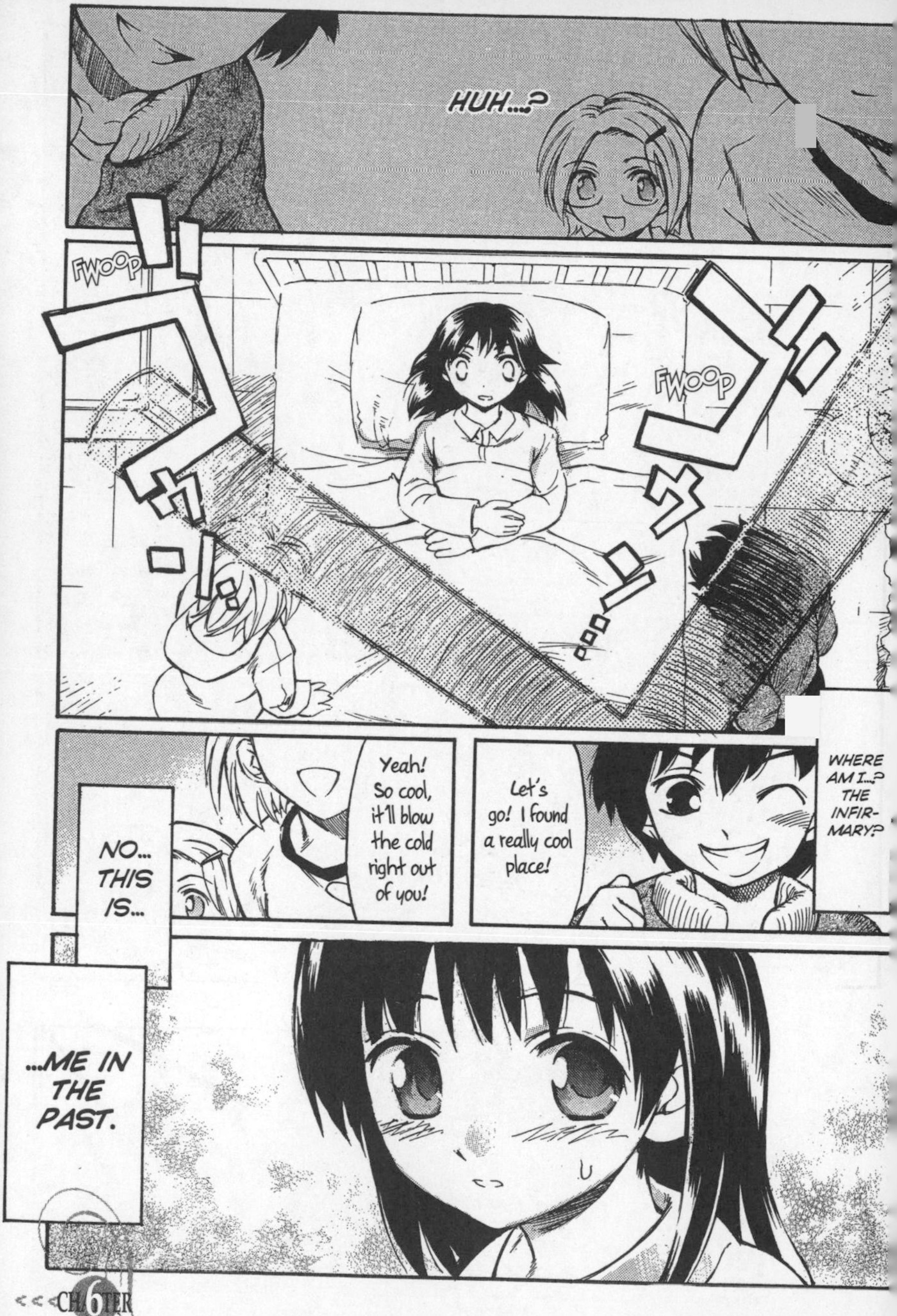
HUH...?
FWOOP
FWOOP
WHERE AM I...? THE INFIRMARY?
Let's go! I found a really cool place!
Yeah! So cool, it'll blow the cold right out of you!
NO... THIS IS...
...ME IN THE PAST.

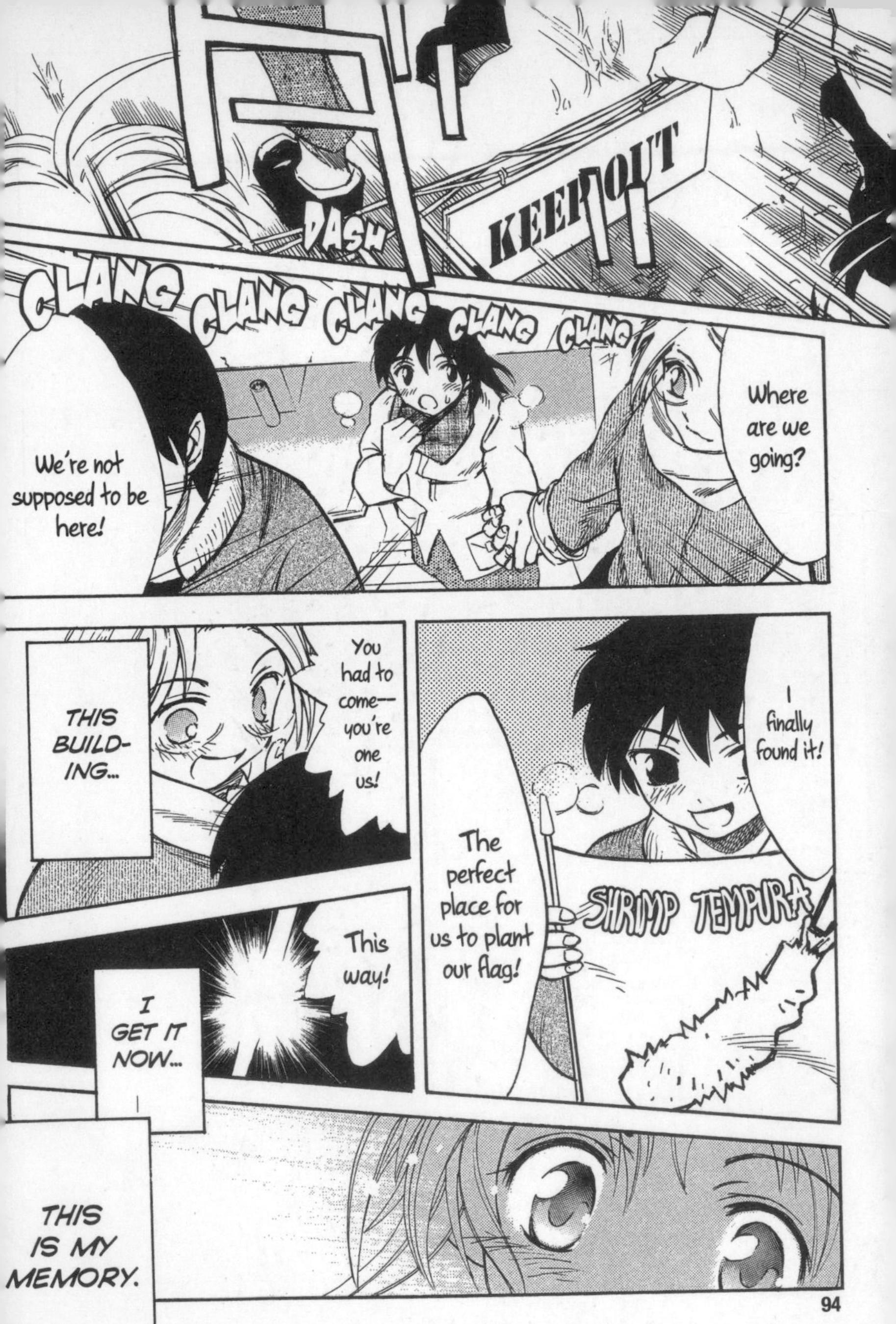
DASH
KEEP OUT
CLANG CLANG CLANG CLANG CLANG
Where are we going?
We're not supposed to be here!
I finally found it!
The perfect place for us to plant our flag!
SHRIMP TEMPURA
You had to come--you're one us!
THIS BUILDING...
This way!
I GET IT NOW...
THIS IS MY MEMORY.

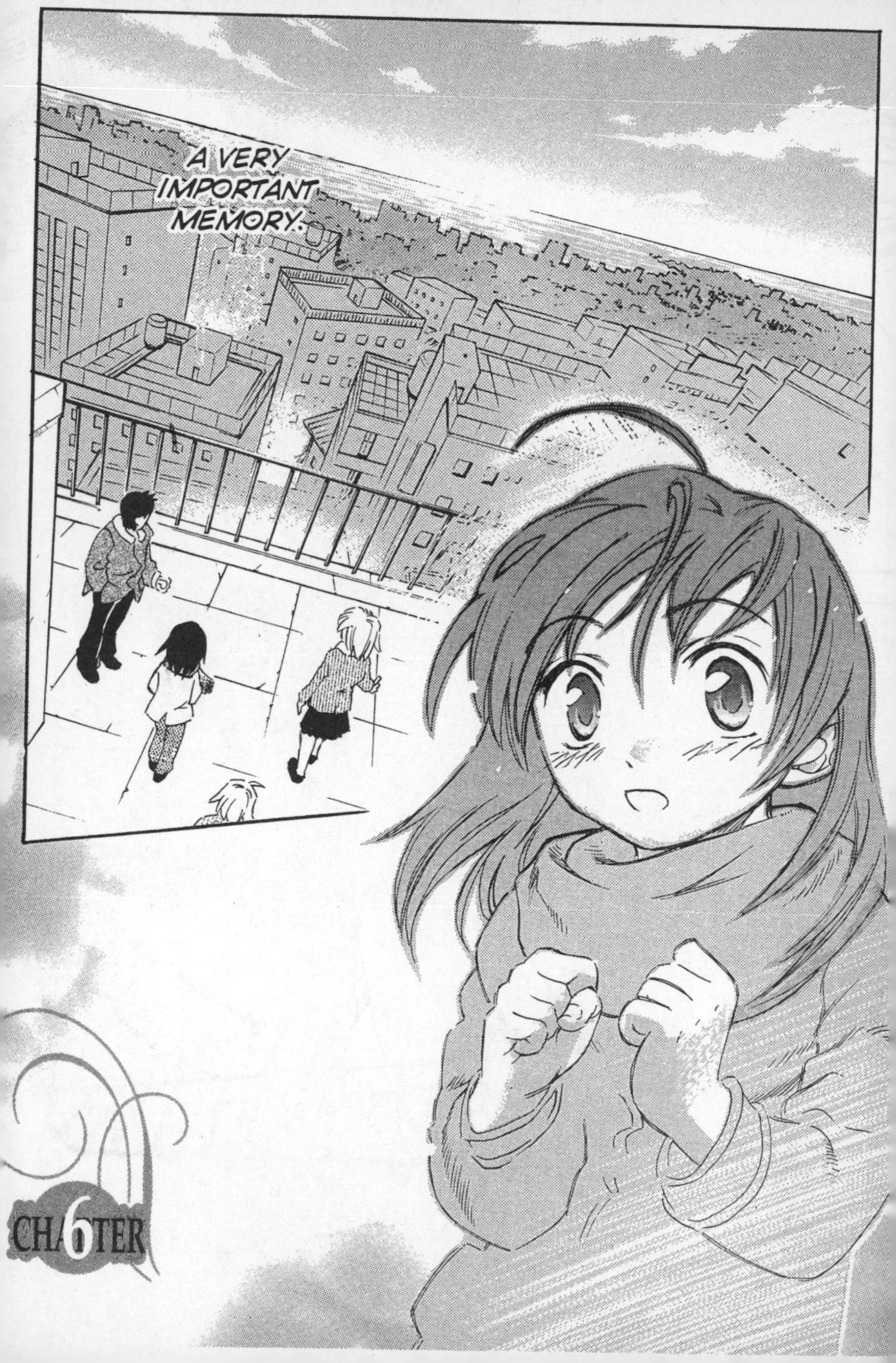
A VERY IMPORTANT MEMORY.
CHAPTER 6

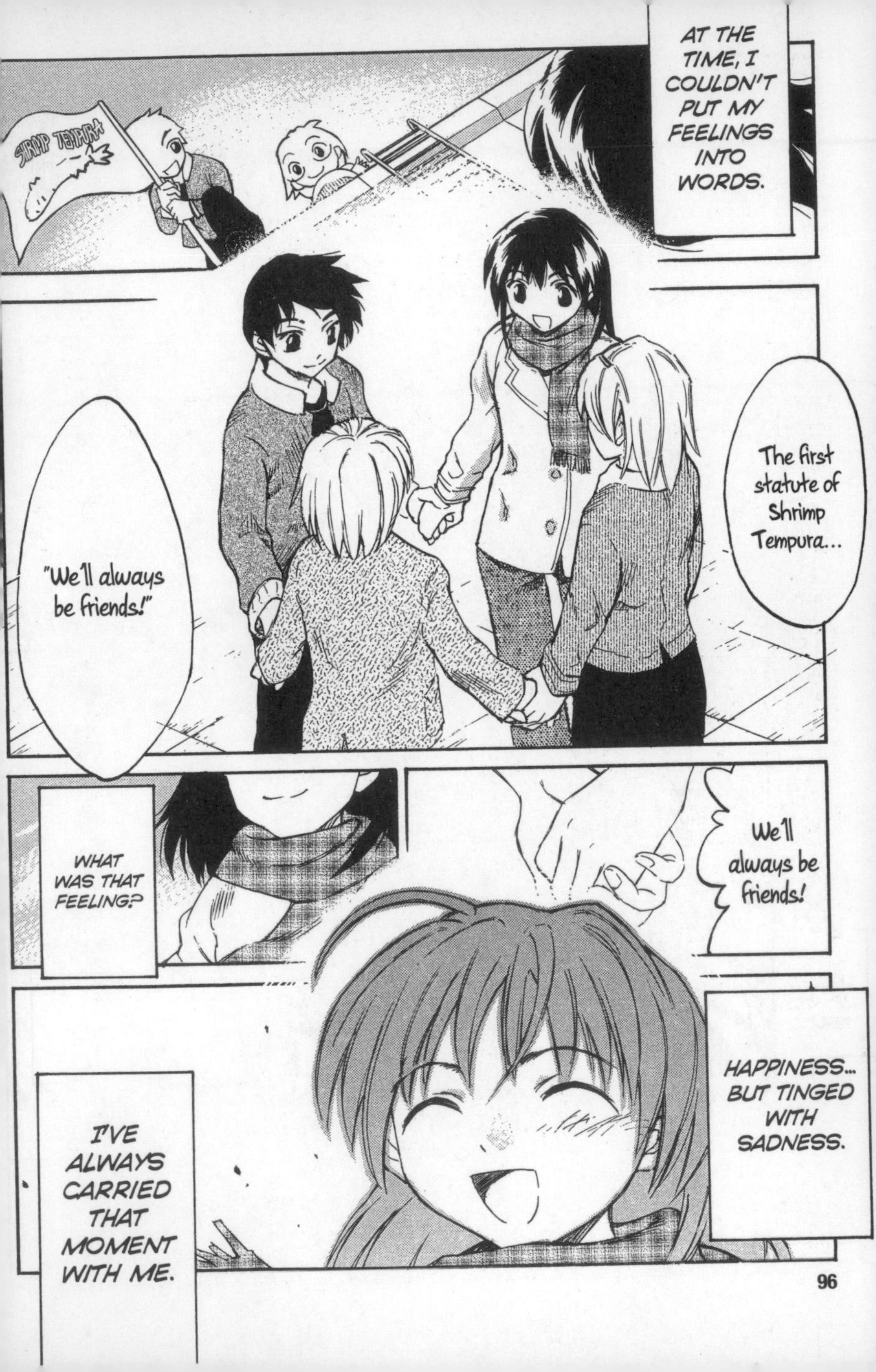
AT THE TIME, I COULDN'T PUT MY FEELINGS INTO WORDS.
SHRIMP TEMPURA
The first statute of Shrimp Tempura...
"We'll always be friends!"
We'll always be friends!
WHAT WAS THAT FEELING?
HAPPINESS... BUT TINGED WITH SADNESS.
I'VE ALWAYS CARRIED THAT MOMENT WITH ME.

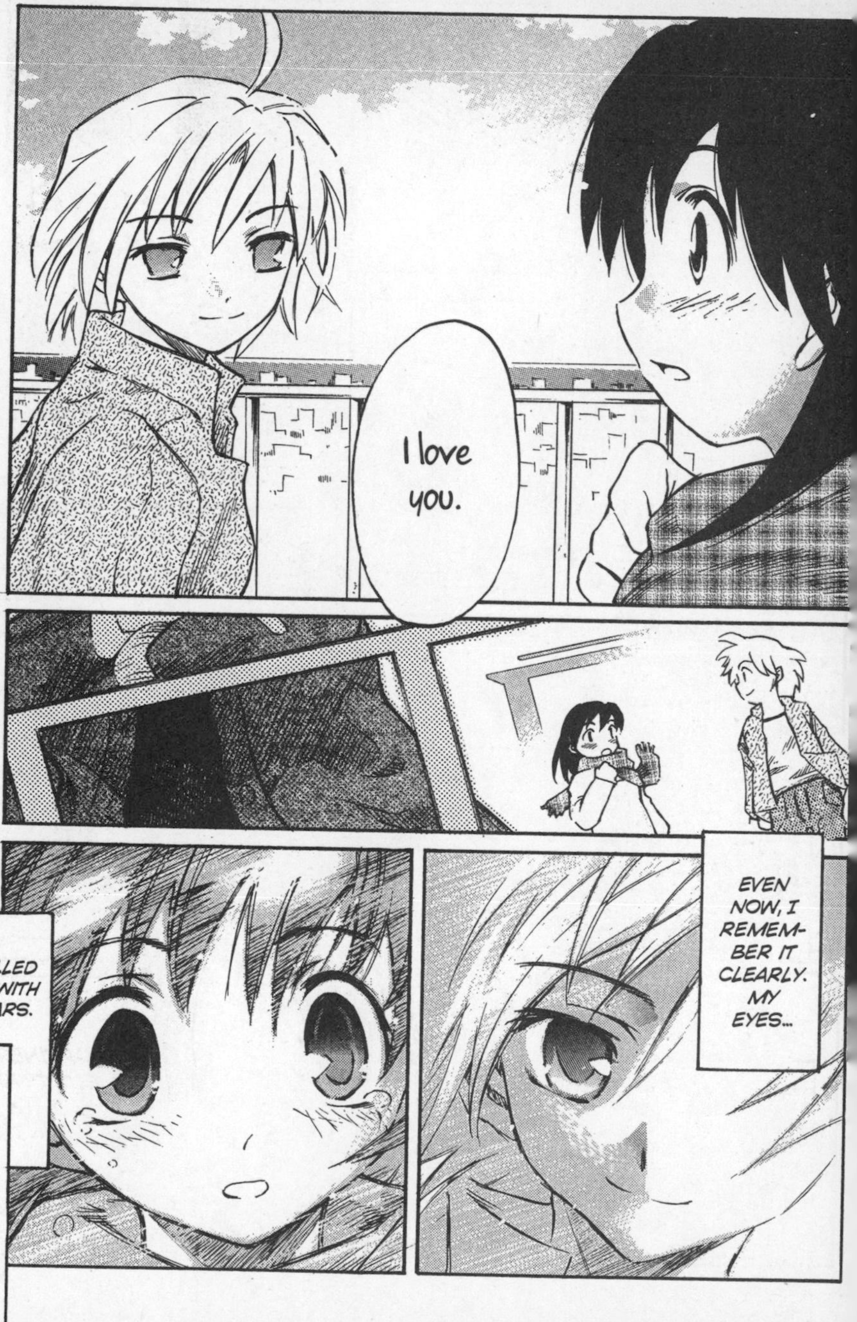
I love you.
EVEN NOW, I REMEM-BER IT CLEARLY. MY EYES...
...FILLED UP WITH TEARS.

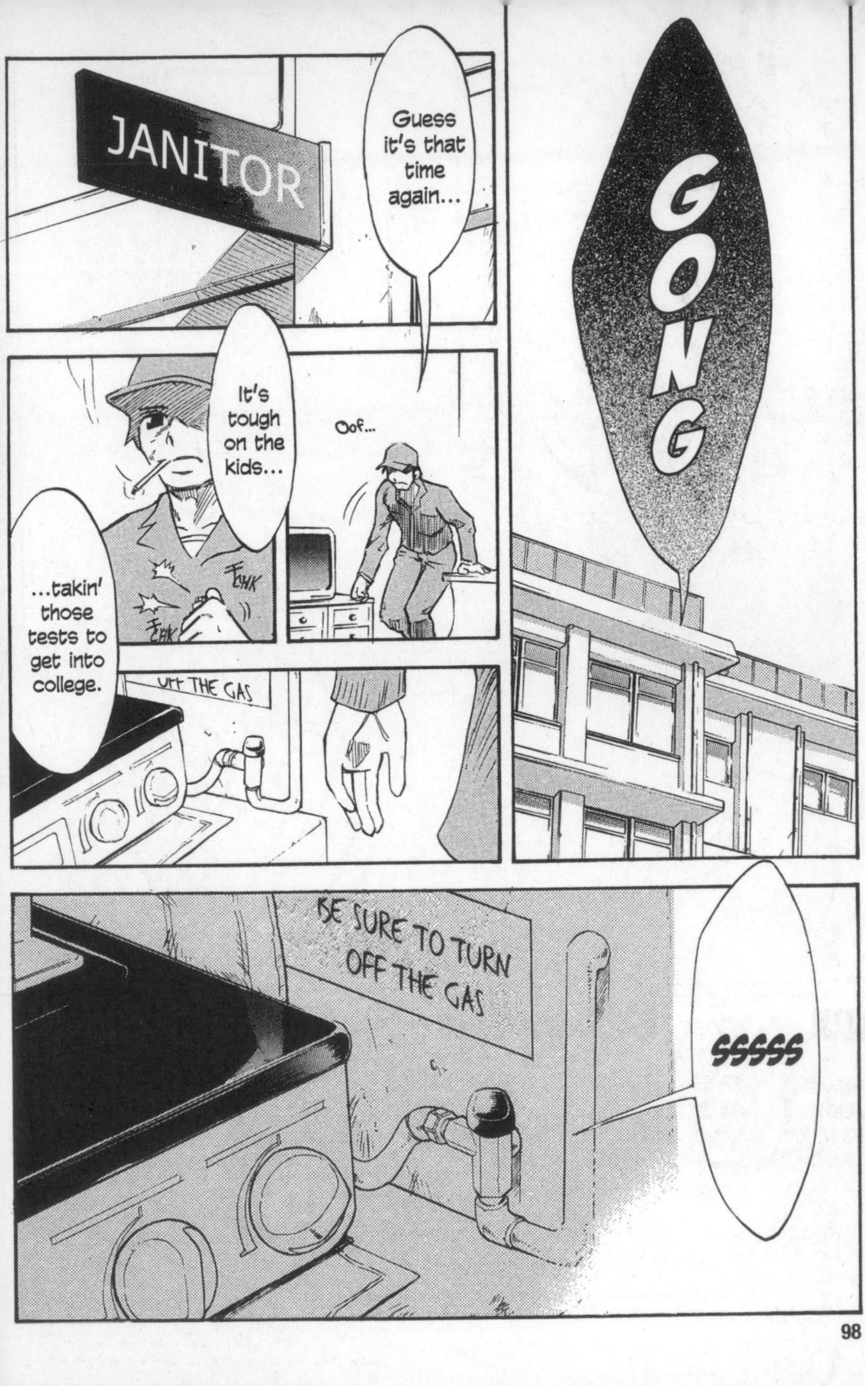
GONG
JANITOR
Guess it's that time again...
Oof...
It's tough on the kids...
...takin' those tests to get into college.
OFF THE GAS
BE SURE TO TURN OFF THE GAS
SSSSS

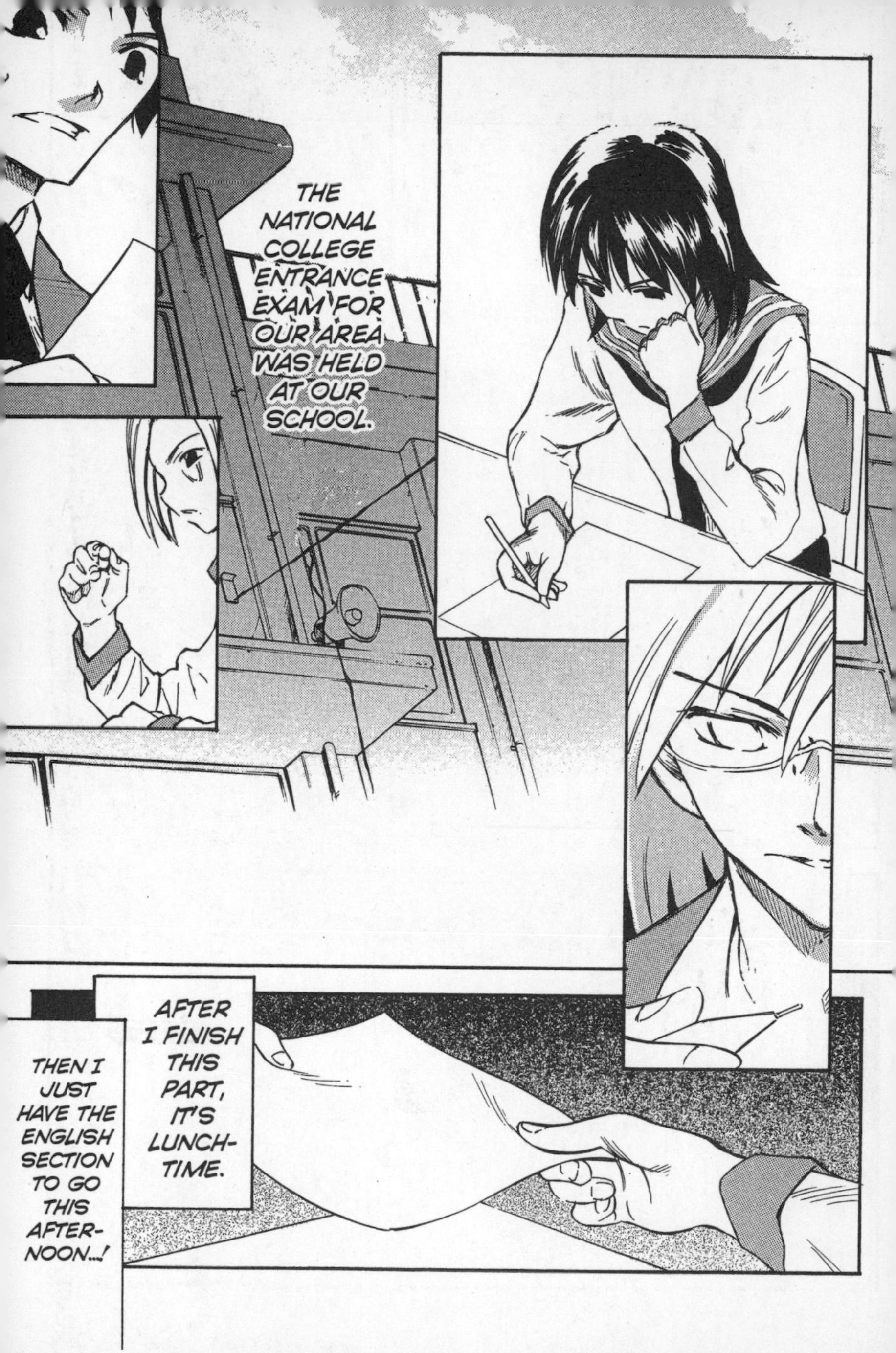
THE NATIONAL COLLEGE ENTRANCE EXAM FOR OUR AREA WAS HELD AT OUR SCHOOL.
AFTER I FINISH THIS PART, IT'S LUNCH-TIME.
THEN I JUST HAVE THE ENGLISH SECTION TO GO THIS AFTER-NOON...!

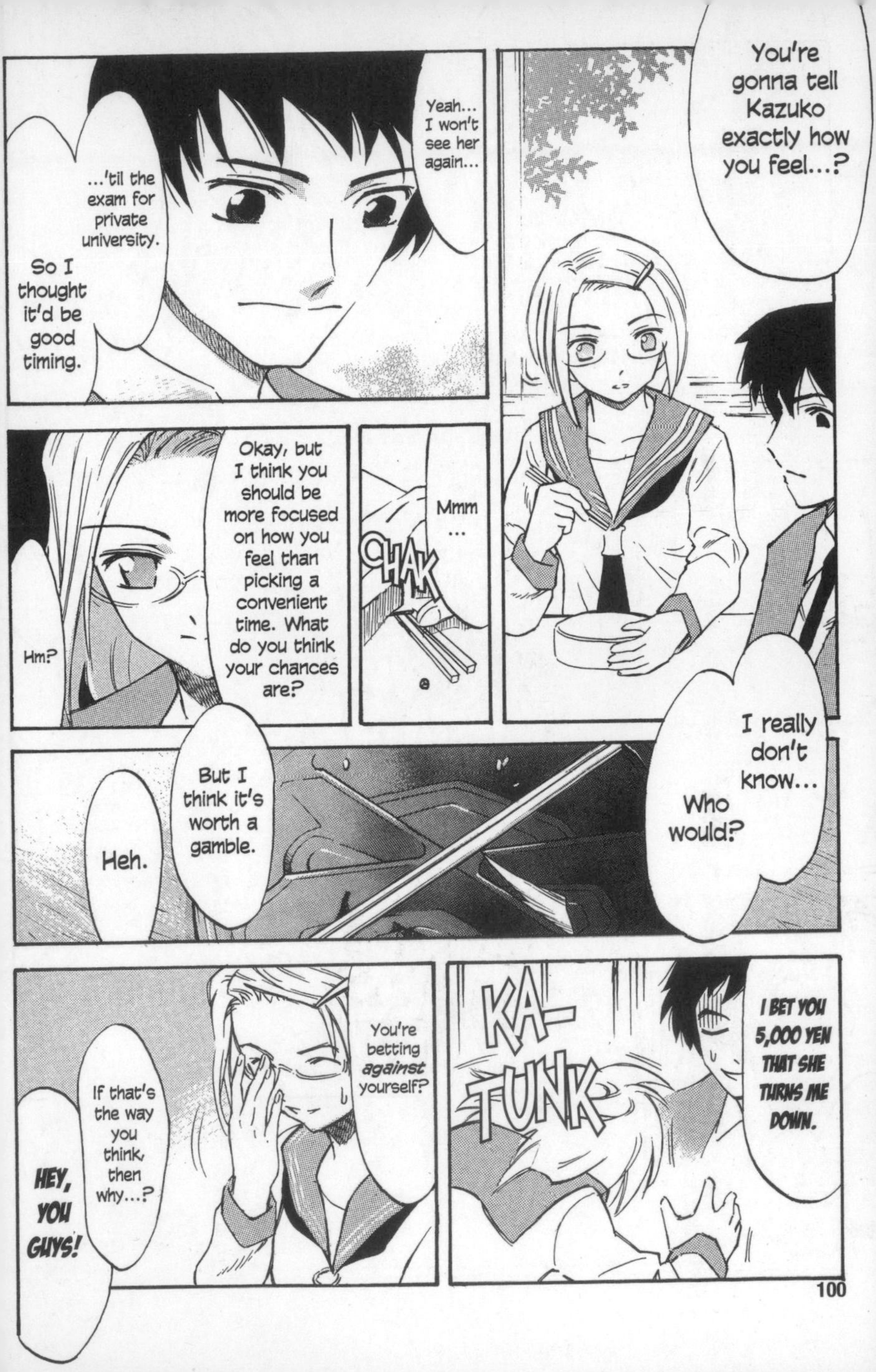
You're gonna tell Kazuko exactly how you feel...?
Yeah... I won't see her again...
...'til the exam for private university.
So I thought it'd be good timing.
Mmm ...
CHAK
Okay, but I think you should be more focused on how you feel than picking a convenient time. What do you think your chances are?
Hm?
I really don't know...
Who would?
But I think it's worth a gamble.
Heh.
I BET YOU 5,000 YEN THAT SHE TURNS ME DOWN.
KA-TUNK
You're betting *against* yourself?
If that's the way you think, then why...?
HEY, YOU GUYS!

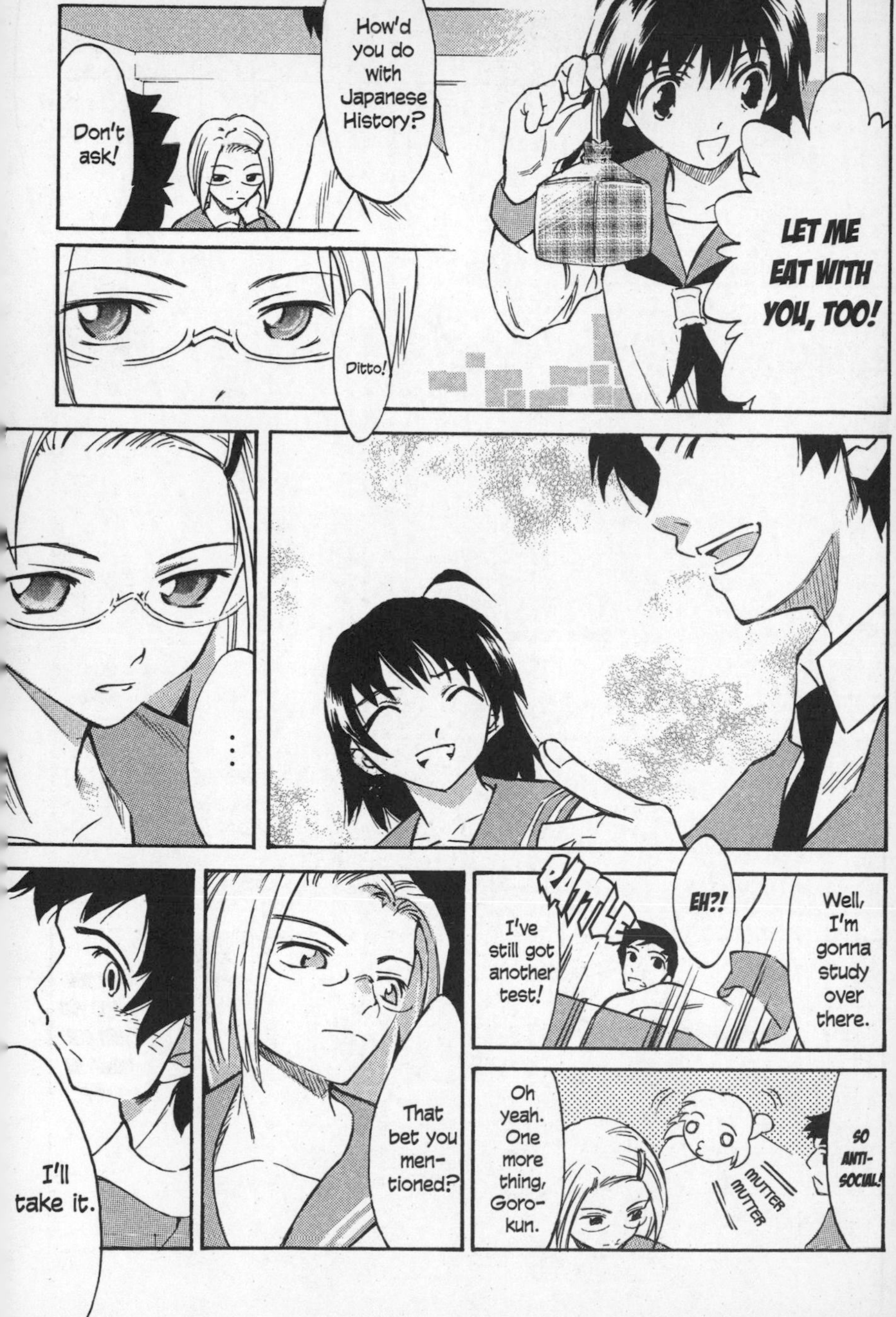
LET ME EAT WITH YOU, TOO!
How'd you do with Japanese History?
Don't ask!
Ditto!
...
Well, I'm gonna study over there.
EH?!
RATTLE
I've still got another test!
SO ANTI-SOCIAL!
MUTTER MUTTER
Oh yeah. One more thing, Goro-kun.
That bet you mentioned?
I'll take it.

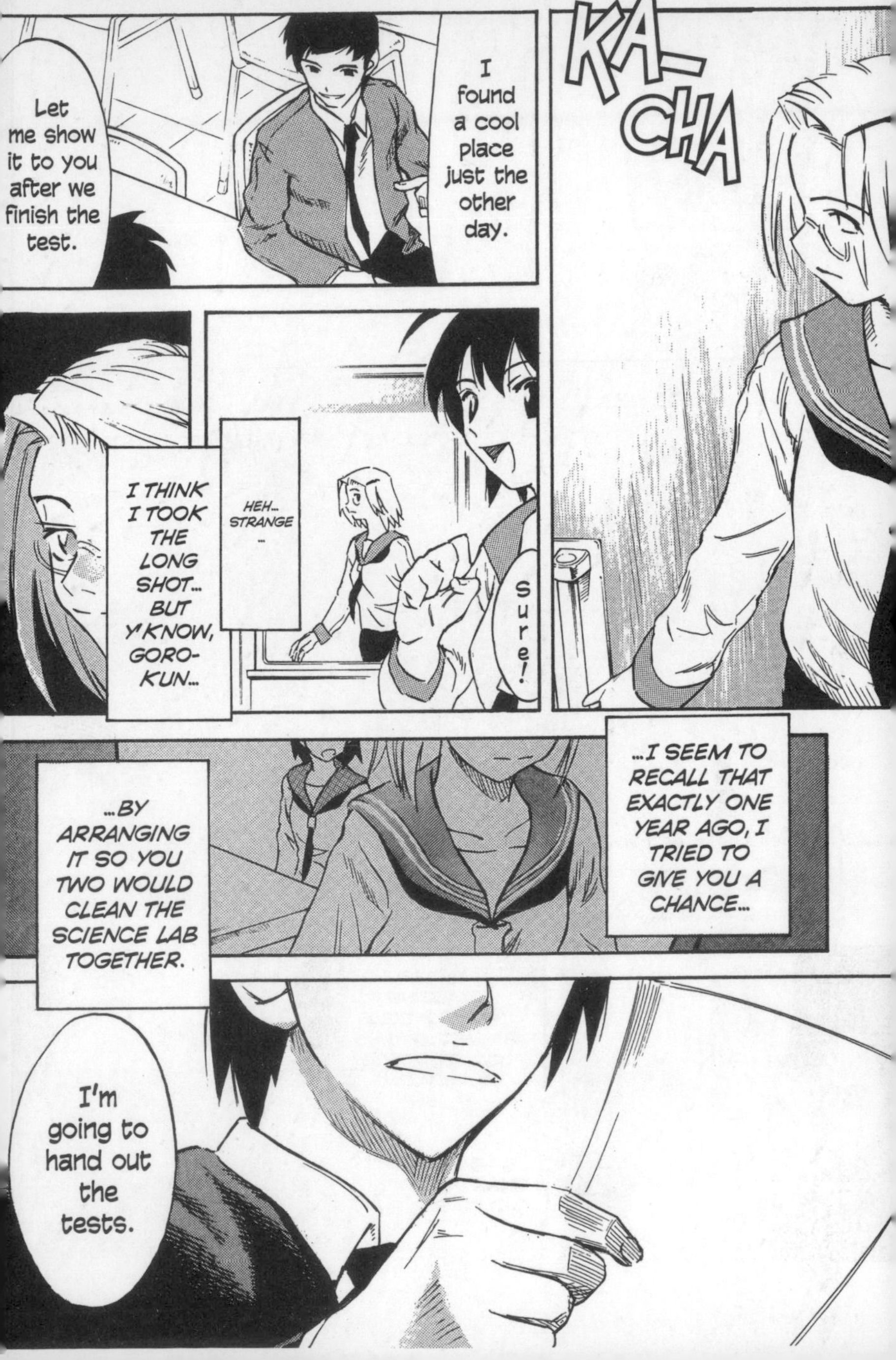
KA-CHA
I found a cool place just the other day.
Let me show it to you after we finish the test.
Sure!
HEH... STRANGE...
I THINK I TOOK THE LONG SHOT... BUT Y'KNOW, GORO-KUN...
...I SEEM TO RECALL THAT EXACTLY ONE YEAR AGO, I TRIED TO GIVE YOU A CHANCE...
...BY ARRANGING IT SO YOU TWO WOULD CLEAN THE SCIENCE LAB TOGETHER.
I'm going to hand out the tests.

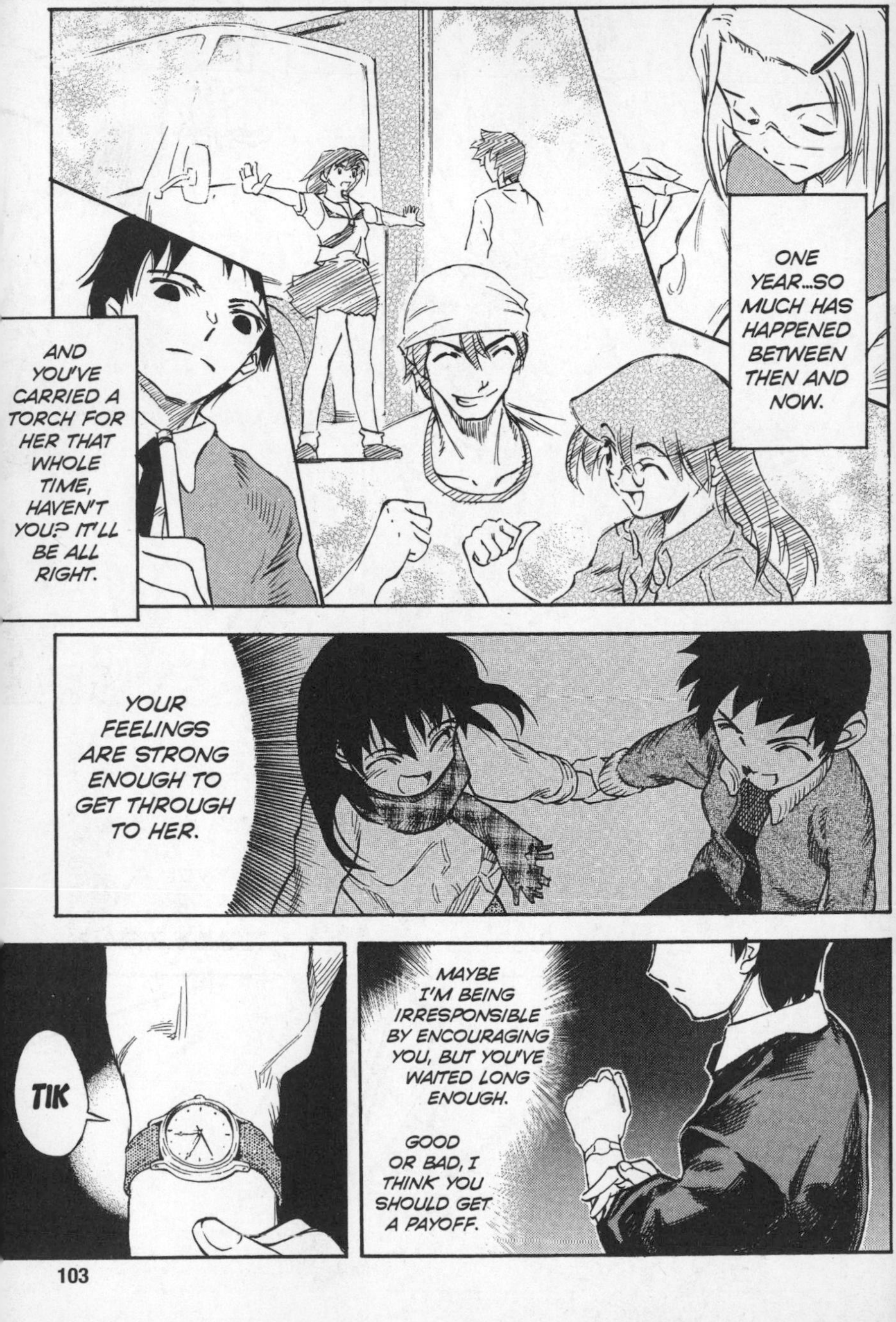
ONE YEAR...SO MUCH HAS HAPPENED BETWEEN THEN AND NOW.
AND YOU'VE CARRIED A TORCH FOR HER THAT WHOLE TIME, HAVEN'T YOU? IT'LL BE ALL RIGHT.
YOUR FEELINGS ARE STRONG ENOUGH TO GET THROUGH TO HER.
MAYBE I'M BEING IRRESPONSIBLE BY ENCOURAGING YOU, BUT YOU'VE WAITED LONG ENOUGH.
GOOD OR BAD, I THINK YOU SHOULD GET A PAYOFF.
TIK

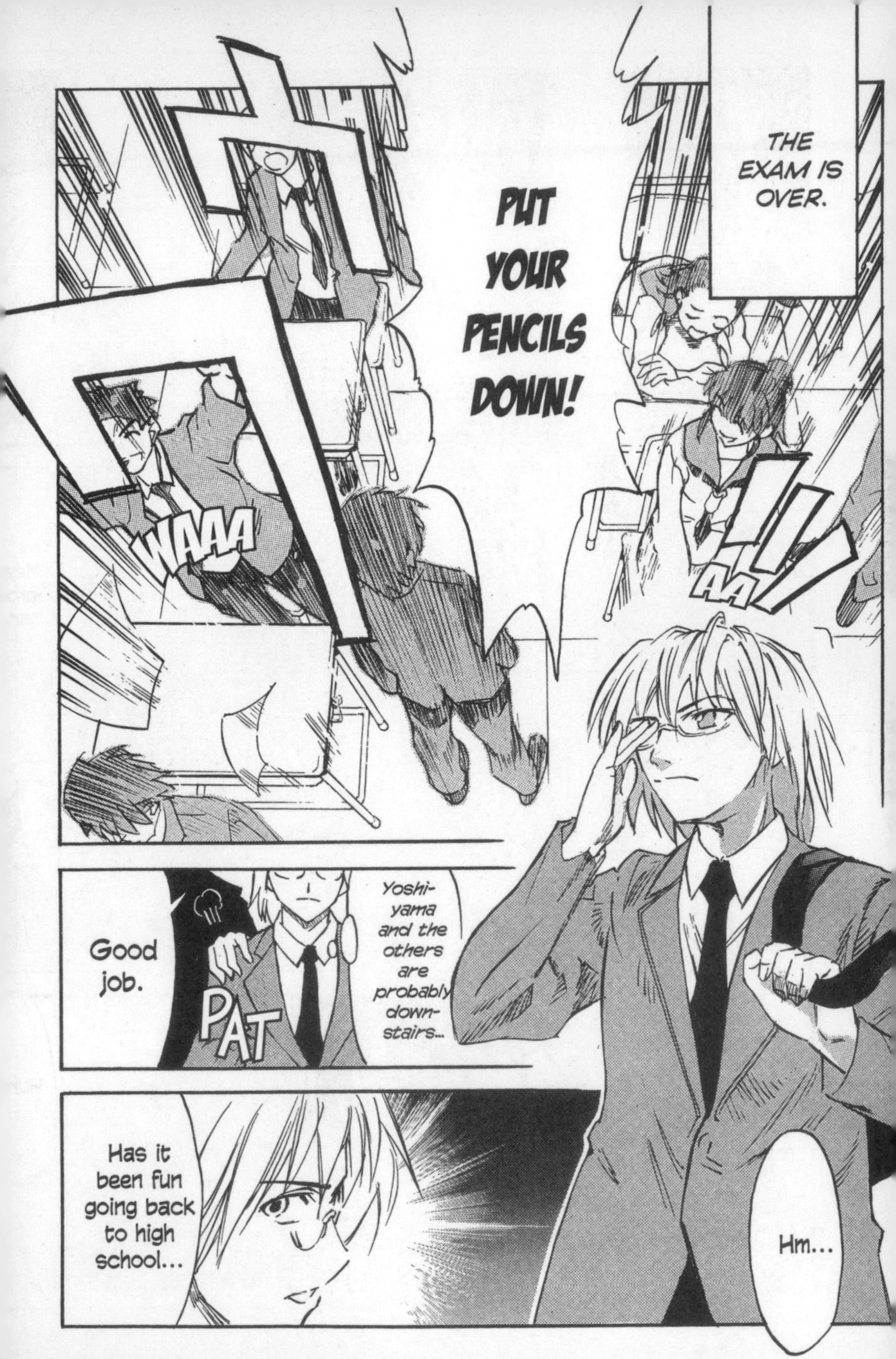

THE EXAM IS OVER.
PUT YOUR PENCILS DOWN!
AA!!
WAAA
Hm...
Yoshi-yama and the others are probably down-stairs...
Good job.
PAT
Has it been fun going back to high school...

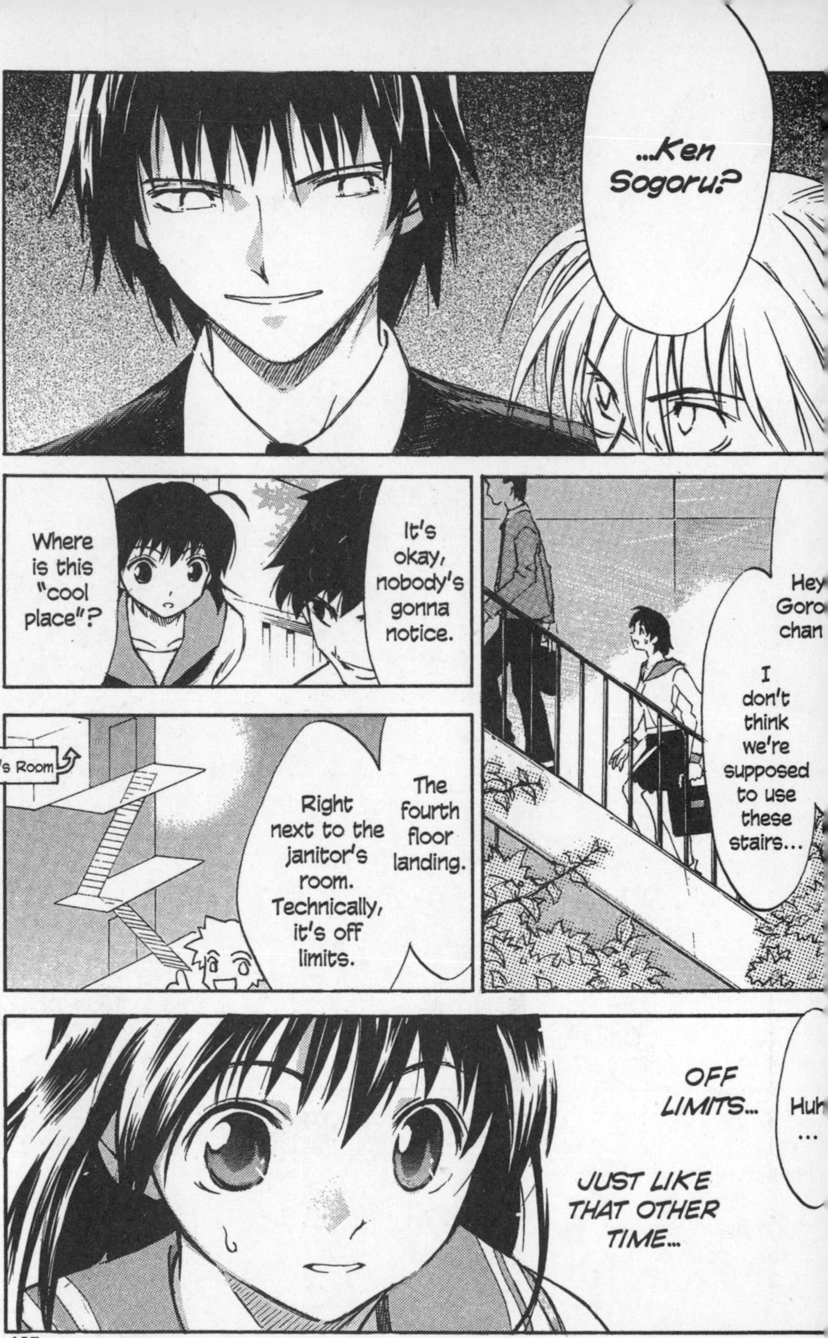
...Ken Sogoru?
Hey Goro chan
I don't think we're supposed to use these stairs...
It's okay, nobody's gonna notice.
Where is this "cool place"?
The fourth floor landing.
Right next to the janitor's room. Technically, it's off limits.
Janitor's Room
Huh ...
OFF LIMITS...
JUST LIKE THAT OTHER TIME...

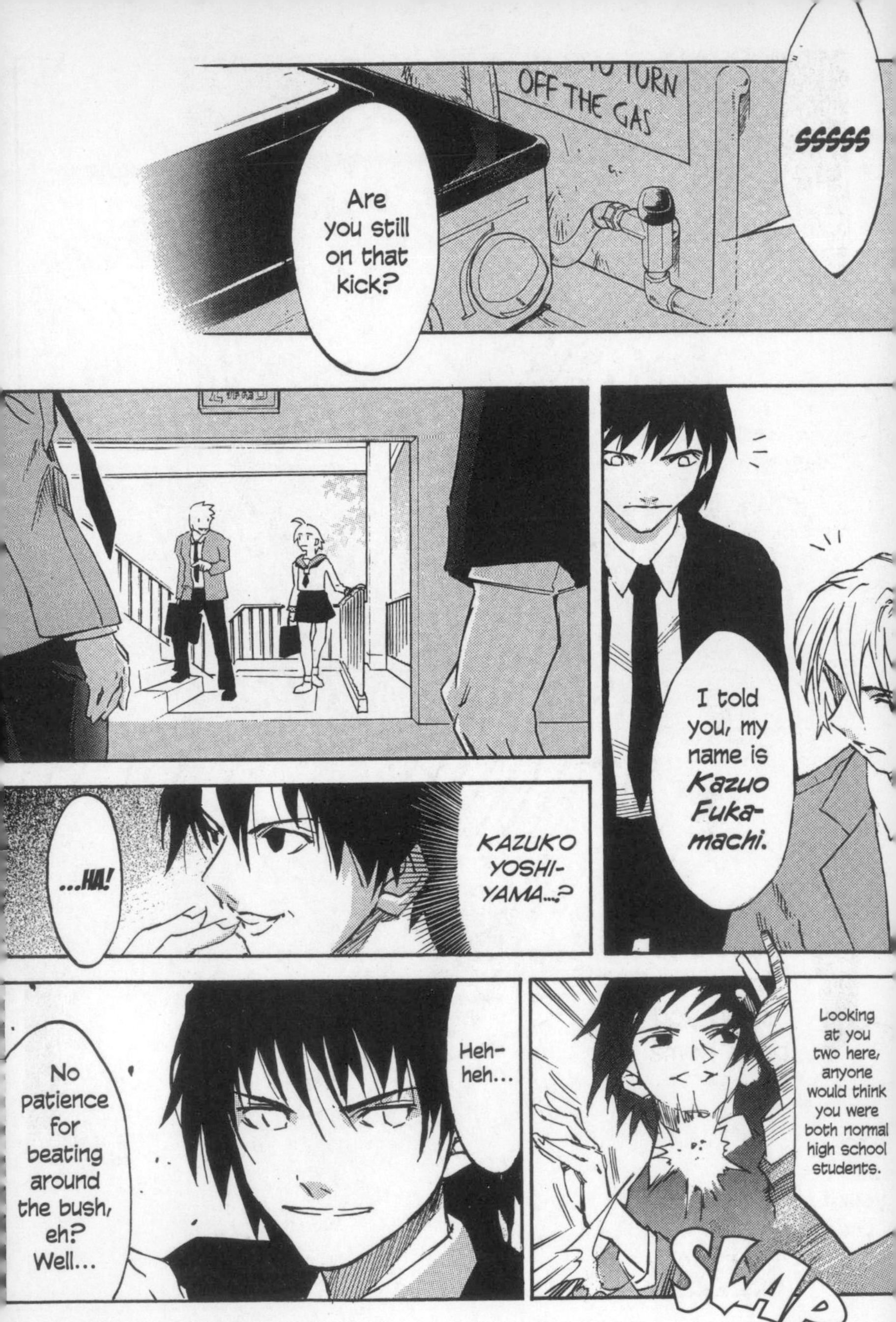
SSSSS
TURN OFF THE GAS
Are you still on that kick?
I told you, my name is Kazuo Fukamachi.
KAZUKO YOSHIYAMA...?
...HA!
Looking at you two here, anyone would think you were both normal high school students.
SLAP
Heh-heh...
No patience for beating around the bush, eh? Well...

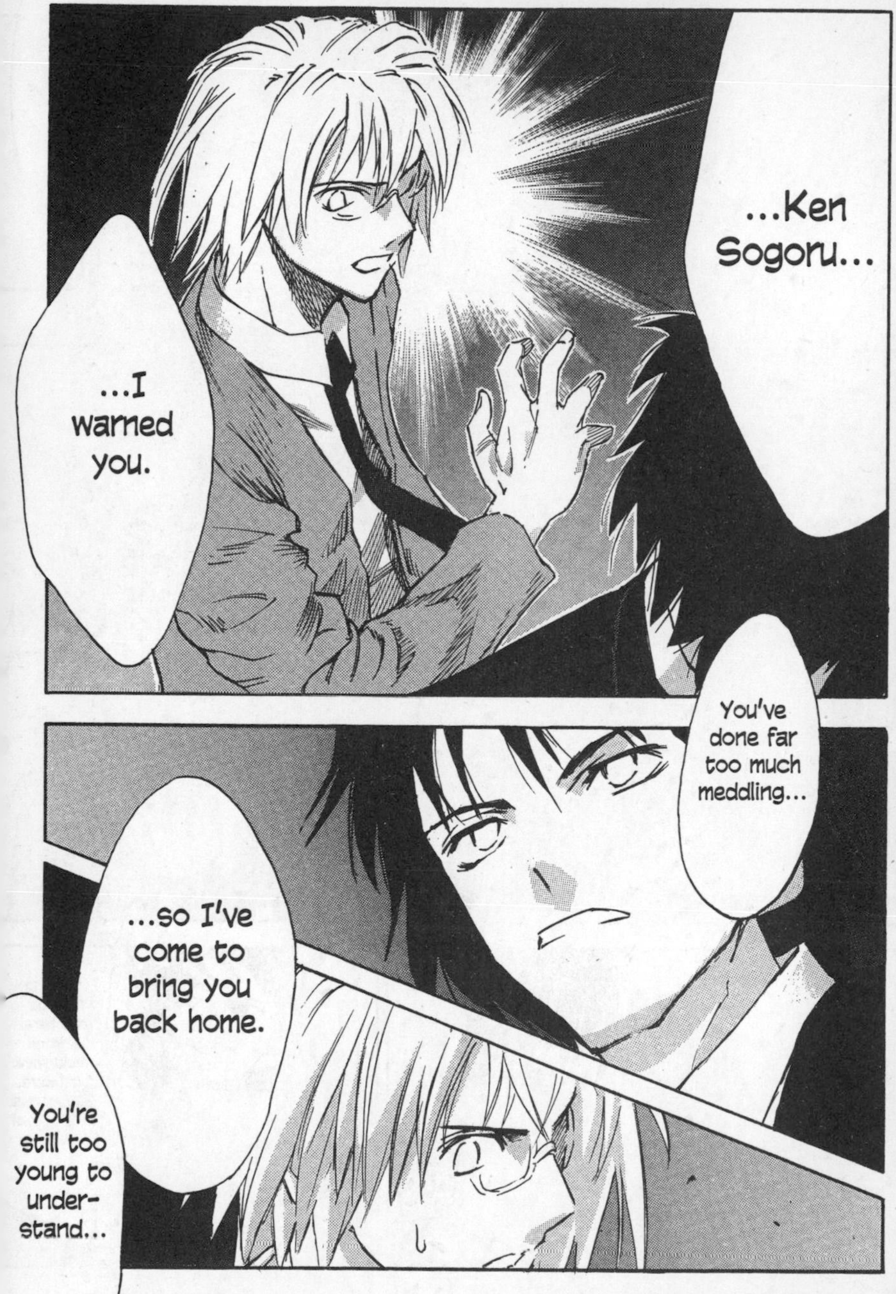
...Ken Sogoru...
...I warned you.
You've done far too much meddling...
...so I've come to bring you back home.
You're still too young to under-stand...

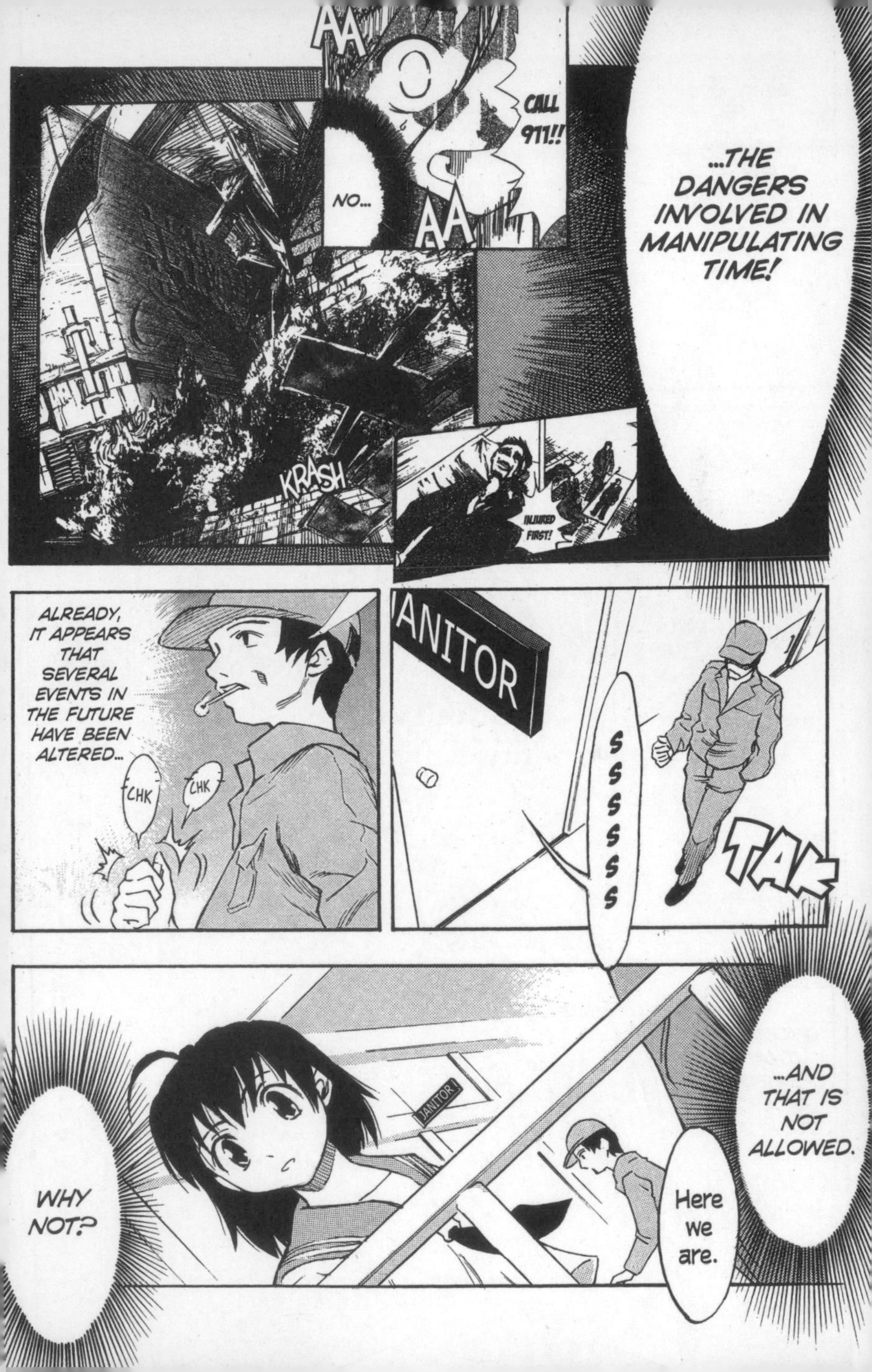
...THE DANGERS INVOLVED IN MANIPULATING TIME!
AA
CALL 911!!
AA
NO...
KRASH
INJURED FIRST!
JANITOR
SSSSSS
TAK
ALREADY, IT APPEARS THAT SEVERAL EVENTS IN THE FUTURE HAVE BEEN ALTERED...
CHK
CHK
...AND THAT IS NOT ALLOWED.
JANITOR
Here we are.
WHY NOT?

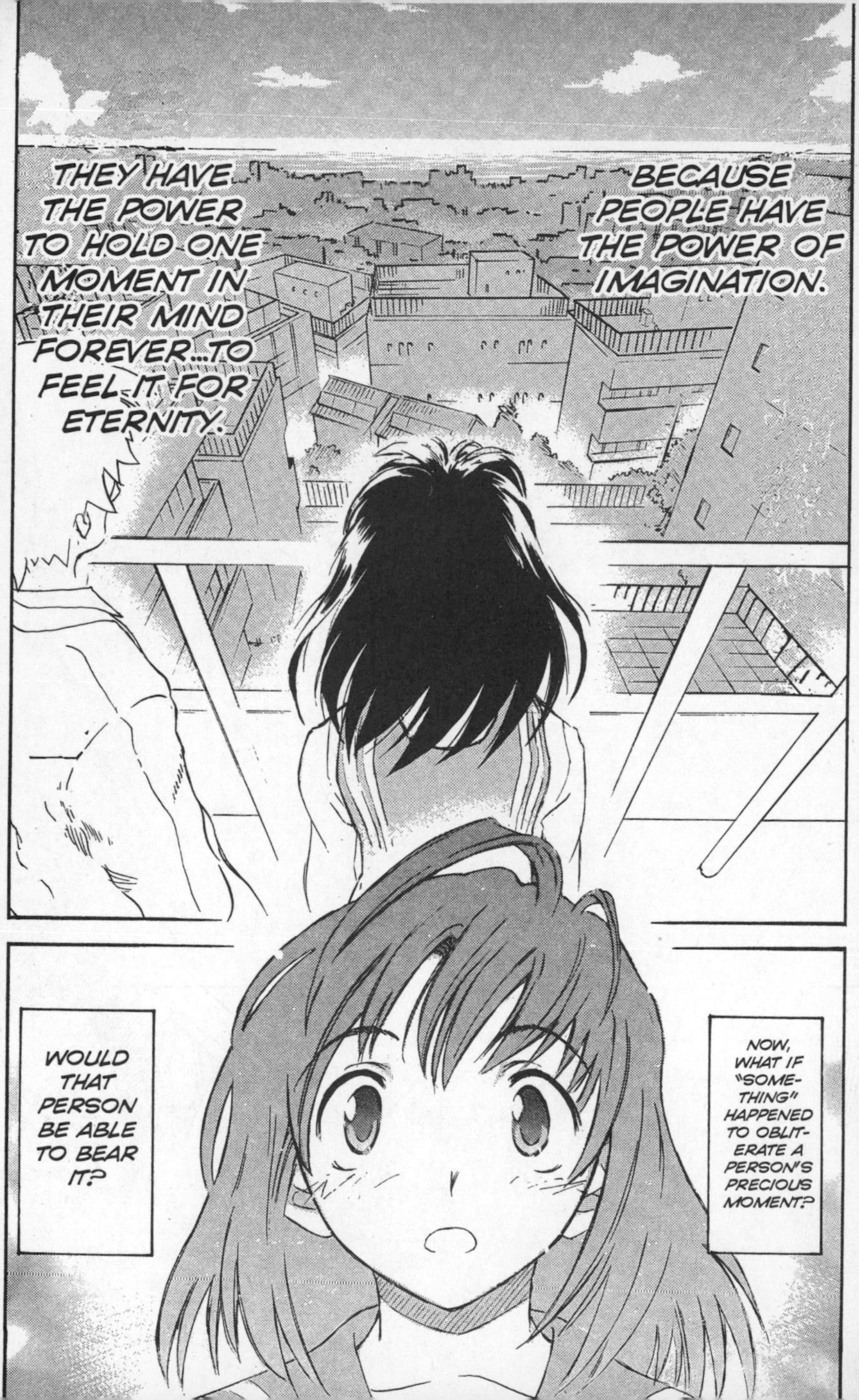
BECAUSE PEOPLE HAVE THE POWER OF IMAGINATION.
THEY HAVE THE POWER TO HOLD ONE MOMENT IN THEIR MIND FOREVER...TO FEEL IT FOR ETERNITY.
NOW, WHAT IF "SOME-THING" HAPPENED TO OBLIT-ERATE A PERSON'S PRECIOUS MOMENT?
WOULD THAT PERSON BE ABLE TO BEAR IT?

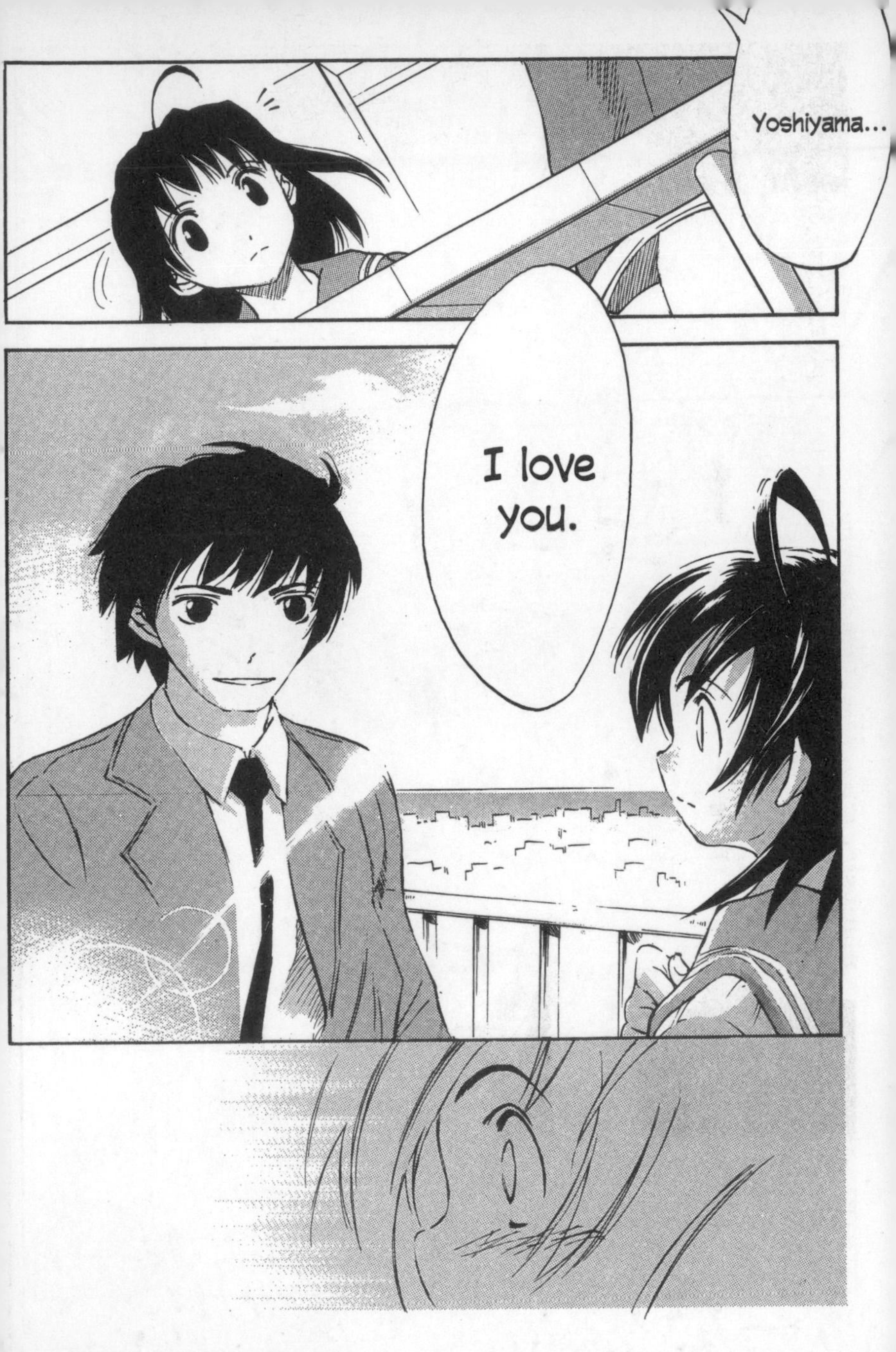
Yoshiyama...
I love you.

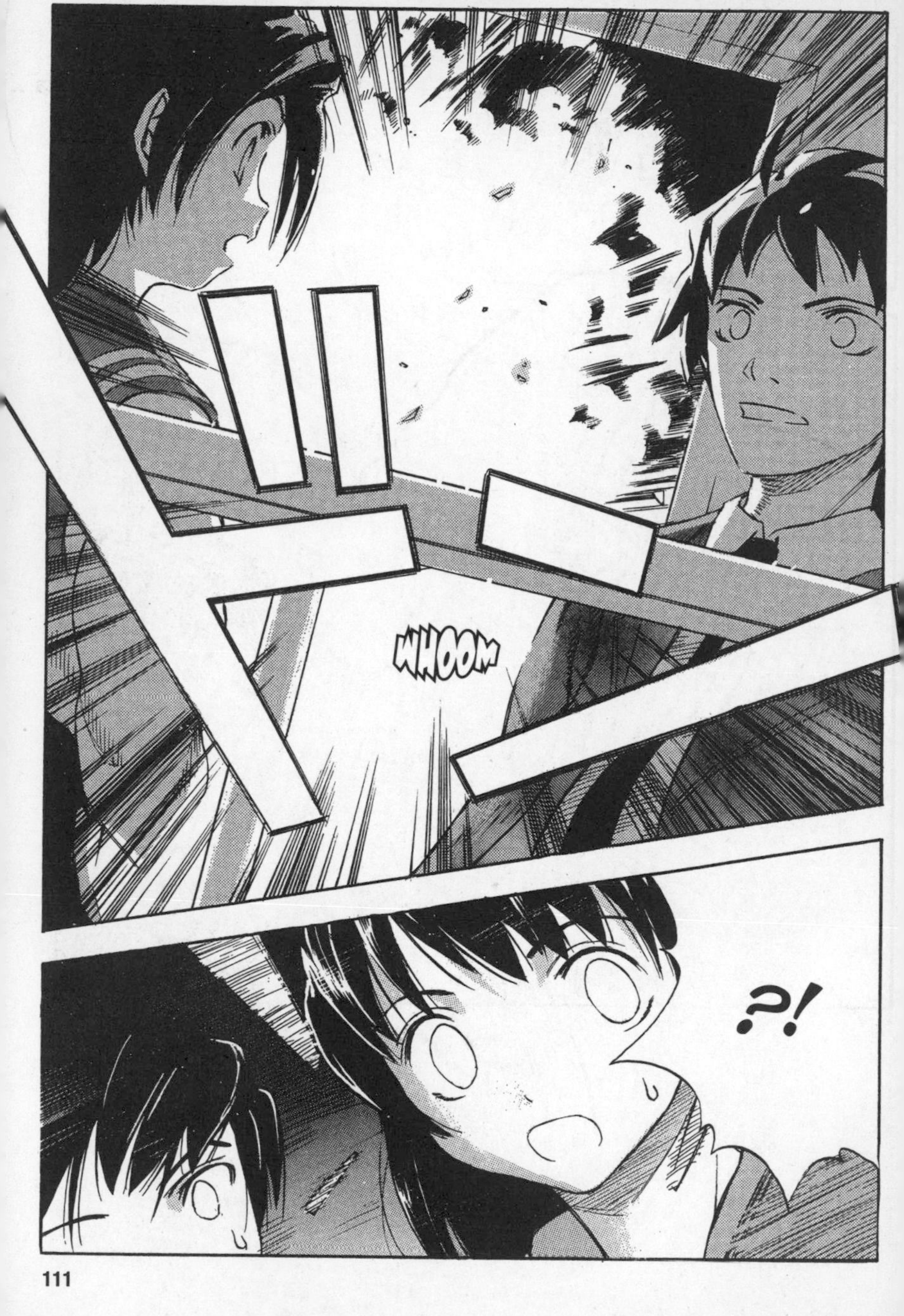
WHOOM
?!

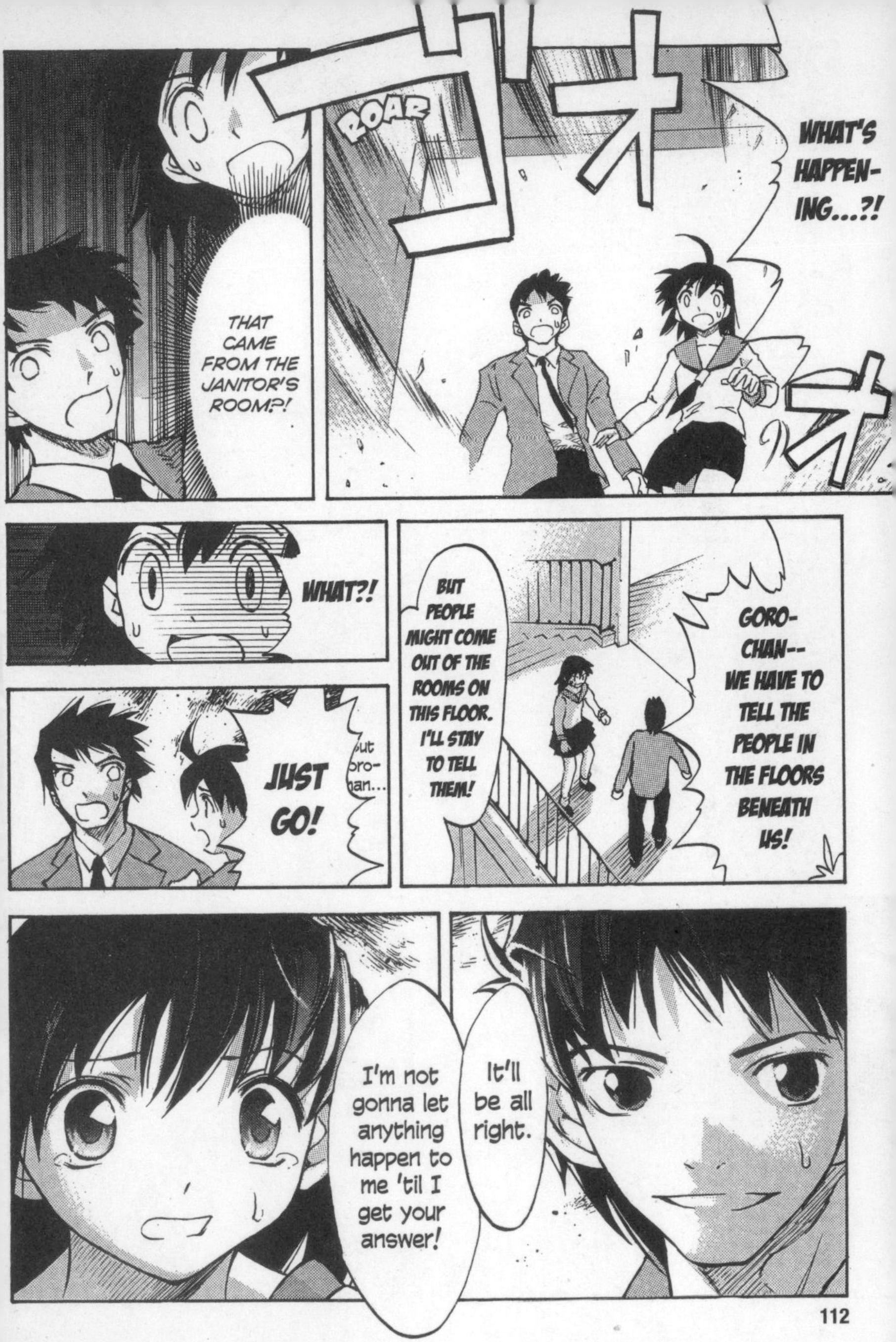
ゴオ
ROAR
WHAT'S HAPPENING...?!
オ
THAT CAME FROM THE JANITOR'S ROOM?!
GORO-CHAN-- WE HAVE TO TELL THE PEOPLE IN THE FLOORS BENEATH US!
BUT PEOPLE MIGHT COME OUT OF THE ROOMS ON THIS FLOOR. I'LL STAY TO TELL THEM!
WHAT?!
ut oro- an...
JUST GO!
It'll be all right.
I'm not gonna let anything happen to me 'til I get your answer!

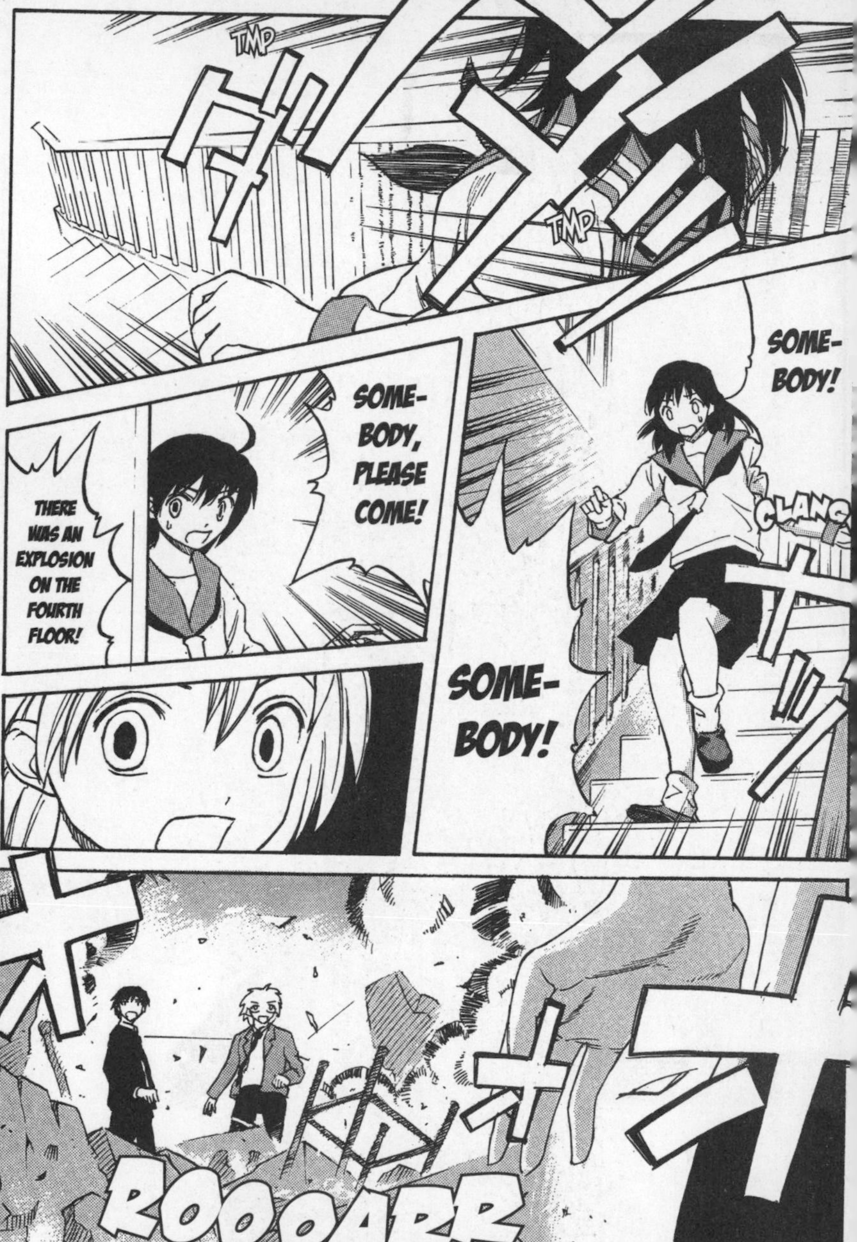
TMP
TMP
SOME-BODY!
CLANG
SOME-BODY!
SOME-BODY, PLEASE COME!
THERE WAS AN EXPLOSION ON THE FOURTH FLOOR!
ROOOARR

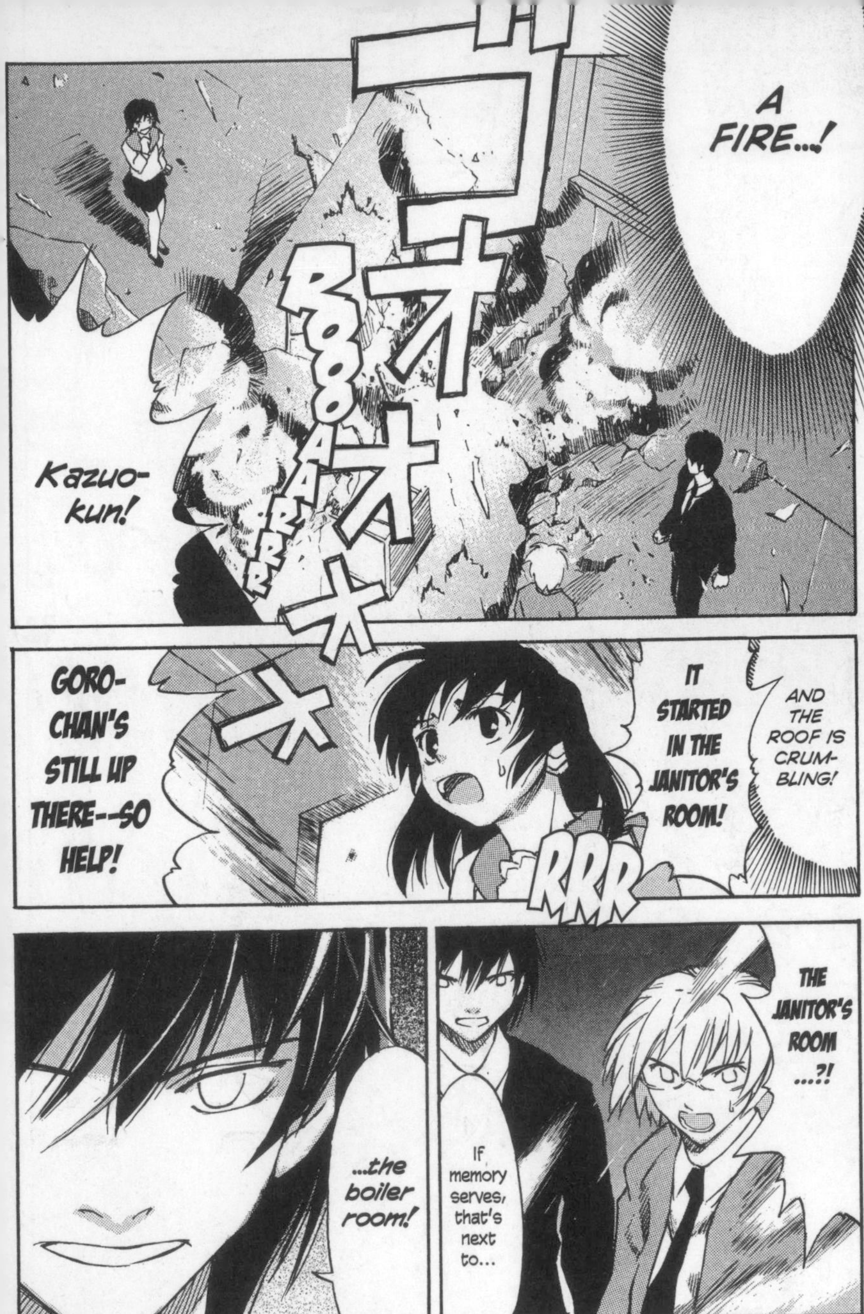
A FIRE...!
ROOOAARRRR
Kazuo-kun!
AND THE ROOF IS CRUM-BLING!
IT STARTED IN THE JANITOR'S ROOM!
RRR
GORO-CHAN'S STILL UP THERE--SO HELP!
THE JANITOR'S ROOM ...?!
If memory serves, that's next to...
...the boiler room!

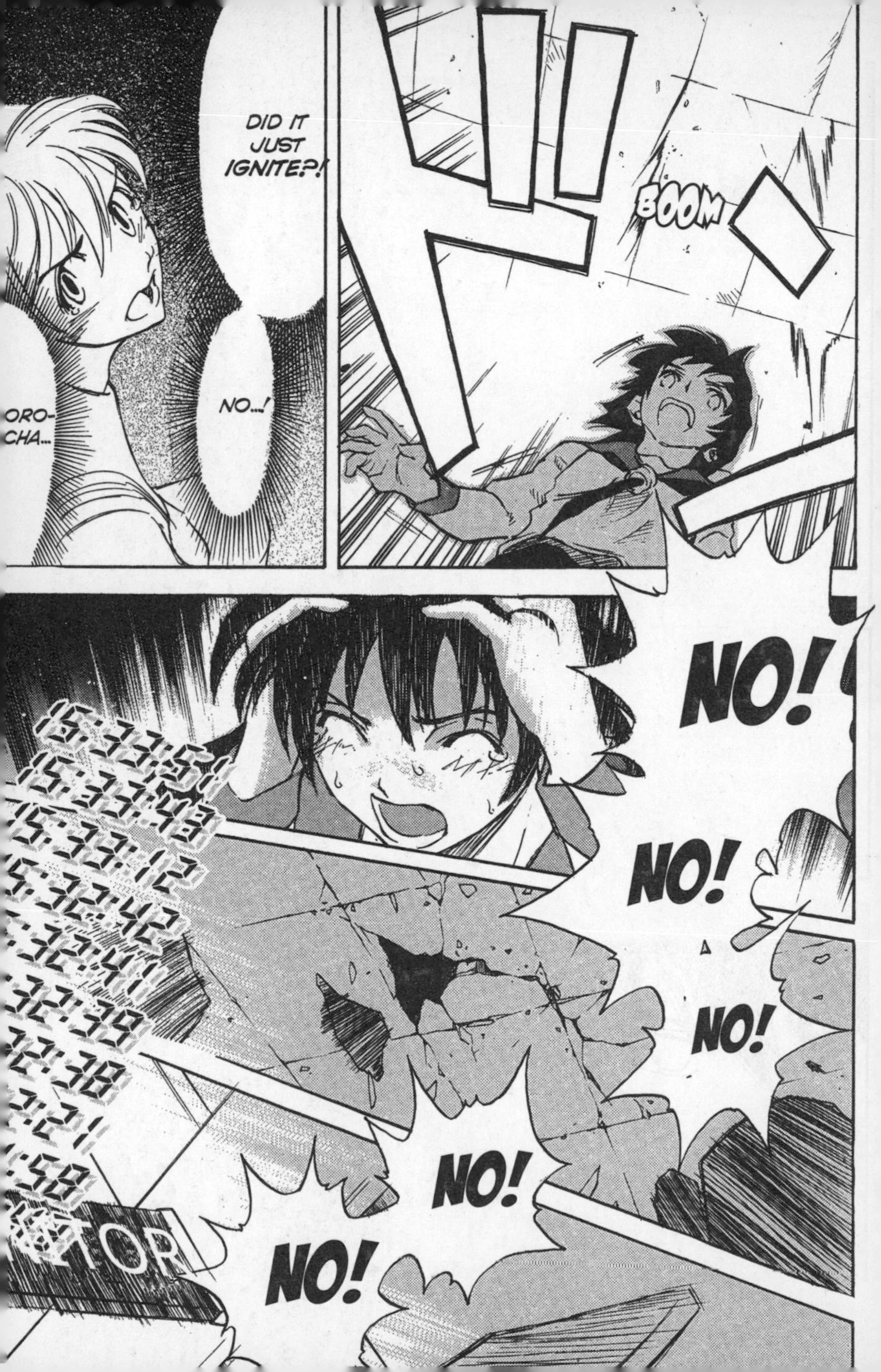
BOOM
DID IT JUST IGNITE?!
NO...!
ORO-CHA...
NO!
NO!
NO!
NO!
NO!

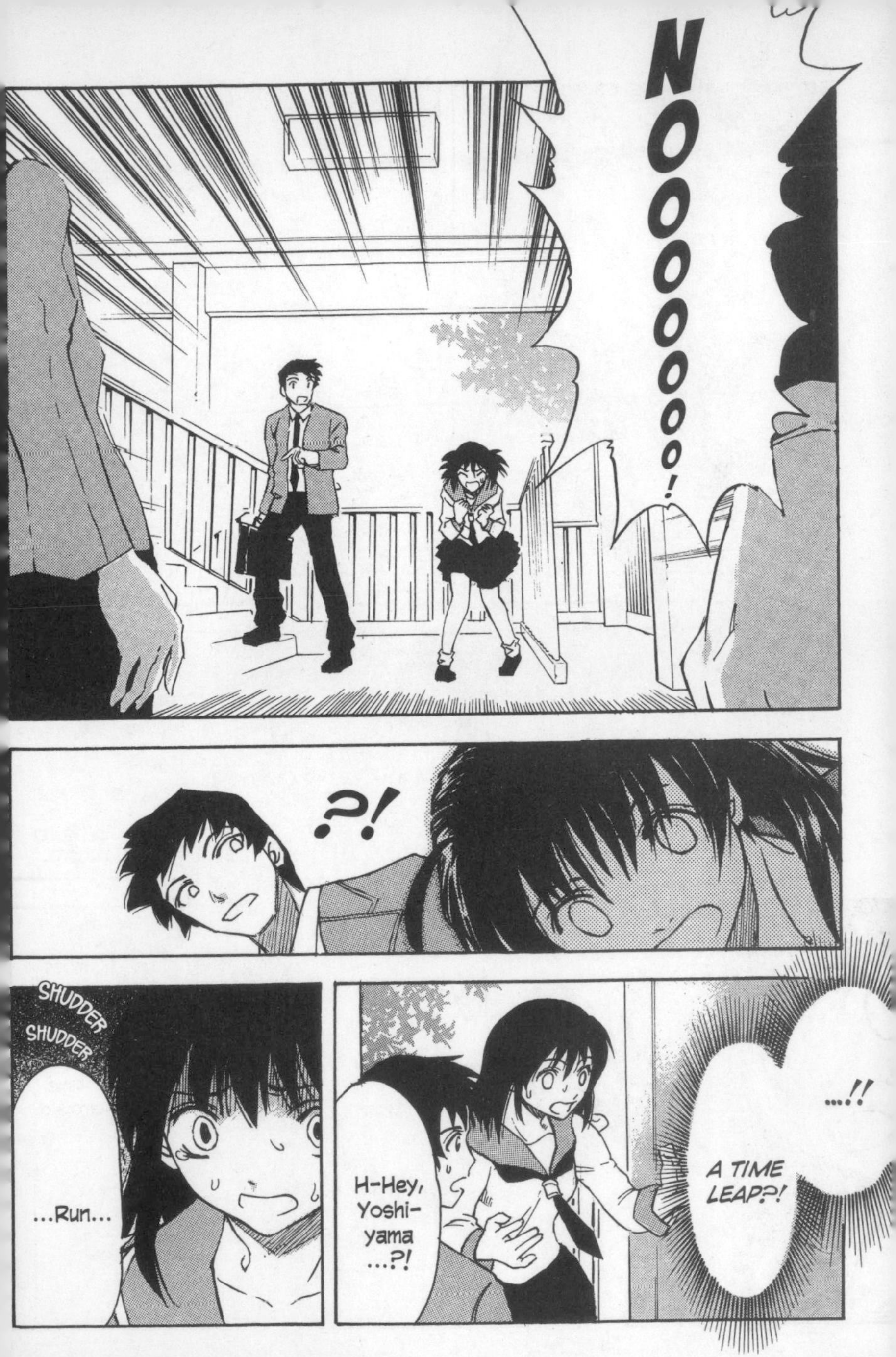
NOOOOOOOOOO!
?!
...!!
A TIME LEAP?!
H-Hey, Yoshi-yama ...?!
SHUDDER SHUDDER
...Run...

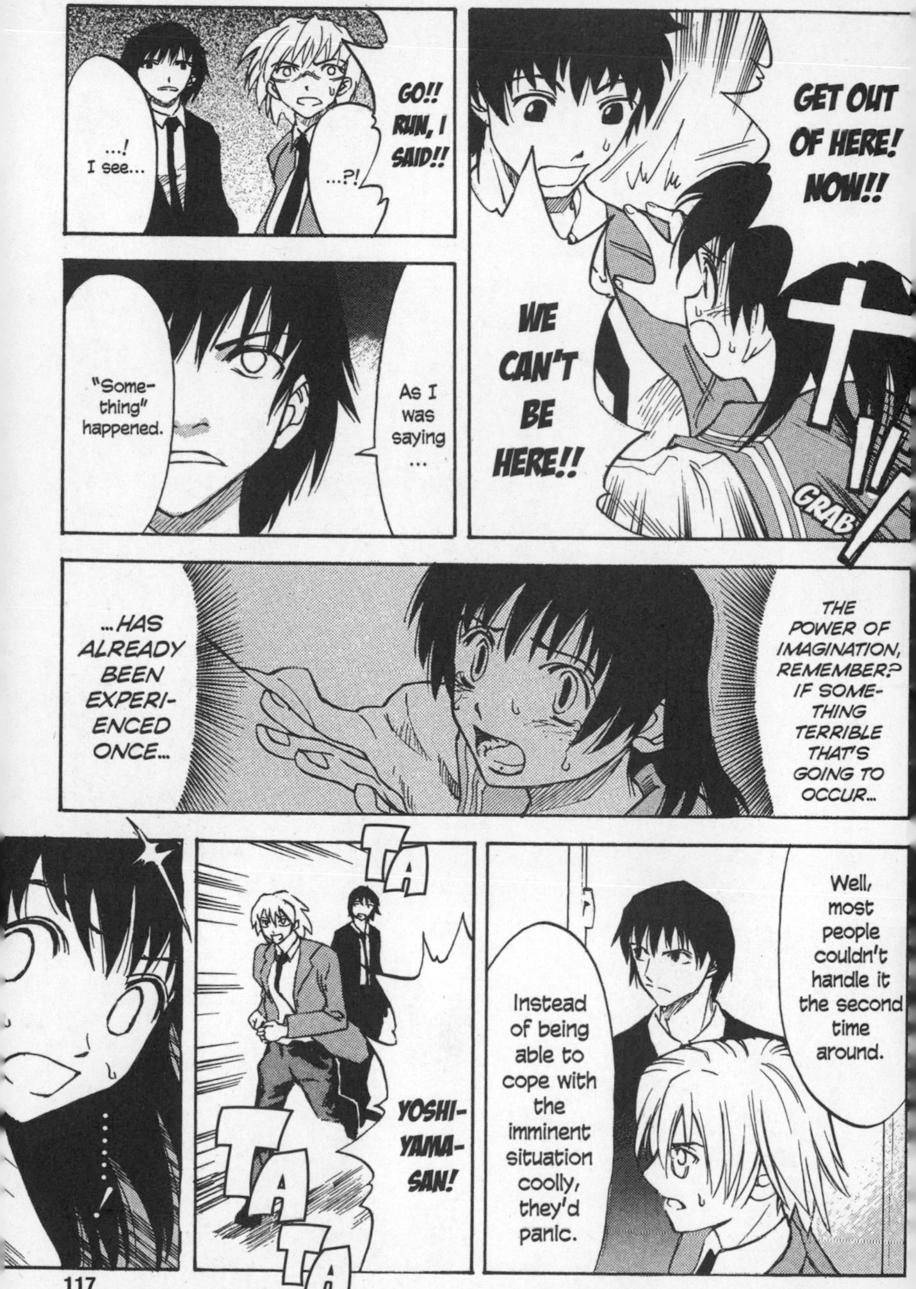
GET OUT OF HERE! NOW!!
WE CAN'T BE HERE!!
GRAB
GO!! RUN, I SAID!!
...?!
...! I see...
As I was saying ...
"Something" happened.
THE POWER OF IMAGINATION, REMEMBER? IF SOMETHING TERRIBLE THAT'S GOING TO OCCUR...
...HAS ALREADY BEEN EXPERIENCED ONCE...
Well, most people couldn't handle it the second time around.
Instead of being able to cope with the imminent situation coolly, they'd panic.
TA
YOSHIYAMA-SAN!
TA TA TA TA
......!

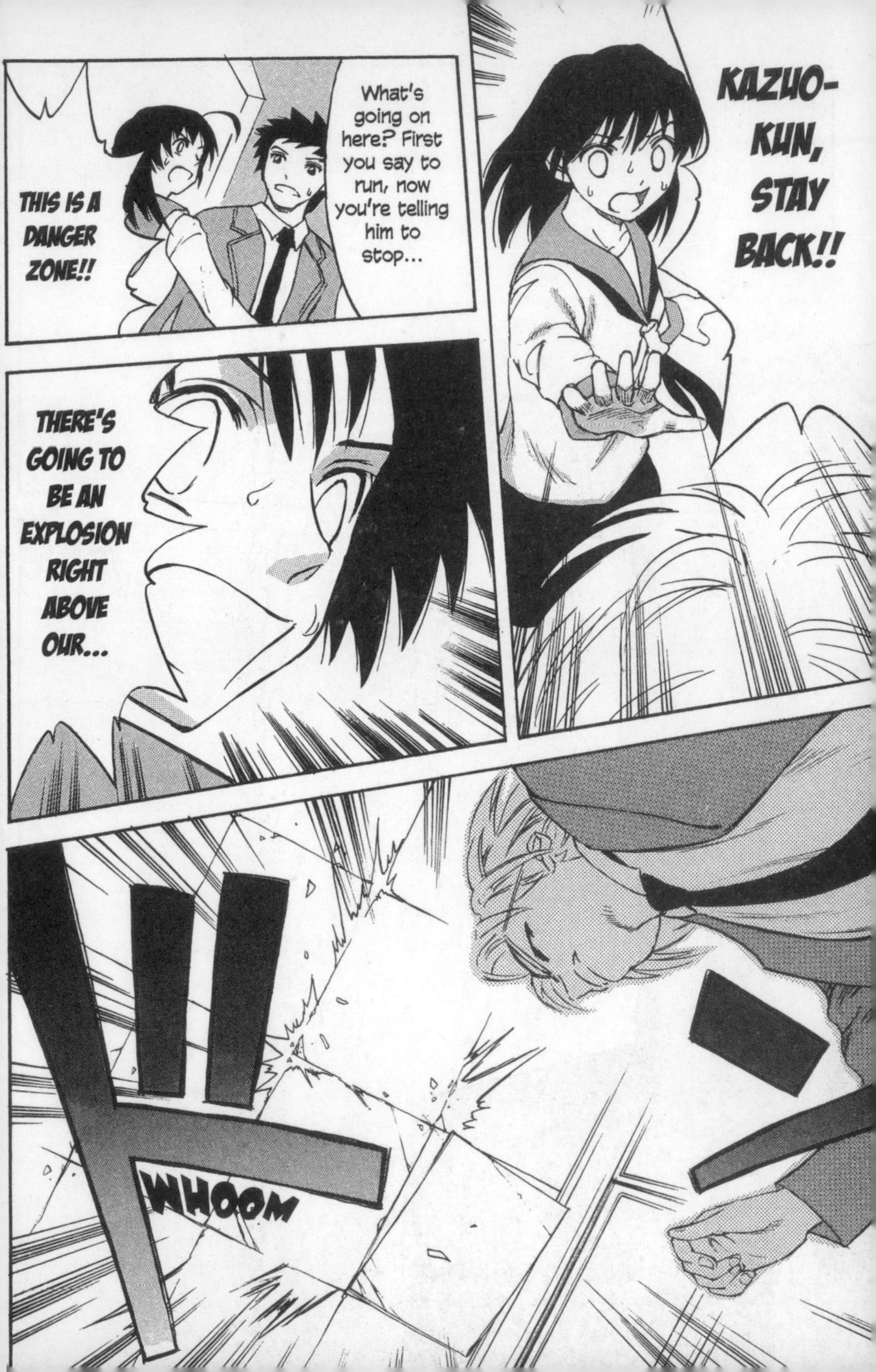
KAZUO-KUN, STAY BACK!!
What's going on here? First you say to run, now you're telling him to stop...
THIS IS A DANGER ZONE!!
THERE'S GOING TO BE AN EXPLOSION RIGHT ABOVE OUR...
WHOOM

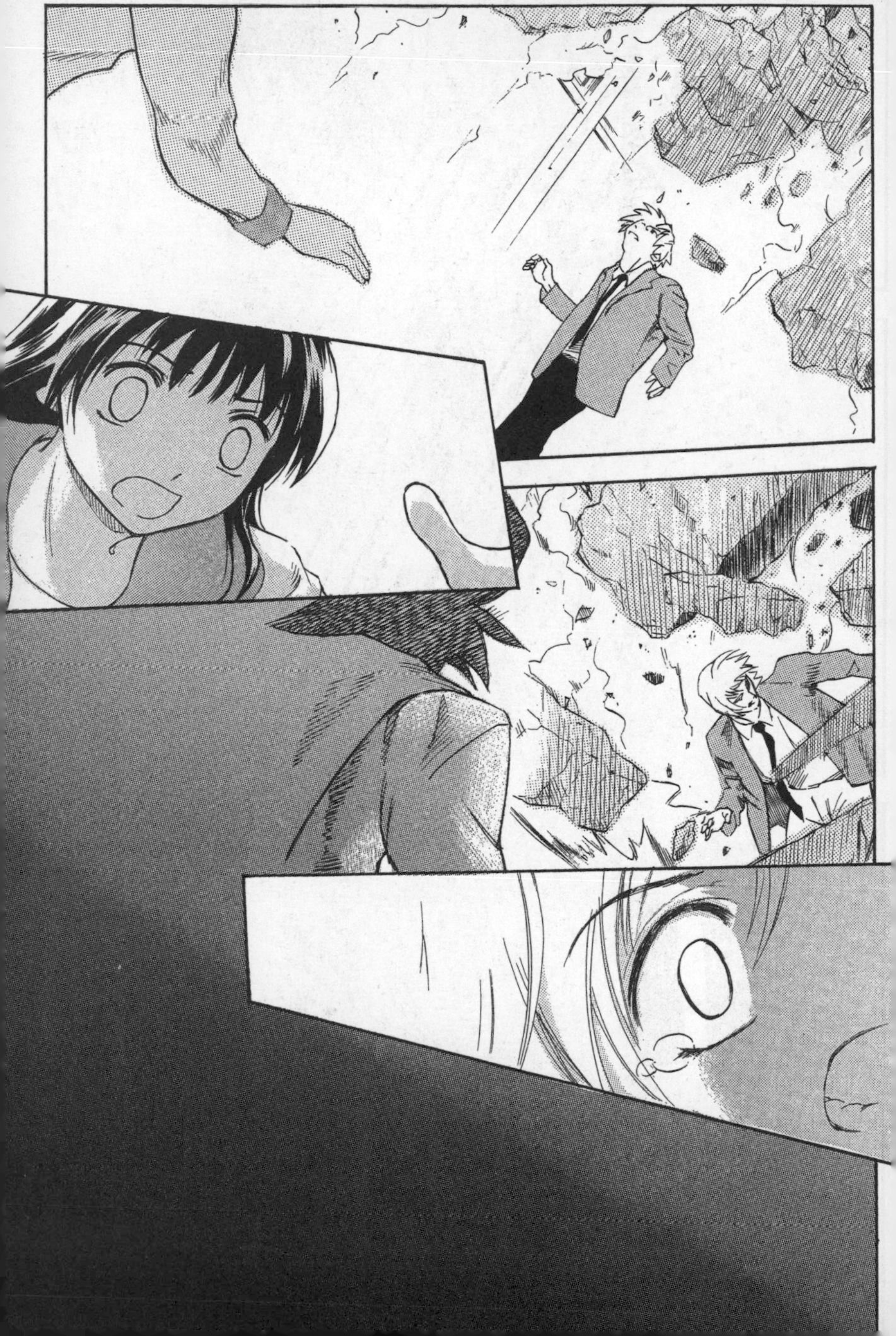

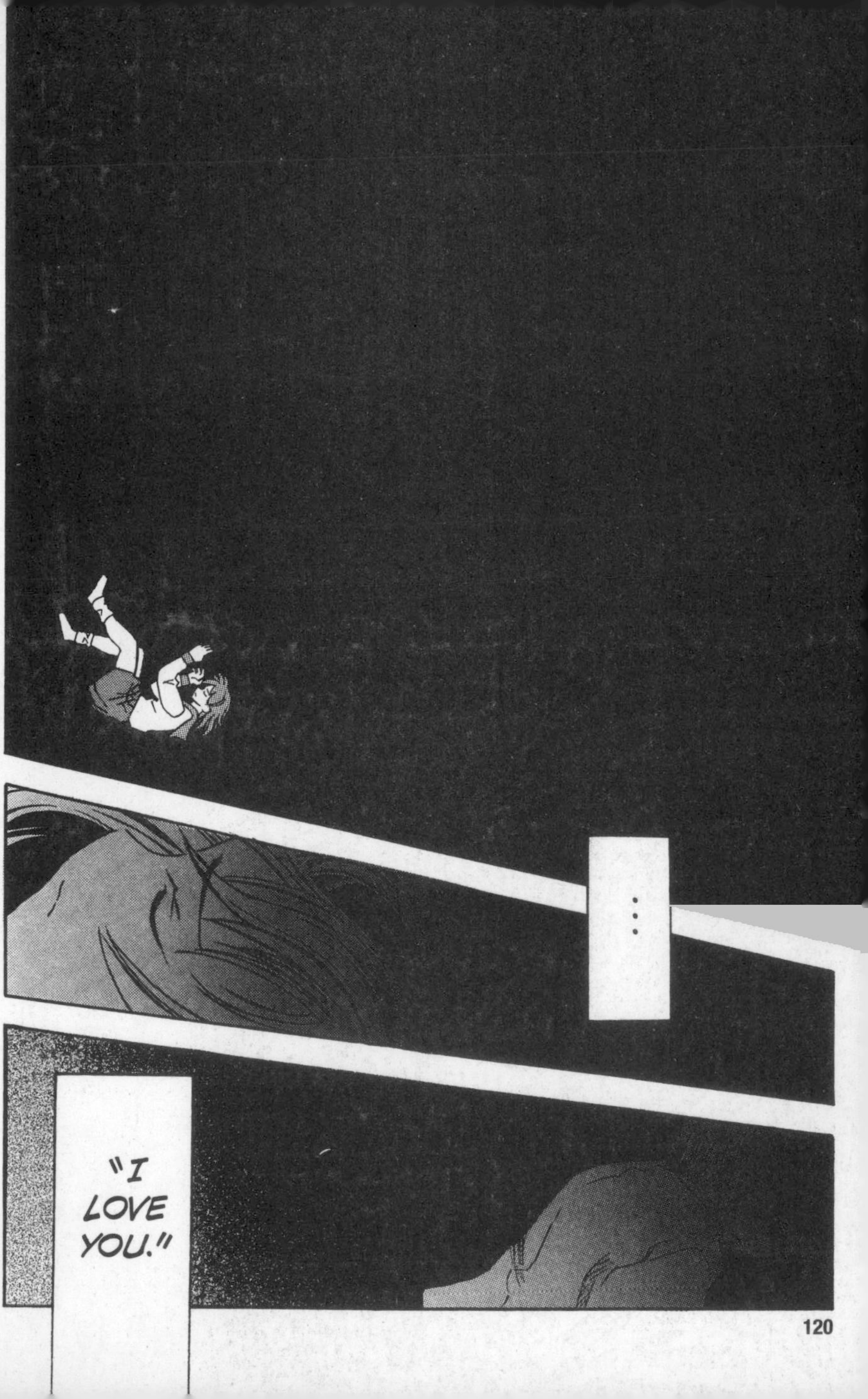
...
"I LOVE YOU."

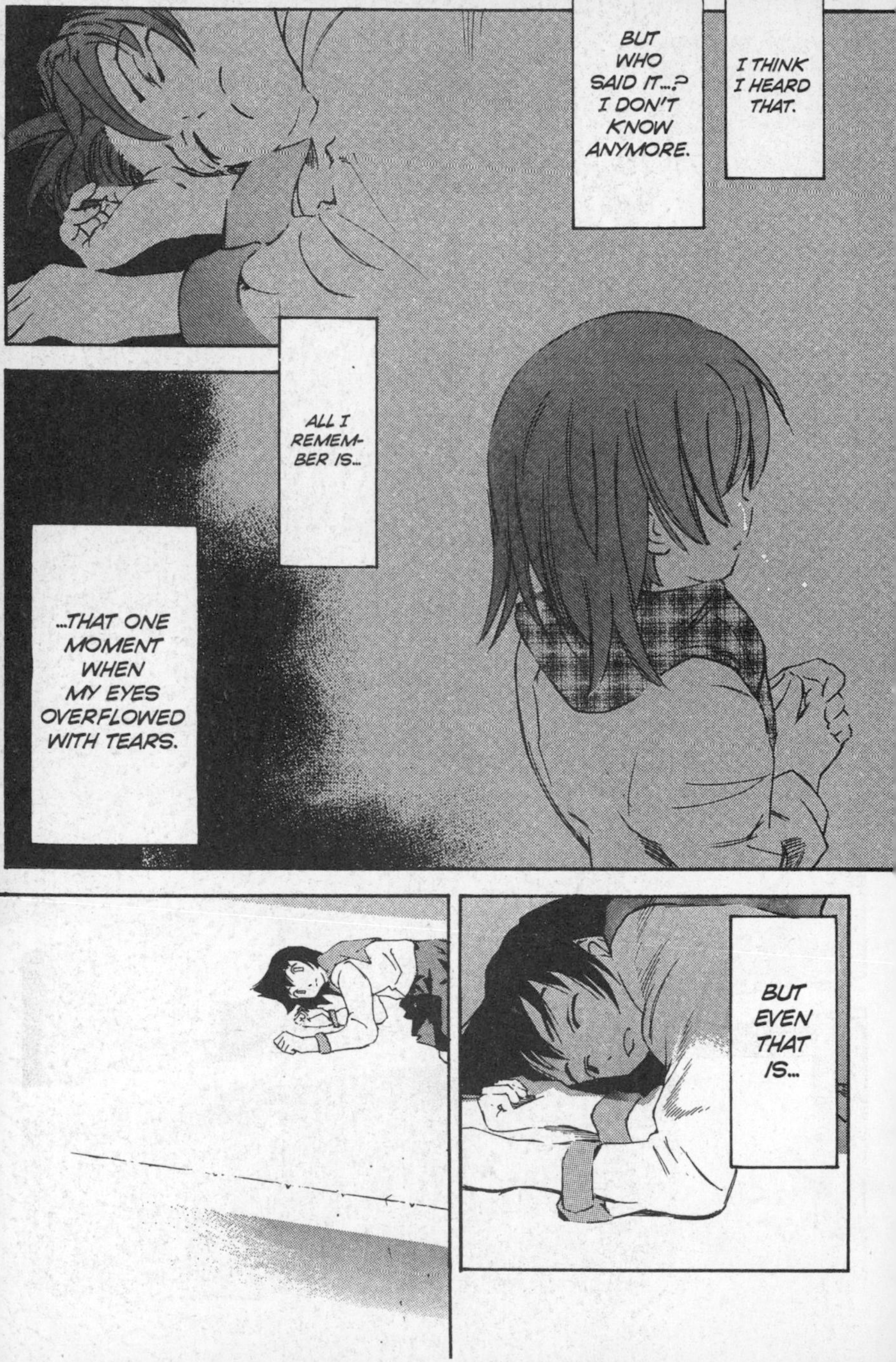
I THINK I HEARD THAT.
BUT WHO SAID IT...? I DON'T KNOW ANYMORE.
ALL I REMEMBER IS...
...THAT ONE MOMENT WHEN MY EYES OVERFLOWED WITH TEARS.
BUT EVEN THAT IS...

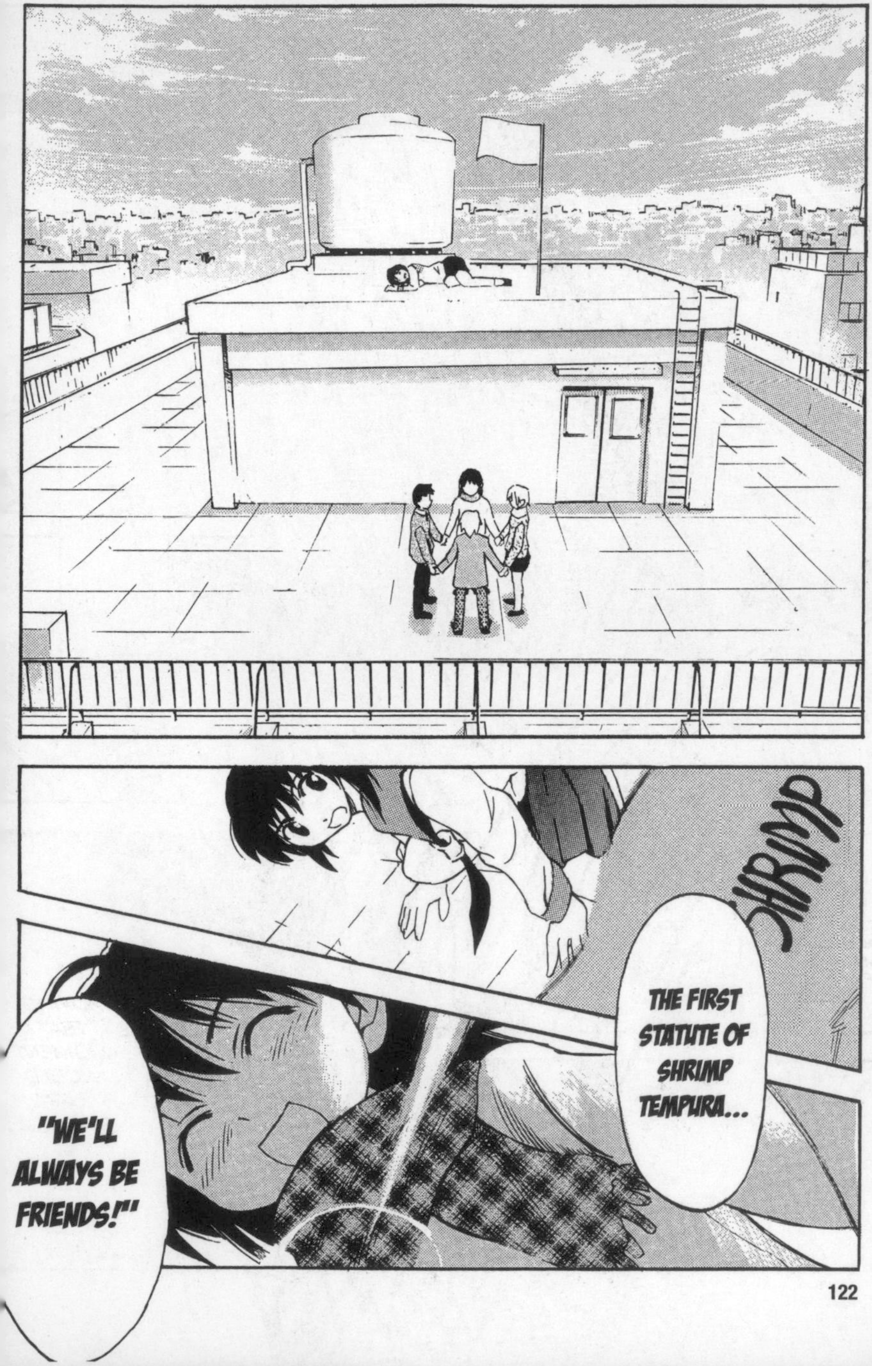
SHRIMP
THE FIRST STATUTE OF SHRIMP TEMPURA...
"WE'LL ALWAYS BE FRIENDS!"

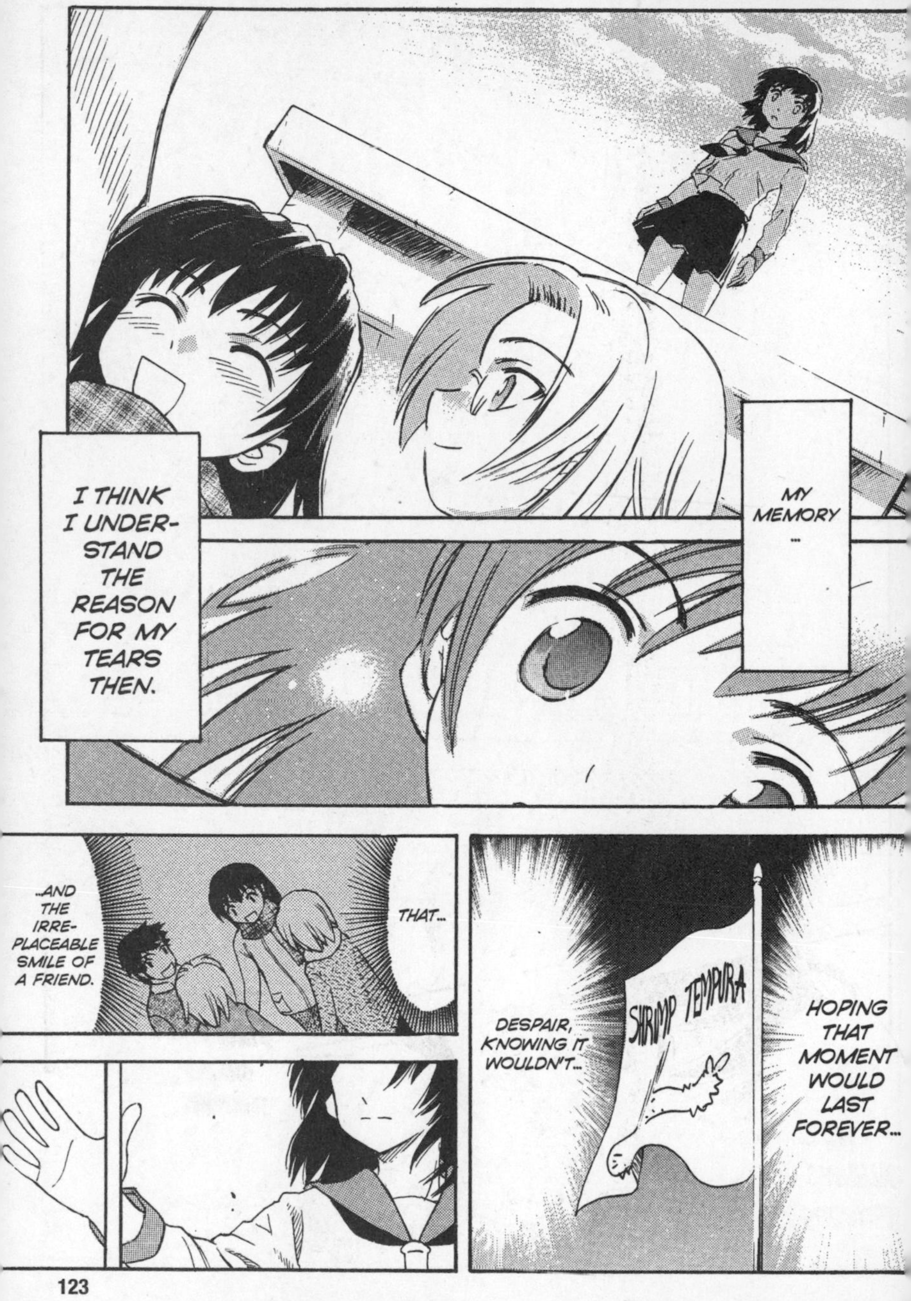
MY MEMORY...
I THINK I UNDER-STAND THE REASON FOR MY TEARS THEN.
HOPING THAT MOMENT WOULD LAST FOREVER...
SHRIMP TEMPURA
DESPAIR, KNOWING IT WOULDN'T...
THAT...
...AND THE IRRE-PLACEABLE SMILE OF A FRIEND.

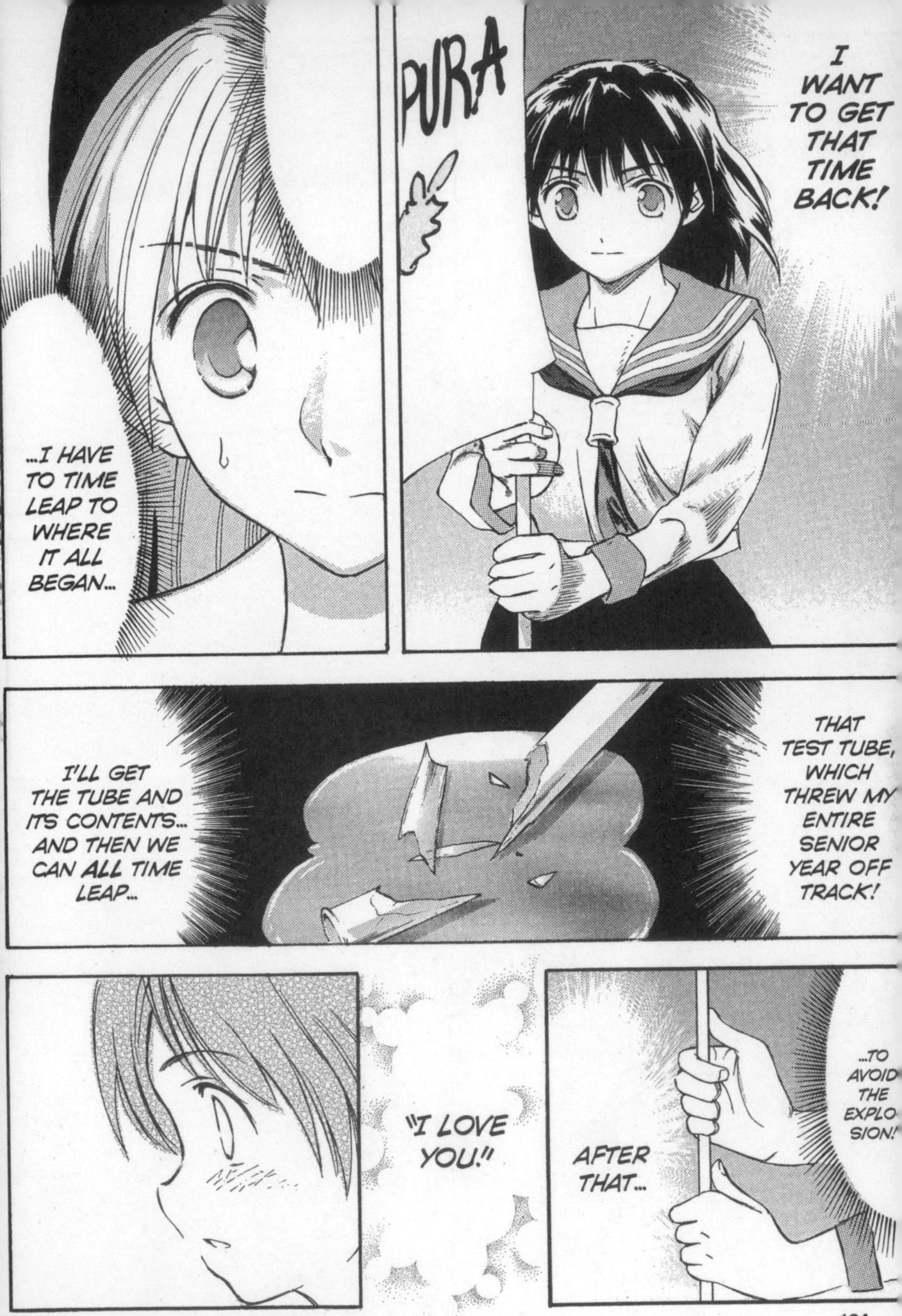
PURA
I WANT TO GET THAT TIME BACK!
...I HAVE TO TIME LEAP TO WHERE IT ALL BEGAN...
THAT TEST TUBE, WHICH THREW MY ENTIRE SENIOR YEAR OFF TRACK!
I'LL GET THE TUBE AND ITS CONTENTS... AND THEN WE CAN **ALL** TIME LEAP...
...TO AVOID THE EXPLO SION!
AFTER THAT...
"I LOVE YOU!"

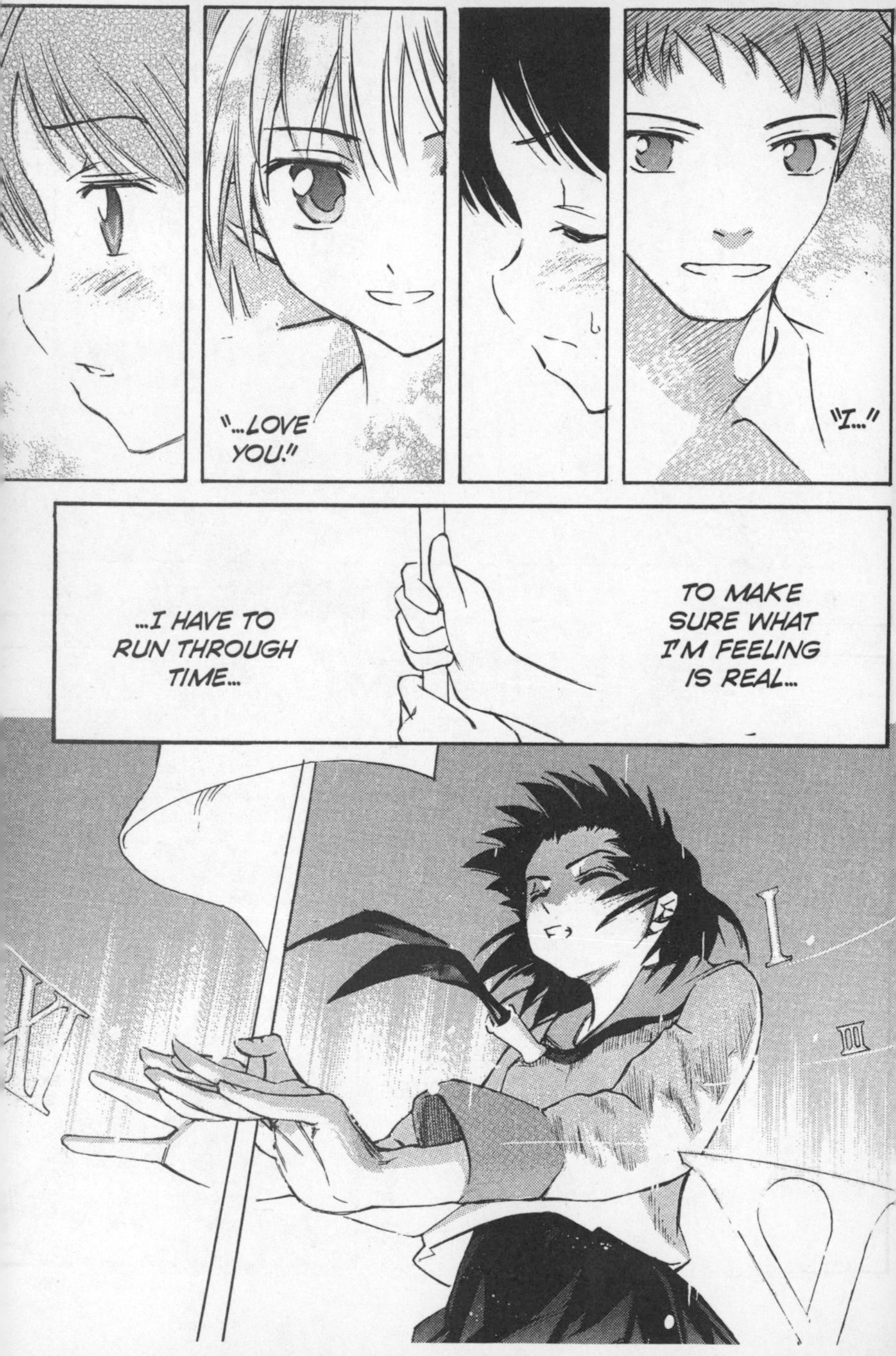
"I..."
"...LOVE YOU."
TO MAKE SURE WHAT I'M FEELING IS REAL...
...I HAVE TO RUN THROUGH TIME...

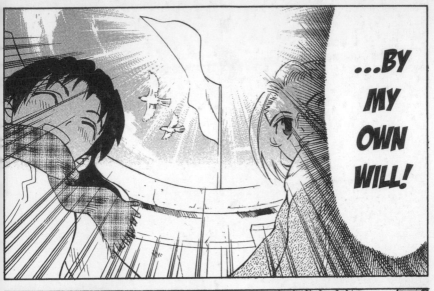

...BY MY OWN WILL!

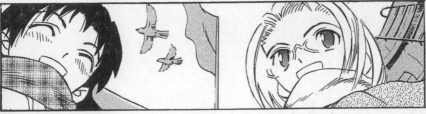

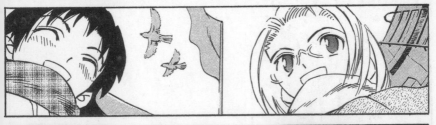

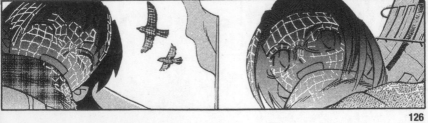

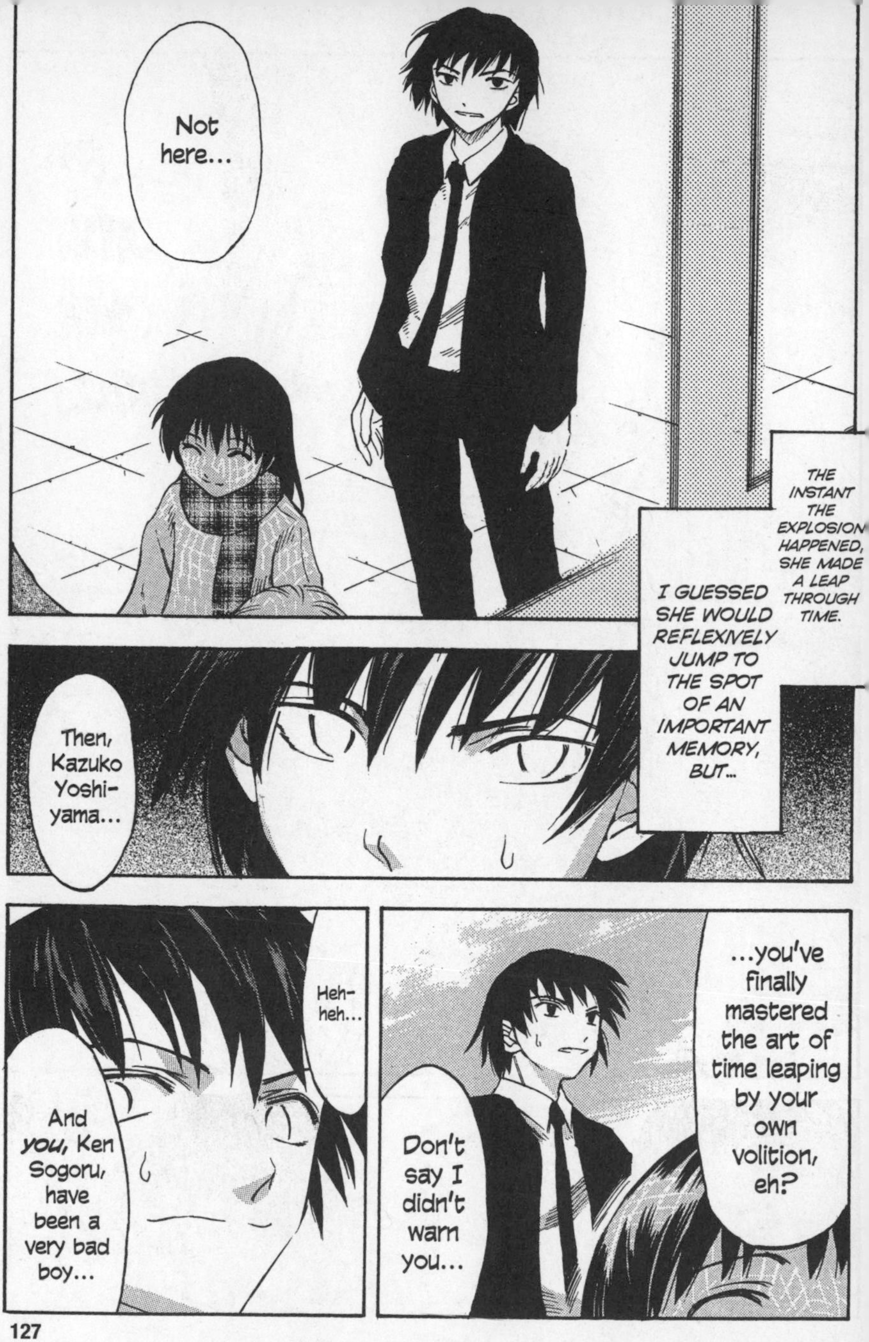
Not here...
THE INSTANT THE EXPLOSION HAPPENED, SHE MADE A LEAP THROUGH TIME.
I GUESSED SHE WOULD REFLEXIVELY JUMP TO THE SPOT OF AN IMPORTANT MEMORY, BUT...
Then, Kazuko Yoshi-yama...
...you've finally mastered the art of time leaping by your own volition, eh?
Don't say I didn't warn you...
Heh-heh...
And *you,* Ken Sogoru, have been a very bad boy...

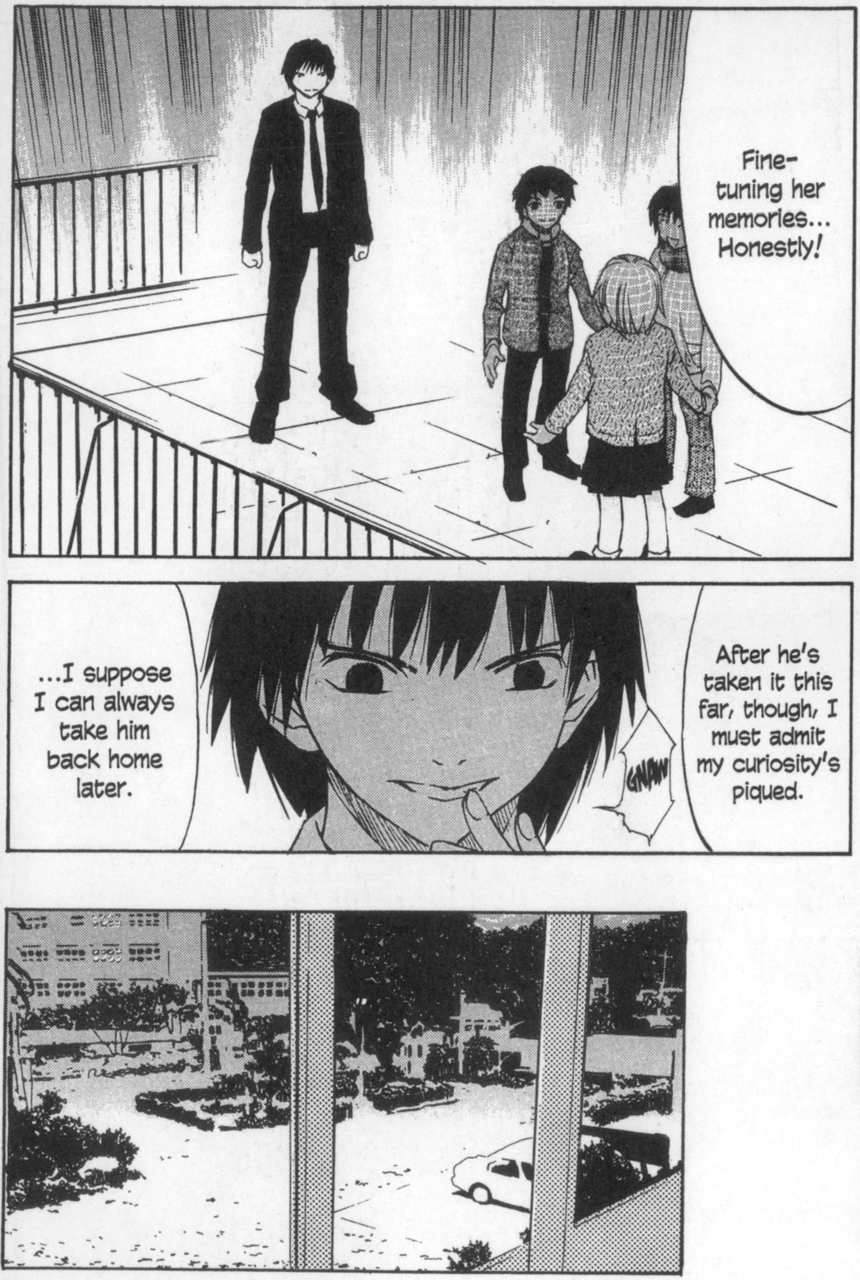
Fine-tuning her memories... Honestly!
After he's taken it this far, though, I must admit my curiosity's piqued.
GNAW
...I suppose I can always take him back home later.

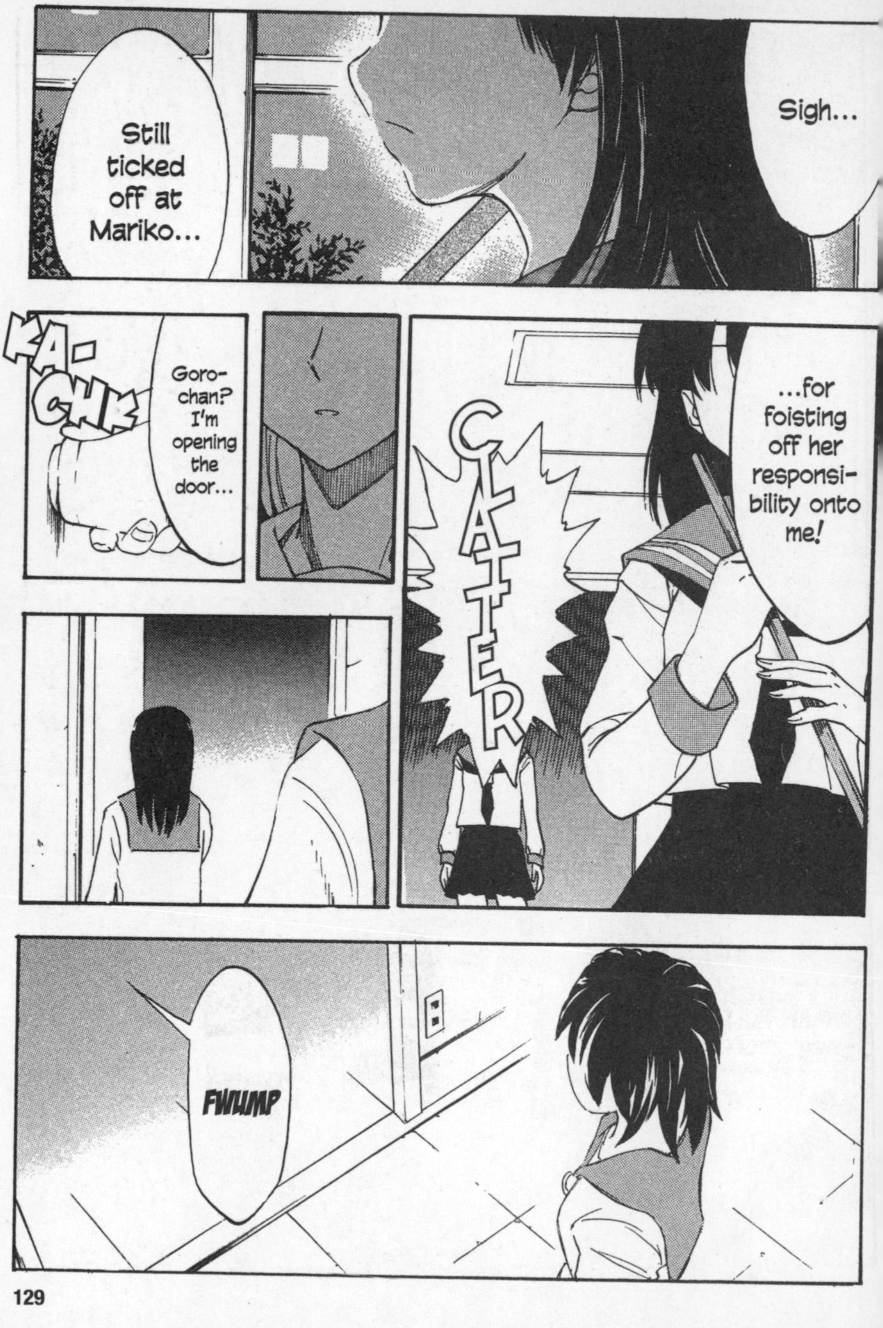
Sigh...
Still ticked off at Mariko...
...for foisting off her responsibility onto me!
CLATTER
KA-CHK
Goro-chan? I'm opening the door...
FWUMP

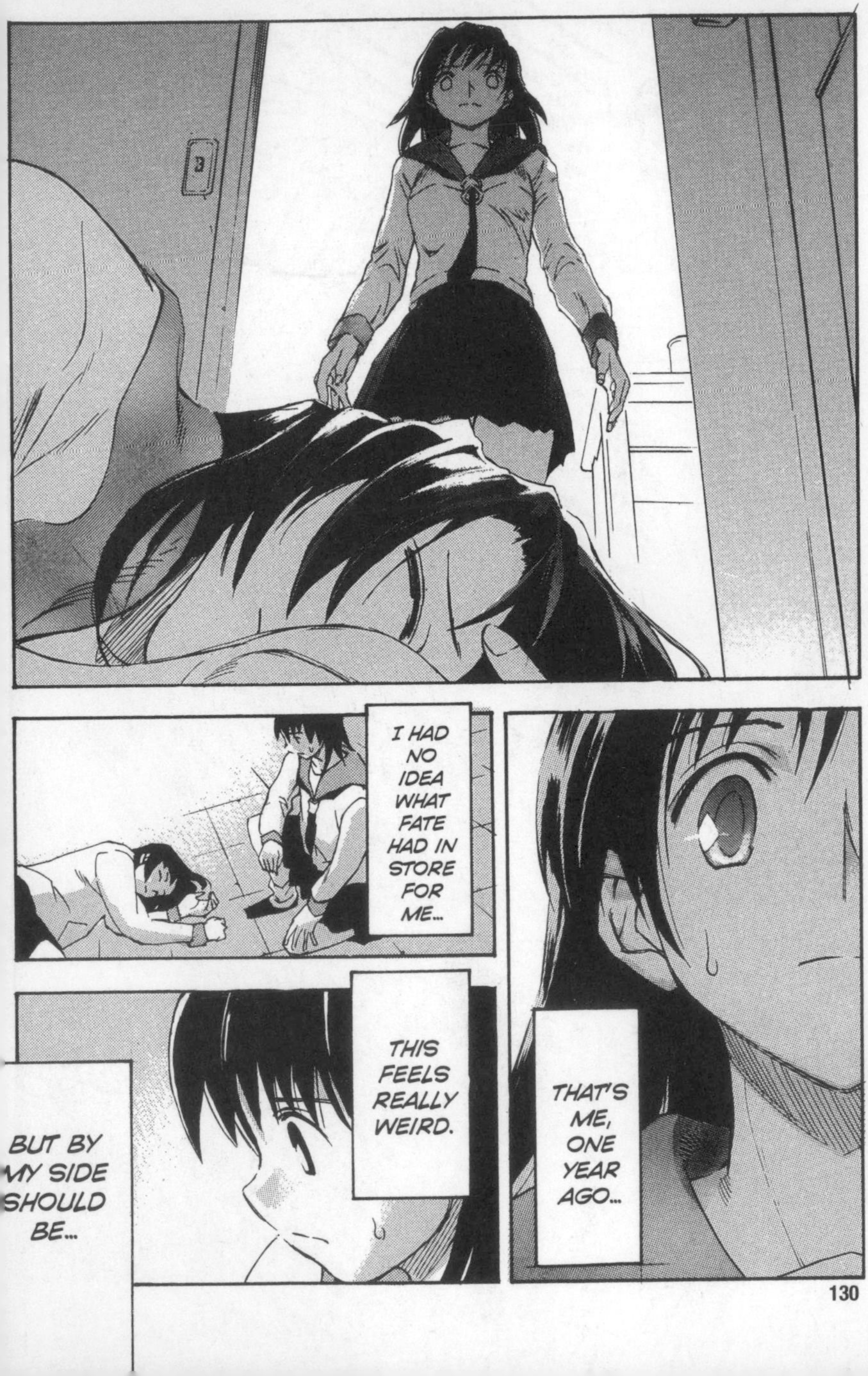
THAT'S ME, ONE YEAR AGO...
I HAD NO IDEA WHAT FATE HAD IN STORE FOR ME...
THIS FEELS REALLY WEIRD.
BUT BY MY SIDE SHOULD BE...

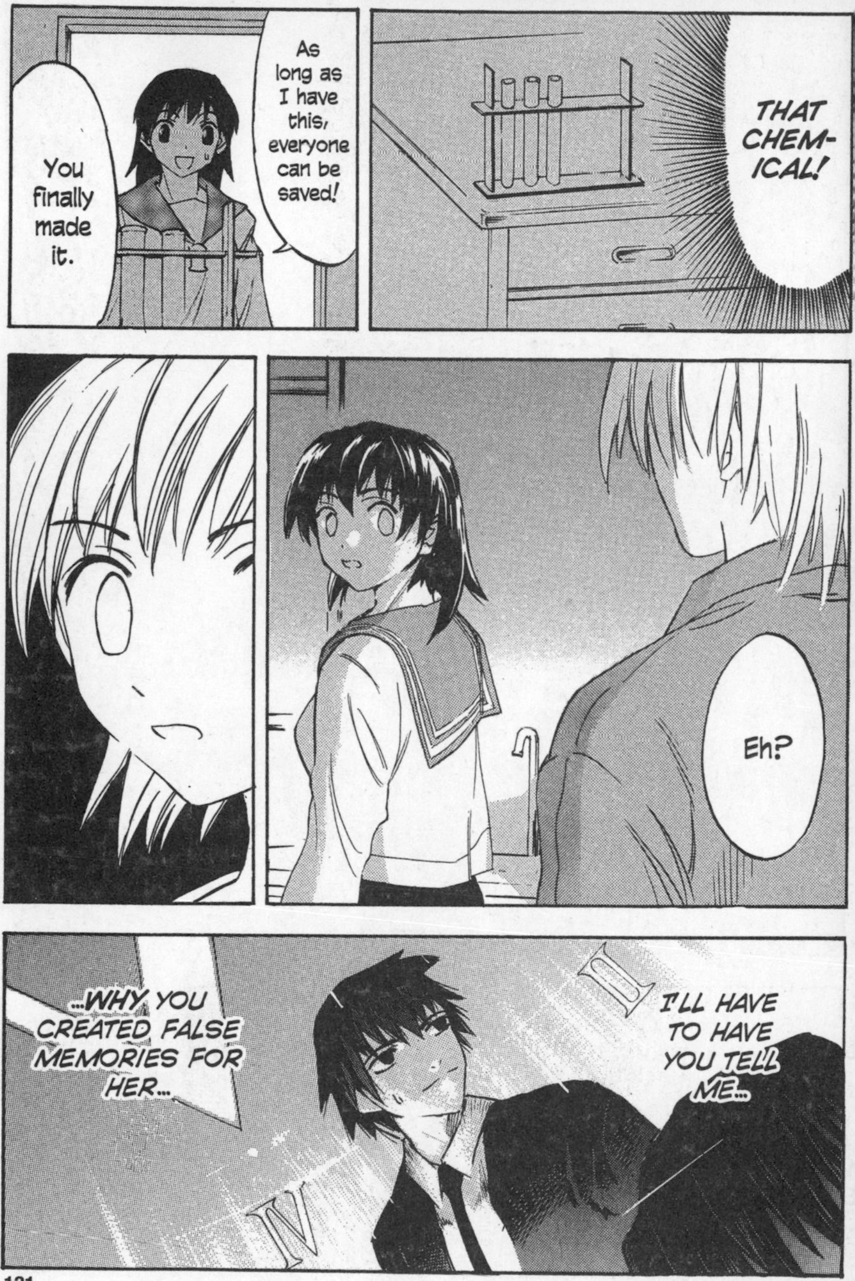
THAT CHEMICAL!
As long as I have this, everyone can be saved!
You finally made it.
Eh?
I'LL HAVE TO HAVE YOU TELL ME...
...WHY YOU CREATED FALSE MEMORIES FOR HER...

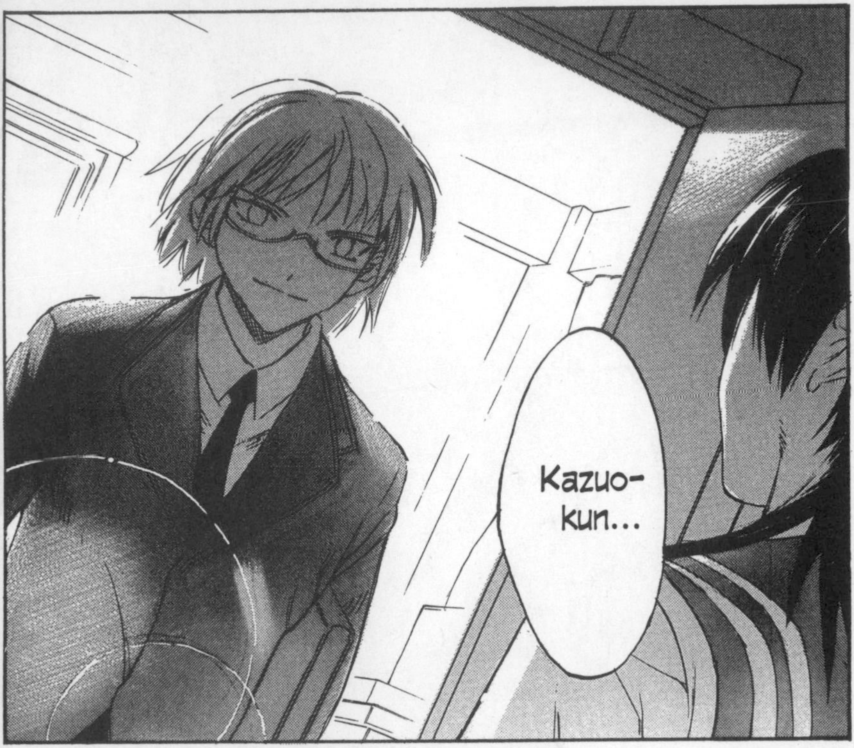
Kazuo-
kun...

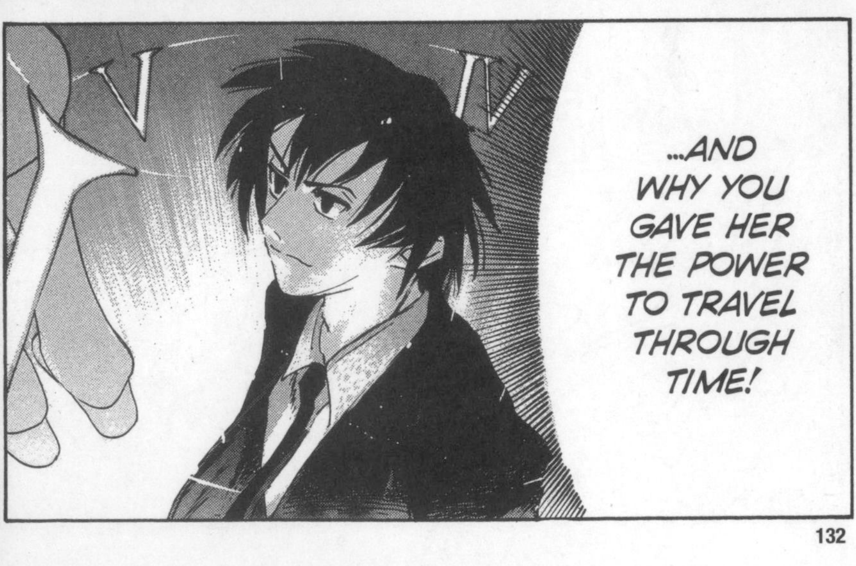
...AND WHY YOU GAVE HER THE POWER TO TRAVEL THROUGH TIME!

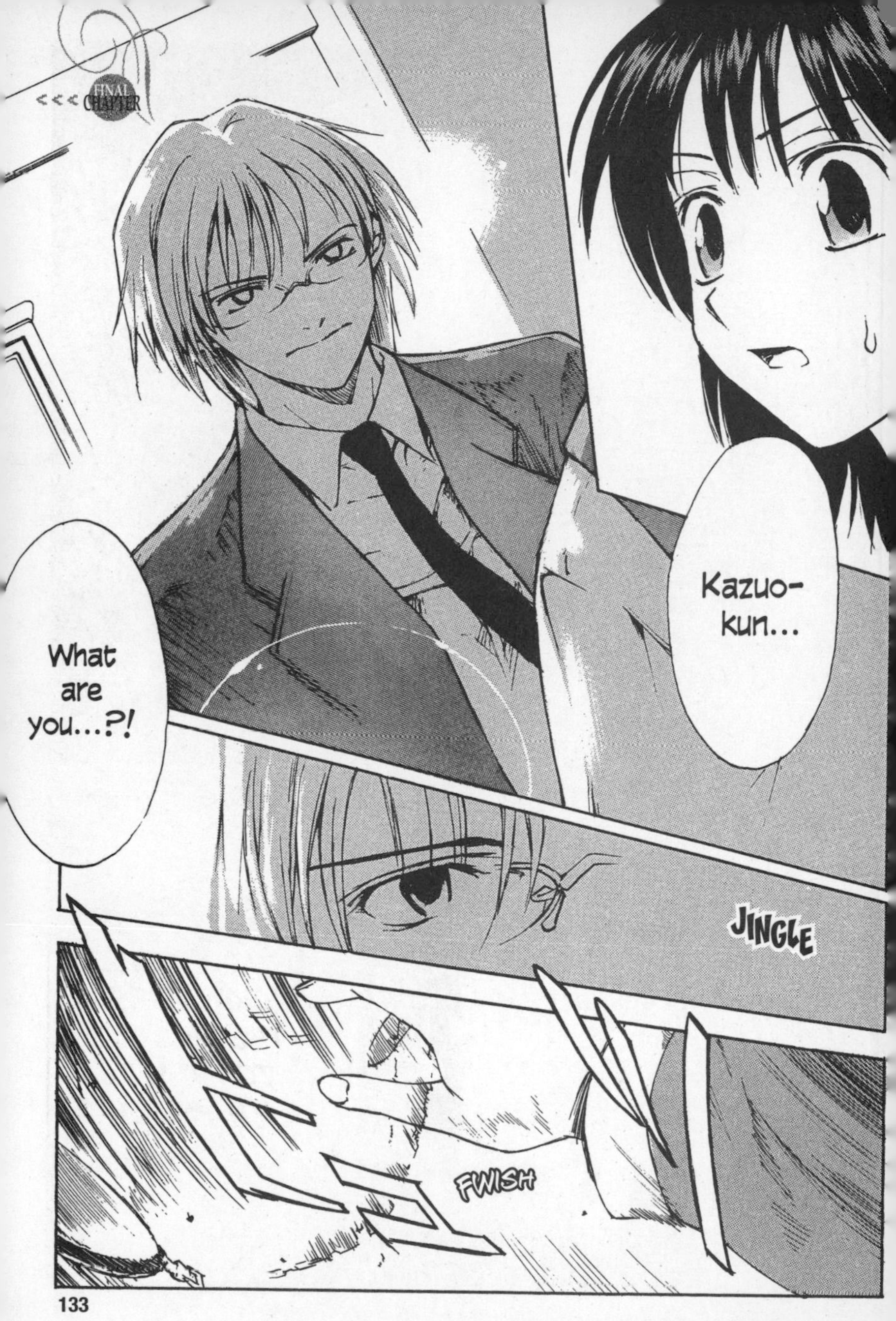
Kazuo-kun...
What are you...?!
JINGLE
FWISH

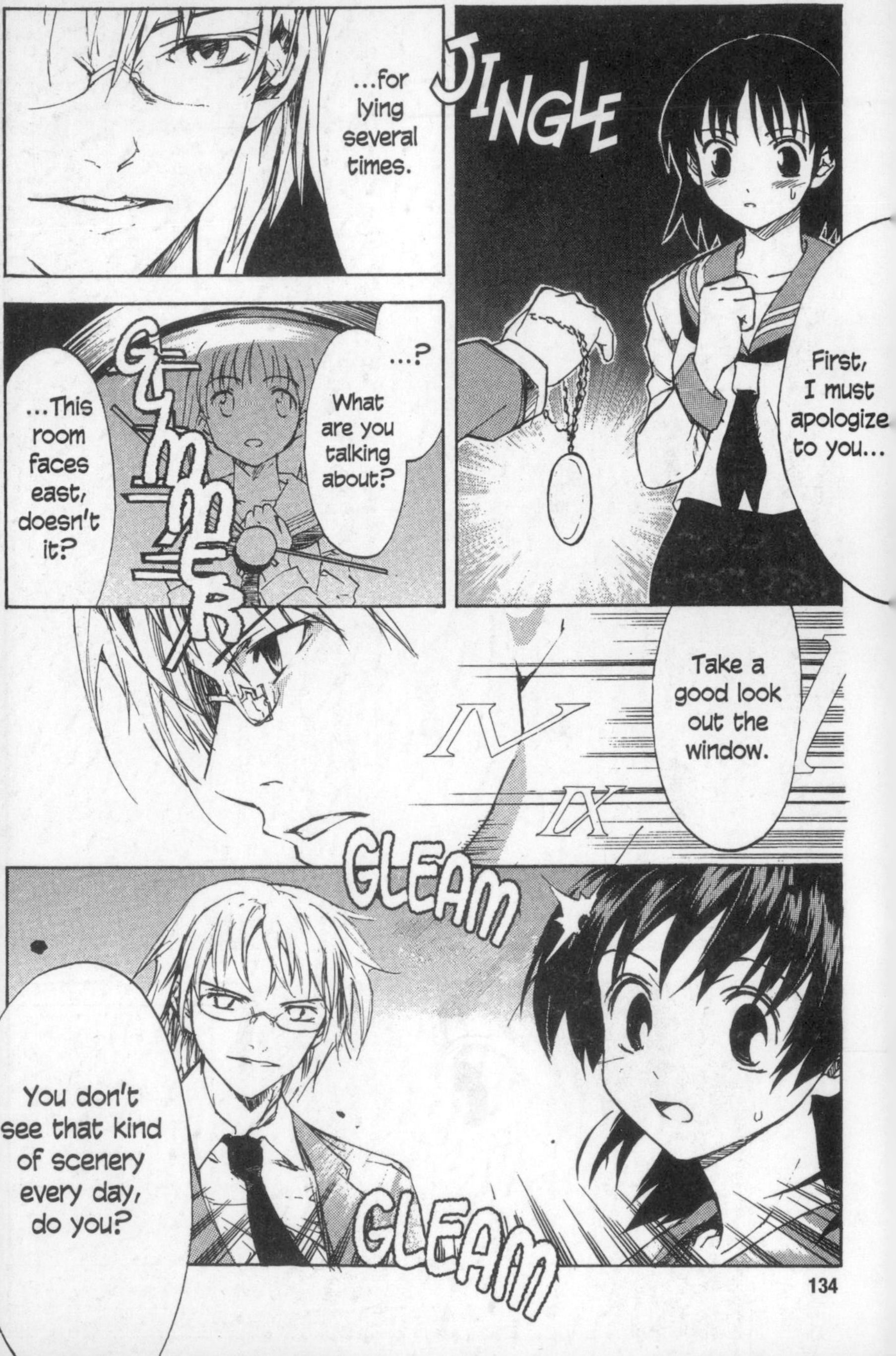
JINGLE
First, I must apologize to you...
...for lying several times.
...?
What are you talking about?
GLIMMER
...This room faces east, doesn't it?
Take a good look out the window.
GLEAM
GLEAM
You don't see that kind of scenery every day, do you?

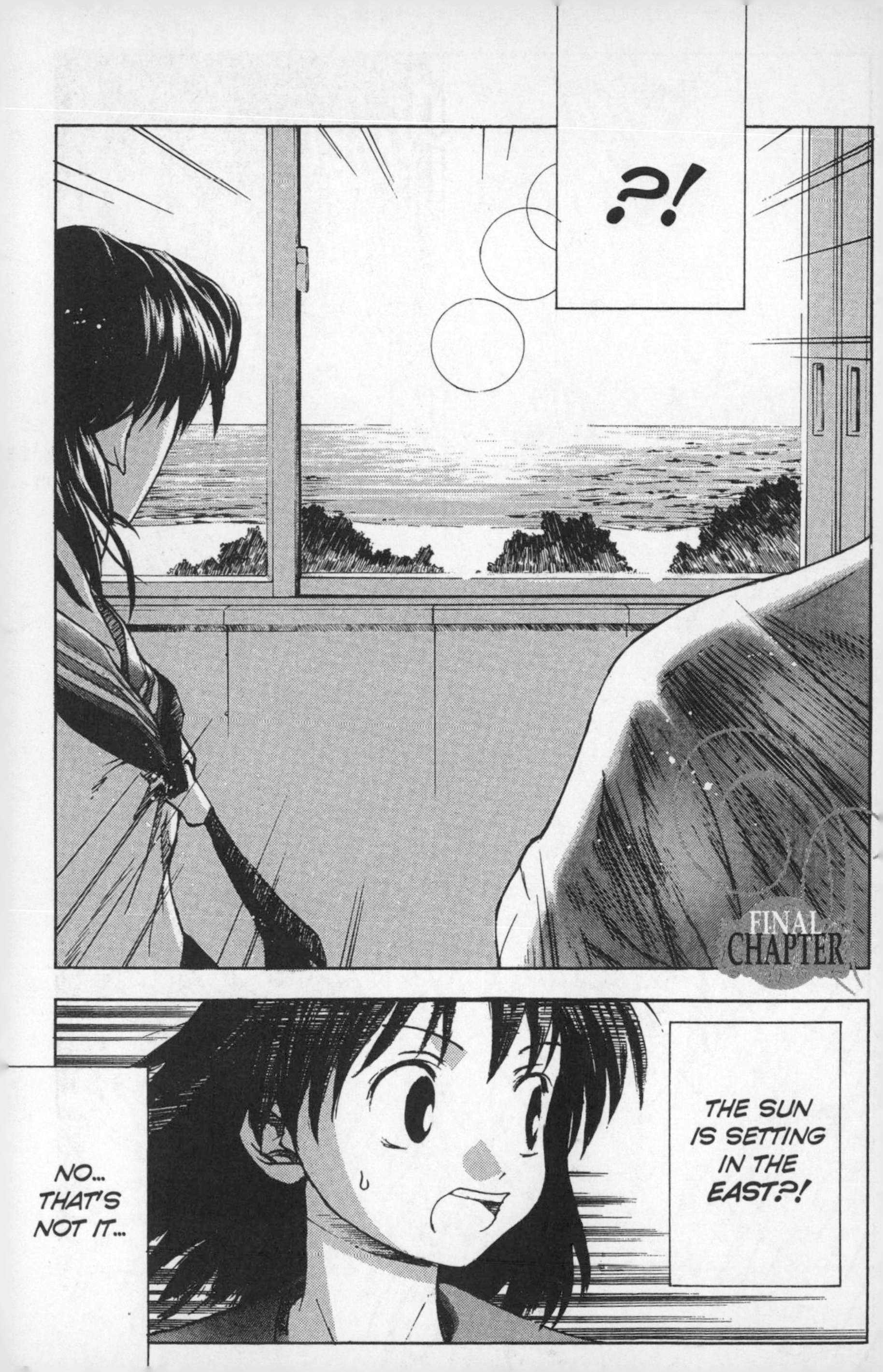
?!
FINAL CHAPTER
THE SUN IS SETTING IN THE EAST?!
NO... THAT'S NOT IT...

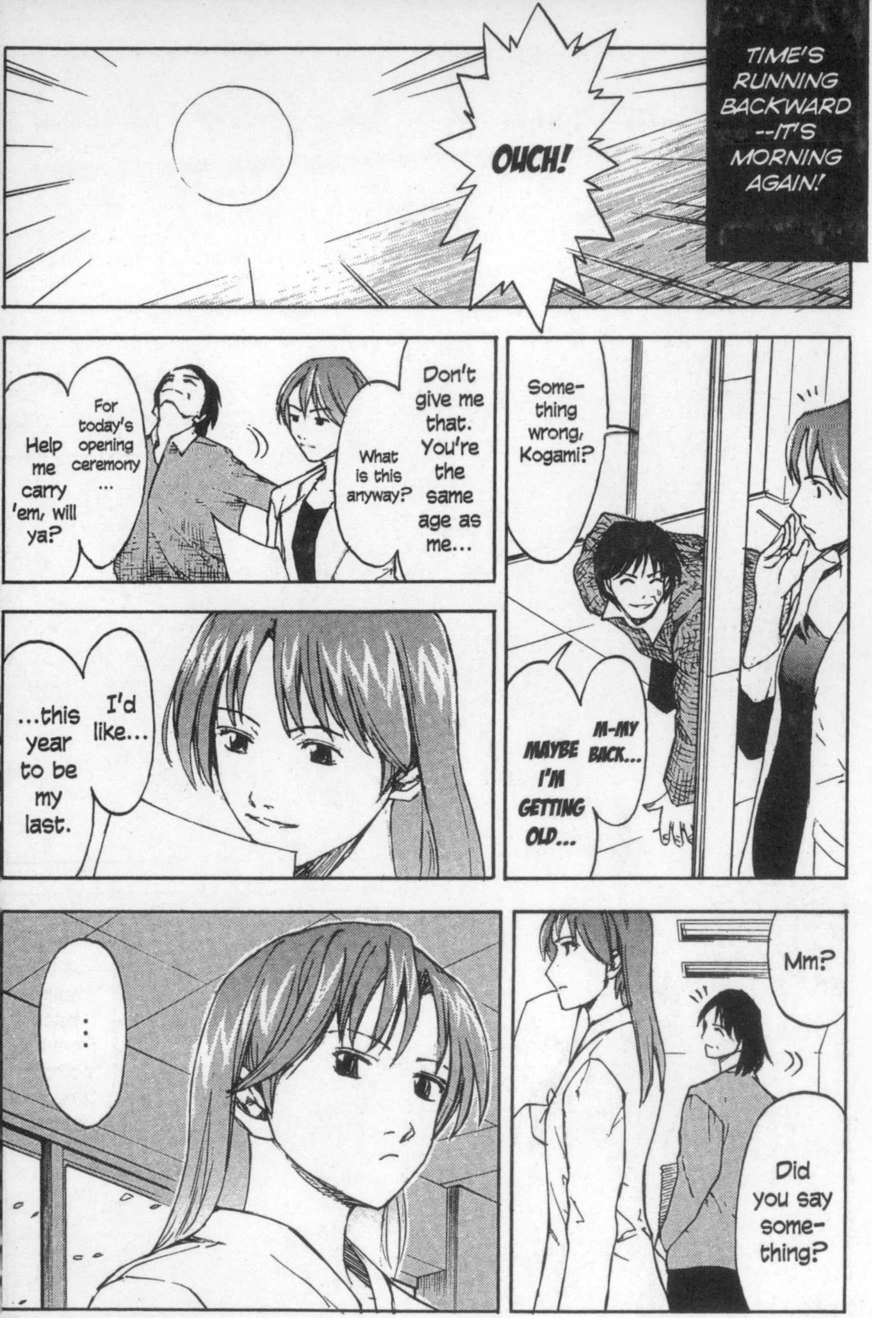
TIME'S RUNNING BACKWARD --IT'S MORNING AGAIN!
OUCH!
Something wrong, Kogami?
M-MY BACK... MAYBE I'M GETTING OLD...
Don't give me that. You're the same age as me...
What is this anyway?
For today's opening ceremony ...
Help me carry 'em, will ya?
I'd like...
...this year to be my last.
Mm?
Did you say something?
...

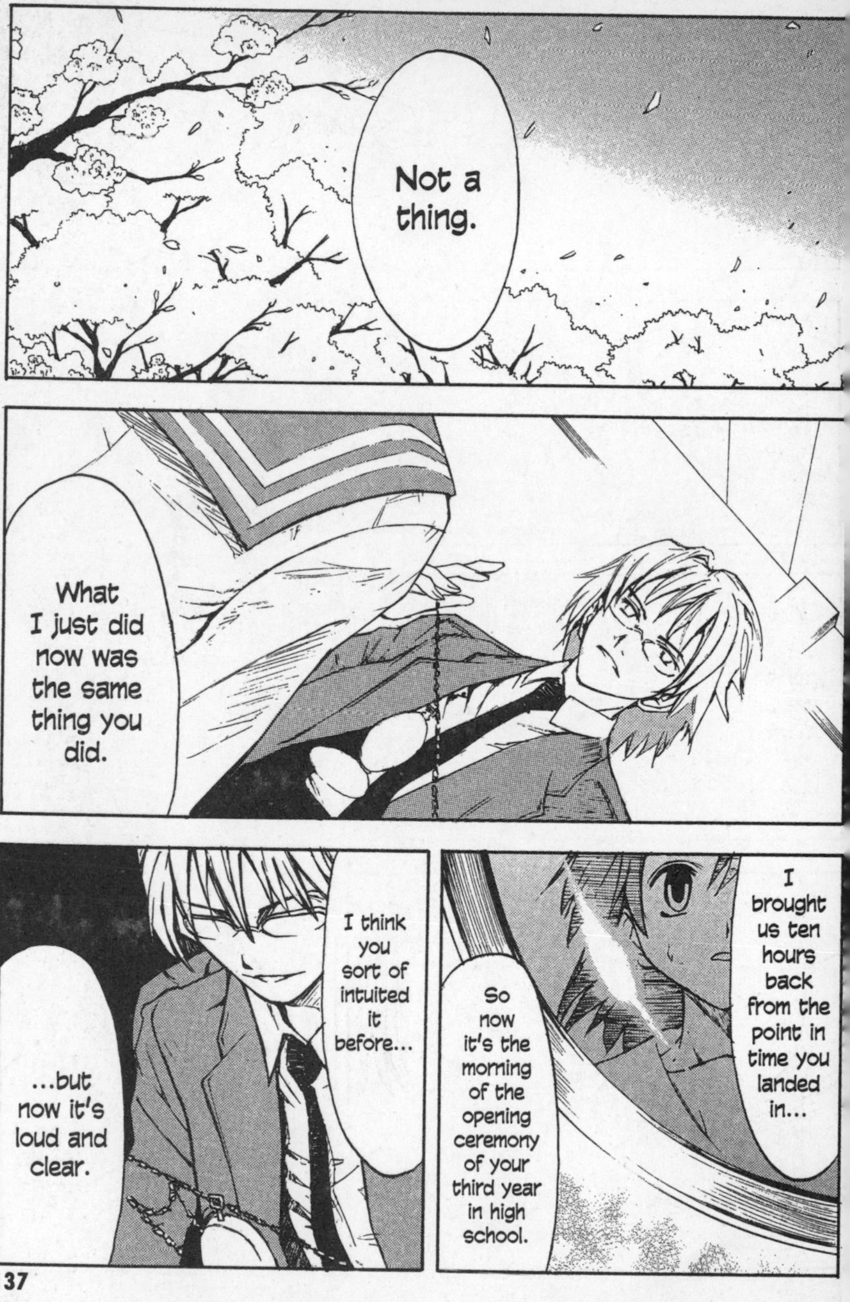
Not a thing.
What I just did now was the same thing you did.
I brought us ten hours back from the point in time you landed in...
So now it's the morning of the opening ceremony of your third year in high school.
I think you sort of intuited it before...
...but now it's loud and clear.

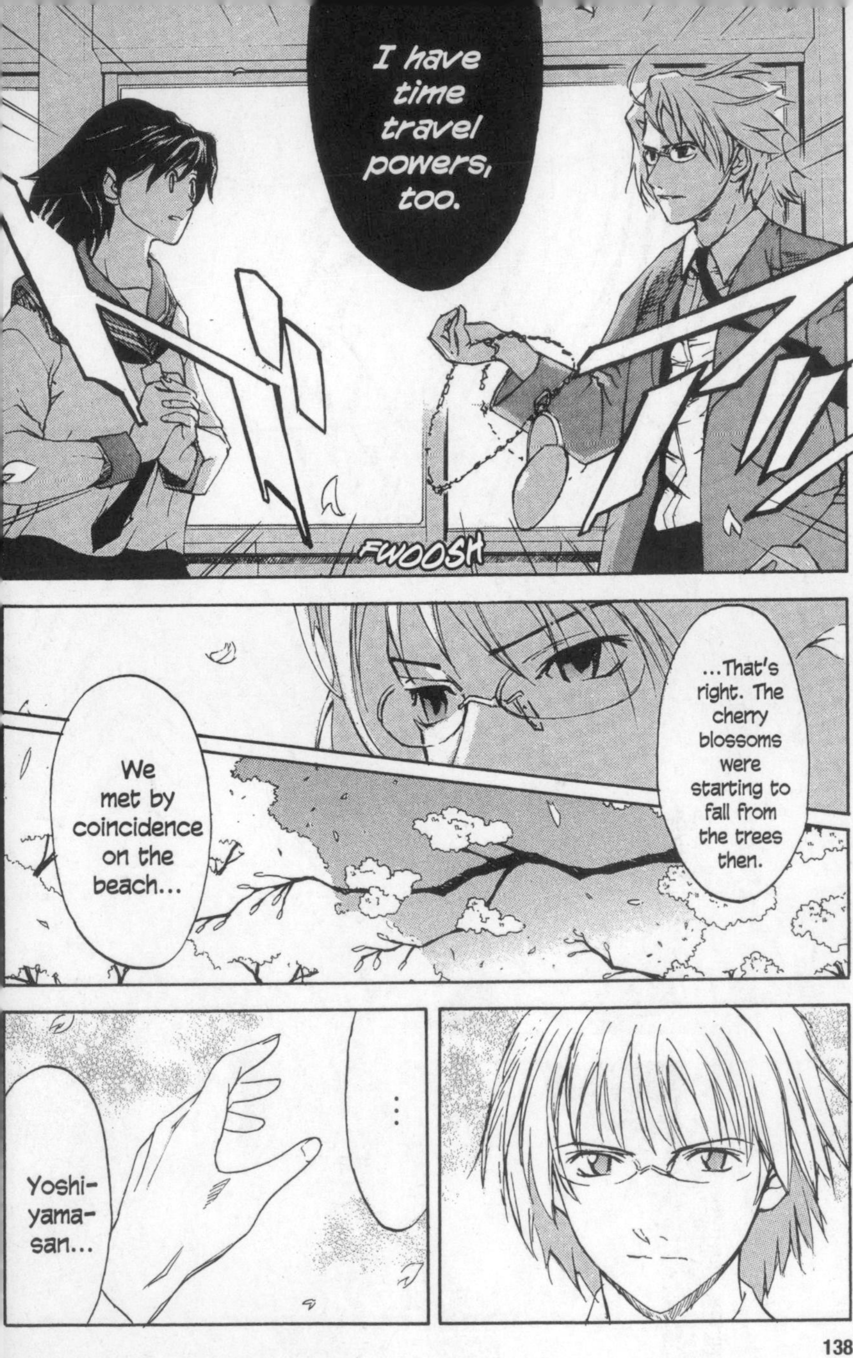
I have time travel powers, too.
FWOOSH
...That's right. The cherry blossoms were starting to fall from the trees then.
We met by coincidence on the beach...
...
Yoshi-yama-san...

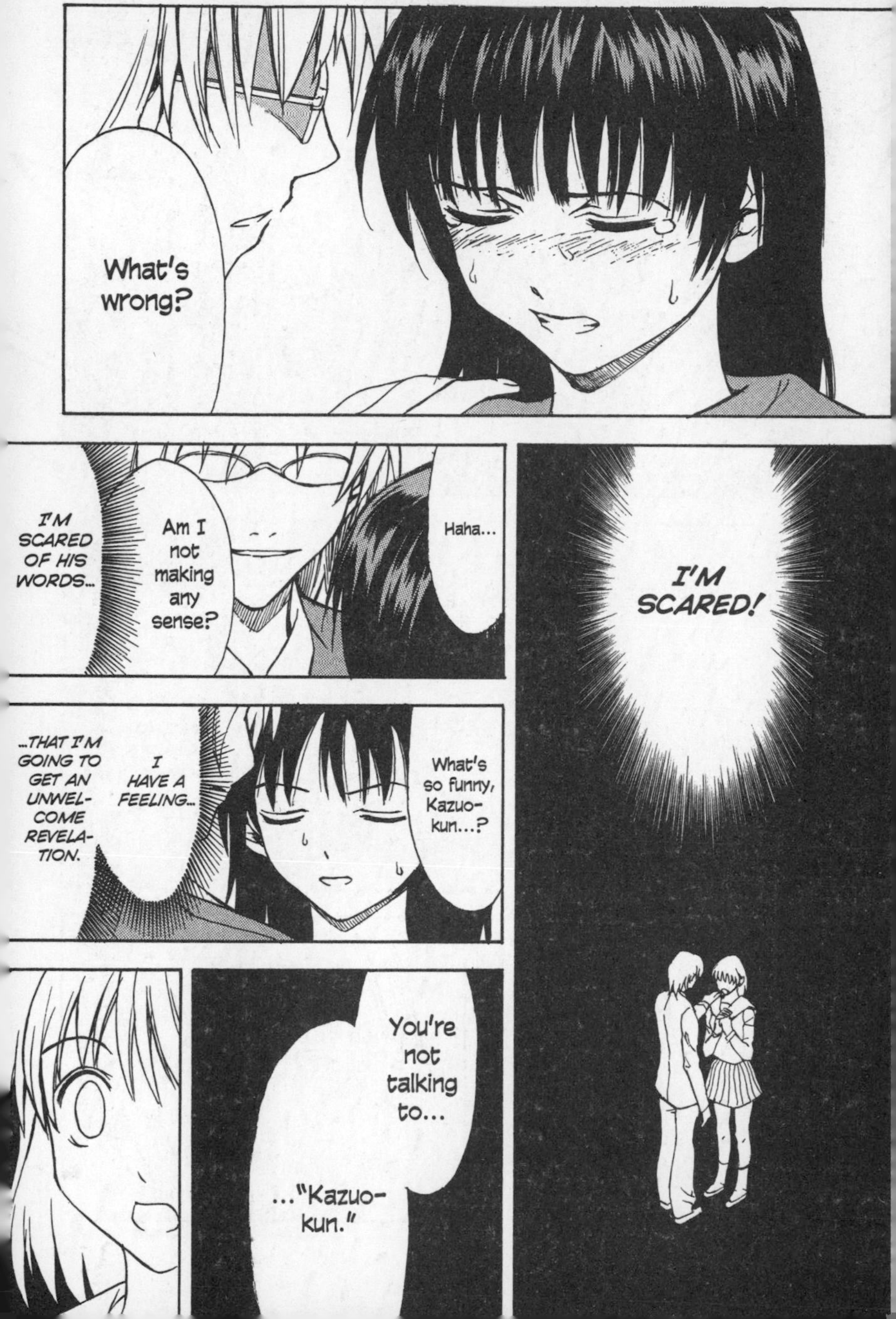
What's wrong?
I'M SCARED!
Haha...
Am I not making any sense?
I'M SCARED OF HIS WORDS...
What's so funny, Kazuo-kun...?
I HAVE A FEELING...
...THAT I'M GOING TO GET AN UNWEL-COME REVELA-TION.
You're not talking to...
..."Kazuo-kun."

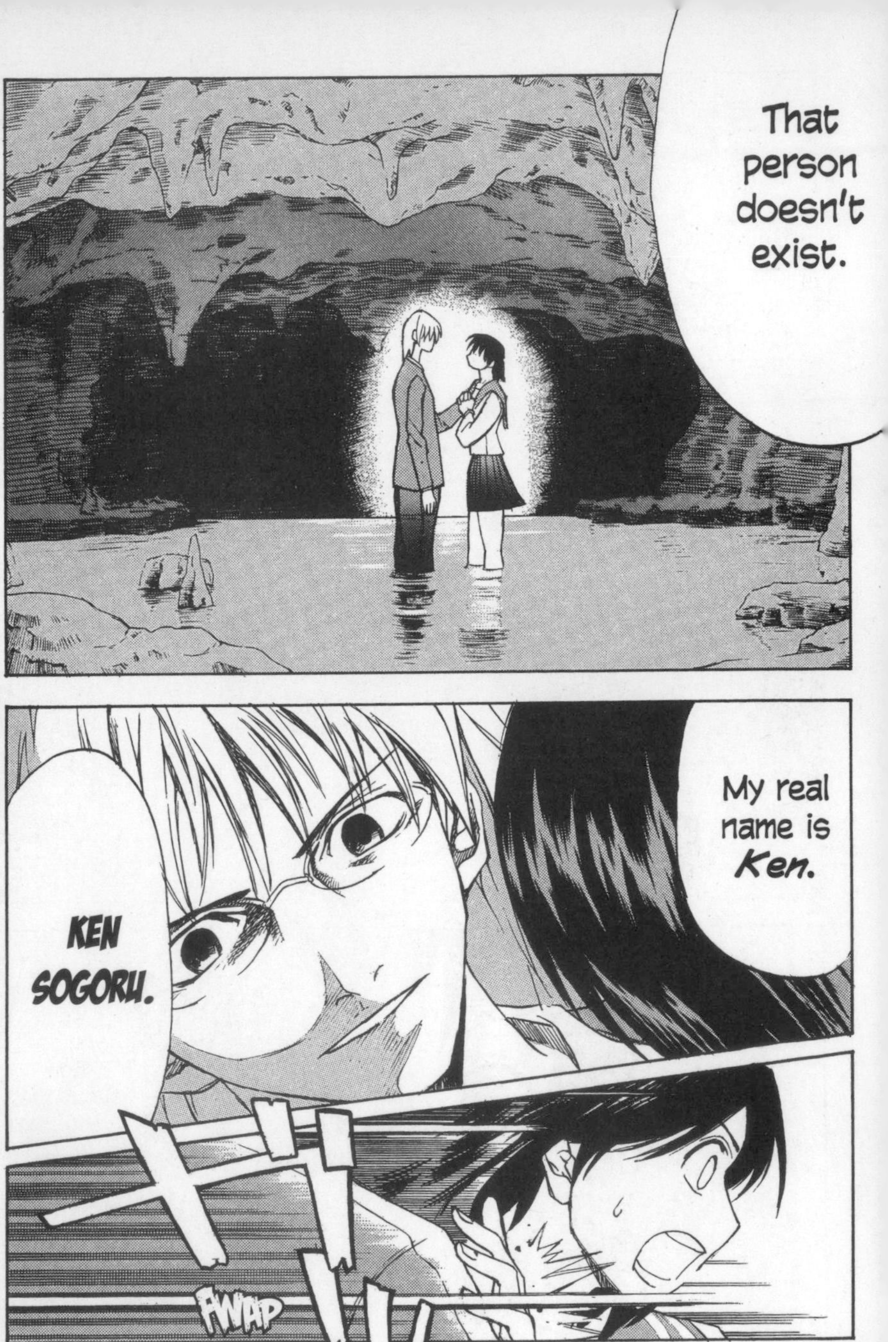
That person doesn't exist.
My real name is *Ken*.
KEN SOGORU.
FWAP

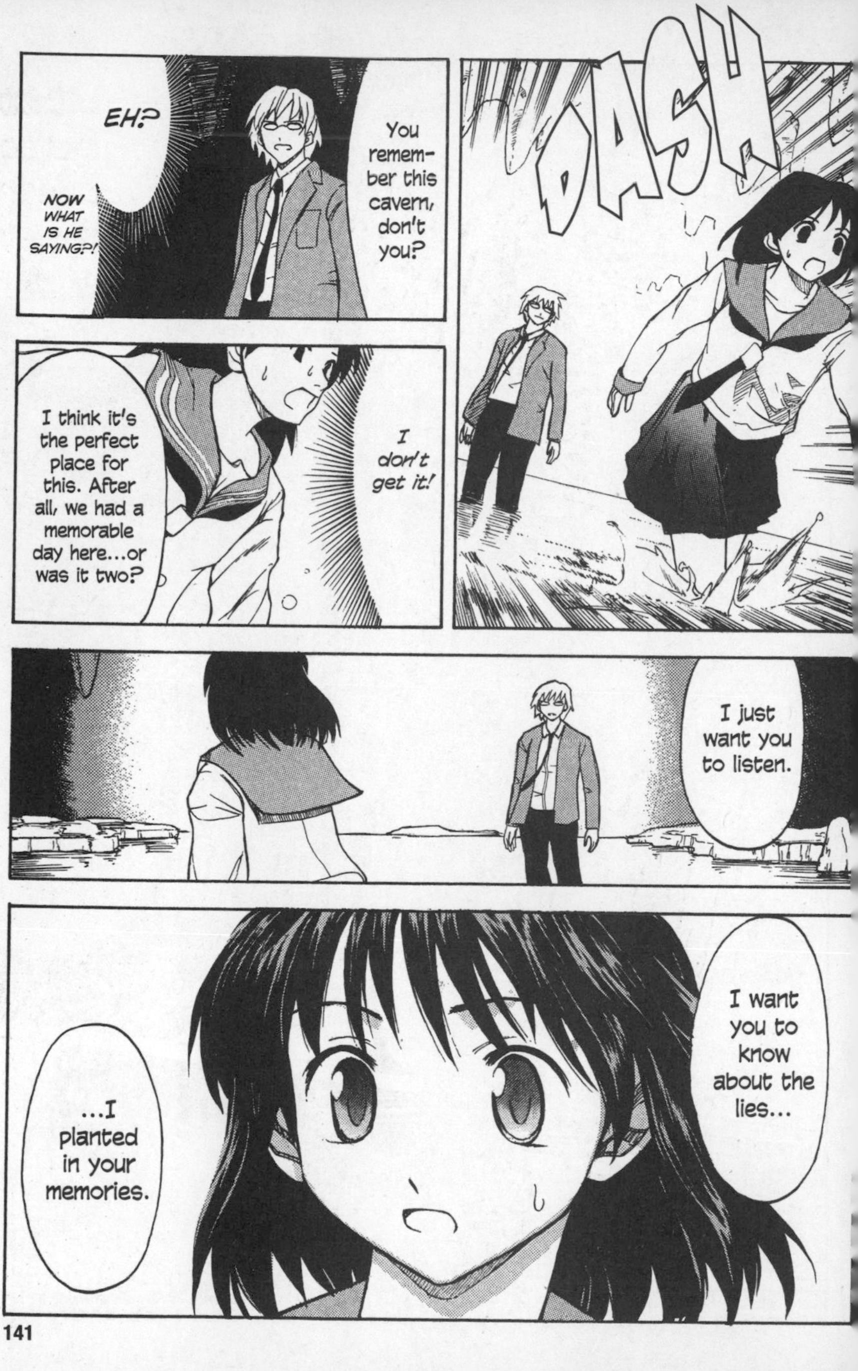
DASH
You remember this cavern, don't you?
EH?
NOW WHAT IS HE SAYING?!
I don't get it!
I think it's the perfect place for this. After all, we had a memorable day here...or was it two?
I just want you to listen.
I want you to know about the lies...
...I planted in your memories.

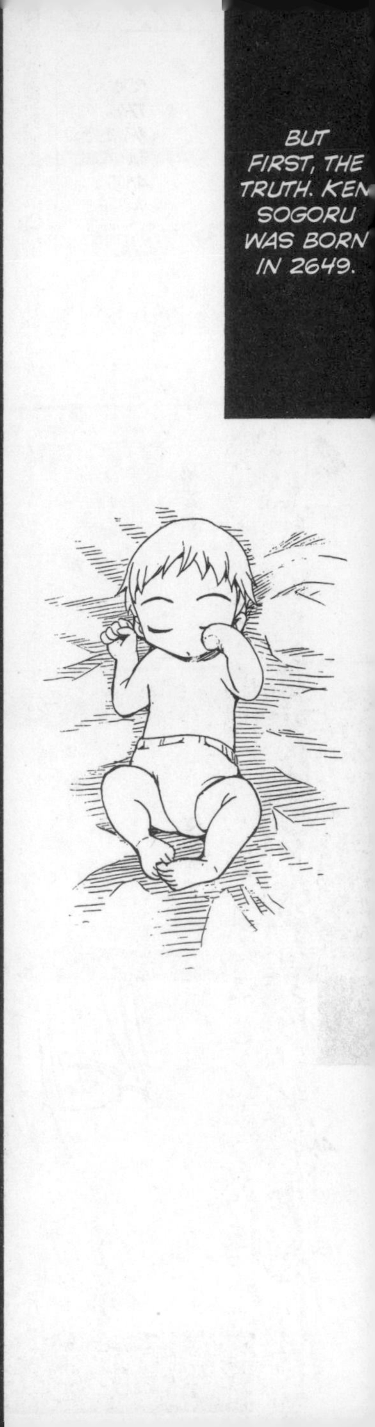
BUT FIRST, THE TRUTH. KEN SOGORU WAS BORN IN 2649.
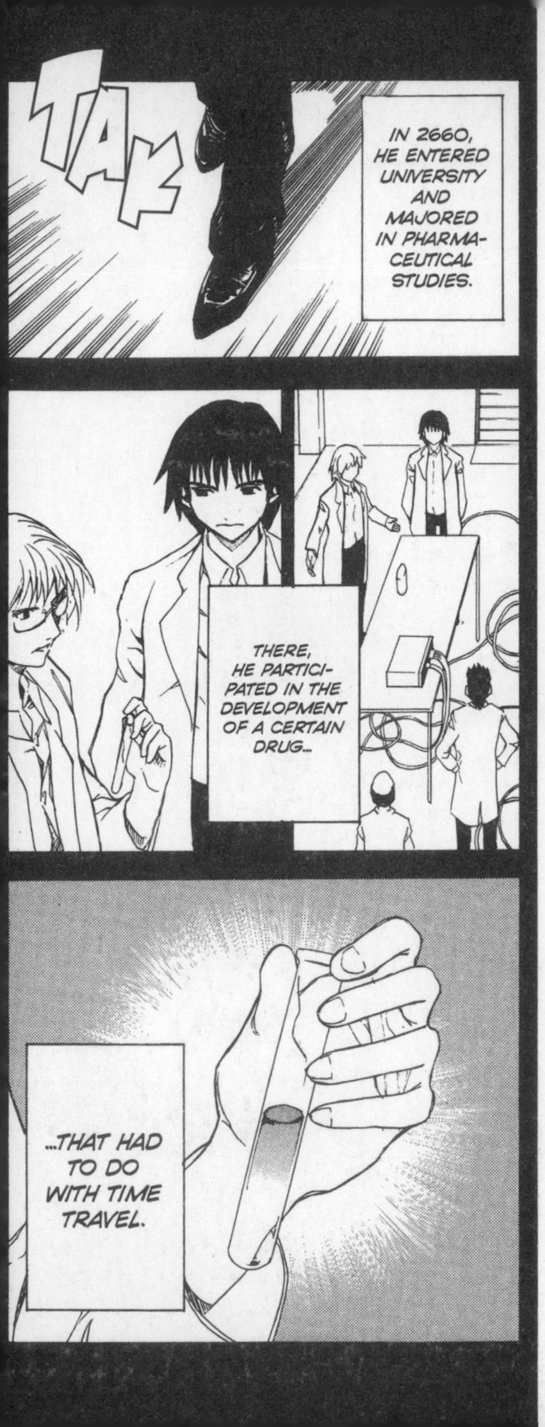
IN 2660, HE ENTERED UNIVERSITY AND MAJORED IN PHARMA-CEUTICAL STUDIES.
TAK
THERE, HE PARTICI-PATED IN THE DEVELOPMENT OF A CERTAIN DRUG...
...THAT HAD TO DO WITH TIME TRAVEL.

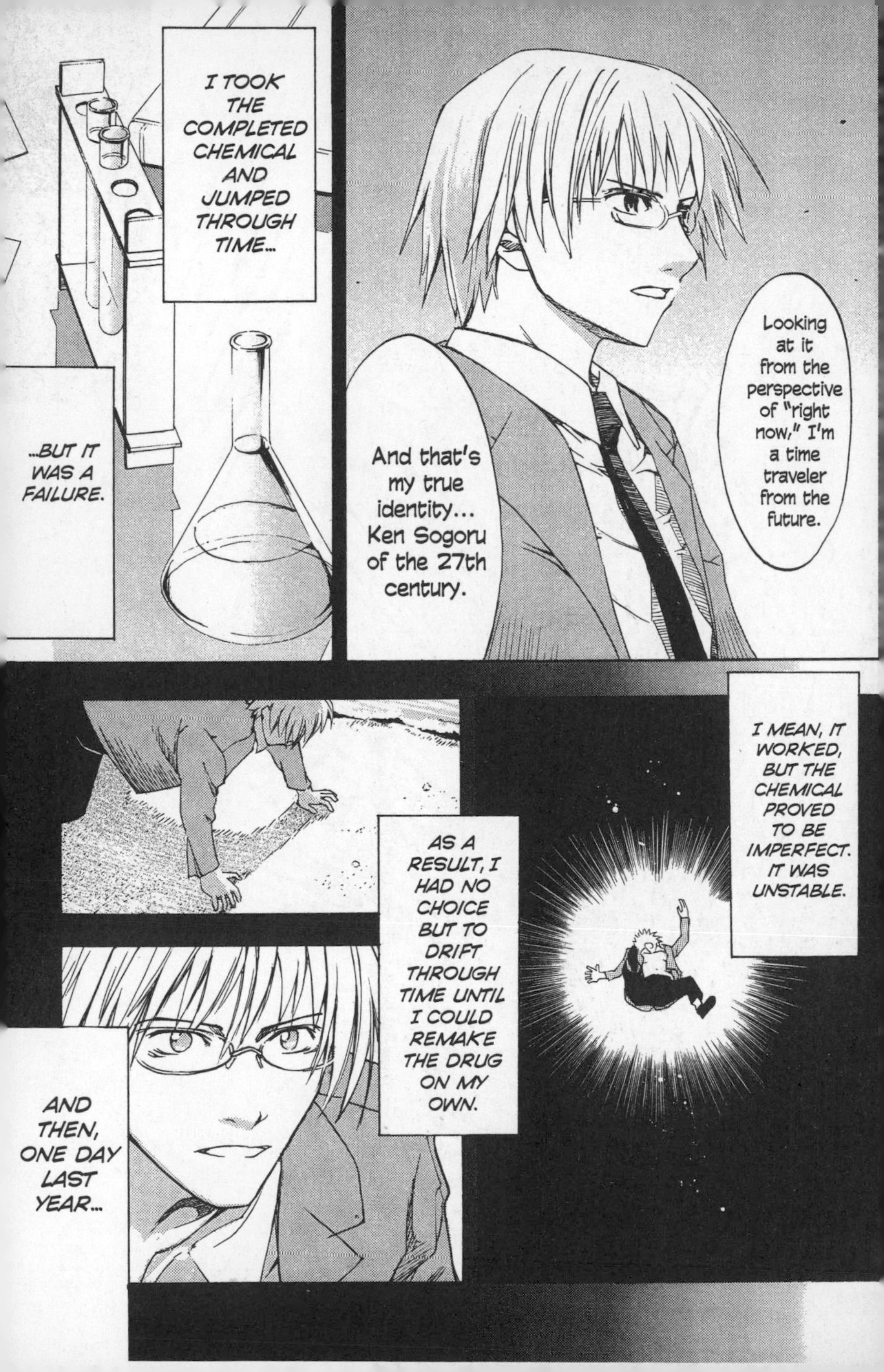
Looking at it from the perspective of "right now," I'm a time traveler from the future.
And that's my true identity... Ken Sogoru of the 27th century.
I TOOK THE COMPLETED CHEMICAL AND JUMPED THROUGH TIME...
...BUT IT WAS A FAILURE.
I MEAN, IT WORKED, BUT THE CHEMICAL PROVED TO BE IMPERFECT. IT WAS UNSTABLE.
AS A RESULT, I HAD NO CHOICE BUT TO DRIFT THROUGH TIME UNTIL I COULD REMAKE THE DRUG ON MY OWN.
AND THEN, ONE DAY LAST YEAR...

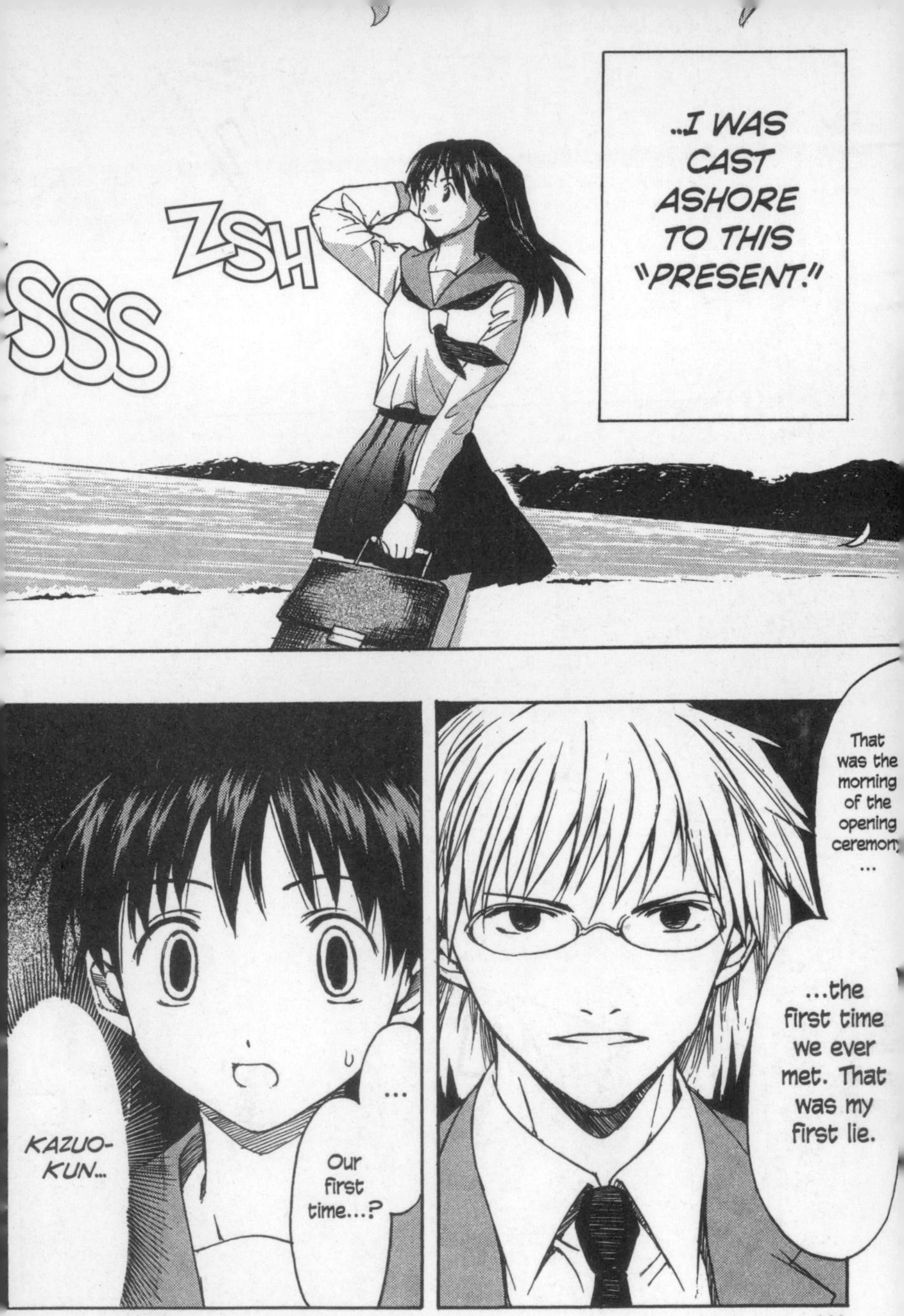
...I WAS CAST ASHORE TO THIS "PRESENT."
ZSH
SSS
That was the morning of the opening ceremony...
...the first time we ever met. That was my first lie.
...
Our first time...?
KAZUO-KUN...

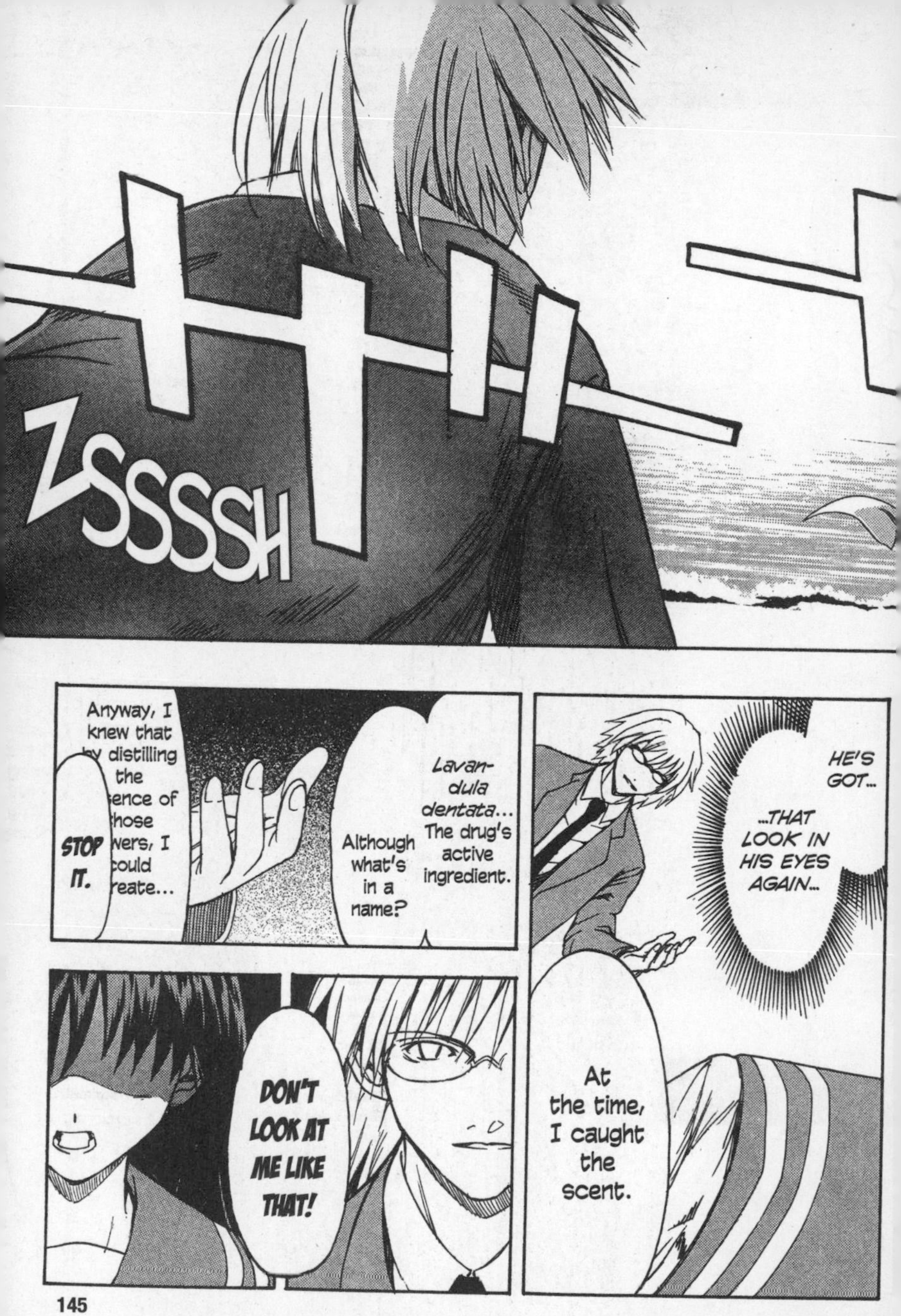
ZSSSSH
HE'S GOT...
...THAT LOOK IN HIS EYES AGAIN...
At the time, I caught the scent.
Lavan-dula dentata... The drug's active ingredient.
Although what's in a name?
Anyway, I knew that distilling the sence of hose wers, I could reate...
STOP IT.
DON'T LOOK AT ME LIKE THAT!

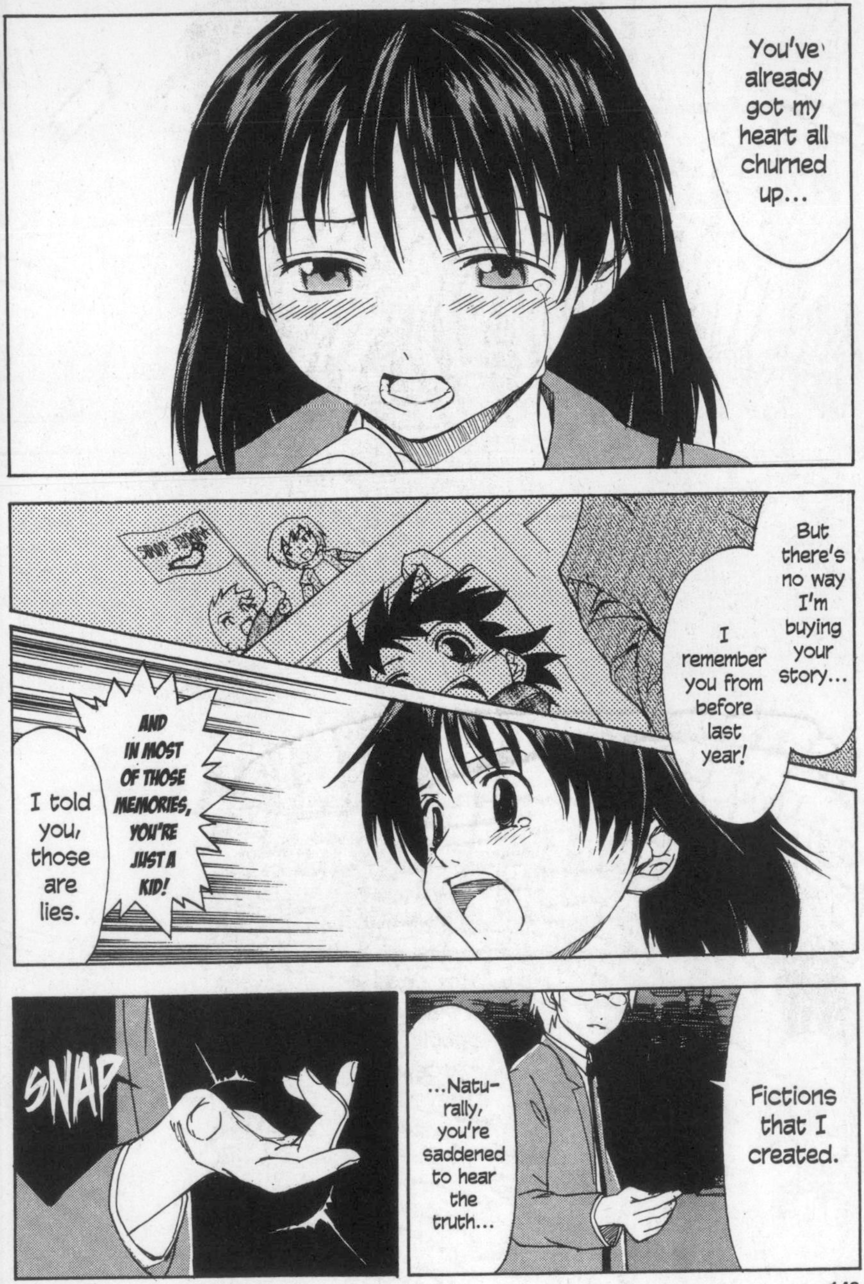
You've already got my heart all churned up...
But there's no way I'm buying your story...
I remember you from before last year!
AND IN MOST OF THOSE MEMORIES, YOU'RE JUST A KID!
I told you, those are lies.
Fictions that I created.
...Natu-rally, you're saddened to hear the truth...
SNAP

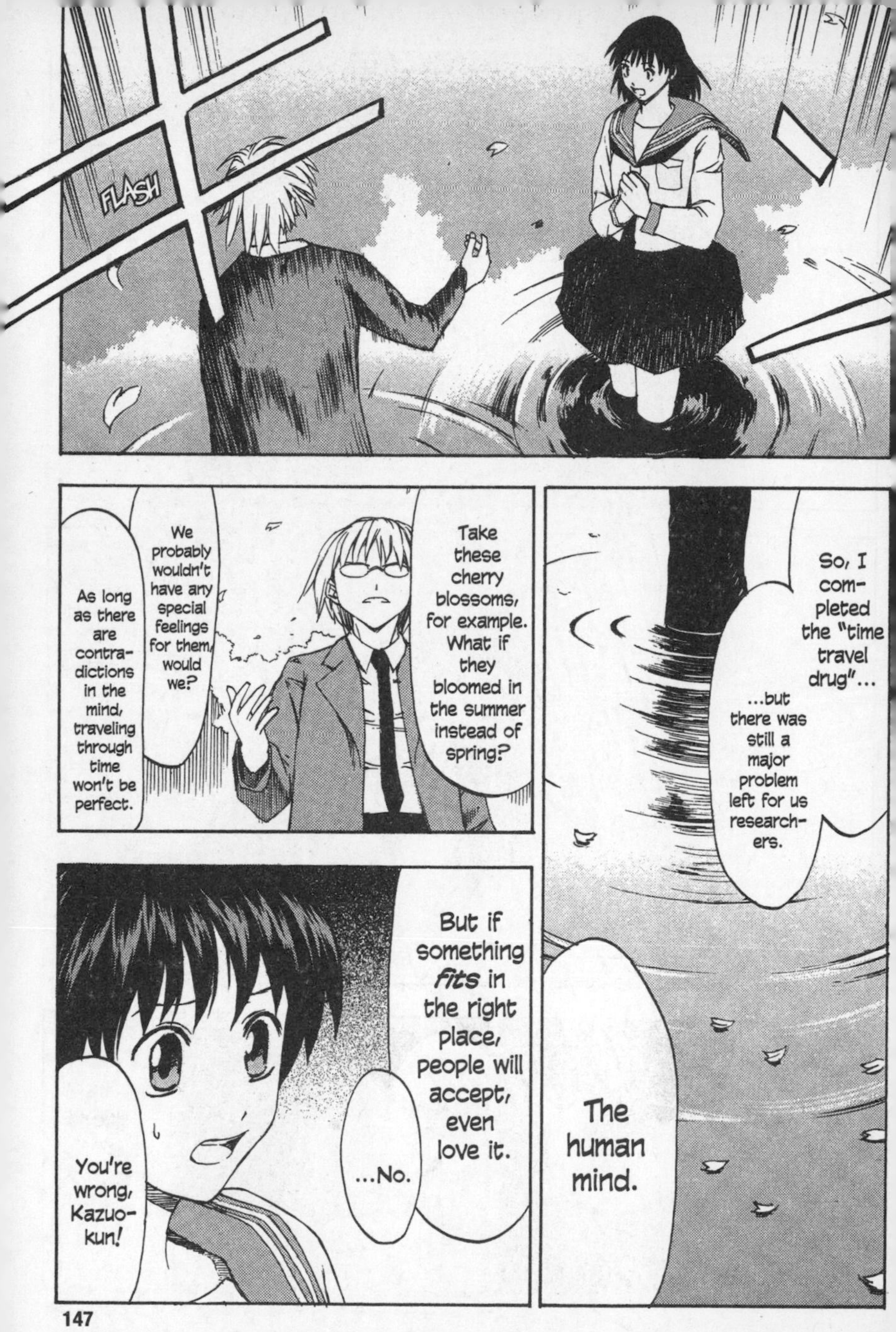
FLASH
So, I completed the "time travel drug"...
...but there was still a major problem left for us researchers.
The human mind.
Take these cherry blossoms, for example. What if they bloomed in the summer instead of spring?
We probably wouldn't have any special feelings for them, would we?
As long as there are contradictions in the mind, traveling through time won't be perfect.
But if something *fits* in the right place, people will accept, even love it.
...No.
You're wrong, Kazuo-kun!

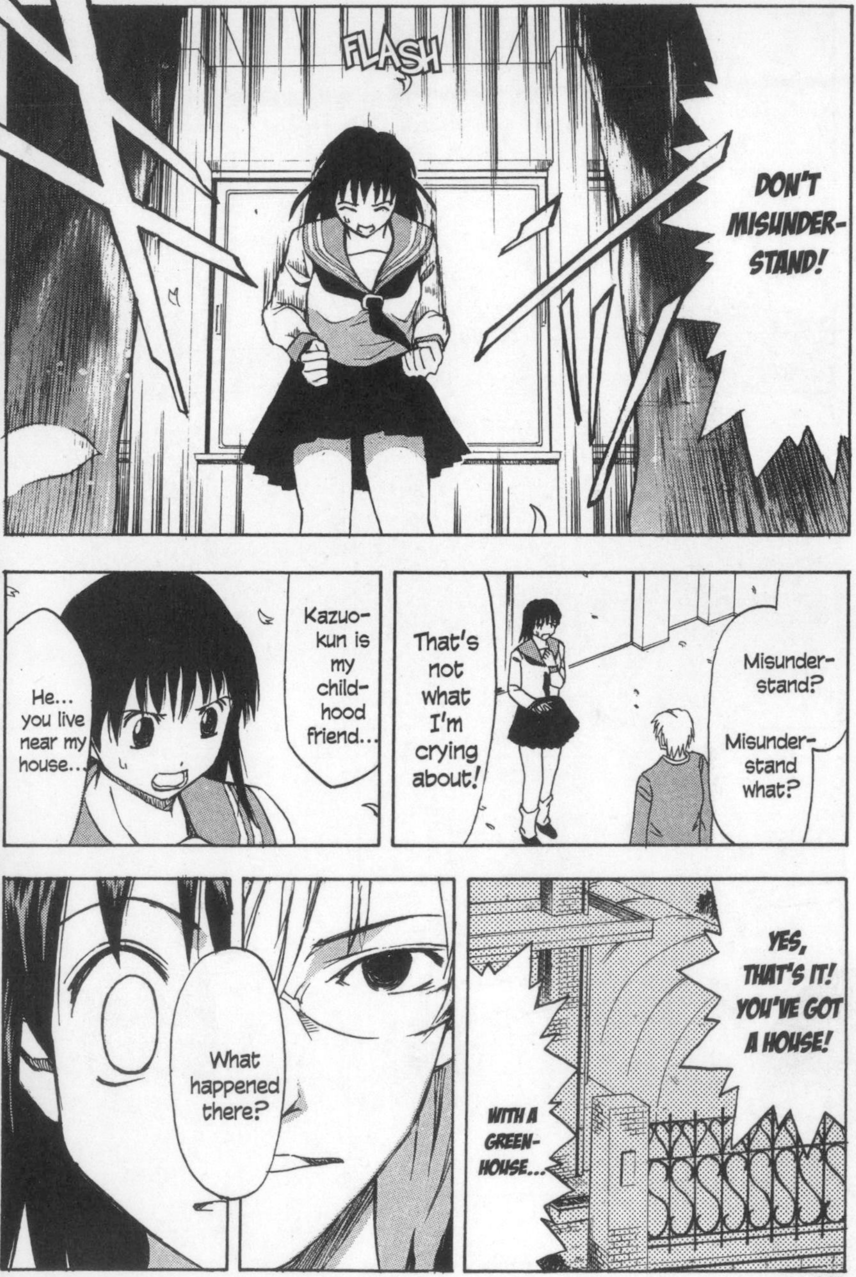
FLASH
DON'T MISUNDERSTAND!
Misunderstand?
Misunderstand what?
That's not what I'm crying about!
Kazuo-kun is my childhood friend...
He... you live near my house...
YES, THAT'S IT! YOU'VE GOT A HOUSE!
WITH A GREENHOUSE...
What happened there?

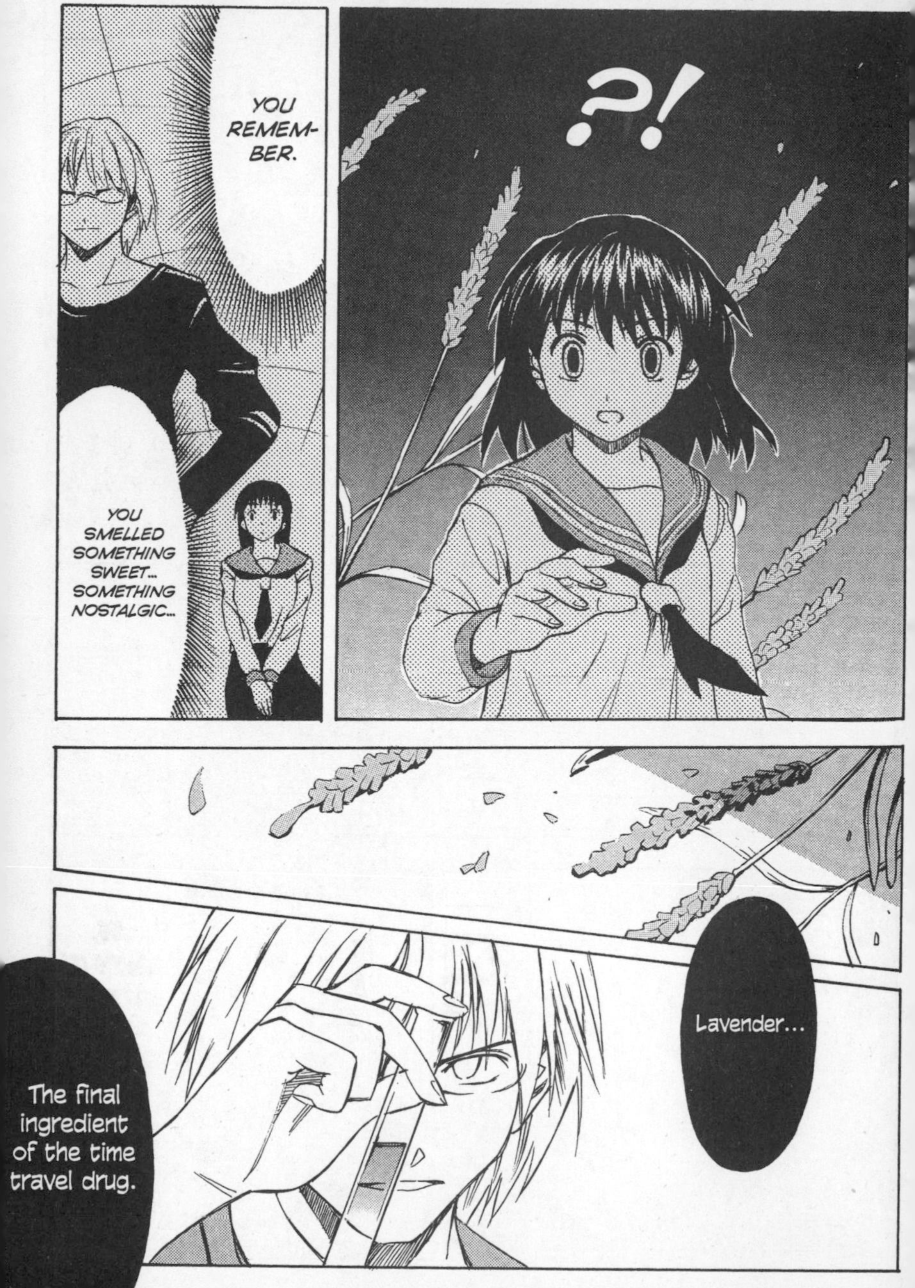
?!
YOU REMEMBER.
YOU SMELLED SOMETHING SWEET... SOMETHING NOSTALGIC...
Lavender...
The final ingredient of the time travel drug.

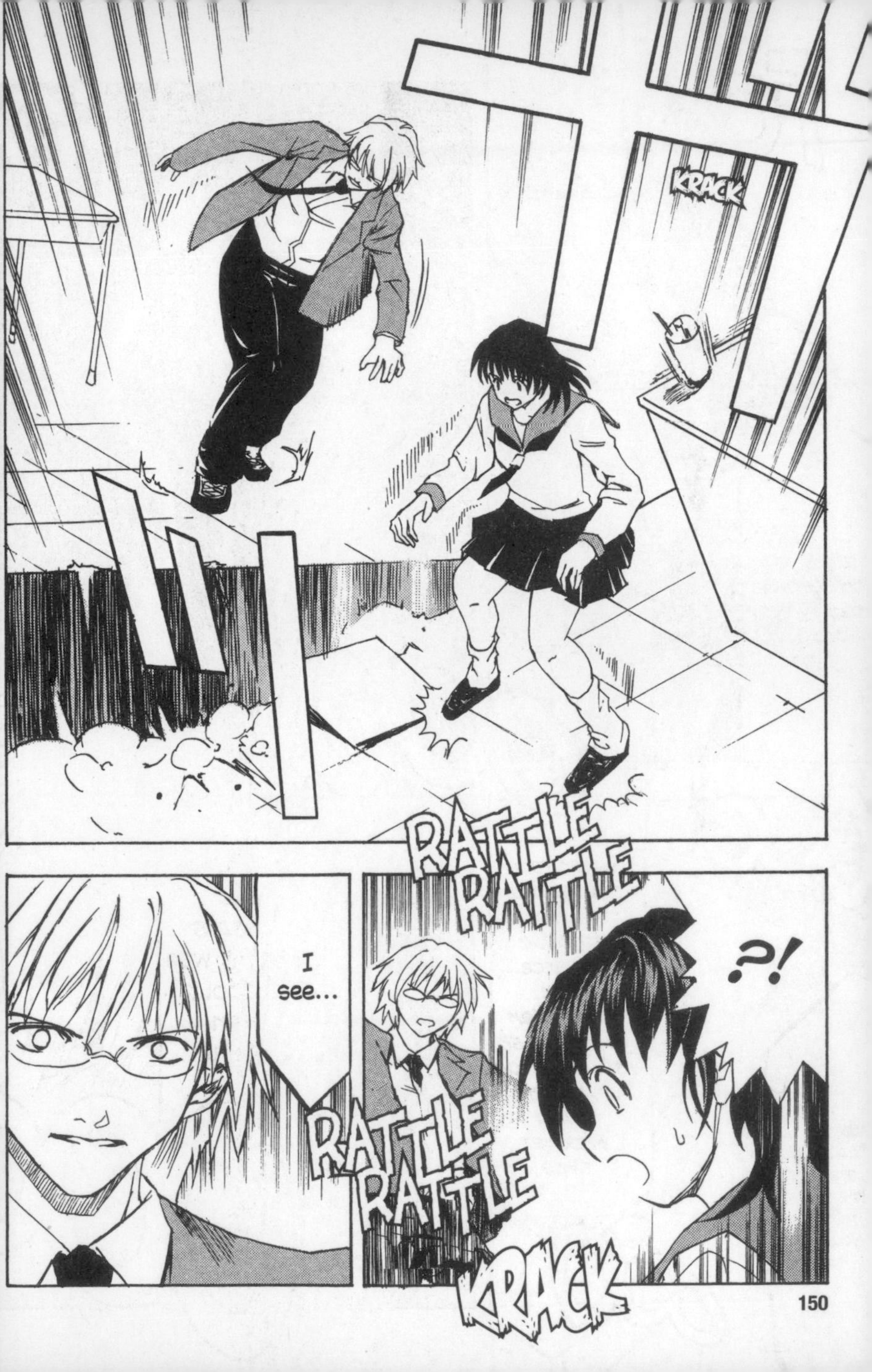
KRACK
RATTLE RATTLE
?!
RATTLE RATTLE
KRACK
I see...

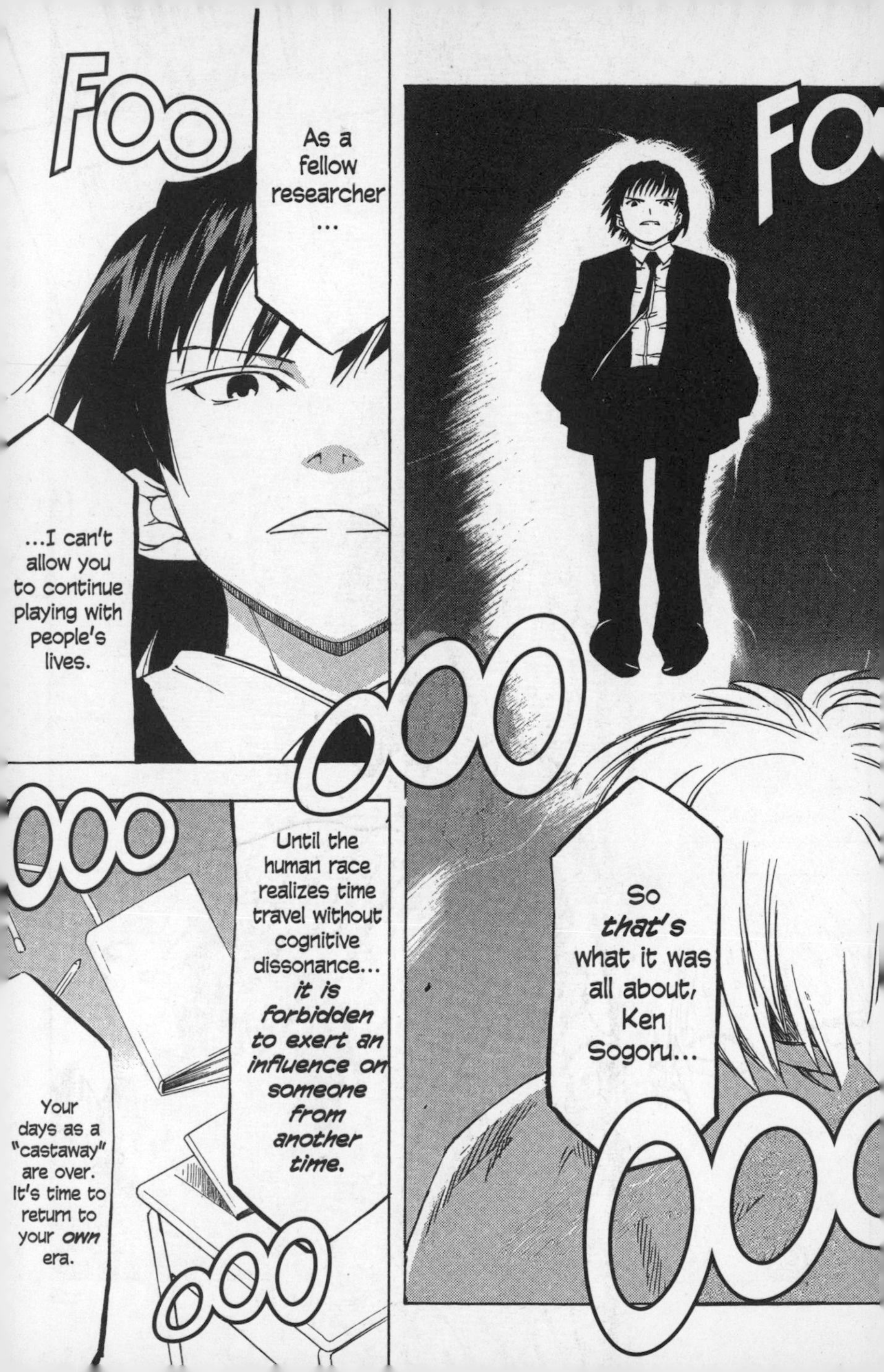
FOOOOOO
So *that's* what it was all about, Ken Sogoru...
FOOOOOO
As a fellow researcher...
...I can't allow you to continue playing with people's lives.
OOOOOO
Until the human race realizes time travel without cognitive dissonance... *it is forbidden to exert an influence on someone from another time.*
Your days as a "castaway" are over. It's time to return to your *own* era.

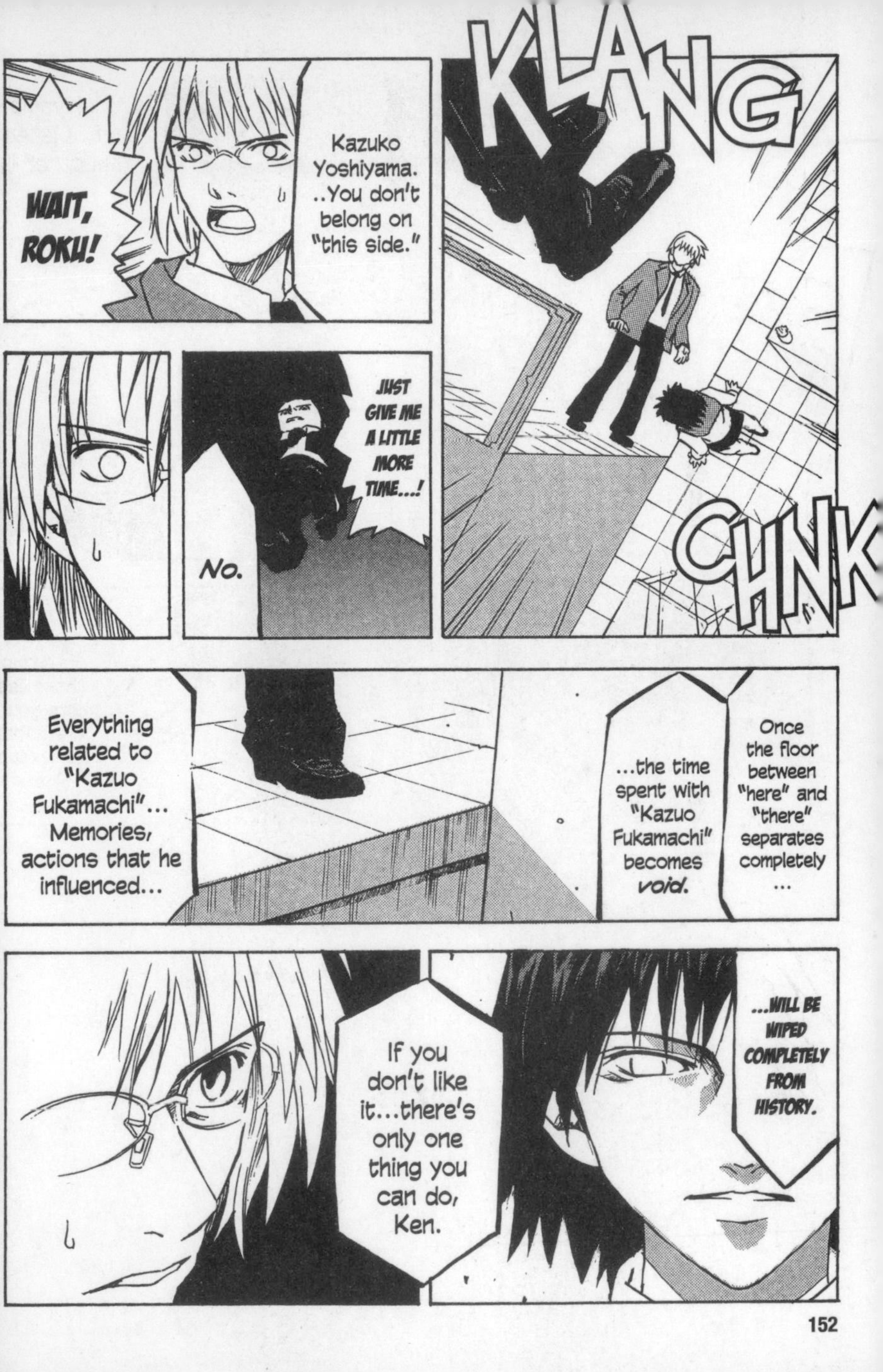
KLANG
CHNK
Kazuko Yoshiyama. ..You don't belong on "this side."
WAIT, ROKU!
JUST GIVE ME A LITTLE MORE TIME...!
No.
Once the floor between "here" and "there" separates completely ...
...the time spent with "Kazuo Fukamachi" becomes *void*.
Everything related to "Kazuo Fukamachi"... Memories, actions that he influenced...
...WILL BE WIPED COMPLETELY FROM HISTORY.
If you don't like it...there's only one thing you can do, Ken.

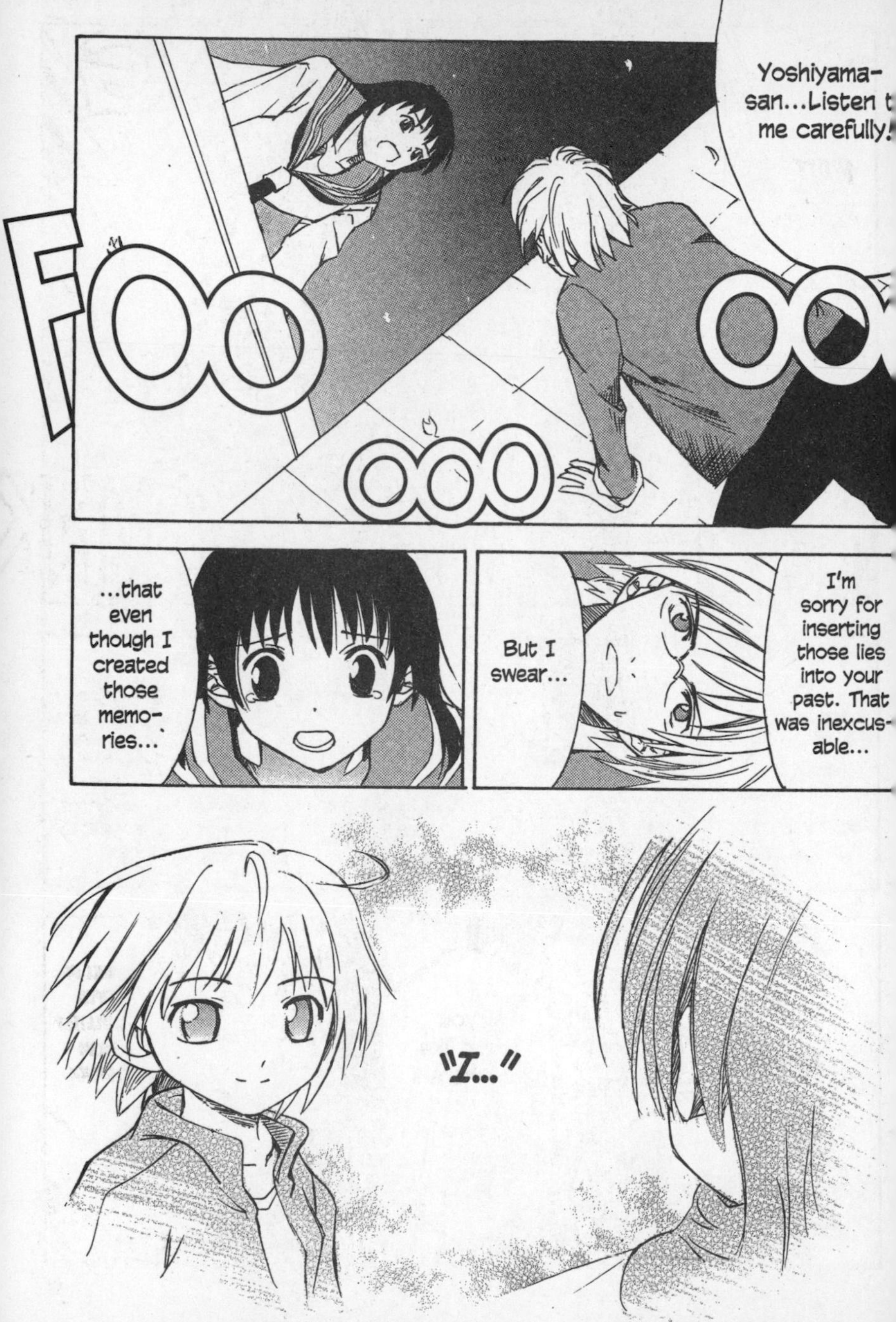
Yoshiyama-san...Listen t me carefully!
FOOOOOOO
I'm sorry for inserting those lies into your past. That was inexcusable...
But I swear...
...that even though I created those memories...
"I..."

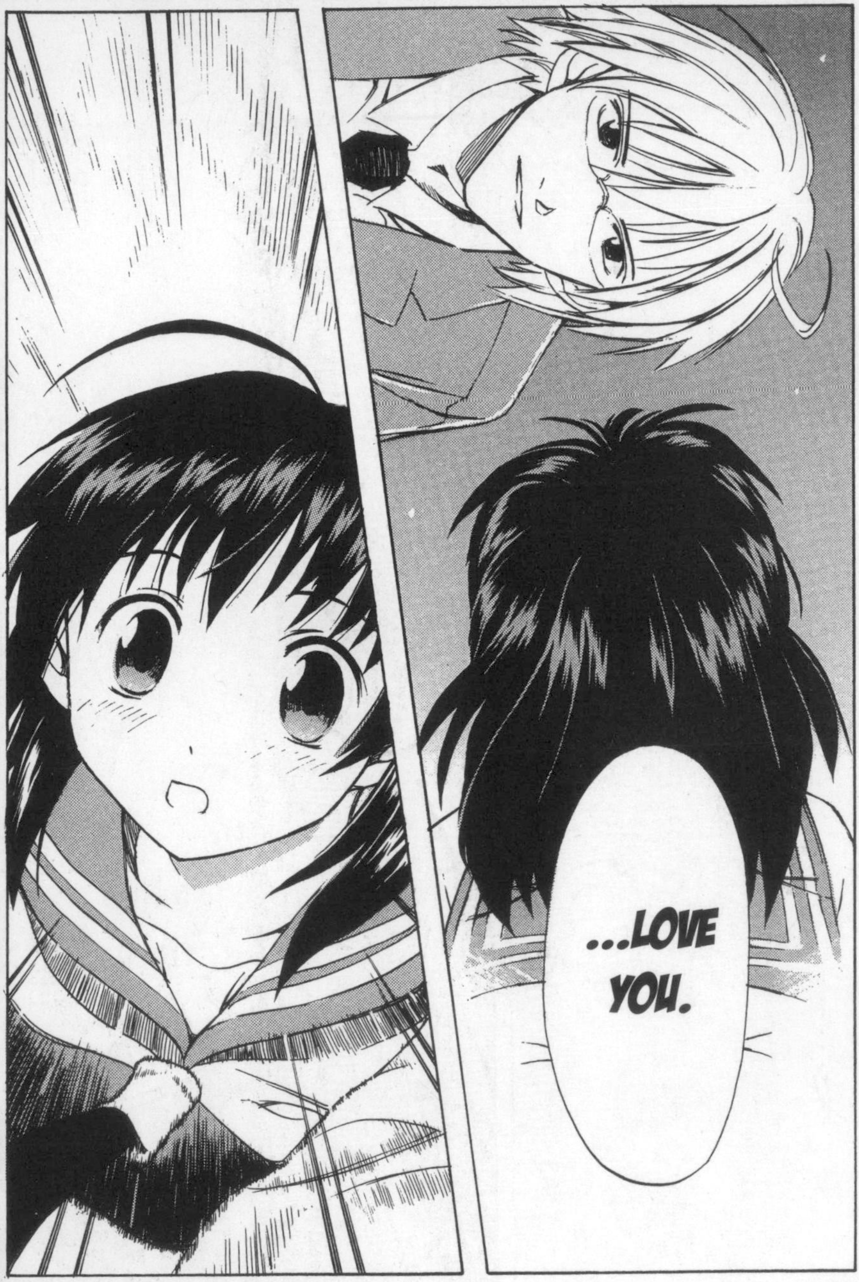
...LOVE YOU.

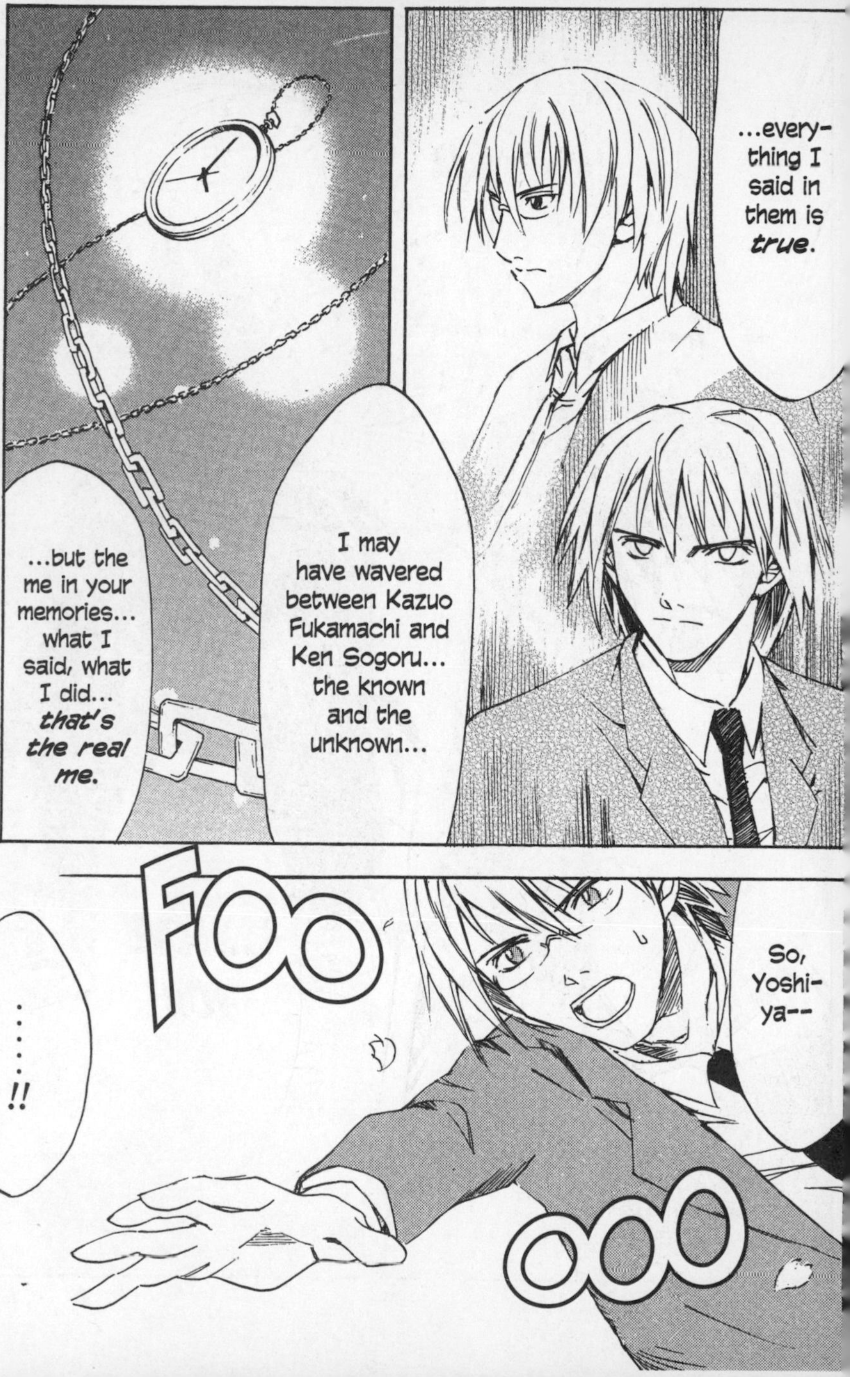
...every-thing I said in them is *true*.
I may have wavered between Kazuo Fukamachi and Ken Sogoru... the known and the unknown...
...but the me in your memories... what I said, what I did... *that's the real me.*
So, Yoshi-ya--
FOOOOO
......!!

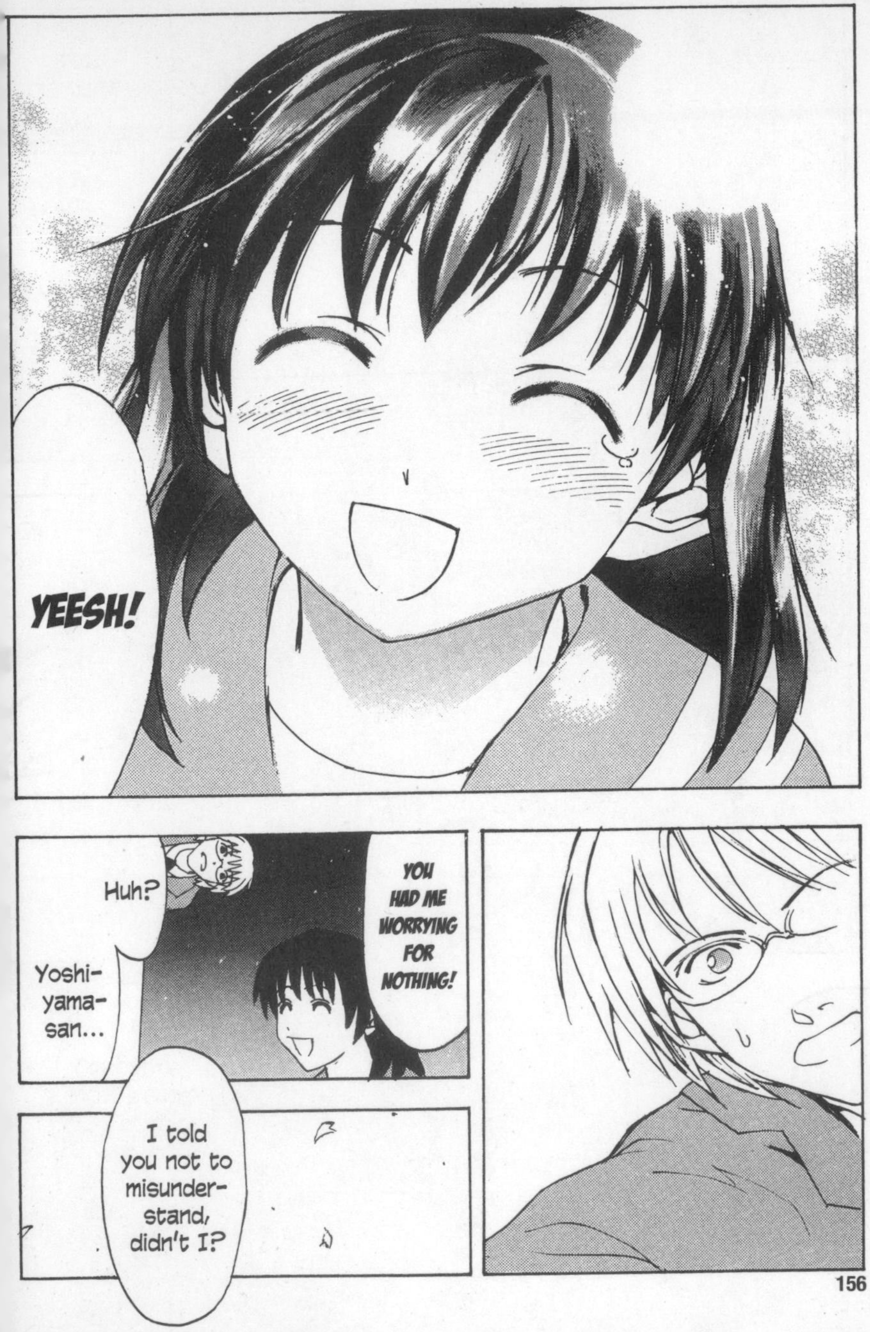
YEESH!
YOU HAD ME WORRYING FOR NOTHING!
Huh?
Yoshi-yama-san...
I told you not to misunder-stand, didn't I?

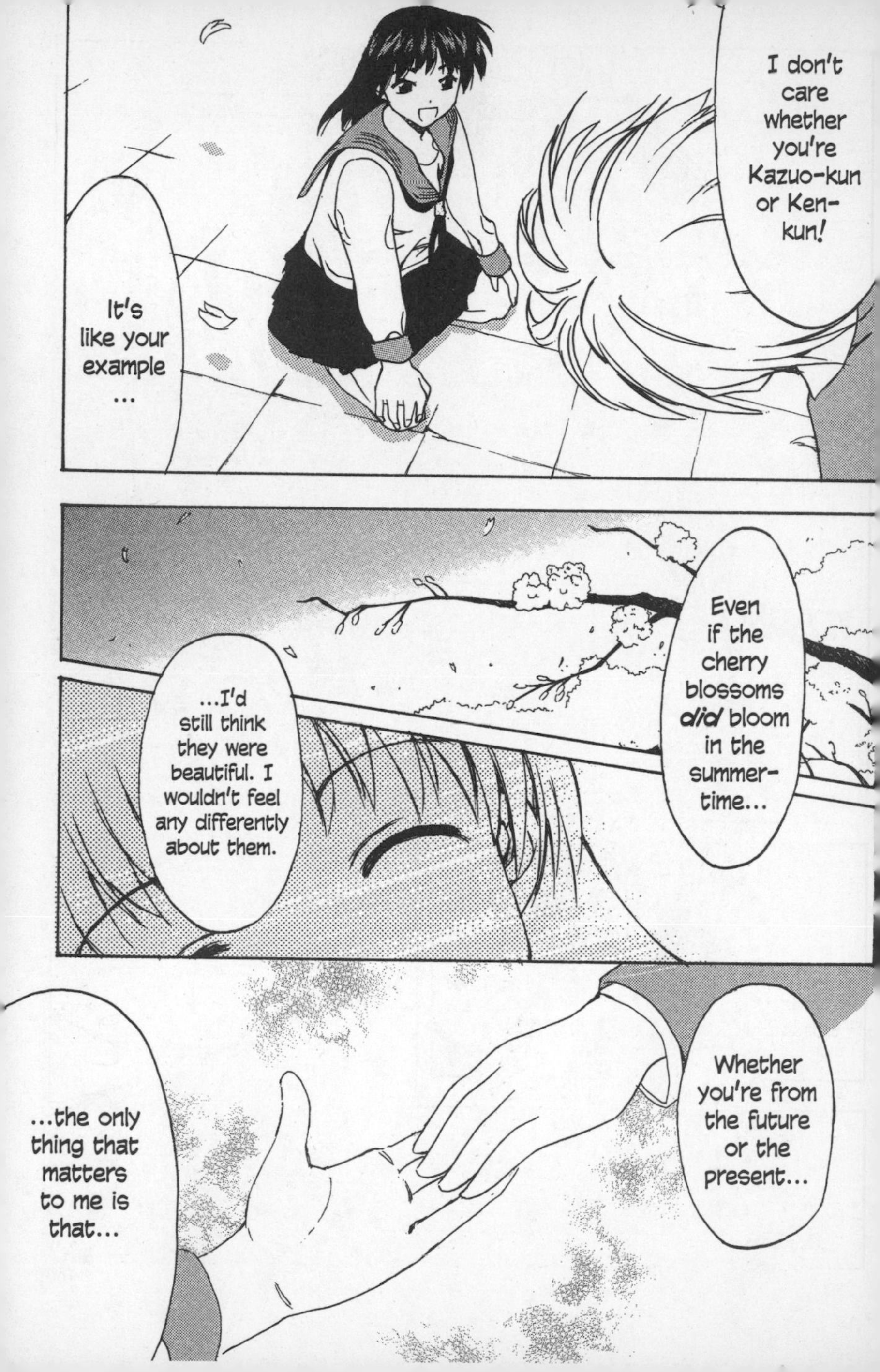
I don't care whether you're Kazuo-kun or Ken-kun!
It's like your example ...
Even if the cherry blossoms *did* bloom in the summer-time...
...I'd still think they were beautiful. I wouldn't feel any differently about them.
Whether you're from the future or the present...
...the only thing that matters to me is that...

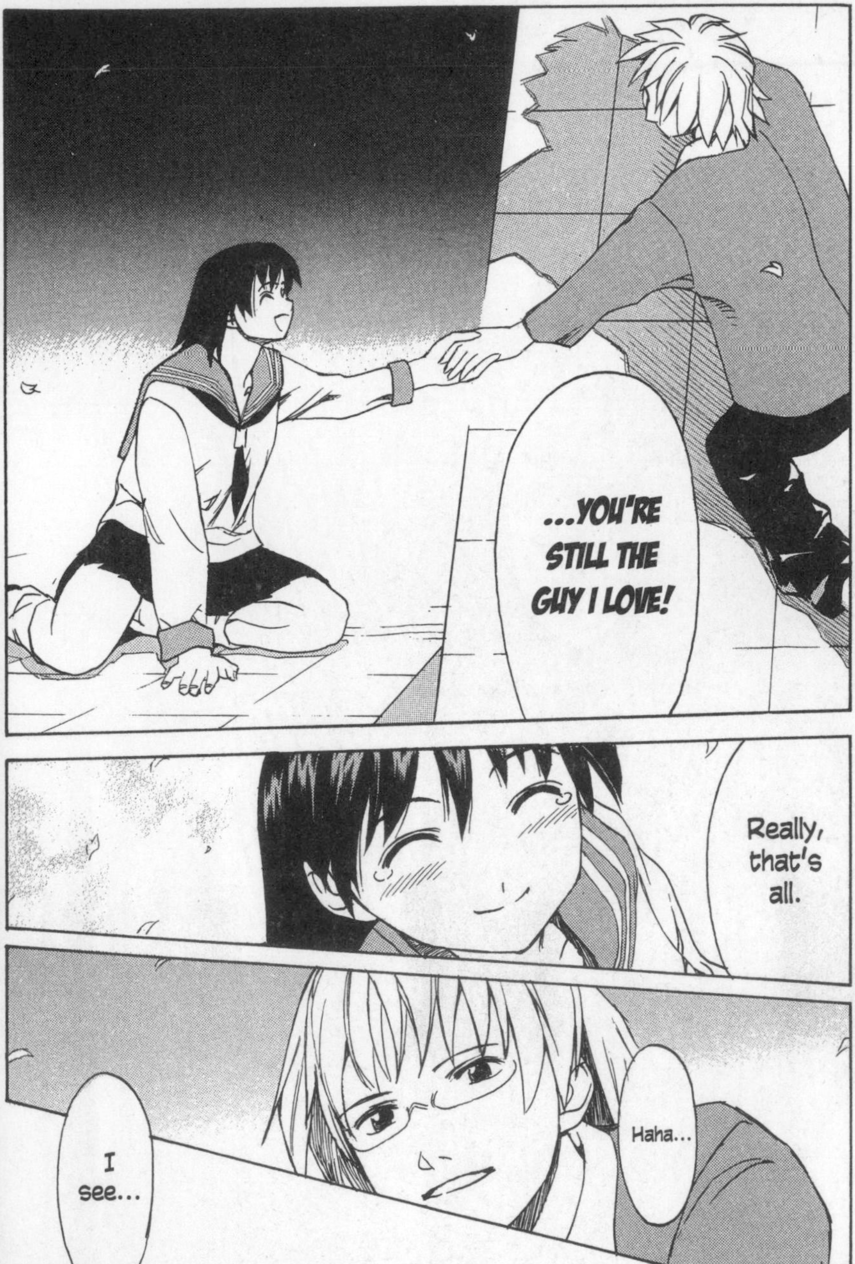
...YOU'RE STILL THE GUY I LOVE!
Really, that's all.
Haha...
I see...

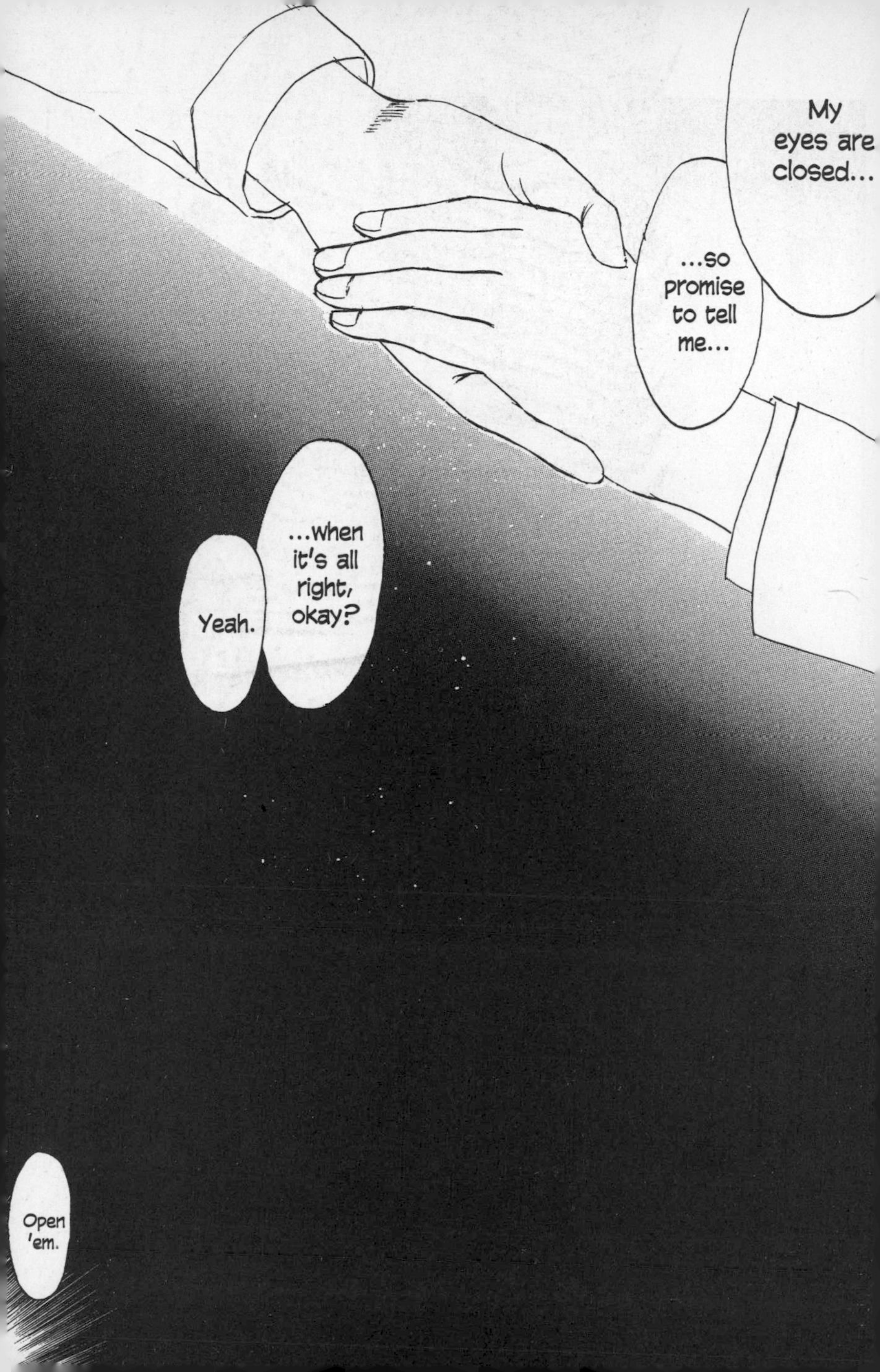
My eyes are closed...
...so promise to tell me...
...when it's all right, okay?
Yeah.
Open 'em.

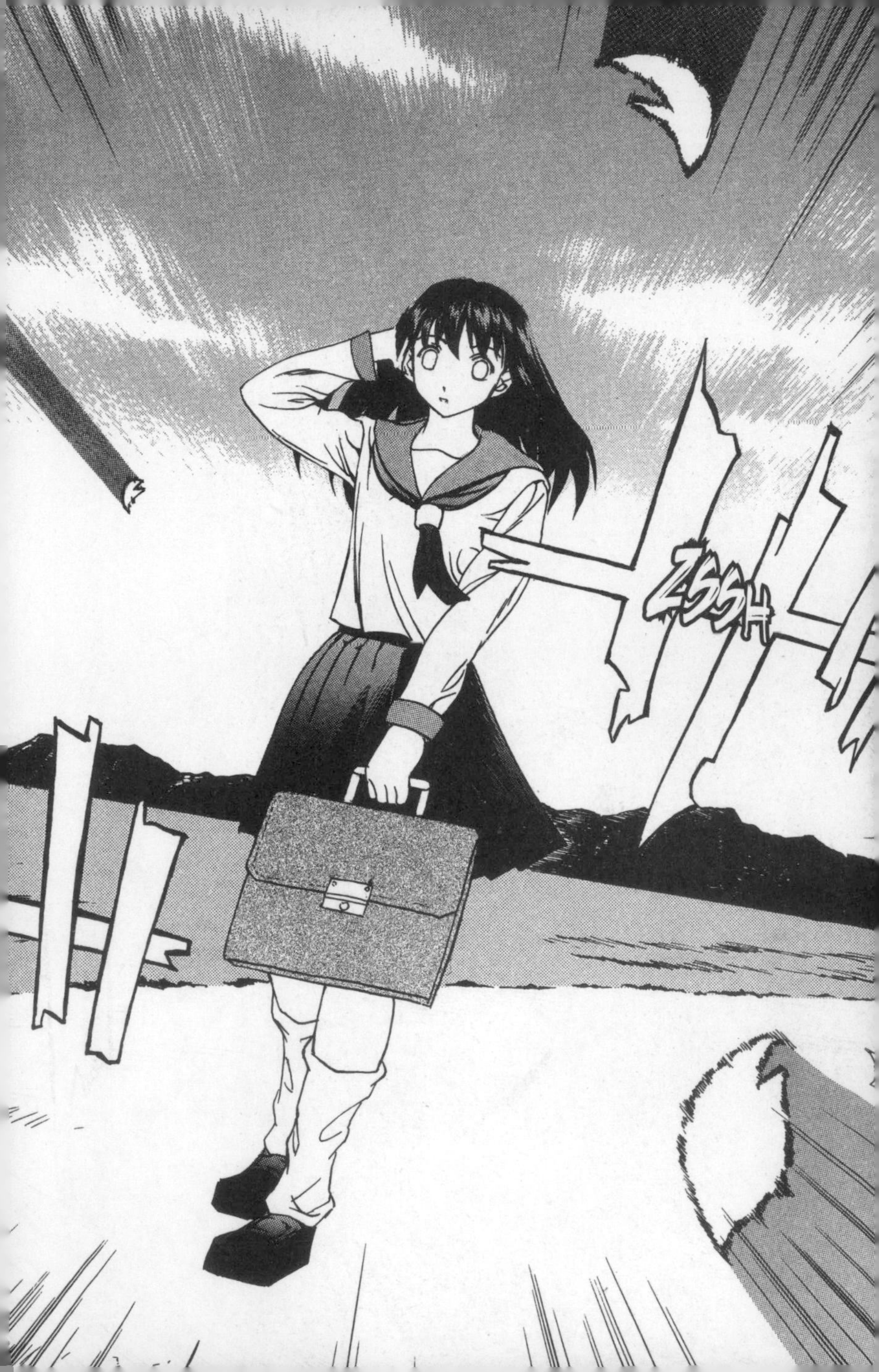
ZSSH

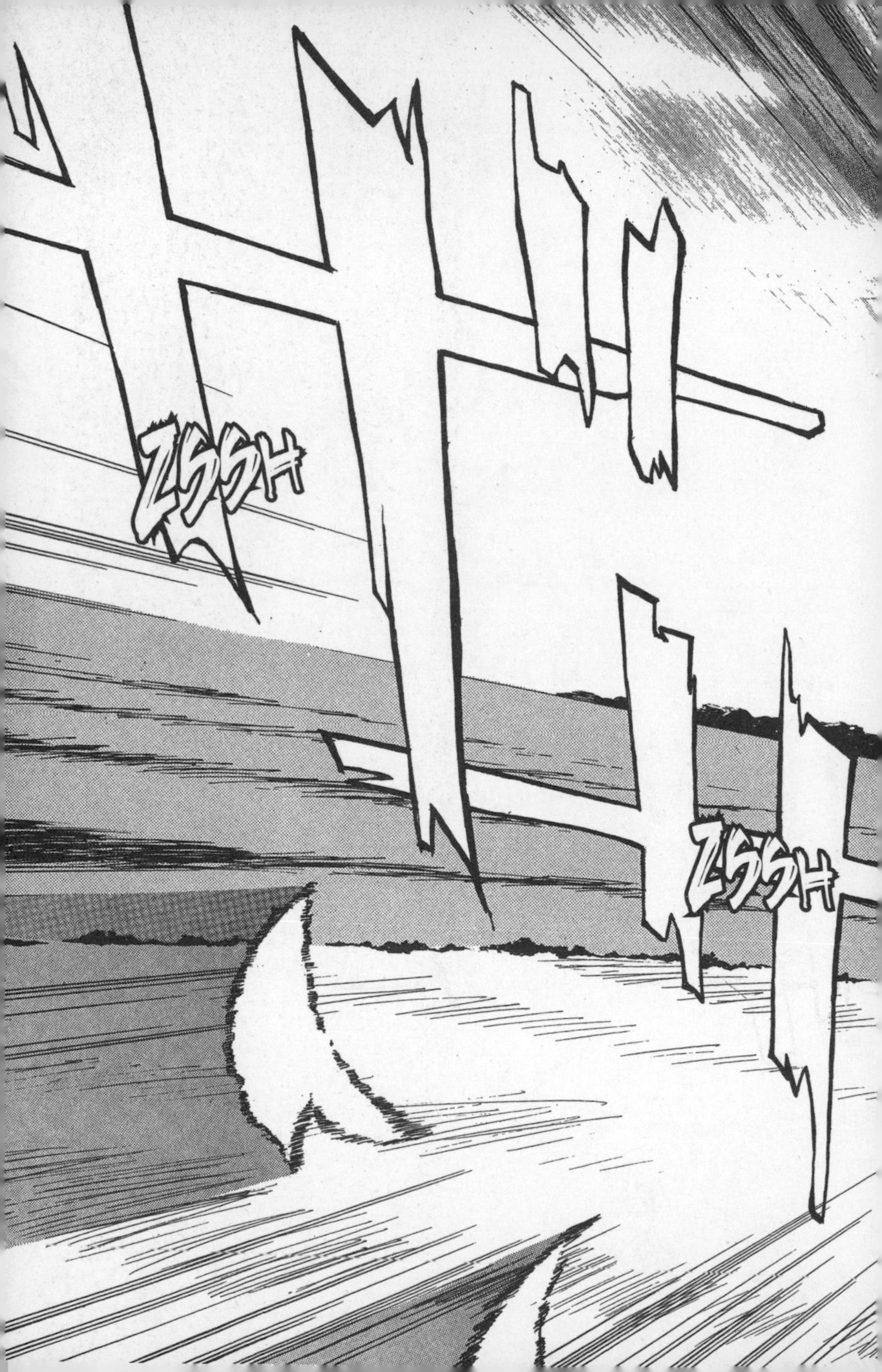
ZSSH
ZSSH

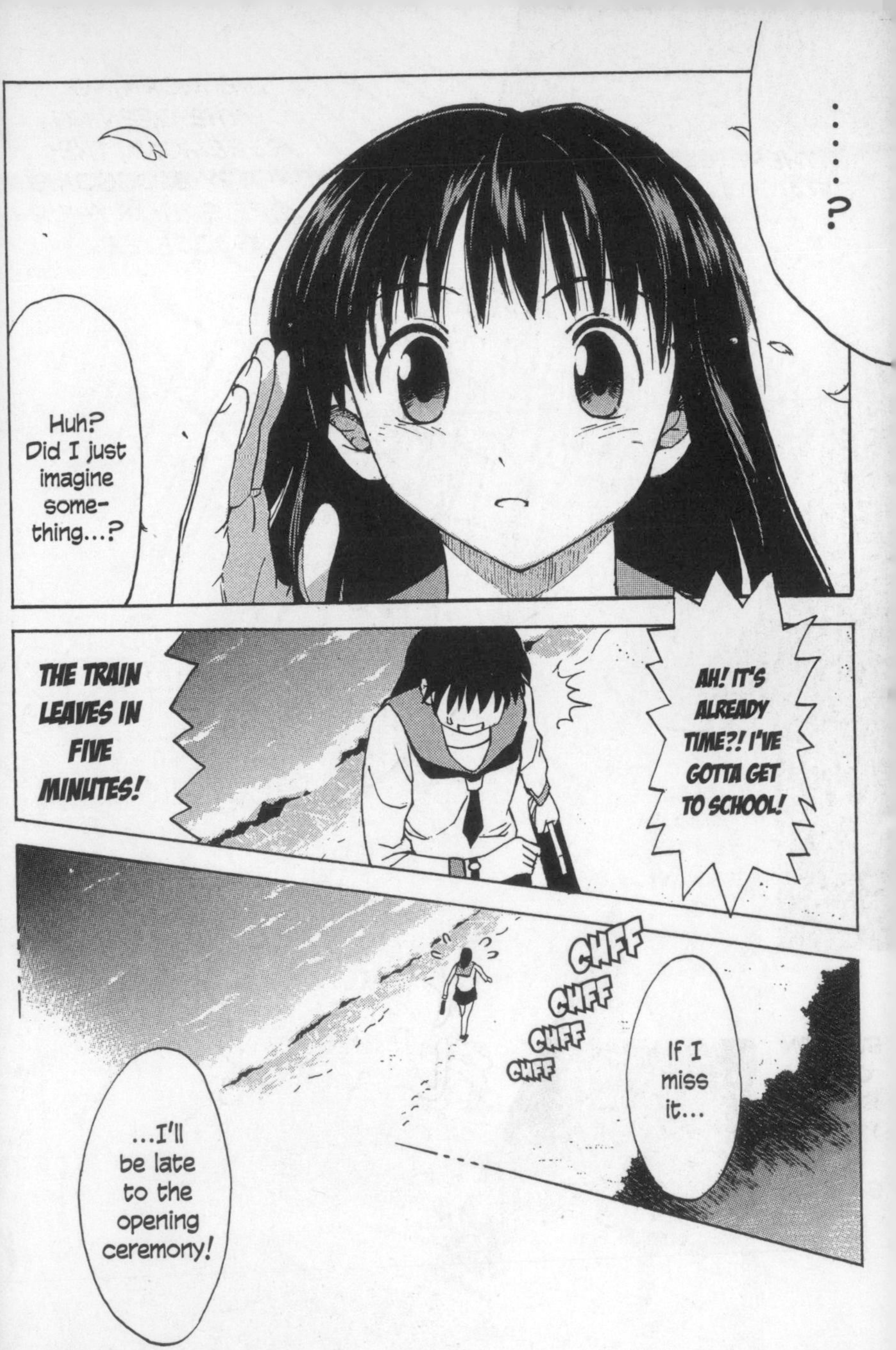
....?
Huh? Did I just imagine some-thing...?
AH! IT'S ALREADY TIME?! I'VE GOTTA GET TO SCHOOL!
THE TRAIN LEAVES IN FIVE MINUTES!
CHFF
CHFF
CHFF
CHFF
If I miss it...
...I'll be late to the opening ceremony!

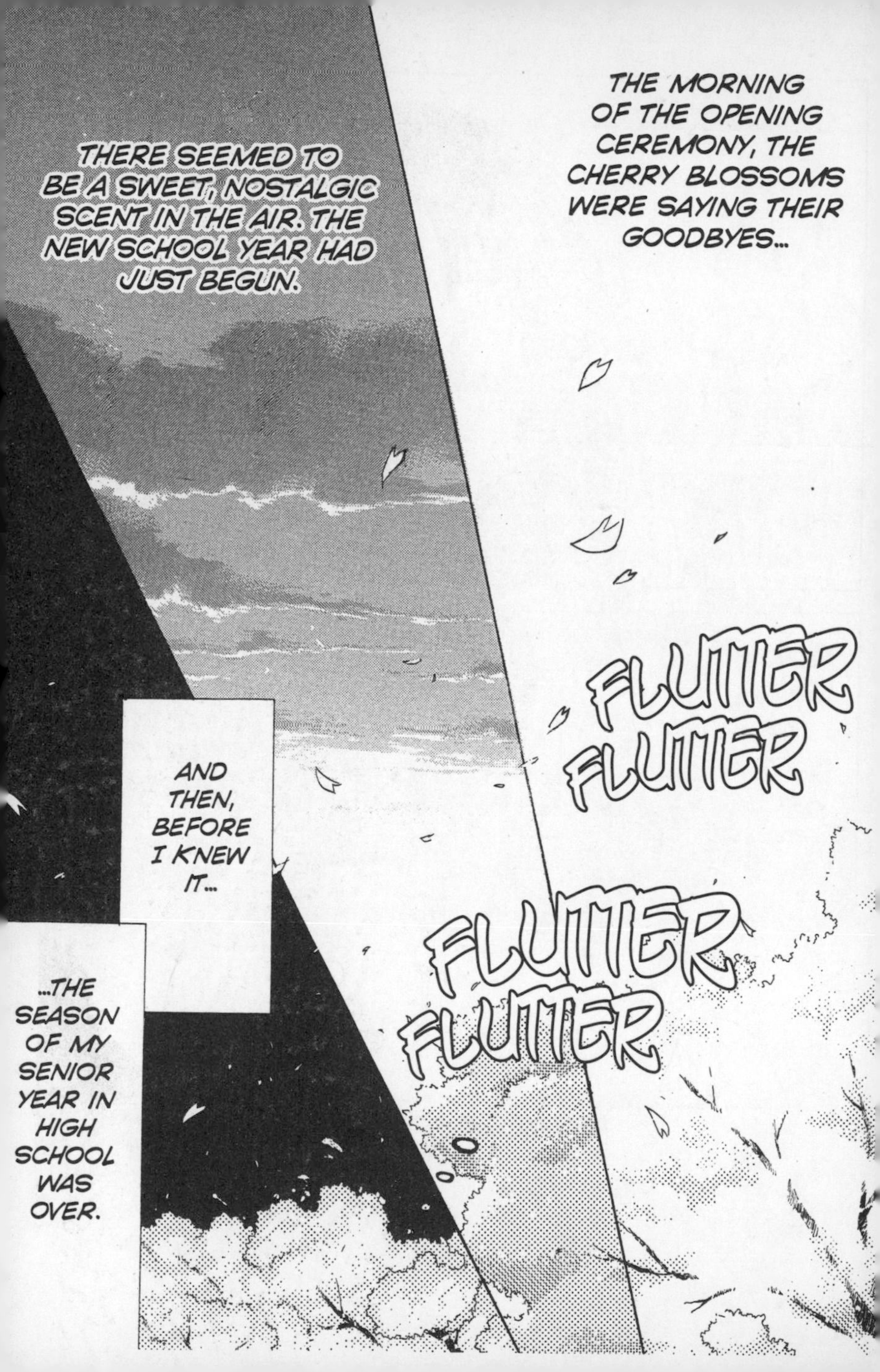
THE MORNING OF THE OPENING CEREMONY, THE CHERRY BLOSSOMS WERE SAYING THEIR GOODBYES...
THERE SEEMED TO BE A SWEET, NOSTALGIC SCENT IN THE AIR. THE NEW SCHOOL YEAR HAD JUST BEGUN.
FLUTTER FLUTTER
FLUTTER FLUTTER
AND THEN, BEFORE I KNEW IT...
...THE SEASON OF MY SENIOR YEAR IN HIGH SCHOOL WAS OVER.

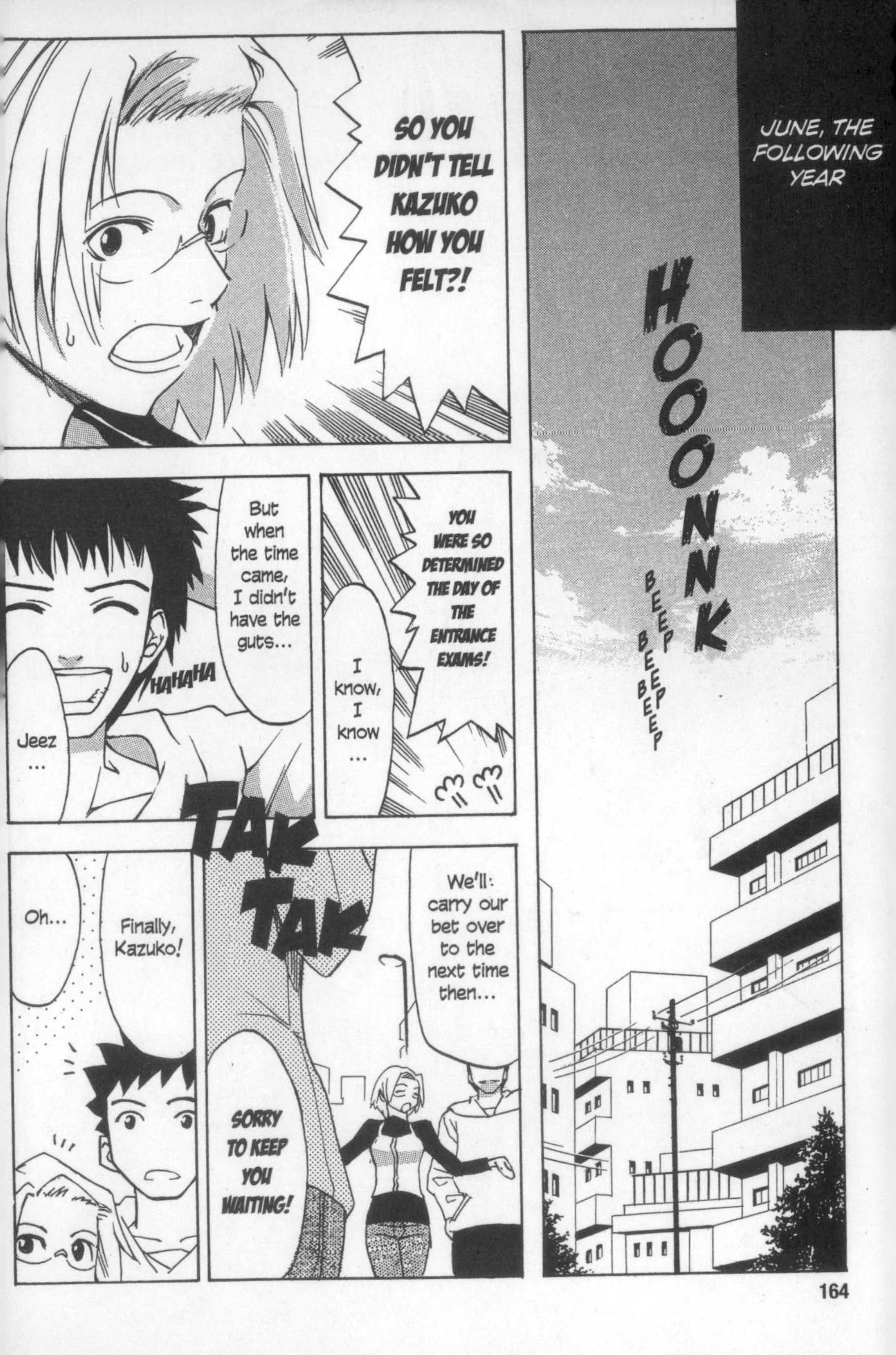
JUNE, THE FOLLOWING YEAR
HOOONNK
BEEP BEEP BEEP
SO YOU DIDN'T TELL KAZUKO HOW YOU FELT?!
YOU WERE SO DETERMINED THE DAY OF THE ENTRANCE EXAMS!
I know, I know...
But when the time came, I didn't have the guts...
HAHAHA
Jeez...
TAK TAK
We'll carry our bet over to the next time then...
SORRY TO KEEP YOU WAITING!
Finally, Kazuko!
Oh...

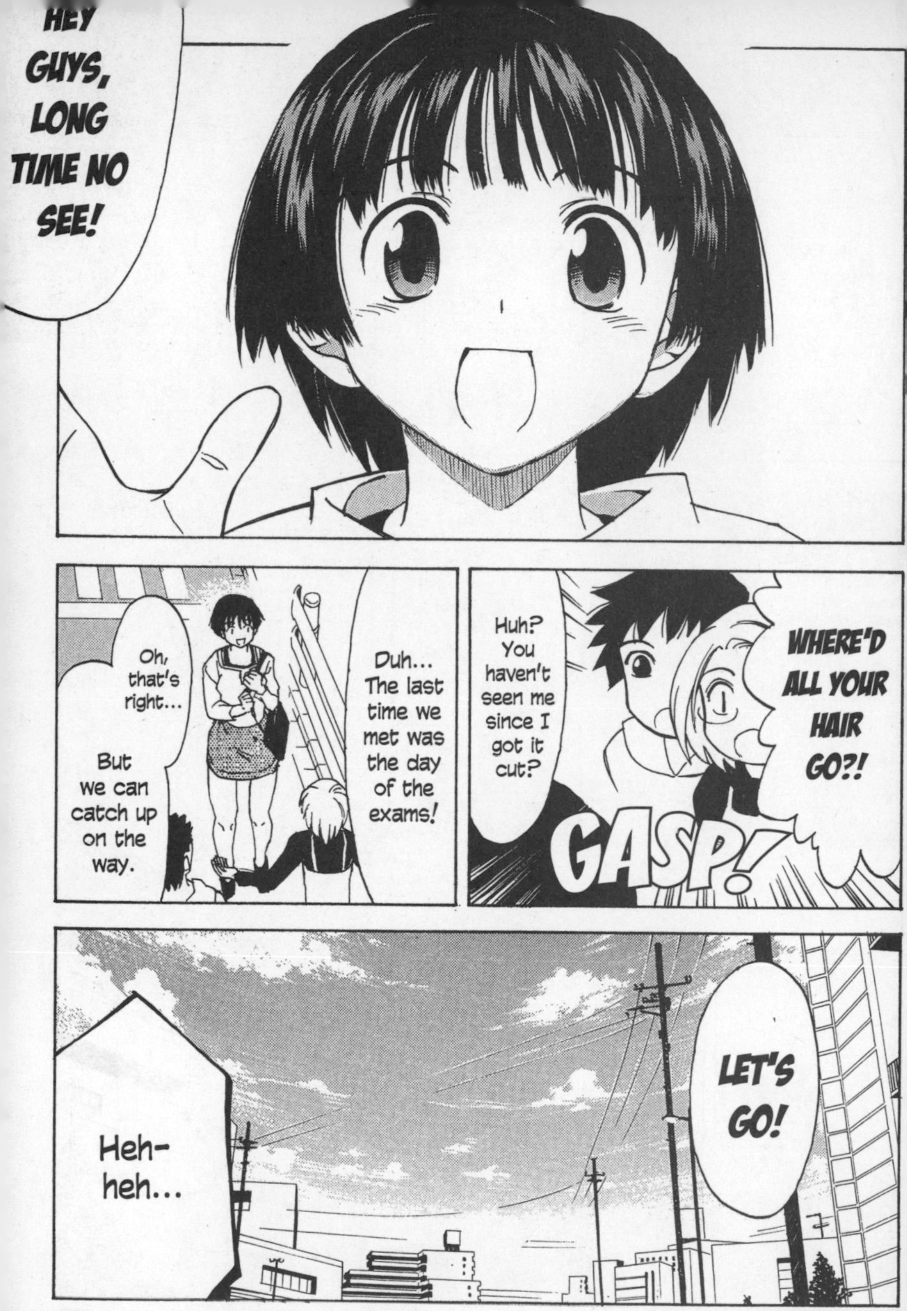
HEY GUYS, LONG TIME NO SEE!
WHERE'D ALL YOUR HAIR GO?!
GASP!
Huh? You haven't seen me since I got it cut?
Duh... The last time we met was the day of the exams!
Oh, that's right...
But we can catch up on the way.
LET'S GO!
Heh-heh...

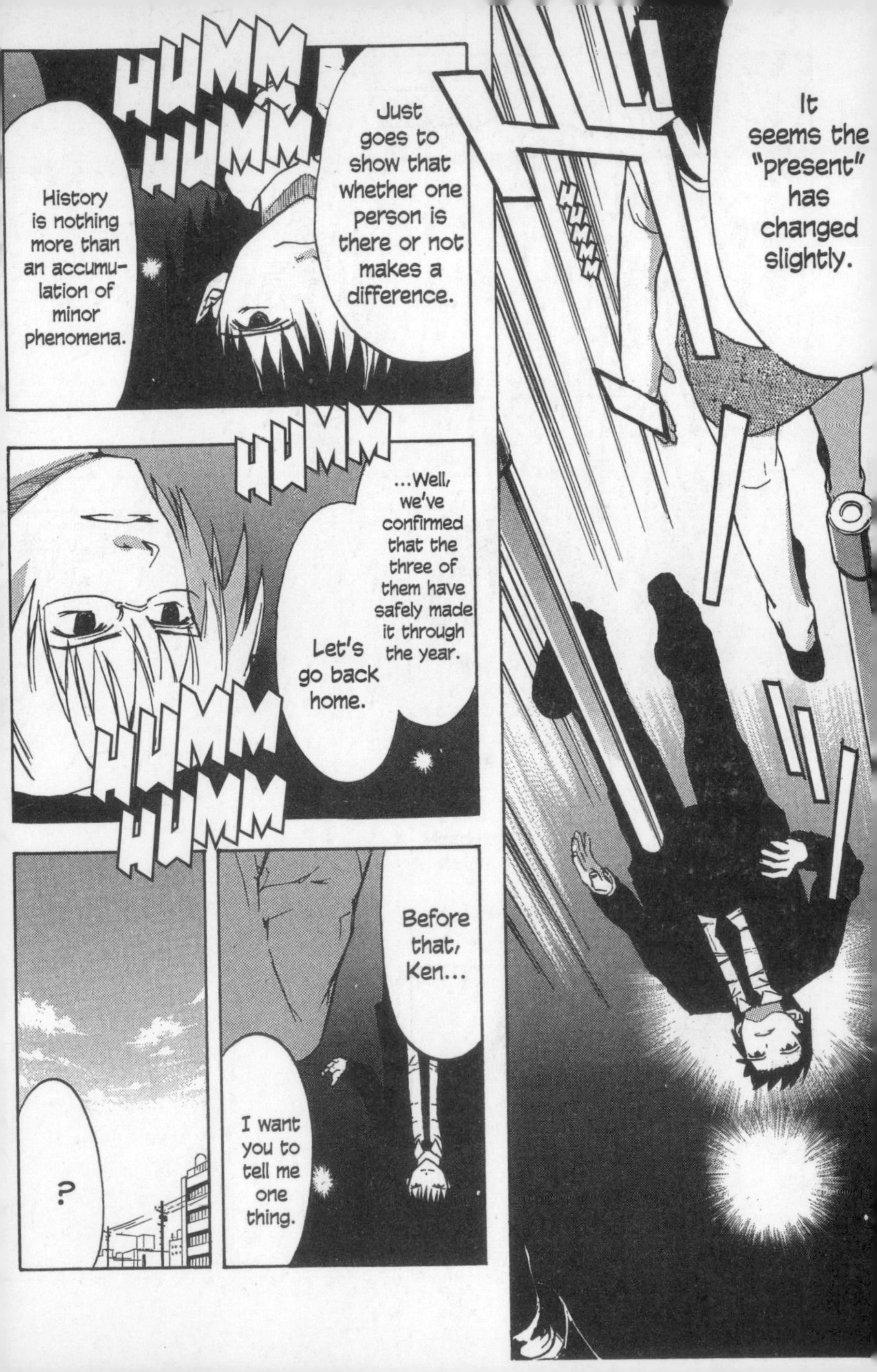
It seems the "present" has changed slightly.
HUMM
HUMM HUMM
Just goes to show that whether one person is there or not makes a difference.
History is nothing more than an accumulation of minor phenomena.
HUMM
...Well, we've confirmed that the three of them have safely made it through the year.
Let's go back home.
HUMM HUMM
Before that, Ken...
I want you to tell me one thing.
?

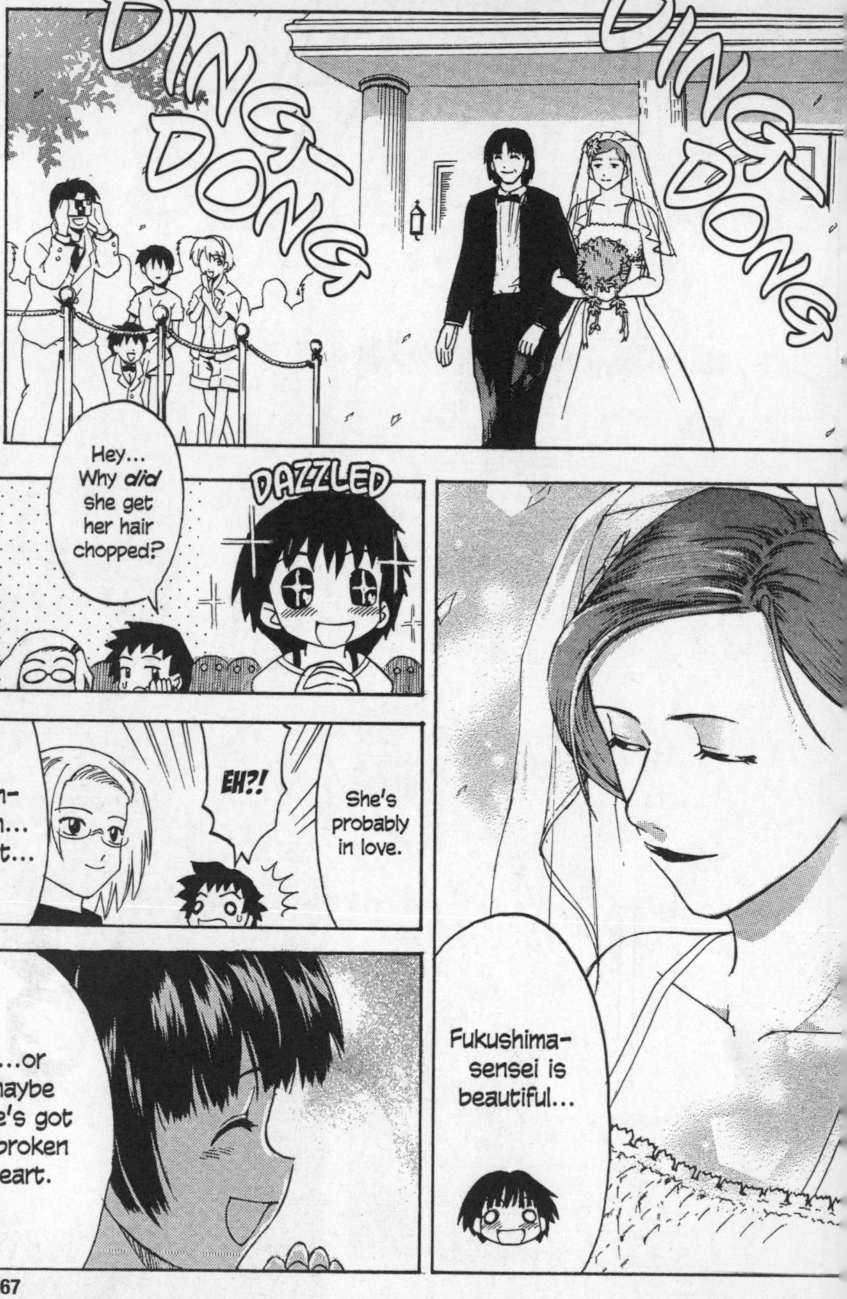
DING DONG
DING DONG
Fukushima-sensei is beautiful...
DAZZLED
Hey... Why did she get her hair chopped?
Hm ...
She's probably in love.
EH?!
Heh-heh... That...
...or maybe she's got a broken heart.

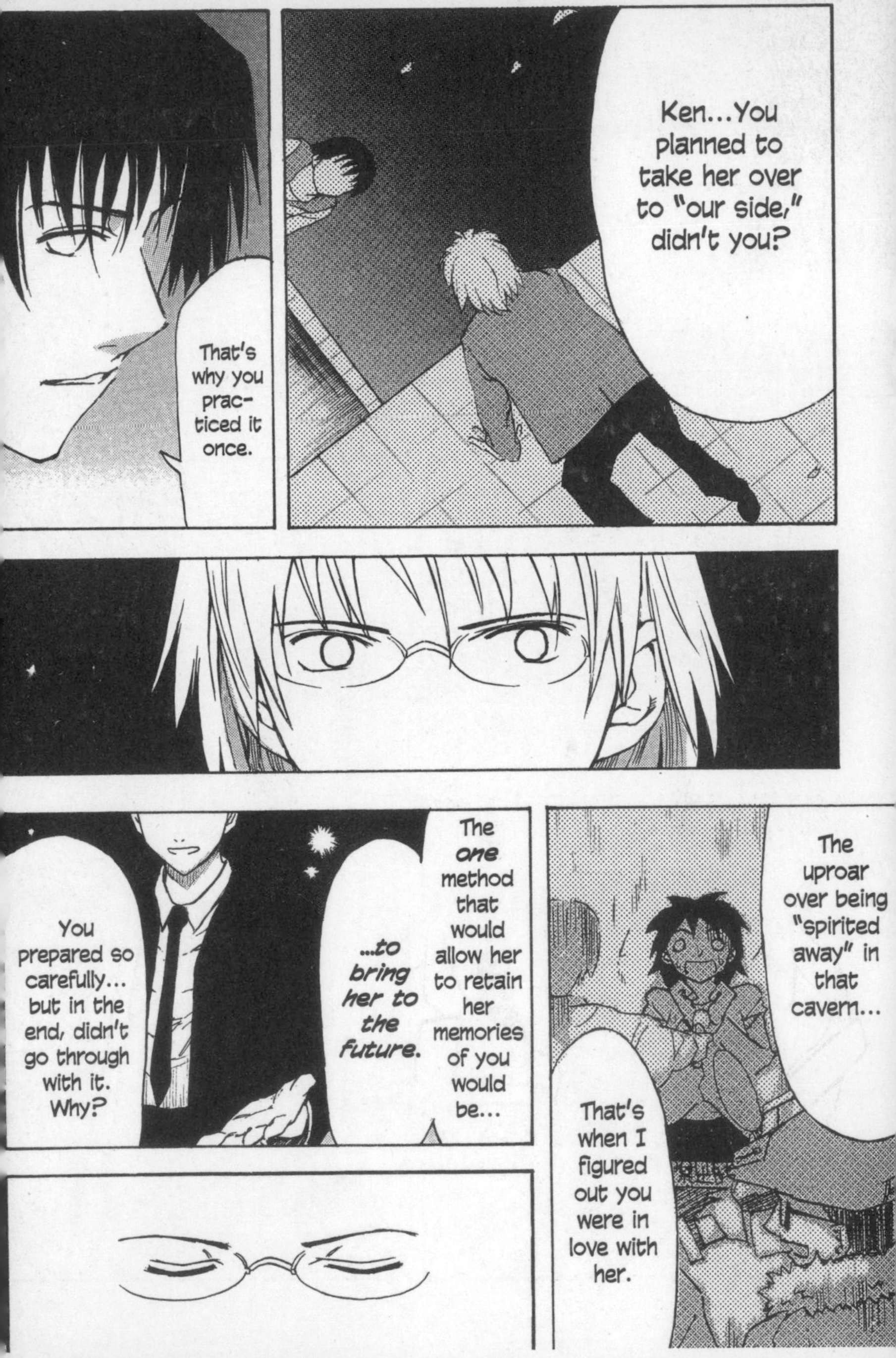
Ken...You planned to take her over to "our side," didn't you?
That's why you prac-ticed it once.
The uproar over being "spirited away" in that cavern...
That's when I figured out you were in love with her.
The *one* method that would allow her to retain her memories of you would be...
...to bring her to the future.
You prepared so carefully... but in the end, didn't go through with it. Why?

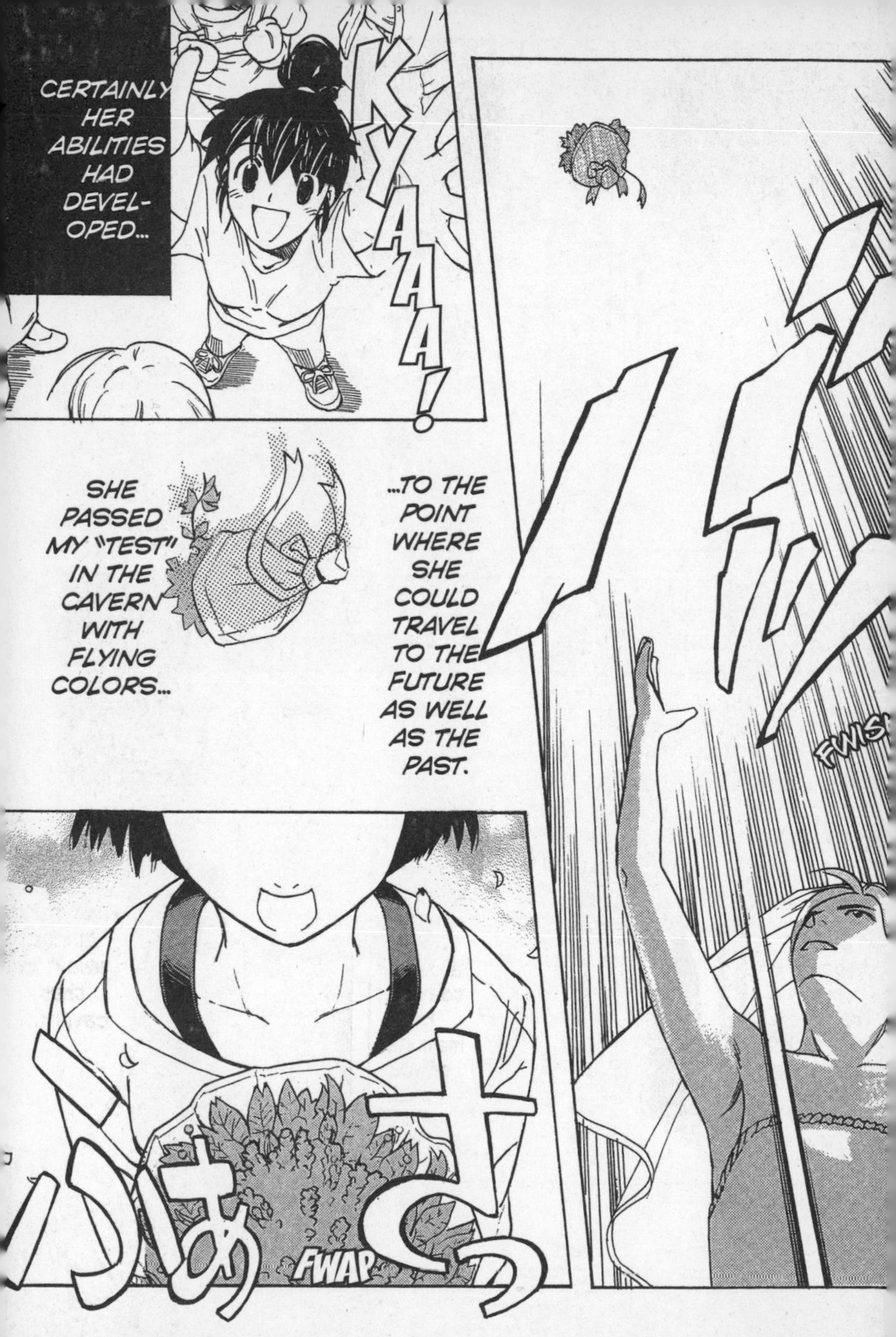
KYAAA!
CERTAINLY HER ABILITIES HAD DEVEL-OPED...
...TO THE POINT WHERE SHE COULD TRAVEL TO THE FUTURE AS WELL AS THE PAST.
SHE PASSED MY "TEST" IN THE CAVERN WITH FLYING COLORS...
FWAP

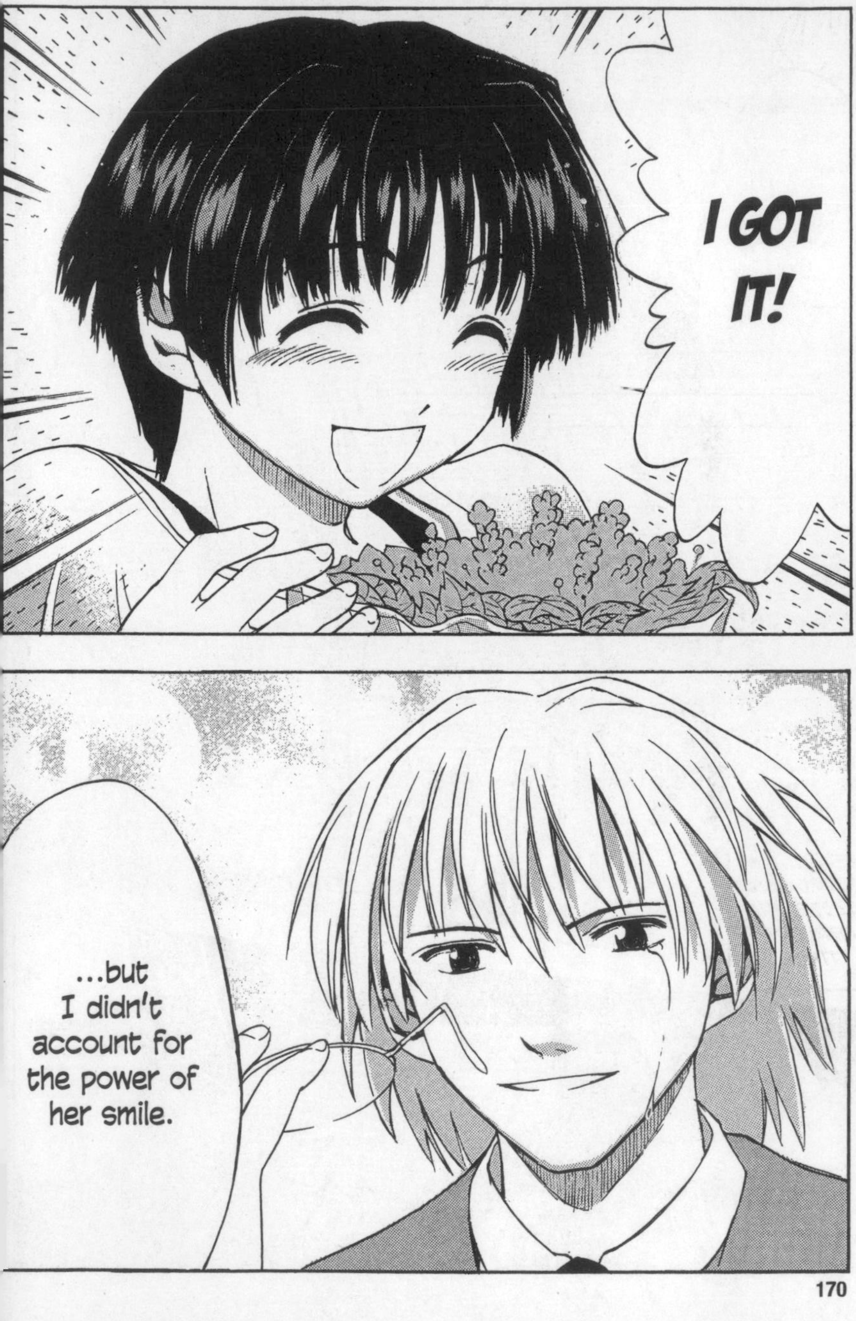
I GOT IT!
...but I didn't account for the power of her smile.

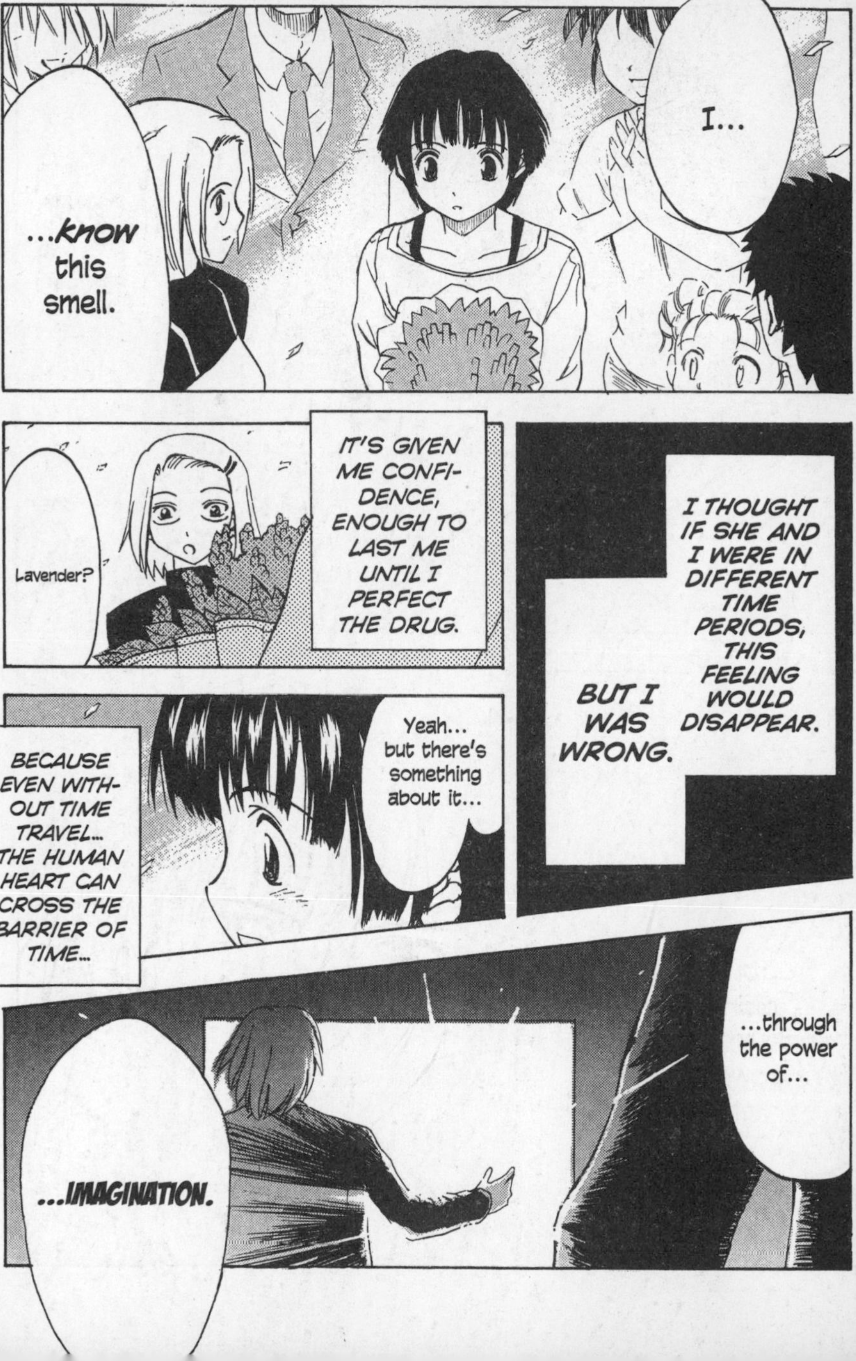
I...
...know this smell.
I THOUGHT IF SHE AND I WERE IN DIFFERENT TIME PERIODS, THIS FEELING WOULD DISAPPEAR.
BUT I WAS WRONG.
IT'S GIVEN ME CONFIDENCE, ENOUGH TO LAST ME UNTIL I PERFECT THE DRUG.
Lavender?
Yeah... but there's something about it...
BECAUSE EVEN WITHOUT TIME TRAVEL... THE HUMAN HEART CAN CROSS THE BARRIER OF TIME...
...through the power of...
...IMAGINATION.

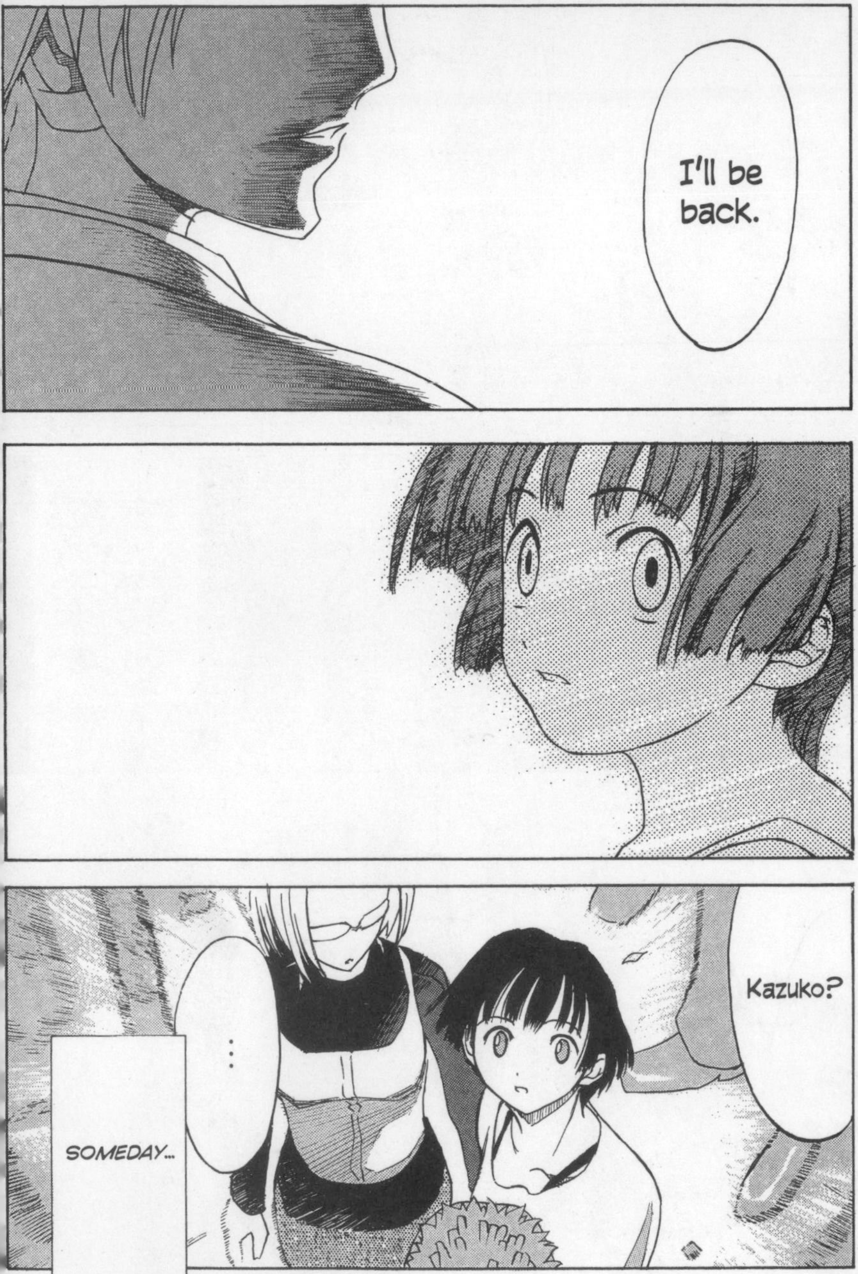
I'll be back.
Kazuko?
...
SOMEDAY...

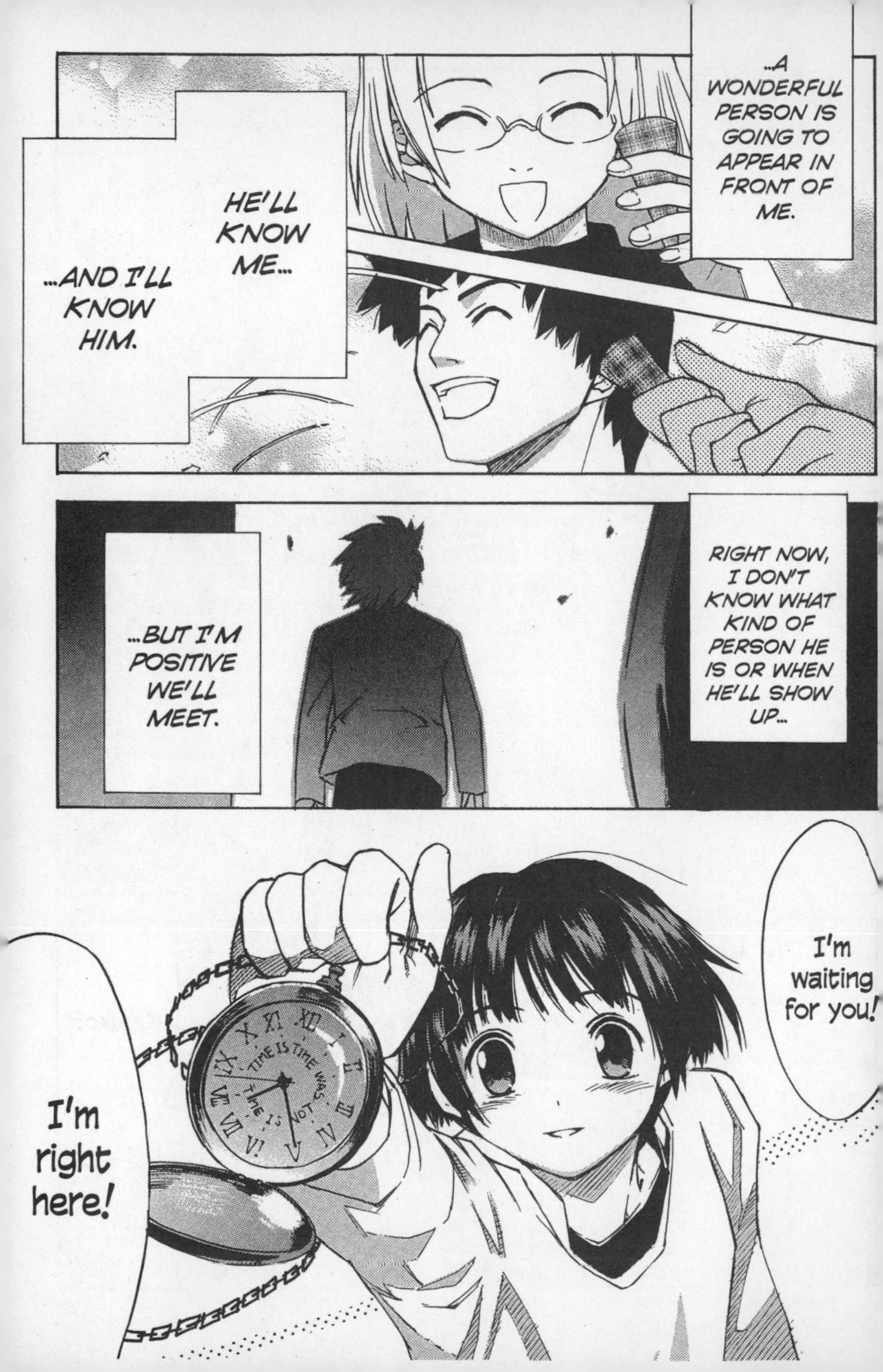
...A WONDERFUL PERSON IS GOING TO APPEAR IN FRONT OF ME.
HE'LL KNOW ME...
...AND I'LL KNOW HIM.
RIGHT NOW, I DON'T KNOW WHAT KIND OF PERSON HE IS OR WHEN HE'LL SHOW UP...
...BUT I'M POSITIVE WE'LL MEET.
I'm waiting for you!
I'm right here!

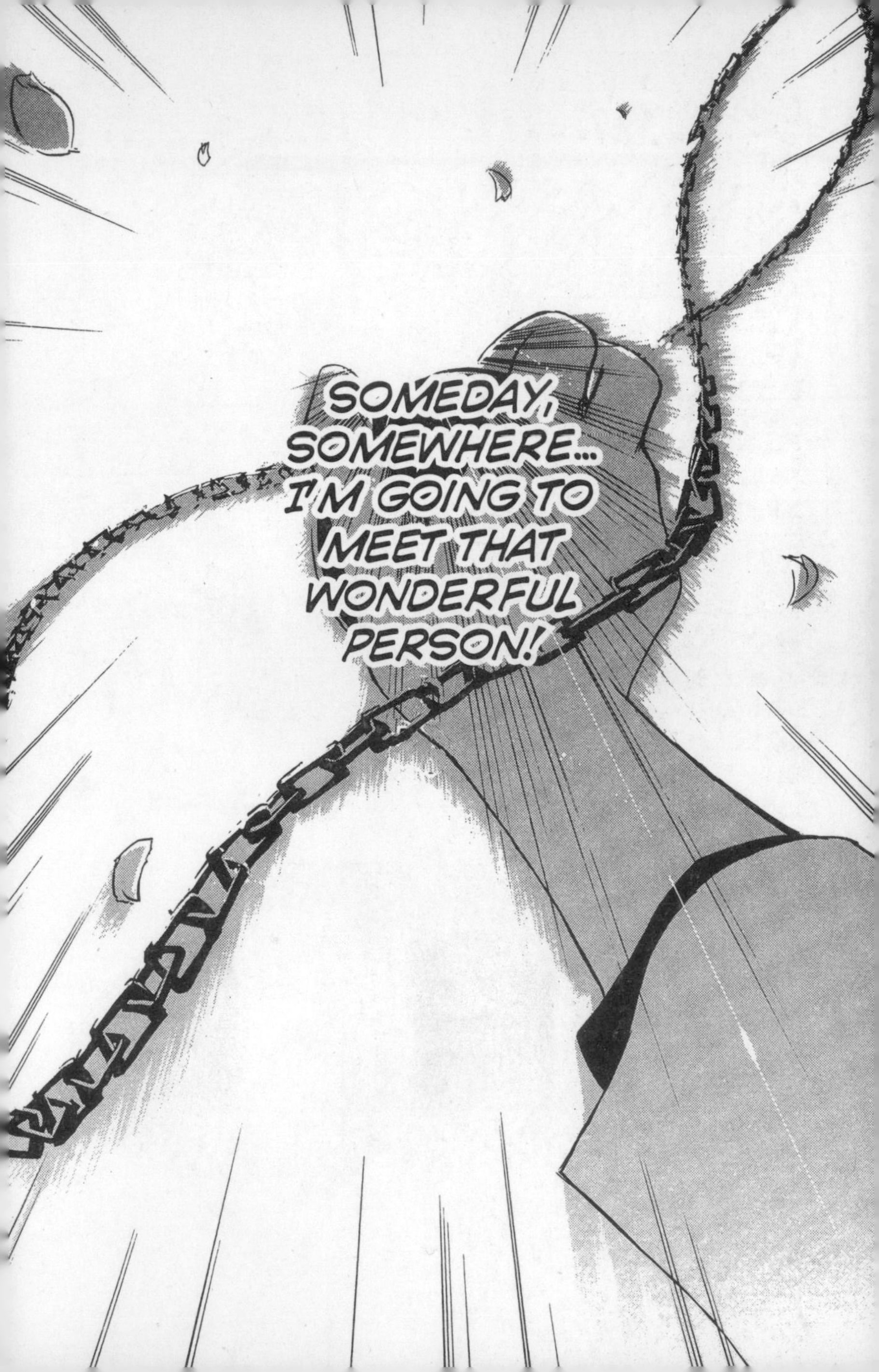
SOMEDAY, SOMEWHERE... I'M GOING TO MEET THAT WONDERFUL PERSON!

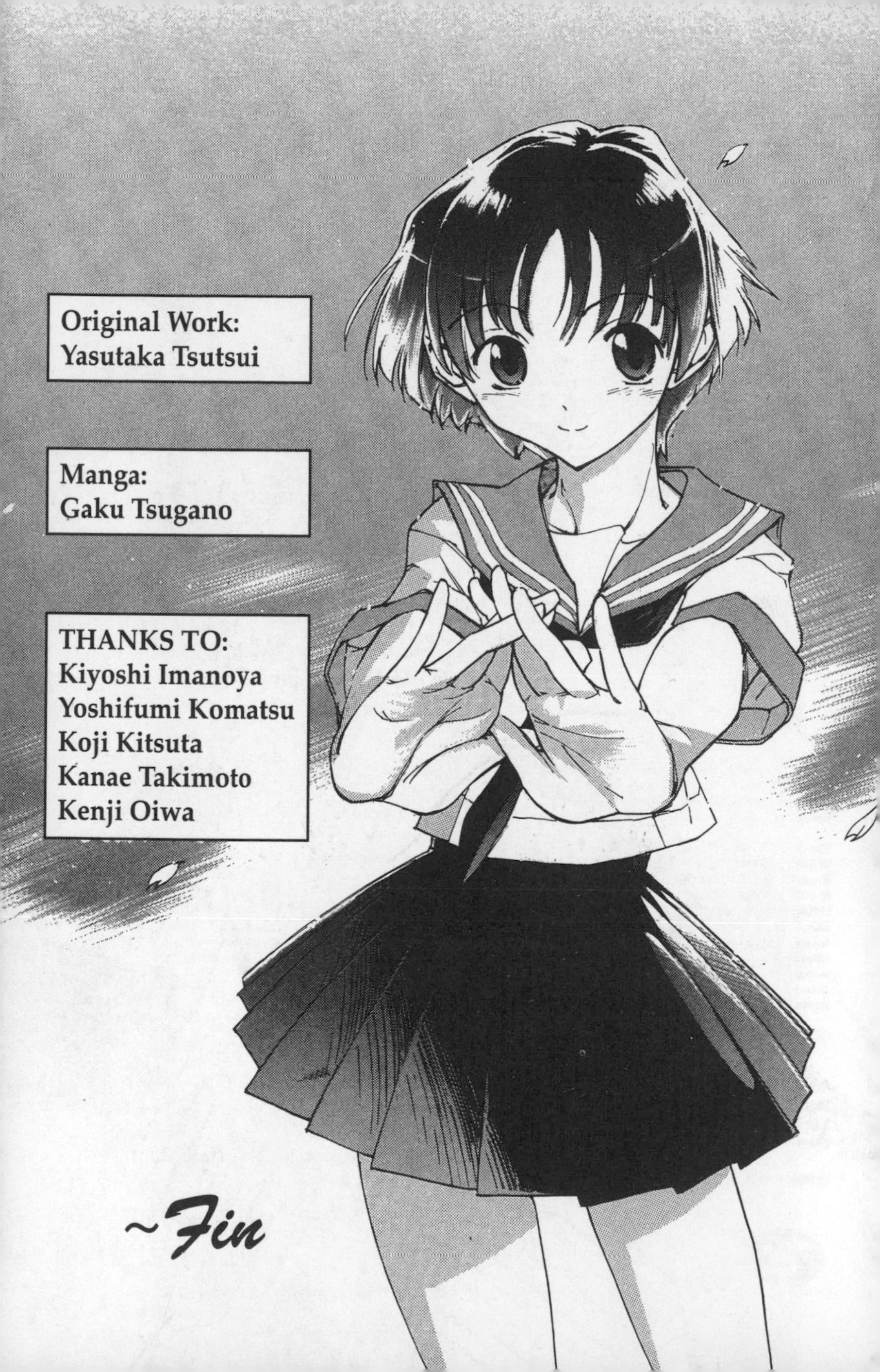
Original Work:
Yasutaka Tsutsui
Manga:
Gaku Tsugano
THANKS TO:
Kiyoshi Imanoya
Yoshifumi Komatsu
Koji Kitsuta
Kanae Takimoto
Kenji Oiwa
~Fin

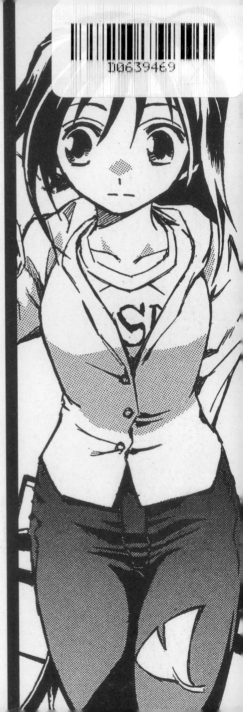

...WO KAKERU SHOJYO Vol. 2 © GAKU TSUGANO
...© YASUTAKA TSUTSUI 2004. First Published in Japan
...4 by KADOKAWA SHOTEN PUBLISHING CO., LTD.,

...irl Who Runs Through Time Volume 2, published by
...torm Productions, an imprint of DC Comics, 888
...ect St. #240, La Jolla, CA 92037. English Translation
...9. All Rights Reserved. English translation rights in
... arranged with KADOKAWA SHOTEN PUBLISHING
...LTD., Tokyo, through TUTTLE-MORI AGENCY, INC.,
... CMX is a trademark of DC Comics. The stories,
...cters, and incidents mentioned in this magazine are
...ly fictional. Printed on recyclable paper. WildStorm
...not read or accept unsolicited submissions of ideas,
...s or artwork. Printed in Canada.

...omics, a Warner Bros. Entertainment Company.

...ldon Drzka – Translation and Adaptation
...k Gianllongo – Lettering
...y Berry – Design
...icia Duffield – Editor

...I: 978-1-4012-2029-7